STRANGE FRUIT OF THE BLACK PACIFIC

NATION OF NATIONS: IMMIGRANT HISTORY AS AMERICAN HISTORY

General Editors: Rachel Buff, Matthew Jacobson, and Werner Sollors

Strange Fruit of the Black Pacific

Imperialism's Racial Justice and Its Fugitives

Vince Schleitwiler

NEW YORK UNIVERSITY PRESS

New York

NEW YORK UNIVERSITY PRESS
New York
www.nyupress.org

© 2017 by New York University

References to Internet websites (URLs) were accurate at the time of writing.
Neither the author nor New York University Press is responsible for URLs that
may have expired or changed since the manuscript was prepared.

ISBN: 978-1-4798-6469-0 (hardback)

ISBN: 978-1-4798-5708-1 (paperback)

For Library of Congress Cataloging-in-Publication data, please contact
the Library of Congress.

New York University Press books are printed on acid-free paper,
and their binding materials are chosen for strength and durability.
We strive to use environmentally responsible suppliers and materials
to the greatest extent possible in publishing our books.

Manufactured in the United States of America

10 9 8 7 6 5 4 3 2 1

Also available as an ebook

A book in the American Literatures Initiative (ALI), a collaborative publishing project of NYU Press, Fordham University Press, Rutgers University
Press, Temple University Press, and the University of Virginia Press. The
Initiative is supported by The Andrew W. Mellon Foundation. For more information, please visit www.americanliteratures.org.

THE
AMERICAN
LITERATURES
INITIATIVE

Some people manage to stay free.
—*Mosquito* (Gayl Jones)

CONTENTS

ACKNOWLEDGMENTS

Any book worth reading must be the expression of a desire to become indebted to others. Whether this is such a book is not for me to decide, but I am lucky to have accumulated the tally that follows. As always, the greatest debts remain unaccounted and nameless.

Over the years, my teachers have given me more than a student should ask, particularly one so incorrigible as myself. I am honored by their patience and friendship, and grateful for their steadfast kindness through adversity. Joycelyn Moody taught me that reading could be a calling, and the pursuit of literacy a life's task; I am still learning. Chandan Reddy's terrifying intellect is surpassed only by his inexhaustible generosity, and I am better for having drawn upon both. From Johnnella Butler I learned that integrity can be sustained with grace at the highest levels of institutions not designed for your survival, a reminder that has saved me on more than a few occasions. Vince Rafael is the most literary thinker I have been fortunate to meet, and his restless mind pushed this project in profound ways. Eva Cherniavsky's steady and exemplary mentorship steered me through many difficult challenges.

Kiko Benitez was an invaluable guide to my early incursions into Filipino literatures, and Alys Weinbaum showed me how to draw my first maps of the planet Du Bois. Steve Sumida, Gail Nomura, Peter Kwong, and Dušanka Miščević have been generous and supportive since my undergraduate years. Student organizers at the University of Washington and Oberlin, including Diem Nguyen, Genji Terasaki, Robin Russell, Marc Philpart, Dana Arviso, and many others provided me with the greater part of my education. I will never be done thanking my old friends from GO-MAP, especially Jerry Pangilinan and Cynthia Morales. In and beyond Seattle, Jeff Chiu, Amy Reddinger and Rhonda Mellinger, Lesley Larkin, Seema Sohi, Caroline Yang, Andrea Opitz and Stacy Grooters, Marites Mendoza, Ryan Burt, Trang Ta, and Keith Feldman allowed me to understand friendship as a form of study. Tamiko Nimura continues to show me the way forward. As a teacher, I have been fortunate to learn alongside many fine students, including Jacquelin Magby Baker, Rhassan Hill, Claire Schwartz, Charlotte Silverman, Kaveh Landsverk, Naima McFarland, Lauren Zachary, Christopher Holland, Sophia Rosenfeld, Jackie Harris, Logan Lawson, Alina and Amber Penny, and too many others to name.

Much love and respect to the Willliamstown diaspora, and to those still holding it down in the Berkshires: Tracey and Devyn Spence Benson, Stéphane Robolin and Evie Shockley, Travis and Jessica Gosa, Neil Roberts and Karima Barrow, Jackie Hidalgo and Sourena Parham, Kiara Vigil and Blake Johnson, Jennifer Randall Crosby, Lillian-Yvonne Bertram, and Manu Vimalassery. The peerless Joyce Foster, learned and wise, is a beacon to me, as to many. Dorothy Wang is fearless and always true. Laylah Ali, Allan Isaac, Wendy Raymond, Greg Robinson, Lisa Lowe, and Elena Creef offered timely encouragement. Mike Phillips, Rebecca Zorach, and Cauleen Smith swung through town when I needed them most.

I am fortunate for the refuge provided, as this book neared completion, by Sarita See and her formidable crew at the Center for Art and Thought: Jan Christian Bernabe, Clare Counihan, and Sarah Lozier. Thanks, too, to Juan Guerro and everyone at UW's department of American Ethnic Studies; to Nayan Shah, Viet Nguyen, and Lanita Jacobs at USC's Department of American Studies and Ethnicity; Christina Hanhardt and everyone at the first Critical Ethnic Studies Association Summer Institute; Vince Rafael and everyone at the Carlos Bulosan centennial conference in Seattle; and Joe Jeon, Yoon Sun Lee, and the participants in the 2014 AALAC workshop at Wellesley, for sanctuary and fellowship.

Daphne Brooks's enthusiasm for this project could not have been more timely. I am honored to have worked with Matt Jacobson, Eric Zinner, Alicia Nadkarni, and everyone at NYU Press. Joe Ponce and Brent Edwards kindly shared their thoughts on a version of the entire manuscript. Amy Reddinger, Ryan Burt, Trevor Griffey, Irena Percinkova-Patton, Georgia Roberts, and Trang Ta also provided helpful feedback on various manifestations of this research. Conversations and collaborations with Keith Feldman, Andrea Opitz, and Dalila Scruggs helped me elaborate its consequences. Brian Norman's advice on an early version of Chapter 5 was invaluable.

Working with Michelle May-Curry and Taylor Bundy, brilliant research assistants, was an honor. Support for this project was provided by the Hellman Fellows Fund, the Oakley Center at Williams College, and the Simpson Center and the English Department at the University of Washington. Essential logistical help was provided by Pat Malanga, Robin Keller, Krista Birch, Susan Williams, Annee Fisher, and Kathy Mork. I am indebted to Lori DuBois of the Williams College Libraries, and to the Special Collections staff at the University of Washington Libraries. This book would not have been possible without the work of gifted teachers at the Preschool at Claremont United Methodist Church and at the Williams College Children's Center, especially Shana Shippee and Ellen Richardson.

My late grandparents, Rose and Vince Tajiri, have been a tangible presence in the writing of these pages. The love and support of Sarah and Brad DeKoter, Midori Tajiri-Byrd and Marc Byrd, Rea Tajiri, Brion Tajiri, Rev. Dae Yong and Youngsook Um, and my mother, Caryn Schleitwiler, have never wavered. But what a small thing is a book! It seems redundant to acknowledge, in a book, those to whom I owe so much more.

As with Ji-Young Um, who has been central to all areas of my life, intellectual and otherwise, since before we went off to graduate school, and who has done more to bring this project into the world than anyone, including its author. Then there is Yuuna, who has been its most cherished impediment. For them both, I will be *forever grateful*.

Overture

The Good News of Empire

Diversity is America's manifest destiny.
—Ronald T. Takaki

cipher

They built a wall so they could keep him on the inside.	(Justice.)
From time to time they try to get him to come out.	(Love.)
When they see him they want to kill him.	(Justice.)
Instead they give him a woman, so they can imagine	
what he does to her.	(Love.)
Some of them think a blonde one is worth six	
of the black ones.	(Race.)
Some of them think that's a poor trade.	(Gender.)
Now they want him on film.	(Love.)
Now they want him on stage.	(Justice.)
Now they want him in the air.	(Freedom.)
Now he is in the air.	

What happened to the women? What happened to the monkey? What
    happened to the cook?

    Somewhere on the island, the women all live together. There are caves
and a hidden beach. Before they came here, they used to work as extras.
    "Where have they taken him?" asks one.
    "To their own home," says another.
    "Will he come back?" asks the one.
    "I think they have killed him," says another.

"Should we find a new one?" asks the one.
"They will make a new one," says another.
"Will we protect him?" asks the one.
"He will find care," says another.
"Where will he find it?" asks the one.

in want of a map

The best-loved celebration of lynching in U.S. popular culture locates the origins of its savage victim-hero on a fictional island in Southeast Asia. If you read this character as black, as the logic of white terror has commonly been understood to imply, then *King Kong* must be the most famous black figure to hail from the Asia/Pacific region until the rise of a Hawai'i-born, Jakarta- and Honolulu-raised law professor, organizer, and memoirist named Barack Obama. Of course, the election of the first African American commander in chief surely signifies hope in the unfolding promise of racial justice—in the teeth of a national history of not only slavery and Jim Crow but also ongoing imperial warfare in Asia. By contrast, admitting the presence of race in Kong's story privileges a history of sexualized violence, white supremacy, and conquest that appears as the very antithesis of racial justice. Between these oddly paired icons and the seemingly incompatible forces they represent lies a terrain of forgotten and forgetful desires, of vivid and resonant shadows, out of which is inscribed a hundred years or more of the history of race—that epoch heralded in 1899 by W. E. B. Du Bois as the century of the color line. It is a space and a time that this book asks you to enter.

Tempting as it may be, the "black Pacific" is not the appropriate name for this terrain. That term I will reserve for a specific lure within it, the engendering chaos of the object or essence posited by the erotic violence of imperial race-making. Call it a *historical nonentity*, for it never actually existed except as speculative fantasy, yet its material consequences persist—a paradoxical condition, to be sure, but one that should hardly be unfamiliar to scholars of race. The black Pacific, you might say, is the indispensable blank or blind spot on the map; the empirically observable terrain, within which it makes its absence felt, is a *transpacific* field, charted by imperial competition and by the black and Asian movements and migrations shadowing the imperial powers. Within this field, the fictive lure calls forth contradictory processes of conquest that endlessly pursue it—so attending to this black Pacific may allow you to apprehend the bonds between the unfolding promise of racial justice and the overwhelming sexualized violence heralding the expansion of justice's domain.

In describing this book's geographic reach as transpacific, I refer less to a fixed oceanic unit than to a kind of tilting of space and time, a dizzying pivotal shift in the centrifugal and centripetal forces moving empires and their shadows. Its measure might be taken from Georgia to Luzon via Hong Kong, or, just as surely, between two towns in the Mississippi Delta. The transpacific is not a place, but an orientation—if at times, as you will see, a disorientingly occidented one. Similarly, the historical setting, between the rise of the United States and Japan as Pacific imperial powers in the 1890s and the aftermath of the latter's defeat in World War II, is periodized less in the sense of termination or punctuation than of a course of movement whose roiling currents might toss an observer's vessel to and fro, or of the calculation of an orbit based on the shifting relations of bodies and vantages across vast distances. Put differently, this book conceptualizes its field of inquiry, not through a singular racial, national, imperial, or even oceanic formation,[1] but through the interrelation of competing figures of movement—multiple circuits of black and Asian migrations cutting across Du Bois's meandering, world-belting color line. Because the comparison necessary to this approach is also the method every imperialism seeks to monopolize, this book reads comparison against a horizon of imperial competition, in the period culminating in U.S. ascendancy as heir to Western global power, even as its foregrounded objects of analysis remain territorially bounded within U.S. rule.

Intersectional and contrapuntal readings in African American, Japanese American, and Filipino literatures provide the book's material and method, tracing how each group's collective yearnings, internal conflicts, and speculative destinies were unevenly bound together along the color line. Their interactions—matters of misapprehension and friction, as well as correspondence and coordination—at times gave rise to captivating visions of freedom binding metropolitan antiracisms with globalizing anti-imperialisms. Yet the links were first forged by the paradoxical processes of race-making in an aspiring empire: on one hand, benevolent uplift through tutelage in civilization, and on the other, an overwhelming sexualized violence. *Imperialism's racial justice* is my term for these conjoined processes, a contradiction whose historical legacy constitutes the tangled genealogies of racism, antiracism, imperialism, and anti-imperialism. Because uplift and violence were logically incommensurable but regularly indistinguishable in practice, imperialism's racial justice could be sustained only through an ongoing training of perception in an *aesthetics of racial terror*. This book takes up the task of reading, or learning how to read, the literatures that take form and flight within the fissures of imperialism's racial justice, while straining to hear what the latter excludes, or what eludes it.

The method of this interdisciplinary book is ultimately literary, less in the choice of its objects than the mode of its articulation, marshalling the capacities of a peculiar tradition of reading destined to never stop overreaching its own grasp. By glossing "reading" as "learning how to read," I invoke the characteristic linking of literature, in African American cultural traditions, with a knot of questions around literacy, wherein the task of learning how to read is always problematized, critical, and unfinished, never reducible to formal processes of education. It troubles the privileging of either print or oral media, the visual or the aural; it is associated with mobility, as both dislocation and flight; it signifies both the possibility of freedom and the threat of its foreclosure. Put differently, I emphasize that the task of learning how to read the literatures of black and Asian migrations is not subsidiary to social and historical analysis. It is not simply to use literary texts as evidence for a critique of dominant histories, to mine them for traces of forgotten historical formations, nor to locate their work within proper historical contexts. It is also, and more importantly, to recognize that the work of these texts is not finished, not limited to the past, and to activate them in the present, undertaking one's historical and theoretical preparations so that their unpredictable agency might be called forth in the process of reading.

This book's method, finally, is the expression of a political desire. It is staked on the chance that the practice of reading as learning to read could open social reality to imagination's radically transformative power, even as it pursues this chance by dwelling in moments of subjunctive negation and foreclosure, fingering their jagged grain. While I participate in a broader aspiration to recuperate the antiracist and anti-imperialist visions of twentieth-century black and Asian movements, what I will term their third-conditional worlds, I do not presume that my hindsight suffices to liberate those visions from the racist and imperialist discourses of their emergence, for to do so would be to posit a freedom my present-day politics has not itself achieved. Instead, this book seeks to read them as they take form and flight within structures of thought whose presumptions I find objectionable, on the chance that they might diagnose a predicament of unfreedom I share.

The book is divided into three parts. Chapter 1 provides a historical overview, theoretical framework, and methodology of reading for studying race across U.S. transpacific domains. It turns to the figure of W. E. B. Du Bois on the threshold of the century he gave over to the problem of the color line, recovering the transpacific geopolitical context of that prophetic formulation, and the radical poetics of his response to racial terror. Stepping back, it surveys two major aspects of an Asian/Pacific interest within African American culture, exemplified by imperial Japan and the colonized Philippines, as well as corresponding black presences in Filipino and Japanese American culture. The second part, in two linked chapters, considers the ambivalent participation of African Americans in the colonization of the Philippines, as soldiers, colonial officials, intellectuals, and artists, alongside the development of an Anglophone Filipino intelligentsia from the colony to the metropole. Pressing the limits of the diaspora concept, it asks how these movements shaped emerging gendered forms of Negro and Filipino collectivity over against their conflation by sexualized imperial violence, and how they bore the echoes of alternative realms of belonging-across-difference that did not come into being. The third part, also in two chapters, reads the history of black urbanization alongside Japanese American incarceration and resettlement, complicating the canonical modernizing narratives of the Great Migration and the Internment. It explores how these forms of nonwhite difference provided each other with aesthetic resources to meditate on the distinction between freedom and graduated privilege, and to recall and release the unspeakable violence by which this distinction is elided. Finally, a brief Afterthought reflects on the "passing" of multiculturalism, inquiring into the ongoing transformations of imperialism's racial justice in the aftermath of the Cold War and the election of an African American president.

The remainder of this Overture introduces the book's central themes, in an extended reflection on the glinting opacity of the epigraph, which the late Ron Takaki cheerily sprinkled through his lectures, interviews, and writings. In turn, each section provides a gloss on a keyword from the book's title: *imperialism's racial justice, black Pacific, strange fruit,* and *fugitives.*

spreading gospel

Over the past fifteen years, scholarship across ethnic studies, American studies, and postcolonial studies has critiqued the appropriation of the grammar and lexicon of antiracism by U.S. imperialism, from the consolidation of an official multiculturalism in the first Iraq war and its deployments in the so-called War on Terror, to its historical precedents in Cold War racial liberalism. With the post–Cold War dissolution of a Third Worldist idea predicated on the continuity of antiracism and anti-imperialism, it became necessary to rethink the relation between imperialism and racial justice, within a broader account of the dramatic shifts and mundane continuities of national and global racial orders after the disavowal of segregation and colonialism.

Yet imperialism's reliance on a language of racial justice is nothing new. If you aim to identify what is distinctive or peculiar to a post–World War II or post–civil rights racial regime, you should know that the phenomenon of an imperialism enunciated as the expansion of racial justice, in word and deed, is no recent innovation. In this book, I trace these concerns to a period when terms of racial justice are close enough to seem familiar, even as the more genteel forms of white supremacism were hegemonic, and American exceptionalism found triumphal expression in overseas territorial colonialism. Because the post–World War II U.S. racial order claims the formal equality of races (against white supremacism) and the formal independence of nations (against colonialism) as the foundation of its disavowal of racism, which it thereby represents as the very exemplar of injustice, it seems odd that the language of racial uplift that once motivated an entire spectrum of black political movements was deployed, in the name of Anglo-Saxon superiority, to justify the conquest of the Philippines.

While lingering in this sense of historical disorientation might be instructive, a few brief hypotheses on race, imperialism, and justice should suffice to proceed. First, if the term "racism" refers at once to structured relations of inequality and to patterns of attitude, thought, and representation, then the latter must serve to uphold and extend the former—which is to say, racism must be understood as always a justification of its own material conditions. This means, curiously enough, that racism must always present itself as the proper form of racial justice, its culmination or terminal phase, beyond which lies chaos or decay. So if some of the more insidious recent forms of racist ideology claim the legacy of civil rights, in the name of "color-blindness," this is nothing new, but a feature common to previous racisms—only the historical terms of what is promised as racial justice have changed.

Second, imperialisms are always *in competition*, a claim that holds at least on contingent empirical grounds in recent eras, if not definitionally. The late nineteenth-century rise of U.S. global power involved the incitement of animosity toward Spanish decadence and cultivation of racial fraternity with England, even as it aimed finally to supplant its European predecessors. Such competition is never entirely friendly, but neither is it entirely unfriendly—it served both U.S. and Spanish purposes to stage the conclusion of the 1898 war in the Philippines as an exchange between equals, with Filipinos excluded. Ultimately, imperialisms seek to be universal and to fully and finally monopolize the very terms of universality—an impossible task. Yet because their power cannot be total, because their dominion cannot be coextensive with the universe, imperialisms must always pursue expansion—preemptively countering the threat of encroachment by some other expansionist force, real or imagined, out to universalize dominion on alien grounds. Imperialisms cannot be satisfied with any victory because their aspiration to total power is insatiable; as such, they will invent an enemy if none can be found.

Third, imperialism, in its various manifestations, is necessarily a multiracial, multiracialist project. Imperialism is, among other things, the desire to rule over difference. It seeks to extend its dominion across peoples and territories thereby defined as other, a process necessarily grounded in coercion rather than consent; yet it must always seek to legitimize that extension, however violent, as the arrival of justice. Put differently, *racial justice is imperialism's gospel*, the good news it is compelled to express in and as violence. The claim *to do justice to difference* provides imperialism with its moral authority, political legitimacy, and ideological engine. Writing amid the din of war in 2003, Edward Said asserted, "Every single empire in its official discourse has said that it is not like all the others, that its circumstances are special, that it has a mission to enlighten, civilize, bring order and democracy, and that it uses force only as a last resort" (xxi). Exceptionalism, in other words, is a formal characteristic of *every* imperialism's claim to justice, a kind of hallmark, in what is merely one of the phenomenon's lesser paradoxes.

That the racialized population imperialism would rule must be constructed as incapable, or not yet capable, of giving their consent does not cancel this requirement for justification. Rather, justice emerges, first and foremost, as a terrain of struggle between *competing* imperialisms, and between the imperial subjects who constitute, at least in principle, a transimperial community of judgment. This figurative gathering is positioned above and before the possible engineering of a colonized subject capable—again, in principle—of provisional membership in that hierarchical community. On such terms, it may be easier to understand how *an annihilating violence may be one form of this justice.* Yet even then, the imperative of expansion guides violence in the direction of inclusion. Just as those racializing processes typically understood as inclusion's opposite actually prove to be modes of incorporation—for example, Jim Crow segregation and Oriental exclusion, in practice, bound unfree subjects *within* heavily restricted and regulated socioeconomic locations—so, too, should processes of inclusion be understood as necessitating a differentiating and refining violence.

Readers who seek to refashion and reactivate the allied projects of antiracism and anti-imperialism, rather than merely perform their critical autopsy, may find these propositions disabling. To think of contemporary U.S. imperialism's deployment of diversity-talk as an appropriation requires imagining a chain of appropriations and counterappropriations stretching back to the onset of European imperialism and the transatlantic slave trade, and positing that the conception of racial justice properly originates with the agents of conquest. Such a model may itself be too simplistic, in seeking to secure a transhistorical autonomy of legitimate and illegitimate conceptions of justice—even if, in local practice, it makes sense to oppose the pragmatic compromises of a liberatory movement to the disingenuous propagandizing of an oppressive regime. Nonetheless, I contend that *imperialism's racial justice* should be approached as an animating contradiction, logically necessary but unpredictably volatile. No mere alibi, it must be taken seriously even—especially—if you hope to reject it.

What readers of any political inclination may find most difficult to accept is that imperialism's claims to justice are not immediately and unambiguously debarred by its reliance on forms of excessive, repetitive, and spectacular violence. Even so, it may be acknowledged that civilizing missions past and present have at times been indistinguishable in practice from overwhelming violence. If such violence proceeds from intentions and premises reflexively represented as benevolent, innocent, and idealistic, this paradox may be explained away as betrayal, corruption, or human frailty, or dismissed as deception or bad faith. Across a political spectrum, histories of imperial violence become separable from theories of racial justice. Against this common sense, I contend that violence is the vehicle of imperialism's racial justice, the very means of its actualization, and that the practical identity between the two is experienced as a quotidian reality. How, then, does their separation come to be taken for granted?

To approach this question as a problem of ideology or epistemology may not sufficiently express how deeply the operations of race pervade social experience. What manages the contradictions of race and justice is also a matter of aesthetics: a set of enabling constraints on the senses that conditions perception. Students of black literature and culture will be familiar with its paradox of invisibility and hypervisibility, and scholars of race will recall the duplicitous language of color-blindness, two examples of a larger dynamic not reducible to the visual or to any single sense. Angela Davis captures it succinctly in asking why older forms of racism are called "overt," as if racism is somehow "hidden" in the post–civil rights era ("Civil Rights"). Similarly, Patricia Williams describes the successful police defense in the Rodney King case as less a rationalization than a painstaking lesson in an "aesthetics of rationality" (54). An elaborate system of looking, charged with fear and desire, which intuitively apprehends a prone black body as a threat demanding overwhelming preemptive force; or again, the socialized habits of perception that instruct you to perceive mass incarceration as a natural function of government, and that evoke the specter of the prisoner to teach you to see yourself as free—such are the broader set of phenomena I conceptualize as an *aesthetics of racial terror*, a training of attention that allows its subjects to distinguish between forms of freedom and unfreedom, between differently racialized and gendered bodies, and between the gospel of imperialism's racial justice and its expression as overwhelming violence.

The violence's tendency toward repetition and excess points to its intrinsic inability to fully and finally achieve its ends, revealing an anxiety over the limits of domination and the nonidentity of coercion and consent. By the same token, its corresponding tendency toward spectacle and ritualization suggests how that anxiety demands a periodic renewal of its lessons. These must be compulsively reenacted in an increasingly formalized manner, whose slightly disjunctive relation to any given situation both extends their temporal reach and invites their eventual collapse. Because the violent operation of imperialism's racial justice is unable to fix its terms, they are shown to be historically contingent. What passes for racial justice under imperialism in one period—expulsion, wholesale slaughter, engineered extinction, religious conversion, cultural erasure—might provide the very definition of racial injustice in another, even as the extent to which imperialism dominates the terms of what can be imagined as racial justice in the present is difficult to properly perceive.

This is why I do not turn to the past to recover an exemplary politics. Such an impulse rests on unacknowledged presumptions regarding history as progressive enlightenment, upholding images of freedom's betrayal in an unfree past to train its optics to mistake the privileging of hindsight for freedom of judgment in the present. By contrast, this book seeks to dwell within the strangeness of the past as a means of defamiliarizing the present, casting its lot within the predicaments of the past in order to read a shared condition of unfreedom in the desire to become estranged to it. This task of reading, or learning how to read, draws on the aesthetic resources of black radical traditions that improvise a countertraining of perception, whose appearance may be anticipated within the ritual sites of training in the aesthetics of racial terror—in its very forms, practices, and protocols. It pursues the chance that what imperial inclusion in the violence of its embrace must exclude bears the clues to what yet eludes it.

* * *

The predominant form of imperialism's racial justice discussed in this book, recent enough to seem at once familiar and foreign, is racial uplift.

At the twentieth century's dawn, uplift encompassed both the range of projects to improve the social conditions of African Americans *and* the guiding rationale for U.S. colonialism in the Philippines. Looking back through a perspective shaped by post–World War II conjunctions of formal racial equality and formal national independence, on one hand, and Third Worldist antiracism and anti-imperialism, on the other, these two senses appear incommensurable. Examples of *Negro uplift*, as collective protest or moralizing conservativism, are regularly represented as antecedents of various contemporary strains of African American politics. By contrast, the attitudes and expressions of *Anglo-Saxon uplift*, when not ignored or discarded, are recognized as outmoded or racist. Whether the racial politics of U.S. colonialism are seen as aberrations or vestiges in an essentially benevolent tradition, or as alibis or paternalistic delusions exposing the immorality of power, their discontinuity from traditions of racial justice is taken for granted. Yet at the time, black intellectuals regularly presumed the coherence and continuity of an overarching category of uplift, upholding it most strongly when they subjected its Anglo-Saxon variant to criticism. On what terms can this continuity be understood?

In his influential work on uplift, Kevin Gaines argues that an older sense of the term rooted in "antislavery folk religion" (*Uplifting the Race*, 1) largely gave way, after Reconstruction, to an ideology stressing "self-help, racial solidarity, temperance, thrift, chastity, social purity, patriarchal authority, and the accumulation of wealth." While "espousing a vision of racial solidarity uniting black elites with the masses," Gaines argues, uplift ideology functioned to establish a fragile class division within the race. In the teeth of racism, "many black elites sought status, moral authority, and recognition of their humanity by distinguishing themselves, as bourgeois agents of civilization, from the presumably undeveloped black majority; hence the phrase, so purposeful and earnest, yet so often of ambiguous significance, 'uplifting the race'" (2). Tenuous and aspirational, this social distinction intensified the values and practices of service and duty to the race, inscribing it even as they worked to overcome it.

Anglo-Saxon uplift was similarly concerned as much with its privileged subject as with its benighted objects. While the stated aim of conquest was to better a native deemed unfit for self-government, its underlying objective was to establish a white American racialized capacity for imperial rule, as illustrated by Rudyard Kipling's famously bitter counsel to his Anglo-Saxon brethren to "take up the White Man's burden" in the Philippines. Though ingratitude, sabotage, and failure may be the results of the colonizer's efforts, the poem suggests, he must be satisfied by the "judgment of [his] peers," veterans of other civilizing missions, upon his "manhood." Counterposing this racialized fraternity to the sour travesty of "silent sullen peoples" impassively "weigh[ing] your Gods and you," the poem illustrates how imperialism constitutes white manhood as a transimperial community of judgment, even as judgment is thereby made available to appropriation by the colonized (291).

This understanding of U.S. conquest as a trial of white manhood, a liberating burden, was not merely an invention of the poet. Cast in decidedly sunnier terms, uplift was President William McKinley's own reported justification for the war. In a notorious 1899 interview, first published by James Rusling in 1903, McKinley insists he had no initial interest in colonization. After nights of soul searching, however, he finds no alternative: returning the islands to Spain "would be cowardly and dishonorable," handing them to another European power "would be bad business and discreditable," and recognizing their independence would be disastrous, as "they were unfit for self-government." "There was nothing left for us to do," he concludes, "but to take them all, and to educate the Filipinos, and uplift and civilize and Christianize them, and by God's grace do the very best we could by them, as our fellow-men for whom Christ also died" (22–23). However authentic the anecdote, it accurately illustrates the official rationales for war, recast as a moral challenge— encountered first before a transimperial community of whiteness, as a test of manhood (the gendered capacity for valor, honor, and credit), and second, in the face of a racialized population, recognized only as the object of responsibility. Uplift, in other words, is a moral duty, in the form of conquest.

Broadly speaking, what's historically particular to uplift as a form of racial justice is its imagination of a benevolent relationship between subjects positioned differently in a hierarchy of civilization. As it worked to establish, certify, and justify inequality, its internal logic cast this relationship as a form of tutelary love. McKinley's official policy of "benevolent assimilation," as Vicente Rafael glosses it, is "a moral imperative" devoted to a "civilizing love and the love of civilization" (21), manifested primarily in education—the governing trope and signature policy concern of Anglo-Saxon uplift in the Philippines, as well as a primary field of debate for competing visions of Negro uplift.

The problem of tutelage holds an inherent paradox, what you might call uplift's miraculous core: it aims to produce a free, self-determining subject through an imposed, coercive process disallowing that subject's capacity to evaluate its fitness for self-rule. While this process may function in retrospect—an autonomous subject can narrate its passage from dependence to independence—it is impossible when imagined prospectively: to require another's recognition of your capacity for self-determination is to be incapable of self-determination. To wait upon the grace of uplift is endless, for it is only ever bestowed after the fact.

In the colony, Anglo-Saxon uplift always deferred the autonomy it claimed to produce. One way to resolve this problem required internalizing tutelage within the collective and individual racial body, which is how Negro uplift sought its autonomy. By taking autonomy as a given, retrospective accounts tend to obscure the unstable intraracial split such tutelage produces—whether between the black middle-class subject and the benighted masses or within that precarious middle-class subject itself—behind the unifying force of racial pride as self-love. Both Anglo-Saxon and Negro uplift, then, heralded the emergence of an internally divided nonwhite subject who belongs in and to a transimperial realm of civilization while remaining marginal to any existing state capable of recognizing that subject as its citizen.

To be clear, I am not suggesting that these forms of uplift are equivalent, nor that one is less authentic or derivative of the other. Negro uplift differs in its primary emphasis on intraracial relations, though it was nonetheless profoundly shaped by interactions with colonized nonwhite populations, as well as the Anglo-Saxon uplift whose hypocrisies it exposed—black observers could excoriate white soldiers and officials in the Philippines while upholding the imperial mission's ideals. But just as Negro uplift saw itself as more fully and properly embodying the ideals proclaimed by Anglo-Saxon uplift, it also shared an essential relationship to violence, moralized and moralizing: unable to recognize the autonomy of its inter- or intraracial object, racial uplift construes its prerogative of coercion as benevolent. Similarly, their shared historical conditions make them alienating to present-day sensibilities in analogous ways. As the prevailing form of racial justice in a period when white supremacism was hegemonic, both forms of uplift contain elements that appear to hindsight as unmistakably racist.

They also shared a more curious feature: the presumption, as a structural premise, of inevitable European civilizational decline, against which uplift's subject was positioned as subordinate but rising, through a generative relation with its own, less civilized wards. Where uplift offered its lowly objects a tutelage in civilization leading, someday, to autonomous selfhood, it promised its advanced subjects protection from decadence or "overcivilization" through reinvigorating contact with primitive vitality. Underwriting uplift was a model of civilization joining hierarchical classification and the forward, upward movement of historical progress to the cyclical rhythms of birth, maturation, reproduction, and death. To be at the pinnacle of this civilizational schema is to anticipate a natural decline. Both varieties of uplift sought to engineer new forms of racial privilege as heirs-apparent to European empires, known and constituted by intercourse with more primitive groups. Among African American intellectuals in the period, the word "Occidentalism" was sometimes used to distinguish a desire for Western ideals from a disdain for white people who claimed them,[2] a term even more striking if you recall its etymological origin—the identification of the west as the direction of the setting sun. Hence, I take *occidented* as my term for this shared orientation, upholding the primacy of Western civilization as the very promise of its downfall.

the missing link

The recent resurgence of an Afro-Asian comparative interest out of disparate investments within African American and Asian American studies, black diaspora studies and critical Asian studies, and American studies and ethnic studies[3] has largely evaded the gravitational pull of the term "black Pacific," as a parallel formation to Paul Gilroy's phenomenally successful if often misunderstood 1993 book, *The Black Atlantic*.[4] However, the phrase appears in two critical interventions worth noting. In "Toward a Black Pacific," his afterword to Heike Raphael-Hernandez and Shannon Steen's *AfroAsian Encounters*, Gary Okihiro points out that "the Pacific" as metonym "often and mistakenly stands in place of or in reference to Asia, especially East Asia" (313). As a brief corrective to this erasure of indigenous histories, he sketches "three intersections between Pacific Islanders and African Americans" (316): overlapping histories of bonded labor migration linking enslaved Africans, Chinese "coolies," and Polynesian captives in Peru; networks of colonial education tying Tuskegee and Hampton to Hawai'i; and circuits of popular culture bringing new styles of Hawaiian and African American music in contact since the nineteenth century. Unfortunately, an excavation of the historical confluences of Pacific Islander and black cultures is beyond the capacity of this book, whose comparative scope is already ambitious. Though it cannot substantively redress the erasures of indigenous Pacific histories and perspectives, I hope at least to unsettle their reinscription, and I follow Okihiro in emphasizing the multiplicity of racial categories that "the Pacific" invokes.

Another intervention is signaled by Etsuko Taketani's essay, "The Cartography of the Black Pacific: James Weldon Johnson's *Along This Way*," which tracks the multiple accounts Johnson gave of his participation, as consul, in the 1912 U.S. intervention in Nicaragua that led to twenty years of military occupation—an incident, he argued, that partly responded to rising Japanese influence, and that would be cited to defend Japan's 1931 invasion of Manchuria. Challenging the tendency in recuperative scholarship to explain black sympathy for Japanese imperialism as "mistaken," Taketani rejects the unexamined assumption that "African Americans are not accountable for globe-carving imperialism" (82), arguing that Johnson's agency cannot be severed from its position within, and influence upon, a politics hindsight finds objectionable. Recognizing "the complicity of imperial modes and a black internationalism" (103) leads her to an instructive reading of Johnson's interrogation of "the very continuity between his position and a position he repudiates as evil" (91).[5]

In this book, I refer to *the transpacific* to account for differentiations within imperial racial formation—noting, for example, that certain features characterizing Filipino and Hawaiian racialization correspond with Negro racialization in this period, by contrast with the racialization of Chinese and Japanese. Acknowledging African Americans' productive complicity in U.S. imperialism reveals how this correspondence conditioned the agency of black soldiers, colonial officials, and intellectuals, as they recast the meanings and destinies of race through encounters with Philippine colonization, as well as how advocates of uplift pursued autonomy through imaginative affinities with imperial Japan. Attending to the transpacific allows me to extend Taketani's exploration of black internationalism's alignments with various imperialisms, while to negotiating the continuity of black and Asian theories and representations of race with positions that now appear unambiguously racist.

By contrast, this book poses *the black Pacific* with a certain irreducible irony. In its inherent volatility, the term might most precisely be described as a joke. If it functions in scholarly endeavors as a lure that misapprehends its own "discoveries," then rather than disavowing the desire that produced it, you might allow it to turn back on that desire as instruction—in the same way the "joke" of passing played by the narrator of James Weldon Johnson's *Autobiography of an Ex-Colored Man* turns back on his narrative as a bitter lesson on distance between racial privilege and freedom. I propose "the black Pacific" to name, not a subfield of academic enterprise, but a mythic preserve within which the desired object of U.S. imperial violence was imagined to live and breed.

Like "race" more broadly, this black Pacific is a social fiction with material consequences, though none of the groups ensnared under its particular manifestations sought to appropriate it as a category of affirmative collectivity. Hence it can be described more emphatically as a *historical nonentity*, in that its existence, as a fantasy with real effects, was recognized only through negation and disavowal. Indeed, it was an *indispensable negativity* for a range of modernizing projects, the specter each needed to invoke in order to exorcize. It was the object of a white imperial desire, which sought at once to consume it and to banish it from perception, whether through overwhelming violence or benevolent tutelage. As the violent tropical zone where Negro and Filipino racialization did not merely overlap but actually converged, it was the slanderous precondition of would-be autonomous forms of Negro and Filipino uplift, which sought to disprove it through the performance of civilized gender norms. In extravagant revenge fantasies of the Negro incarnation of Japanese imperial might, it offered a teeming cache of speculative fancies to projects of Negro and Nisei self-imagining, which learned to disavow it as the price of fashioning a serious politics. Finally, it gave birth to alternative political solidarities, from world-belting social movements to inchoate aesthetic impulses, which aimed to displace it in the name of the "darker races," the "Afro-Asian," or the "Third World"—names that have come to evoke a nostalgia for worlds that never came to pass, a feeling that bears whatever is left in these histories that still gives itself to the chance of another world.

The black Pacific, to repeat, existed only as fantasy; it entered history to the extent that the denial of its entry into history was imagined as history's inauguration. Its sheer unreality, moreover, allowed it to function as—to borrow Jacqueline Goldsby's elaboration of Du Bois's phrase—"a terrible real" (166). Lest this seem too obscure, note that its most celebrated denizen has already made an appearance on these pages, passing under the cover of familiarity. You know him as Kong.

* * *

Invented for the classic 1933 film that bears his name, King Kong's broad appeal and wide-ranging cultural afterlife have never been significantly hampered by the widespread recognition that he serves as a metaphor for racist fantasies of violent black sexuality. Nor has that metaphor been disrupted by the largely ignored fact that Kong's imagined origins lie not in Africa but in Southeast Asia—more specifically, the fictitious Skull Island somewhere west of Sumatra.[6] A heart of darkness never penetrated by white explorers, it proves irresistible to Carl Denham, a fast-talking New York movie producer whose technological expertise, entrepreneurial spirit, and cocky disregard for tradition embody U.S. modernity. His dream of capturing on film something "no white man has ever seen" expresses the ambitions of U.S. whiteness in an arena of imperial competition, and he guards the secret of their destination from his crew until just before their arrival, aware that its existence has circulated in obscure rumor. The captain, for example, admits to having heard the name Kong, which he skeptically identifies as "some native suspicion."

These words appear to be a minor alteration from the shooting script, which refers instead to "some Malay suspicion" (22)—Malay being the dubious racial-scientific category of the period that included Filipinos and other Southeast Asians and Pacific Islanders. Within days of *King Kong*'s March 24, 1933, premiere at Grauman's Chinese Theatre in Hollywood, the California Supreme Court ruled, in *Roldan v. Los Angeles County*, that because Filipinos were "Malays" rather than "Mongolians," they did not fall under antimiscegenation laws targeting Chinese; less than two weeks passed before the legislature amended California law to bar Malay-white marriages (Baldoz 98–101). Threats of miscegenation reinvigorated anti-Asiatic exclusion movements, which converged with the complex politics of colonial nationalism to produce the Hare-Hawes-Cutting Act of 1933 and its successor, the 1934 Tydings-McDuffie Act, promising the Philippines formal independence within a decade while terminating Filipino labor migration. In short, a consensus had formed that colonial rule in the Philippines was more trouble than it was worth. The disappearance of the word "Malay" from the film's dialogue parallels its broader elision of the Philippines and other U.S. colonial possessions in the Pacific. Similarly, the film never purports to represent Negro characters, but cast African American actors to portray Skull Island's natives, in a notorious conflation of minstrel and savage stereotyping that recalls the black-skinned, bug-eyed, wide-lipped Filipino natives of U.S. political cartooning during the Philippine-American War.[7]

The accumulation of these elliptical references ultimately allows Kong to emerge from a dense network of racial signifiers, transubstantiating empirical knowledge and imperial histories of race. The island's edges are littered with the wreckage of past imperial expeditions, circuited by a wall the men hesitantly compare to "Egyptian" ruins or "Angkor," built by some "higher civilization" lost in the mists of time. While the current islanders "have slipped back," they ritually maintain the fortifications sealing off the interior, and their language resembles that of the nearby (nonfictitious) Nias Islanders enough for the captain to engage them in crude dialogue. Their distance from the sleepy decadence of East Asian civilization is further established by contrast with the ship's cook, Charley, a stock Chinese stereotype.

This distinction develops through a complex staging of racial and gendered dynamics involving the frustrated romance between Ann Darrow, the beautiful unknown cast by Denham as his film's lead, and Jack Driscoll, the macho first mate, a committed sailor hesitant around modern women. In an extended sequence after the crew's initial encounter with the islanders, whose chief had offered six native women to purchase Ann for the still-unidentified Kong, the shooting script shows Ann speculating about Kong's identity with Charley, who exits suddenly in pursuit of a playful monkey named Ignatz (*King Kong* shooting script

38–39). On a ship full of men, only the reassuringly asexual cook and the comical simian mascot allow her to relax. The film elides this introduction, getting straight to the dramatic action: a chance encounter on the moonlit deck, where Ann tells Jack the islanders' drumming has kept her awake. Jack confesses to fearing for her safety, then to fearing her, and finally, to being in love. When she retorts, "You hate women," he awkwardly replies, "I know, but you aren't women," and they kiss. Then, after the captain calls him away, two islanders suddenly appear to kidnap her. Jack returns, finds only Charley, and heads off to her cabin, but then Charley discovers a cowrie bracelet on the deck and sounds the alarm, declaring: "Crazy black man been here!"

The modifier *black*, in the Chinese cook's broken English, does not identify the absent kidnapper as African or Negro. Rather, it signifies his racialized capacity to violently assert masculine heterosexual prerogative—unlike Jack or Charley, who are not *man enough* to act upon their natural desires to possess the white woman. This racialized capacity is merely transferred to the kidnappers as the agents of Kong, to whom the white woman will be offered; at a further remove, it transfers from the islanders to Ann and Jack via the drumming that aurally conditions their previously blocked embrace. While Charley's own interest in Ann is laughable—in a comic bit of business, he tries to join the search party, waving his meat cleaver and babbling, "Me likey go too. Me likey *catch Missy*," before the white men, armed with guns and explosives, wave him away—he provides a cautionary tale for Jack's white manhood. Just as the decline of Asiatic civilization resulted in emasculated, servile "Chinamen," Western modernity risked falling into decadence through its supposed disruption of traditional gender roles. The figure of a beautiful young woman, driven by ambition to venture, without husband or father, first to New York City and then to a savage ocean on a boat of rough men, is terrifying enough to send the valiant, virile Jack scampering to the company of other sailors. What might forestall this collapse into decadence is a tonic infusion of primal, violent sexuality, the essence of a blackness embodied by Kong—"neither beast nor man," Denham puts it, but "monstrous, all-powerful."

Kong's blackness thus emerges through careful differentiation from all existing racial categories to embody the ideal blackness posited by U.S. imperial desire. His dominion is the fabled blank spot on the map that eluded all previous empires, an untouched state of nature, abstracted from all the ongoing "race problems" left over from historical iterations of the civilizing mission—genocidal conquest, enslavement and Reconstruction, colonial rule in the Philippines. By implicit contrast to such historical complications, Kong's blackness appears as a fictive distillate of the longed-for real: the primal essence that might rejuvenate a U.S. whiteness imperiled by the perversions of overcivilization.

This essence must therefore be captured and carried to the metropolitan center, its violent mastery enacted before an excited public. When his film is ruined and his crew ravaged, Denham redoubles his ambitions, capturing and exhibiting not the image but the creature himself. Back in New York, before a packed theater, he displays Kong in chains: "He was a king and a god in the world he knew, but now he comes to civilization merely a captive, a show to gratify your curiosity." This performance is heightened, for the *cinematic* audience, when Kong escapes, seizes Ann, and runs amok in the city.[8] Finally, he climbs the Empire State Building, symbol of modern U.S. ascendancy, and briefly fights off a squadron of planes before falling to his death below.

By the rules of the narrative, Kong's death had already been assured, if not by his status as a figure of terror, then by the notorious scene on Skull Island where he partially undresses his blonde captive. In staging a fantasy of white womanhood imperiled by black sexual violence, which calls forth an overwhelming retributive violence to destroy the black threat in public spectacle, the film unmistakably repeats the logic—or the training in an *aesthetics of rationality*—that structures ritualized lynching. This structure manifests as a narrative trajectory from prehistoric to modern, vertiginously captured in the iconic image of the great ape battling airplanes from the top of the skyscraper, and mediated by the white woman's body, as Dunham famously concludes: "It wasn't the aviators. It was Beauty killed the Beast." The sacrifice and consumption of a primal essence redeems a white nation threatened by overcivilization, restoring its organic capacity for growth and regeneration: civilization's sublimation of the savage is a life-giving act of sexual violence. Kong's capture and killing make Jack *more* of a man, Ann *more* of a woman, and their resulting heterosexual union *more normatively white*. This ritualized narrative, what you might call *the lynching form*, miraculously births whiteness through the violent incorporation of blackness, a ceremony of communion whose celebration constitutes a white—that is, imperial—nation.[9]

The resemblance between spectacle lynching and other communion rites has long been noted, an analogy highlighting both the desire invested in the sacrificial object and the endless repetition of ritual. Because the reproduction of whiteness is the *effect* of a ceremonial performance constituted by the screening of the film, it is not actually represented within the narrative: the conjugal union of Jack and Ann takes place only after the story ends. If audiences tend to forget Jack, who is largely superfluous to the climactic sequence in Manhattan and never achieves normative masculinity on screen; if their desires tend to fix on Kong and his captive, a primitivized figure of female sexual vulnerability not yet restored to a properly gendered norm; if the film reads as a tragedy whose hero's death is rescinded in the afterlife of innumerable remakes and new adventures across genres and media—all this may be a consequence of the lynching form's ritual temporality: it is cyclical, mortal, always insufficient, requiring repetition, again and again and again.

Just as Filipinos and African Americans do not actually appear in the film, as signifiers rendered "nonfictional" by troublesome histories of racialization, the fictional Kong appears extraneous to historical analyses of U.S. imperialism and its production of racial categories. But Kong, you might say, is the fabled "missing link" that makes the logic of U.S. imperial racism coherent: because the black Pacific did not exist, he had to be invented. His story portrays the logic, or aesthetic, of the bond between discrepant racial subjects forged by the violence of the U.S. civilizing mission, held together by the abstract ideal of a primal essence posited by imperial desire. In seeking the embodiment of its sexual fantasy, this violence functioned to conflate Negro and Filipino racialization, and yet all its ritual recurrences, whether in cinematic and literary representations or in grisly live reenactments, could never conjure the fantasy into existence.

Indeed, for those African Americans who journeyed across the ocean, on ships or in the pages of print or the shadows of the cinema, and for Filipinos across empire, writing at the seam of metropolitan and colonial racial formations, it was the *discrepancy* between racial forms, the disjunctive doubling of savage stereotype in the superimposition of Negro and Filipino, that provided motive and mobility. Drawing on Brent

Edwards's theorization of *décalage* as the discrepancy or gap in articulations of diaspora enabling movement, understood as the absence of some artificial "prop or wedge" ("Uses" 65–66), you might say that it was the removal of the black Pacific "missing link" that allowed articulations of Negro-Filipino relations to be set in motion. If the identity posited by the fusion of these racial forms could only be a trap, the incitement of violence, the difference between them might serve as a pivot in another direction. How this difference was operated, in what manner and toward what ends, I will take up throughout this book.

freedom from love

To state that *King Kong* is a celebratory reenactment of lynching is merely to express an open secret, one consistent with lynching's own logic: as Jacqueline Goldsby has shown, the simultaneity of spectacle and secrecy is crucial to understanding this violence. In the film and its remakes, audiences are called upon to simultaneously see and not see lynching's manifestation, the same training of perception that made the perpetrators of spectacle lynching disappear before the sight of the law. Yet this history of violence seems incompatible with the curious love adhering to the character, in all his unlikely vagabondage through global popular culture. Where audiences' love for the renegade ape largely serves to dissociate their narrative investment in lynching's reenactment, it is the perceptual foregrounding of lynching, the insistent calling of attention to the visual, olfactory, and kinesthetic evidence left in its wake, that banishes explicit recognition of the erotic dynamics suffusing Billie Holiday's performance of "Strange Fruit." To love Kong, viewers of the film must all but forget they are enjoying a lynching; to attend to lynching, listeners to the song must all but forget that its performance gathers in a space consecrated to love.

As a reader of such reenactments, learn not to forget there is danger here.

The danger inheres, first of all, in the condition of being overwhelmed, which any attempt to speak the violence struggles to restrain but cannot fully deny. *When I sing it, it affects me so much I get sick*, Holiday writes.[10] *It takes all the strength out of me* (95). Earnestness or anger, a politics of righteousness, may disavow its insufficiency only by substituting the work of exorcism for the appeal to justice. For the dead have not been saved, and justice has not come. *It reminds me of how Pop died.* To say otherwise, to proclaim justice's establishment in a haunted land, on behalf of those living who would claim the name of the dead—as a nation, race, or species; as rightful heirs—is to willfully misperceive your privilege as freedom. To be open to the radical force of the appeal to justice demands the vulnerability of understanding the violence as ongoing. *But I have to keep singing it, not only because people ask for it but because twenty years after Pop died the things that killed him are still happening in the South* (95). In short, to speak of lynching is to render your own ethical failure, whether you admit it or not—not only to acknowledge justice's failure to redress a harm but to bear forward the work of the violence out into the world.

Coming after the first is a second danger, weaving leisurely in its course, but swiftly registered by a certain attentive presence within Holiday's audience. For example, the civil rights journalist and community leader Evelyn Cunningham recalled: "Many times in nightclubs when I heard her sing the song it was not a sadness I sensed as much as there was something else; it's got to do with sexuality. Men and women would hold hands, they would look at each other, and they would pretend there was love going on, or something sexual. They would get closer together and yet there was a veneer—and just a veneer—of anger and concern" (qtd. in Margolick 81). The hesitance in Cunningham's guarded testimony pauses over what seems to be an actual confusion, another presence in the crowd, *something else* that is not but has *got to do with sexuality*. Righteousness, a thin skin of affect as the badge of a politics, fails to conceal what is nonetheless only pretense: *as if* "there was love going on, or something sexual." Looking at the stage and at each other, holding hands, the men and women perform for Cunningham's gaze, in the dark, as if they do not know they are being watched, as if they do not know what possesses them.

In her characteristically blunt memoirs, Holiday remarks on this strange presence:

> Over the years I've had a lot of weird experiences as a result of that song. It has a way of separating the straight people from the squares and cripples. One night in Los Angeles a bitch stood right up in the club where I

was singing and said, "Billie, why don't you sing that sexy song you're so famous for? You know, the one about the naked bodies swinging in the trees."

Needless to say, I didn't. (95)

It is tempting to imagine the woman as merely unknowing, deficient in awareness or ability, what Holiday refers to as a *square* or *cripple* or both. But her request, as Holiday reports it, suggests a more deliberate cruelty.[11] Unlike the cautious Cunningham or the unwitting couples she observes, the figure called *bitch* bears knowledge but lacks care, setting loose a force she cannot really control. Meeting her affront with greater knowledge and equal fearlessness, Holiday's account enacts a curt dismissal whose brevity contains volumes—outstripping speech not because there is nothing to say but because there is too much, an excess of meaning. Yet it is *needless to say* because Holiday works the song to elude the domain of what is said. How so?

Consider, for contrast, James Baldwin's "Going to Meet the Man," in which a white deputy sheriff's childhood memory of a lynching bee remedies an episode of impotence, summoning figures of racist fantasy to mediate intercourse with his wife. Or consider Kara Walker's shameless exhumations of the imaginative domains of power, violence, and sexual desire bequeathed by the history of slavery, loosed demons fluttering free from the profound moralism of Baldwin's redemptive vision. You might take such work as extrapolations of the knowledge implicit in Holiday's performance, in her auditory and kinesthetic shaping of the words and again in the way she inhabited the iconicity the song helped define for her. These extrapolations extend the knowledge's reach by diminishing its ineffable force. Where Baldwin names white interracial desire as the motive force formalized in lynching, exposing the racializing and sexualizing violence on which white reproduction depends, Holiday's performance refrains from such naming, as it refrains from putting its most powerful message into words, even as it enacts the exposure of the history of sexuality that the song and all it reenacts has *got to do with.*

In the words of the song, lynching's *bitter crop* disrupts the *pastoral scene* of trees and flowers and birds and weather, its reversion to nature leaving a perverse remainder: these *bodies* are not persons, but *fruit*, and what makes them *strange* is what makes them *black*. There must have been persons here, once, in the bodies dehumanized in their blackening, and as the agents of that blackening—absented, monstrous, horrific, one feels obliged to say, inhuman. Although there must have been persons here once, the song cannot imagine them in words. Blackness as death is what the words can picture as presence; blackness as life-giving essence has been absconded with by whiteness. In this way the words of the song enact the same perceptual protocols that render the perpetrators of lynching invisible before the eyes of the law, passing unmarked into the community of whiteness after enacting its social reproduction, with the same effortless slide of a movie camera away from the conjugal act.

The words were written by the leftist writer, lyricist, and composer Abel Meeropol, published as a poem under his given name, and later set to music under his professional name, Lewis Allan.[12] By his own account, they were written in response to a lynching photograph (N. Baker 45), commonly taken to be the notorious image of the 1930 lynching of Thomas Shipp and Abram Smith in Marion, Indiana, which prominently features a festive crowd of onlookers. Meeropol's Jewishness surely modulates the lyrics' critical restaging of the lynching rite's aesthetic training—elsewhere, he put it quite succinctly: "I am a Jew, / How may I tell? / The Negro lynched / Reminds me well / I am a Jew" (qtd. in N. Baker 45). Yet even if this ethnoracial shading passes unremarked, at least two varieties of whiteness already appear in the space evacuated by the lyrics, each constituted against the other. One gathers to celebrate the violence, its communal rejuvenation in defiant defense against the threat of decadence manifested in the other, which is constituted by the horrified desire to read the participants in the lynching bee out of history. That the latter form of whiteness has become hegemonic may be registered by the quicksand fascination experienced by present-day viewers of lynching photographs for their figures of white onlookers.[13] In the aftermath of the civil rights era, that latter form still shares in the national commemoration of lynching's death through the ritual consumption of the sacrificed black body, but the presence of the former as an audience within the photographs exposes, for better or for worse, lynching's function to reproduce whiteness.

As written, the words respond to the photograph, to the experience of its observation at a remove, within an alternate gathering of racial community, completing the process of the perpetrators' disappearance. As sung, Kevin Young proposes, the words constitute "a symbolic lynching photograph" that, "confronted with the crime of looking, . . . resorts . . . to the abandoning of a self altogether" (219). That is, Young's reading attributes to Holiday's voice the agency of a withholding of both "I" and "you,"[14] whose result he glosses precisely in an ambiguous riffing quotation, "*Look away, Dixieland*" (220). "Lady Day embodies a strategy of silence," he argues, that in the *performance* of the words "talk[s] back to the silence of lynching, which you can almost see in a lynching photograph" (220). Her performance, he concludes, "shelters and smuggles meaning beyond the borders of what is acceptable—or even seen" (224). Because the violence itself establishes these enabling borders, perceptual before epistemological or ideological or moral, its agency lies outside what can be seen or shown or said. Holiday's performance moves outside to confront it.

Simply put, it does so through a contrast between the words of the song and the conditions of its performance—the milieu from which it emanates and the genius of its embodied voice—that improvises an aesthetic countertraining within the very observation of ritualized racial terror. "I wondered then whether it made sense to sing a song in such a milieu," comments a listener quoted by David Margolick. "I thought it belonged instead in a concert setting, without beer and whiskey and cigarette smoke" (52). Presumably meant as a compliment—for jazz music, it was prophecy—the attitude has many precedents. Before his encounter with lynching, James Weldon Johnson's ex-colored man, for one, hoped to uplift the music from nightclub to concert hall. But it is the music's association with less respectable environments, of good times and ill repute, that gives the performance its force. The association of racial transgression, political radicalism, and the nightlife that defined Café Society, the Greenwich Village nightclub where Holiday made the song famous, was a recipe that set Harlem in vogue over a decade earlier. To ask whether the amplification of sexual desire served transgressive politics or political sentiment merely licensed sexual transgression is only to attempt to impose narrative order on what was, for good or ill, an undeniably transformative historical dynamic.

For its part, jazz, like other forms of popular music and dance, has historically flourished in spaces organized to profit on its aphrodisiac qualities, often involving fixation on the singer. The nightclub, rather than the concert hall, is the privileged setting for Holiday's music, and if this space sanctions alternative arrangements of social life experienced, in all their ephemerality, as liberatory, it is only because the space itself is dedicated to celebrating, conjuring, evoking, and enhancing erotic feeling. While the music cannot be reduced to its aphrodisiac qualities or their instrumentalization in courting or seduction, these qualities are irreducible from its conditions of production and reception, even in the devotions of a solitary fan.[15]

More than other singers, Holiday attracted such devotion, whose most disturbing product is the condescending, often bizarre equation of her artistry with the most salacious and tragic details of her biography—physical and sexual abuse, child prostitution, drug addiction. It places her in the front rank of a long tradition of singing black women, icons shaped between the violently hypersexualizing attention of white desire and the impossible resources of a longer tradition of black women's vocality.[16] The racialized, gendered, sexualized dimensions of this attention are structural, preceding the intentions or identifications of any listener, but Holiday's genius, as a prerequisite to its expression, involves the reflection, redirection, and reappropriation of this attention, working and reworking it for other purposes, turning and transforming its force.

It is here that the impact of her performance becomes unavoidable. The song's lyrics observe the lynching form, evoking the racist fantasies of black male sexual violence toward white women accompanying and justifying it, against which any respectable antilynching politics, white or black, needed to reaffirm the boundaries of racial and sexual propriety. Yet the song's performance—the embodied voice issuing from the nightlife milieu—exposes another history of sexual violence and interracial desire, culminating in the fetish of a hypersexualized black girl whose gift of singing beautifully is equated with her vulnerability to sexual exploitation and sexual violence. By setting these two contradictory histories in unbearable proximity, Holiday's "Strange Fruit" renders each radically unstable. On the one hand, she bends the most violently sexist and racist desires conditioning her consumption as a performer into a profound affective identification with opposition to lynching. On the other, she wrenches open a politics of respectability that stifled and suppressed poor black women in the name of uplift, schooling the ideology that would deny her the moral standing and personal dignity to bear witness against lynching's violence. In both cases, the work of Holiday's "Strange Fruit" turns on an insight left unspoken, that refrains from entering speech or sight: the violent, sexualizing, and racializing desire that drives the formalization of lynching is the same mysterious presence structuring the audience's relation to the singer, incarnating her as a singing body laid open to violence.

What *works* this presence, turning on an insight that may remain unavailable to the audience, is a genius extending back, insistently previous, before the incarnation of the singing body. The figure of the hypersexualized, broken, helpless girl is revealed as a mere veil, flung like a net over the Lady. In claiming her title, Lady Day did not wait on recognition; she did not seek inclusion or acceptance within respectability so much as she rebuked it, put it to shame. Neither does the work of her song depend on the audience's conscious recognition of what's happening, the effect of the words dissociating from the dynamics of the performance, even as both at once demand the audience's engagement. That space where the lynchers are, the same perceptual nowhere inhabited by persons unknown, is where the work of Holiday's song takes place, even as sight and speech remain trained on the lynched body, that bitter crop.

* * *

For twenty years she carried it with her, a gift and a curse, filial duty and liberating burden, this song that helped make her a star and a target for the law. She died young with a wrecked voice, everyone says, and if you listen to recordings of the song over the course of her career it's easy to imagine you can feel the weight of it, borne across that time, all those miles, all that way from poverty and scorn to international fame. This is, of course, only an element of her artistry, to evoke a feeling that, sad or happy, joyful or melancholy, is so full of longing it seems like intimacy, like the most ecstatic identification. Rather than art.

Perhaps this is why so many of Lady's ardent devotees want to believe that the music killed her—made her suffer, rode her down, burned her up, ruined her, leaving her a defiant shell of herself, far older than the forty-four years given to her. To believe the music killed her is to imagine she died for love, for a love she shared with you. But she was just poor, and black, and a woman, which is explanation sufficient to a life of struggle and an early death, and there ought to be tragedy enough in that statement if you would just leave the music out of it. For if there is any *freedom* beyond *mystery* in her art, it is freedom *from* this love: the music itself as her freedom from the engulfing love it conjured up in her audience.

But the dead have not been saved, her song continues to tell you. To marshal all of her artistry to sustain this perception, this condition of being overwhelmed and unbearable longing for response, must have been a perilous act. Dwelling in peril, in preparation and performance, in her long commitment to the song, brought her fame and criticism, celebration and condescension, often in the same breath. The song was too serious, or not serious enough; it was ponderous or pandering; it was beneath her, bad art, or it ruined her for the lighter and faster material to which she was better suited. What frightens critics of the song most of all, it seems, is its relation to that ambivalent yet terrifyingly intense love it engendered, and perhaps this has as much to do as racism and sexism and snobbery in explaining the bizarrely persistent notion that the song's full meaning was somehow beyond her ken.[17]

The controversial white promoter John Hammond famously dismissed the song. "The beginning of the end for Billie was 'Strange Fruit,' when she had become the darling of the left-wing intellectuals," he asserted, leading her to begin "taking herself very seriously, and thinking of herself as very important." Opposing her to his icon of primitive authenticity, Bessie Smith, he bemoaned her contamination by this love, by her "success with white people," and, worst of all, by "homosexuals," who "just *fell* for Billie" (qtd. in Margolick 78–79). By contrast, Cunningham, whose courageous reporting for the *Pittsburgh Courier* won her the ironic title "lynching editor," earned the right not to listen: "There comes a time in a black person's life where you're up to your damned ears in lynching and discrimination, when sometimes you were just so sick of it, but it was heresy to express it. She was a great artist and she did great things with that song, but you would not admit you did not want to hear it." Yet Cunningham calls the song "an attention grabber," "a marketing device," suggesting that Holiday never "really understood or anticipated the serious attention" it brought. Against the evidence of her own comments about the presence of something *to do with sexuality* in the interracial audience, she insists, "The song did not disturb me because I never had the feeling that this was something she was very, very serious about" (qtd. in Margolick 81).

Earnest and self-flattering yet prurient and titillating, condescending in its benevolence and insatiable in its desire for violence—such contradictions only feed the intensity of this love. What boggles me is that would-be sympathetic auditors of Holiday so regularly turn away, in fear, to presume her ignorance—as if her performance, night after night and year after year, never prepared for such responses, as if there was no sophistication to Lady's rigorous education in and of this love. But her artistry does not rely on the audience's capacity to cognize its response, being concerned, instead, with training their perception and responsibility. The agency of her artistry may not be abated even as the audience falls short of what it asks of them, or reports to have closed their ears. And if sometimes Holiday refused to perform "Strange Fruit," whether out of frustration with the crowd or mere exhaustion, at other times you might imagine her response to the desires of both critics and fans in the phrases of a love song just as difficult to hear: *hush now, don't explain.*

Is this what is meant when it is said that her voice sounds wise? Even those convinced she didn't understand the words she sang speak of her singing in this fashion, but what does it mean to attribute wisdom to the quality of her sound? (*Lazy*, they also call it, which may be easier to understand, if you can recognize preparation and skill in achieving the effect. "Lazy" sounds scornful, and often is, because *laziness* names the confrontation between fantasies of imperial privilege and everyday resistance, revolted and envious desire gazing down on a dream of freedom catching like a tune in the back of your head.) What kind of wisdom is this?

Formally speaking, schools would not teach it, though it might be learned there; what education Holiday received, in any case, is a matter of lore. Schools were part of a complex of uplifting institutions given to violent intervention in Holiday's transient family life; eluding one's embrace only brought on the attentions of another. Not yet ten, as Eleanora Gough, "cutting school on . . . a spectacular scale" got her hauled to juvenile court and sentenced to a year at Baltimore's House of the Good Shepherd for Colored Girls, where, "for protection and confidentiality," she was known as "Madge" (Nicholson 23). After nine months, she was returned to her mother, Sadie. The following year, on Christmas Eve, Sadie interrupted a neighbor in the act of raping her, and called the police, who arrested the rapist but took his victim back to the reformatory (25). It would take until February for Sadie to secure her daughter's release, after borrowing money for a lawyer (27).

In *Lady Sings the Blues*, the stays at the House of the Good Shepherd are conflated, and the institution, run by Catholic nuns, is a place of nightmares. A girl, forced to wear a tattered red dress, is warned by the Mother Superior that God will punish her, before flying from a swing and breaking her neck. Later, Holiday is made to wear the same dress, locked overnight in a room with a dead girl, and beats her hands against the door until they bleed (17–18). In Stuart Nicholson's biography, however, the reformatory is a positive influence, "a disciplined environment" offering "the guidance and security that were missing in her life"; the truancy bringing her there is a "cry for help" resulting from a lack of maternal attention (23). Her departure from the institution is reported with melancholy impassivity—"The House of [the] Good Shepherd marked her file, 'Did not return to us'" (27)—as the poor girl follows her neglectful mother into an underworld of nightlife and prostitution. Alternately reported as benevolent and cruel, the reformatory, an explicitly gendered and racialized institution of education and incarceration, embodies all the contradictions of uplift from Baltimore to the Philippines.

In Julia Blackburn's *With Billie*, the school is simply "an awful place, very bleak and grim" (23); one of Holiday's contemporaries recalls the Mother Superior's harsh discipline and systematic physical and sexual abuse by the older inmates (24–25). Another interviewee recalls Holiday's visit to the institution a quarter-century later, seeking documentation for a passport. In this anecdote, the singer agrees to an impromptu performance for the girls, choosing "My Man," a song now notorious for lyrics professing devotion to an abusive lover (28).[18] Could this be true, and if so, what lesson passes from an alumna to a group of girls eager to identify with her escape? In the words of the song, love forecloses freedom.

Returning to Nicholson, you will find that the path from the reformatory leads to a different education, set in a brothel but conducted by Victrola: Holiday runs errands for the local madam so she can listen to her recording of Louis Armstrong's "West End Blues" (27). Nicholson notes that Holiday herself particularly favored this anecdote, recounting it in her autobiography and multiple interviews, and though the juxtaposition with the reformatory is his own, it seems clear she meant it as a fable or origin myth of her own education. Its central elements include the setting, extravagant beauty defying disreputable poverty, the aesthetic experience of wonder, and a lesson in technique: Armstrong's scat singing outstrips the impoverished meaning-making capacity of words.[19]

So if there is a model, a place of identification, a way out, it appears where the music outruns words. This is what there might be, for those who love the music, for poor black girls caught in uplift's cruel embrace, for everyone not yet free, if you are willing to risk reading too much into stories made of other stories, old lies, cultivated memories, and half-forgotten desires. It should be a relief to know, as Farah Griffin admits in her book on Holiday, that you cannot "escape positing [your] own version of Lady Day," and you should not "want to escape doing so" (6), because it is Holiday herself who escapes from behind all the tales. For myself, I prefer to recall the girl who demanded her mother get her out of that prison they called a school, and the struggling young woman who found a way to do so. Sadie died young, too, six years older than her daughter would, according to Nicholson's careful accounting, or the same age, according to the sly voice of the autobiography: "Mom got to be thirty-eight when I was twenty-five. She would never have more than four candles on her birthday cake. So she was only thirty-eight when she died. I'm going to do the same thing. She never cared what calendars said, and neither do I" (125).[20]

no-way out

If the love of wayward mothers and daughters is to elude reformation, it must be prepared to face an accounting with violence, for the love of uplift is jealous and claims the violence as its prerogative. Even so, uplift's love finds firmer ground when it attempts to intercede between dark fathers and their sons.

As with Kong, whose continuing fame, as well as proof of cultural relevance, relies on a series of remakes, following an underlying logic: he is reincarnated, every few decades, when new cinematic technologies succumb to vertiginous fantasies of a lost, primal embodiment. More forgettable are all the films, cartoons, texts, and products that follow the mercenary logic of the sequel—derivative efforts to extract diminishing revenue from the canon of the original and its remakes. The first in this line was hustled out in months by the original producers: "I don't care what you make," Merian Cooper recalled telling his partner, Ernest Schoedsack; "anything made called *Son of Kong* will make money" (qtd. in Vaz 249).

What they made, it happens, was a comedy, cobbled around the flimsy premise of a racist joke: Kong's son is white. Though still a monstrous ape, he is drastically diminished in size, entirely white in color, and selflessly devoted to the service of Carl Denham, who has fled New York in the aftermath of the first film. Having dragged his father in chains to his doom, Denham discovers mild feelings of obligation to "little Kong," who returns the sentiment in spades, giving his life to save his master in Skull Island's climactic destruction. The film reads as imperialism's affectionate self-parody: white love's chuckling acknowledgment of its comical, loyal offspring.

Though Kong's son deserves a thorough consideration of his own, as a footnote to his father's story, *Son of Kong* merely confirms his entrapment, securing one dubious line of escape: the benevolence of uplift and the spectacle of conquest turn out to require the same sacrifice. That is, despite his long afterlife as a fictional celebrity, bigger than any vehicle paying his way, Kong remains trapped between the logic of the remake, which continually reenacts his lynching under a gauzy veil of color-blindness, and the logic of the sequel, which reimagines him as a pet—two manifestations of the same violence. Is there no way out for Kong?

Well, why should anyone care? Isn't Kong a figure for everything antiracism seeks to abolish? Isn't the task to get beyond Kong and the white supremacist regime that gave him birth?

In a gesture both damning and profoundly generous, the eponymous cycle of poems in Cornelius Eady's *Brutal Imagination* responds to the case of Susan Smith, a white South Carolina woman who drowned her two young sons in 1994, by recovering a voice for the imaginary black male kidnapper Smith invented to take the blame. Like the infamous speakers who observe him in several intervening poems, including "Uncle Tom" and "Uncle Ben," this "black man pour[ed] from a / White woman's head" (27) is granted an autonomous consciousness without agency in the material world. The opening poem, "How I Got Born," establishes that autonomy as a kind of limbo existence from which Smith summons him—"an insistent previousness evading each and every natal occasion," to recite the Nathaniel Mackey epigraph to Fred Moten's *In the Break*. This fabricated black man is confined to Smith's body, though he shares neither her face nor her skin, making him both "a black man" and "a mother" (16), a fantasy with real effects, materialized by her fear and desire: "Everything she says about me is true" (6).

The empirical fixity of this truth does not protect Smith as her story unravels, so the cycle tracks his inexorable reabsorption into the body of her character, as it is inscribed in law and public scandal. The final poem, "Birthing," intersperses his voice among fragments of her actual confession, concluding with his incarnation into their body in the moment she reenters the world after watching the car bearing her children disappear into the lake. In an astonishing act of witness, Eady's poem keeps faith with all of Smith's victims—the drowned children, the African American community onto which she mustered the full force of the police power—even as he finds the only possible way to empathize with the murderer herself. For the black man she has invented to take the blame, who is *no one* if not Smith herself, is the only one who can stand with her as she stares out from the shore.

What the poem is proposing may be as simple as this: it is the task given to a certain line of poetry to stand on the shore, to be the only one standing with this woman, even as she murders her children, even as she surrenders herself to the movement of an overwhelming violence that bursts from her solitary act out into the long-remembered floodways of the civilized world. The poem neither redeems nor excuses; it does not ask if Smith was herself a victim, nor comment on the intimate violence and sexual abuse known to have marked her upbringing. Whatever it is in Smith that has been formed by the violence, in this poem, is that which she surrenders to the violence to place herself on its lee side, the side of mastery, and with it she surrenders her status as a mother and her agency and responsibility as the murderer of her children. It is this surrendered self that her imagination identifies as black. And so what the poem is also proposing is as simple as this: here too is a way blackness is birthed into the world.

To imagine you can properly segregate the blackness that poured from Smith's head from that of the people who bore the violence she unleashed—justice's extension across the darkness, the long arm of the law—is to disavow the everyday lived experience of blackness. But if the truth *did* come out, for once, why concern yourself with this white woman's racist fantasies? Can't you draw a line between this criminal and the community she so recklessly slandered and endangered? You may, the poem replies, but what would that line say if he could speak?

The truth came out, and the criminal was identified as a white woman named Susan Smith, but the poem also witnesses the moment when antiracism is once again seized by the ongoing hatred of blackness. Under a post–civil rights racial order, hegemonic antiracism requires figures such as Smith, who justify the reproduction of whiteness, and lesser forms of racial privilege, by embodying everything the enlightened and civilized love to hate: that bred-in, inbred intellectual and moral deficiency, pitiable but requiring correction unto death, that agency of violence calling an overwhelming violence onto itself as justice. *We know it when we see it*, goes the protocol. *We don't call its name in polite company. We just call the police.* What the poem allows you to see is that the blackness that poured from Smith's head—in the act of explanation, *subsequent* to the murder, as the only possible figure to bear the blame—is still entering the world, and the desire to pretend you can reverse this birth and lock it back up from whence it came, in the name of racial justice, is what secrets and secures the ongoing hatred of blackness beyond the realm of perception.

So the exercise of Eady's imagination, recovering a voice for the fabricated black man, is less about producing a speaking subject than about the task of listening to what is constituted as inaudible, reading as learning how to read, asking how to perceive freedom from his perspective. Eady's unyielding generosity, and the line in which it follows—say, James Baldwin and Toni Morrison; Toshio Mori and Hisaye Yamamoto; Gwendolyn Brooks and Edward P. Jones—serve as the horizon of my clumsy efforts, in this overture, to listen and learn from Kong.

Is there no way out for him? You may look to the book of Billie Holiday, the wisdom of her sound as textualized by black women auditors. Griffin's title, *If You Can't Be Free, Be a Mystery*, cites Rita Dove's poem "Canary," which observes that "women under siege" learn "to sharpen love in the service of myth." Because a question as to anyone's freedom pertains to all, this truth may be gendered but is not only for women.[21] The point is that Holiday could not be free because the world was not. Her "burned voice" (Dove) is lure and lament, alarm and alternative.

What alternative? Freedom is fugitive in an unfree world; it must be denied to her because it is denied anywhere and everywhere short of unfreedom's general abolition, but Holiday did what she could in a world not yet free, like your own, taking her freedom when and where she could, could not. The way out of no way, as Fred Moten riffs in a recent poem, may also be "a way into no way" ("test" 96), or, as he puts it in an interview: "I believe in the world and want to be in it. I want to be in it all the way to the end of it because I believe in another world in the world and I want to be in *that*" (Harney and Moten 118). This is the love sounded in Holiday's music as a freedom from love, slipping from one embrace to a larger one that cannot be seen because it is everywhere all around, a love that does not turn away from the world it shows to be broken but sounds and resounds it.

So Kong, the old trouper, may be released here. Rewind the film to the moment he slips from the skyscraper's pinnacle, and switch it off as he begins to fall.

(Let him take the "black Pacific" with him! Please remember that the term functions, in this book, only in absence, as a prop removed, which never actually existed except as a fantasy of violence. This book holds no brief for a "black Pacific studies," and whatever histories may emerge from this space will refuse this name,[22] eluding its claim of paternity to reach back to a previousness beyond its imagining. In the pages to come, whatever partial recuperations this book offers will concern only what has moved in and through its absence.)

Leave him in the air. Let him surrender to it, as Toni Morrison suggests in *Song of Solomon*, in it all the way to the end of it and to what is there, slipping imperialism's embrace to give himself over to everything you cannot imagine when you say *justice*. For to long for justice without mercy is to surrender the world to a love for empire.

1.

The Violence and the Music, April–December 1899

The quality of light by which we scrutinize our lives has direct bearing upon the product which we live, and upon the changes we hope to bring about through those lives. It is within this light that we form those ideas by which we pursue our magic and make it realized. This is poetry as illumination, for it is through poetry that we give name to those ideas which are—until the poem—nameless and formless, about to be birthed, but already felt.
—Audre Lorde, "Poetry Is Not a Luxury" (36)

Improvisation must be understood, then, as a matter of sight and a matter of time, the time of a look ahead whether that looking is the shape of a progressivist line or rounded, turned. The time, shape, and space of improvisation is constructed by and figured as a set of determinations *in and as light*, by and through the illuminative event. And there is no event, just as there is no action, without music.
—Fred Moten, *In the Break* (64)

a false start

The story with which I begin you'll have heard before, familiar in form even if its content appears as new. It's an old-fashioned story of modernity, an abortive tale about coming of age, a parable of racial meaning as a product of world-belting mass migrations mapped onto the scale of a single body, on a walk down a city street. Well-worn by countless retellings, the story is autobiographical, if admittedly less the way something actually happened than a way to make what happened *move* in the eyes of those who might gather to hear it. It's the story of a false start.

James Weldon Johnson spun a version in his *Autobiography of an Ex-Colored Man*, and Ralph Ellison recorded a cover in *Invisible Man*; Carlos Bulosan never stops telling it in *America Is in the Heart*, repeating it with such frequency and dizzying speed that, by the end, you can't tell if it's finished or just beginning. But the book I open now is by W. E. B. Du Bois, his polygeneric 1940 volume with the teetering, ambiguous title, *Dusk of Dawn: An Essay towards an Autobiography of a Race Concept*. My text is found in a chapter recounting Du Bois's early academic career, his rivalry with Booker T. Washington, and his departure from Atlanta University for the editorship of *The Crisis*, as processes exemplifying the world-historical forces of the chapter's title, "Science and Empire." The plot of the chapter is captured, in miniature, in an anecdote of a walk down Atlanta's Mitchell Street in April 1899—a journey much shorter than anticipated, a detour whose duration would extend beyond his long and eventful life:

> At the very time when my studies were most successful, there cut across this plan which I had as a scientist, a red ray which could not be ignored. I remember when it first, as it were, startled me to my feet: a poor Negro in central Georgia, Sam Hose, had killed his landlord's wife. I wrote out a careful and reasoned statement concerning the evident facts and started down to the Atlanta *Constitution* office, carrying in my pocket a letter of introduction to Joel Chandler Harris. I did not get there. On the way news met me: Sam Hose had been lynched, and they said that his knuckles were on exhibition at a grocery store farther down on Mitchell Street, along which I was walking. I turned back to the University. I did not meet Joel Chandler Harris nor the editor of the *Constitution*.
>
> Two considerations thereafter broke in upon my work and eventually disrupted it: first, one could not be a calm, cool, and detached scientist while Negroes were lynched, murdered and starved; and secondly, there was no such definite demand for scientific work of the sort that I was doing, as I had confidently assumed would be easily forthcoming. I regarded it as axiomatic that the world wanted to learn the truth and if the truth was sought with even approximate accuracy and painstaking devotion, the world would gladly support the effort. This was, of course, but a young man's idealism, not by any means false, but also never universally true. (*Writings* 602–3)

Du Bois's memory is not entirely reliable in this case. A consultation of "the evident facts," heroically compiled by Ida B. Wells, reveals that Hose did not kill his landlord's wife; in fact, while he admitted killing his employer, Alfred Cranford, in self-defense during a dispute over payment, he denied widespread rumors that he'd assaulted Cranford's wife (Wells 14).[1] But in this brief passage, autobiography takes the form of a fable or parable—not the science of history but the higher art of propaganda, in Du Bois's terms.[2] As the rest of *Dusk* makes clear, this anecdote both exaggerates the naïveté of his ambitions and telescopes his long transformation, that *eventual disruption* of his work, to provide his readers with the narrative kernel of an example—not quite *I once was blind, but now I see*, but rather: I thought I could see, but I was blind. Or, more expansively: in the arrogance of my youth, thrilled by the dawn of a modern age, I thought enlightenment would suffice to dispel racism, and that if I served the light, others would be glad to see—but they preferred to see differently.

This *red ray* was cast much farther than Mitchell Street. Wells, for one, made certain of it, catching and projecting it through the global circuits of modern mass media, compiling an account from Atlanta's white newspapers and commissioning a report from a white Chicago detective for her pamphlet *Lynch Law in Georgia*, to spread to the world the news of the migrant laborer known as Sam Hose or Samuel Wilkes. Yet while the transatlantic circuits of Wells's antilynching campaign are better known, news of this case also reached as far as the Philippines, where a nationalist resistance was waging war against U.S. colonial occupation. Indeed, as evidenced by the casual reference to this exceptionally American ritual in José Rizal's incendiary 1891 novel, *El Filibusterismo* (360), Filipino nationalists may have been aware of lynching long before its introduction to the Philippines by the U.S. military.[3] Seizing upon this news, the nationalists reflected it back upon their adversaries. By August, exiled leaders in Hong Kong had composed propaganda imploring African American soldiers to reconsider their loyalties, which appeared in placards concluding, "The blood of your brothers Sam Heose [*sic*] and Gray proclaim vengeance."[4] Among those who responded to this call was a young corporal of the 24th Infantry from Florida, David Fagen, whose exploits as an officer in General Emilio Aguinaldo's forces became legendary both in the Philippines and the United States.[5] Promoted from first lieutenant to captain under General José Alejandrino, he was referred to as "General Fagen" both by his own troops and by the front page of the *New York Times*.[6] An official military investigation, spurred by wild rumors of his escape to California in 1901, revealed that an accused bicycle thief in L.A. had assumed his name in defiant tribute.[7] Fagen persisted in guerrilla warfare even after Aguinaldo and Alejandrino surrendered, bedeviling the U.S. general Frederick Funston, whose vain intentions to lynch him were so well known that his own sister-in-law mocked them at a Christmas dinner, conjuring a vision of Fagen's hanged body in a playful bit of light verse![8]

shades of a world problem

Given the dizzying reflections and refractions of this red ray, how might you begin to theorize the traveling operations of race across the domains of early twentieth-century U.S. imperialism? These movements flicker across what have been historically understood as two regionally distinct racialized regimes: Negro segregation, in the post-Reconstruction U.S. South, was consolidating both in law (as in the 1896 *Plessy v. Ferguson* decision) and in extralegal violence, while in the Philippines, U.S. colonial governance was being established through military conquest. Further, for U.S.-based scholarship, such historical understanding passes through and is inflected by two additional settings: the industrial cities of the Midwest and Northeast, like Wells's Chicago, where small black communities would be dramatically expanded by the long process of African American urbanization known as the Great Migration, and the West Coast, where the Asiatic exclusion movement, already turning from the Chinese to the Japanese, would eventually encounter a wave of Filipino migrants, establishing the conditions for their inscription in what would one day be termed Asian American history.

To draw together these historically and geographically distant domains, you must first acknowledge that the conditions of such articulation have their genesis in acts of overwhelming violence. But while a link between black and Filipino racialization was initially forged by U.S. imperial conquest, it was quickly seized upon by Filipino nationalists, in the Sam Hose propaganda, to foresee a different destiny for both groups, surpassing the telos of inclusion within the United States, as nation or as empire. And it was not only the Filipino nationalists who saw this.

In seeking a theorization of race sufficient for this task, I turn to Du Bois's concept of the color line. Best known from his epochal 1903 *Souls of Black Folk*, it appears in an earlier speech at the 1900 Pan-African Conference in London, "To the Nations of the World,"[9] but its most comprehensive formulation is found in "The Present Outlook for the Dark Races of Mankind," Du Bois's presidential address for the third annual meeting of the American Negro Academy in Washington, D.C., in December 1899.[10] It is likely, if perhaps impossible to definitively prove, that this is the first text in which his oft-quoted declaration of the *problem of the twentieth century* appears.[11] More to the point, where the others merely present this statement as a striking premise, only this text presents it as a thesis to be demonstrated. Indeed, its express purpose is to establish the claim. Read closely, it offers a series of insights upon which the methodological and historical framework of this book is built.

Announcing itself as a characteristically ambitious inquiry into race "in its larger world aspect in time and space" (95), Du Bois's address takes his audience on a whirlwind tour of social conflicts spanning five continents and four centuries of world history, to argue that a crisis of accelerated imperial competition is generating intensified processes of racialization within imperial states, at their borders *and* at their centers, legitimizing both conquest *and* mastery in racial terms, whose ultimate horizon is global. *This* is the crisis he is naming in his proposition that "the world problem of the 20th century is the Problem of the Color line" (104). Crucially, he secures this claim at the end of his section on Europe, where "the question of color" arises unpredictably in a new racialization of metropolitan populations, as in the controversy over "the Jew and Socialist in France," and in aspiring powers' pursuit of global standing—for example, Russia's whiteness is questioned when contrasted with Germany but enhanced in conflicts with "the yellow masses of Asia" (103). Du Bois's color line, then, is better understood not as a binary or a bar to be lifted or crossed, but as *a traveling analytical concept for examining how race is made and remade, in uneven and unpredictable ways, across a global field of imperial competition.*

If this concept helps theorize the circulation and reconfiguration of race in the Philippine-American War, this is no accident. For the war,

Du Bois claims, was the occasion for his address: "But most significant of all at this period is the fact that the colored population of our land is, through the new imperial policy, about to be doubled by our ownership of Porto Rico, and Hawaii, our protectorate of Cuba, and conquest of the Philippines. *This is for us and for the nation the greatest event since the Civil War* and demands attention and action on our part" (102, emphasis added).[12] The text's internal logic and historical context together indicate that what's decisive in this *event* is the U.S. decision to conquer the Philippines. In the transition from the 1898 Spanish-American War to the Philippine-American War, African American popular opinion had largely turned against military-imperial policy, and the Philippines focalized a range of heated debates over U.S. expansion and African Americans' place within it. While Du Bois, who opposed the war, obliquely criticizes its prosecution later in the text, here he takes conquest, if not annexation, as a fait accompli, in order to contemplate the consequences of a massive increase in the nonwhite population including eight million Filipinos.

This event, Du Bois argues, must be embraced as a problem, an opportunity, a duty, depicted in ringing patriotic terms: "What is to be our attitude toward these new lands and toward the masses of dark men and women who inhabit them? Manifestly it must be an attitude of deepest sympathy and strongest alliance. We must stand ready to guard and guide them with our vote and our earnings. Negro and Filipino, Indian and Porto Rican, Cuban and Hawaiian, all must stand united under the stars and stripes for an America that knows no color line in the freedom of its opportunities" (102). What began as a matter of demographics attains world-historical importance, as Du Bois continues, assimilating these new populations to a benevolent project of racial uplift whose privileged American Negro subject ascends to autonomy on the geopolitical stage: "We must remember that the twentieth century will find nearly twenty millions of brown and black people under the protection of the American flag, a third of the nation, and that on the success and efficiency of the nine millions of our own number depends the ultimate destiny of Filipinos, Porto Ricans, Indians and Hawaiians, and that on us too depends in a large degree the attitude of Europe toward the teeming millions of Asia and Africa" (102–3). Here, Du Bois's attitude looks disturbingly similar to McKinley's infamous justification for conquest as a duty "to educate . . . and uplift and civilize and Christianize" Filipinos deemed "unfit for self-government" (qtd. in Rusling). But Du Bois turns from this implicit mimicry of McKinley to signify explicitly on Rudyard Kipling: "No nation ever bore a heavier burden than we black men of America, and if the third millennium of Jesus Christ dawns, as we devoutly believe it will upon a brown and yellow world out of whose advancing civilization the color line has faded as mists before the sun—if this be the goal toward which every free born American Negro looks, then mind you, my hearers, its consummation depends on you, not on your neighbor but on you, not on Southern lynchers or Northern injustice, but on you" (103). In his elegant rhetorical sweep, Du Bois drives the ideology of the civilizing mission to the occidented conclusion that *its manifest destiny is the end of white world supremacy*, and presumes his *American Negro* audience's global solidarity with the *brown and yellow*, while exhorting them to assume self-determining moral agency in achieving it.

This autonomy, a liberating burden, arises as racial uplift shifts from a national struggle for equal opportunities to a transimperial crusade. The global phenomenon of "groups of undeveloped peoples brought into contact with advanced races under the same government, language and system of culture" establishes the world-historical significance of *American Negro* striving: "German Negroes, Portuguese Negroes, Spanish Negroes, English East Indian[s], Russian Chinese, American Filipinos— such are the groups which following the example of the American Negroes will in the 20th century strive, not by war and rapine but by the mightier weapons of peace and culture to gain a place and a name in the civilized world" (107). Note that while the text heralds an internationalism of the darker races—a politics of correspondence and even coordination—the color line does not itself figure that politics, whether as ideology or as organized alliance, but merely its preconditions. As a concept-metaphor, the color line enables a geopolitical analysis that, typically for Du Bois, is coldly pragmatic. For example, the address admits the "rapacity and injustice" of British imperialism, yet insists it is preferable to the alternatives in much of Africa and Asia, and welcomes its triumphs over its rivals (96)—a view that he would not hesitate to reverse when circumstances changed.[13] Moreover, this analysis bears in itself no guarantee of a particular political commitment. Given these caveats, what is most crucial in this passage, for theoretical purposes, is that *the recognition of the* unevenness *of disparate sites of the production and contestation of race*—here, the relatively privileged position occupied by African Americans vis-à-vis colonized populations—*is the basis of potential counter-articulations* along, *rather than across, the global color line.*

The concept's potential for transformative politics is worth pausing over, for its conditions may be counterintuitive, and lead to several further historical and theoretical insights relevant to this inquiry. First, while disparate domains of racialization are initially linked via acts of imperial violence, this violence is inseparable from the benevolence of the civilizing mission, which promised justice through uplift. Vicente Rafael's gloss on McKinley's policy of "benevolent assimilation," as the "moral imperative" for the United States to develop and care for "wayward native children" in the same way "a father is bound to guide his son," is instructive: "Neither exploitative nor enslaving, colonization entailed the cultivation of 'the felicity and perfection of the Philippine people' through the 'uninterrupted devotion' to those 'noble ideals which constitute the higher civilization of mankind'" (21). "White love" is his memorable term for this attitude, which "holds out the promise of fathering, as it were, a 'civilized people' capable in time of asserting its own character. But it also demands the indefinite submission to a program of discipline and reformation requiring the constant supervision of a sovereign master" (23). The difficulty, of course, comes when dark sons—not to mention daughters—presume to ascend to the patriarchal position, asserting autonomy over the operation of racial uplift. In Du Bois's address, this claim is established first within empire, as black men anticipate the dereliction of white love toward little brown brothers, and then beyond it—for like white supremacy, racial uplift is not exclusive to any particular empire, regardless of its claims of exceptionalism. As such, American Negro uplift may forge imaginative links to nonwhite subjects of other colonial powers independently of U.S. geopolitical interests, a perquisite of the structural contradiction between racial and national identity Du Bois elsewhere called double-consciousness.

Second, Du Bois's ideas in this address are relatively unoriginal, even commonplace, just as his play on Kipling's phrase is a conventional trope in black writing in this moment.[14] More generally, as extensive and informed as his awareness of global events and their ramifications for local race politics may seem to a present-day reader, it is hardly exceptional within African American popular intellectual life through at least the mid-twentieth century. Knowledge of international affairs had a different salience before the United States became the global superpower, when it was easier to imagine a higher foreign influence intervening within local hierarchical orders.

Similarly, when Du Bois concludes the address by sketching something of a plan of action, the program is uncontroversial boilerplate. He bemoans the "prevalence of Negro crime," calls for a "great revolution" in "the Negro home," invoking "the right rearing of children" and "the purity and integrity of family life," and closes with a bland cry for a greater "spirit of sacrifice" (108–9). Even when advocating for elite cultural achievement, he is careful to cite the example of "the new book by Booker Washington" (109). If you take the text at its word, the theorization of the color line is offered in the service of an ideological consensus among the American Negro elite, whose name is uplift.

Put differently, I contend that Du Bois's great original intellectual contribution, in this address, is *poetic*. This is one way to read the disarmingly modest opening to "The Negro Mind Reaches Out," his contribution to Alain Locke's 1925 *New Negro* anthology: "Once upon a time in my younger years and in the dawn of this century I wrote: 'The problem of the twentieth century is the problem of the color line.' It was a pert and singing phrase which I then liked and which I have since often rehearsed to my soul and asked:—how far is this prophecy or speculation?" (385).[15] This may also explain why Du Bois did not revise the address for *The Souls of Black Folk*, which abandons the thesis's argumentative grounding, distilling it into a catchphrase, *the problem of the twentieth century is the problem of the color line*, repeated three times in the text.[16] For the insights carefully established by the address are, for Du Bois, embedded in the phrasing itself, remaining available for activation even as its elegance encourages an almost limitless capacity for repetition and recontextualization. Later in the chapter, I will return to the suggestion that Du Bois's radicalism emerges from his poetics.

Rather than citing or reproducing the argument of the 1899 address, "The Negro Mind Reaches Out" is effectively a *remake*, twenty-five years on, suggesting that the thesis's grounding is irreducibly historical.

This time, Du Bois's virtuoso survey of geopolitical events is organized, not by continent, but by empire—reviewing the "shadow" of race
problems in Portugal, Belgium, France, and England—and by the transimperial movements of labor and pan-Africanism. This leads to a third
observation. If the germ of later adversarial "colored" internationalisms
can be traced back to the turn of the century, as in Du Bois's devout
belief in the coming of a "brown and yellow world," then *it is necessary
to account for the* continuity *of their emergence with the ideology of the
civilizing mission.*[17]

If this statement appears as the converse of the earlier observation
that the violence by which U.S. imperialism articulated its transpacific
domains was inseparable from its expression as tutelary uplift, then taken
together, they reveal the structure of what I have been calling *imperialism's
racial justice.* Put differently, imperialism's own self-justifications, the
epistemological and aesthetic production of race that cast this overwhelming violence as the actualization of justice, dominate the discursive realm out of which antiracist and anti-imperialist movements arise
to seize and recast the meanings of race and of justice. Yet to imagine
this domination as total is to complete the work that any existing imperialism necessarily leaves unfinished, to surrender your faith to the
promises no imperialism can ever actually keep. This is a fourth point:
*because imperialisms are always in competition, the realm of racialization
and of justice is transimperial.* As an analytic figure traversing it, *the color
line serves not to ground appeals to a transcendent conception of justice
but to open up the fissures between the disparate sites of racialization that
competing imperialisms are unable to fuse together*—even as the political
programs thereby made possible may only register, in retrospect, as efforts to close up or seal over what has been broken and to complete what
has been promised beyond justice's reach.

Finally, if the color-line concept identifies an intensifying crisis of imperial competition manifested in uneven and unpredictable processes
of racialization, then the term itself serves as an analytical figure for
the production of any number of modern subjects. That is, *the color
line names the site at which new, modern racial subjects are incarnated
and incorporated.* Pride of place in these processes goes not to Du Bois's
American Negro, whose assumption of the burden of uplift heralds the
rise of a new world, nor to his American Filipinos, constituted along

the tutelary paths of uplift, but to whiteness itself, in all its forms. For what drives the processes identified by the color line is the imperative to define imperial mastery in racialized terms. This whiteness is not a singular type, but an expanding category of racial privilege, whose competing forms vie to assume the position of rightful heir to the progressive expansion of civilization—or, as Du Bois succinctly defined it in 1910: "whiteness is the ownership of the earth, forever and ever, Amen!"[18] Yet this heterogeneous production of whiteness also generated unforeseen varieties of nonwhiteness in its wake. The theoretical intervention of the color line, finally, lies not in conceiving of movement *across* it, into new hierarchical forms of racial privilege masquerading as freedom, but *along* it, to ask: What other shades of modernity are produced, and what might happen as their disjunctures gather toward each other in its wandering course?

an Afro-Asian century and a third-conditional world

When the 1899 address lists those peoples expected to follow the American Negro example, there is one notable omission—the only other nonwhite group whose historical agency Du Bois celebrates, a counterpoint to what otherwise passes as an exceptionalism. This group's encounter with "advanced races" had not involved direct colonization or minoritization, and pointedly, it had not disavowed struggle through military force. Identified as the "one bright spot in Asia to-day," it is "the island empire of Japan," whose "recent admission to the ranks of modern civilized nations by the abolition of foreign consular courts within her borders is the greatest concession to the color-line which the nineteenth century has seen" (98).

Unlike the dramatic reference to the Philippine war, the rhetorical climax to the text's discussion of the United States, Du Bois's comment on Japan is relatively unstressed. Because the casual ascription of world-historical significance to current events is central to the text's method, the superlative phrasing barely delays its rapid inventory of the "congeries of race and color problems" (97) that is Asia. Further, Du Bois's rhetorical decision to relegate this recent event to the century that is ending suggests some effort to distance the Japanese example from his model of American Negro striving. Nevertheless, the text may be justifiably described as prescient regarding the significance of Japan's challenge to global white supremacy. In a later section on Russia's designs in northeast Asia, Du Bois muses, "Perhaps a Russia-Japanese war is in the near future," concluding, "At any rate a gigantic strife across the color line is impending during the next one hundred years" (104).

Within five years Russia and Japan were at war, and Du Bois was quick to see a confirmation of his arguments. At the conclusion of a 1905 lecture titled "Atlanta University," Du Bois revisited his color line thesis, warning that a declining interest in African American concerns was ignorant of the direction of global affairs. After a succinct summary of the thesis's geopolitical grounds, he turned to the "epoch-making" event of the moment: "To-day for the first time in a thousand years the great white nation is measuring arms with the yellow nation and is shown to be distinctly inferior in civilization and ability." "The foolish modern magic of the word 'white' is already broken," he averred, "and the color line has been crossed in modern times as it was in the great past." If "the awakening of the yellow races," and eventually their "brown and black" counterparts, was now inevitable, the question is whether this "awakening . . . be in accordance with and aided by the greater ideals of white civilization or be in spite of them and against them." "This," he concludes, "is the problem of the yellow peril and of the color line, and it is the problem of the American Negro."[19]

Returning to the 1899 speech, it becomes clear that, while the format of its global survey runs predictably from Africa through Asia and South and North America to Europe, ascending a hierarchy of race or "civilization," the logic of its geopolitical analysis identifies Asia as the stage upon which the most strategically consequential imperial conflicts are taking place. There, two great events define the historic occasion, that dawning century, that modern black striving must seize. In short, *the color line concept was articulated as a direct response to the transpacific rise of U.S. and Japanese global power amid the shifting dynamics of imperial competition in Asia.*

If this association was merely incidental to the 1899 address, rightly jettisoned as the color-line thesis became a catchphrase, it might hold little interest. Yet subsequent history suggests it was prophetic, as the changing conditions of African American social and political life in the coming century would prove deeply interconnected with events in the region. Corresponding to Du Bois's logic, two major aspects of an Asia/Pacific interest in African American culture may be identified. The first turned toward Asia in a kind of messianic anticipation, entertaining fantasies—usually casual and speculative, though here and there surprisingly devout—of the arrival of a champion of the darker races against white world supremacy. Though occasionally associated with other countries, this racially alien figure was most often identified with imperial Japan. The second aspect traversed the Pacific along U.S. imperial pathways, pursuing opportunities for racial uplift, particularly in the Philippines and Hawai'i.

Through the first half of the century, an intermittent but abiding interest in Japan was present across all the locations of a vibrant African American intellectual life, from the academy to the press, the church to the literary salon, the juke joint to the street corner, and the offices of respectable civil rights organizations to the meetings of ragtag radical groups. Rather than attempting to determine any singular coherence to this interest, it is best approached as a series of debates. For every editorial, lecture, or sermon promoting the modernizing and uplifting lessons Japan could teach, another might reject such claims. Similarly, intellectuals argued for and against the prospect of Japanese leadership of the darker races, and popular and elite sentiment oscillated between identifying with Japanese and Japanese American struggles against white racism and dismissing them for setting themselves above black people.[20]

Primarily shaped by geopolitics, this interest peaked around major events—the Russo-Japanese War; the 1919 Paris Peace Conference, where President Woodrow Wilson defeated the Japanese delegation's proposal of a racial equality clause for the League of Nations Charter; and the 1935 Italian invasion of Ethiopia, in which widespread hopes of Japanese intervention were ultimately disappointed. The latter largely confirmed the attitudes of a younger cohort of intellectuals, whose leftward turn in the 1930s led to critiques of Japanese imperialism, sometimes recasting China or India in familiar pro-Japanese tropes. Yet the earlier influence of Marcus Garvey, who promoted "Asia for the Asiatics" and upheld Japan as a model of racial pride and self-determination, was not entirely dislodged. To a lesser extent, African Americans also monitored the anti-Japanese movement and Japanese American civil rights campaigns against school and housing segregation, restrictions on immigration and land ownership, as well as the Supreme Court 1922 case *Ozawa v. United States*, in which a challenge to racial restrictions on naturalized citizenship, on the grounds that Japanese should be considered white, was denied. These currents crested during World War II, as African Americans contemplated both the mass incarceration of West Coast Japanese Americans and the demands and opportunities of national loyalty in wartime.

Yet the larger historical significance of this interest may lie in its more shadowy and imaginative manifestations. It was given freer rein, for example, in speculative fiction by prominent intellectuals. John Edward Bruce's uncompleted 1912 short story, "The Call of a Nation," and James D. Corrothers's "A Man They Didn't Know," published in *The Crisis* in December 1913 and January 1914, both imagine a race war, in which Japan's initial triumphs in the Philippines and Hawai'i lead to an invasion that the United States can defeat only by abandoning white supremacy to ensure the support of black soldiers. Fifteen years later, Du Bois himself contributed to the genre with *Dark Princess*, whose protagonist, a talented African American in Berlin, stumbles into a secret international council of the darker races plotting the overthrow of the white nations.[21] The greatest influence of this interest may have been in the pro-Japanese activities of a range of religious, nationalist, and emigrationist groups uncovered by Ernest Allen, including the Pacific Movement of the Eastern World, the Ethiopian Pacific Movement, the Moorish Science Temple of America, and the Allah Temple of Islam (a predecessor to the Nation of Islam led by Elijah Muhammad).[22] It almost certainly conditioned Noble Drew Ali's influential theory of "Asiatic" blackness, as well as Muhammad's vision of a Japanese-built UFO or "Mother Plane." Broadly understood, you may recognize its significance in the ways this interest offered imaginative realms for conceptualizing racial difference beyond white supremacy—a necessary condition for recovering an affirmative notion of blackness irreducible to its constitution by white racism. Thus, one of its more surprising variants provided a lexicon for alternative stylizations of female and queer nonwhite sexualities, in the appropriated Orientalisms of writers such as Marita Bonner, Nella Larsen, and Richard Bruce Nugent.

The final collision between U.S. and Japanese imperialisms in World War II, and the subsequent reshaping of the world order, drastically revised the terms of this interest, both dispersing and intensifying it. Sympathies for Japan were largely forgotten, helped by active efforts of suppression during the war, by government officials—over eighty members of black organizations, including Muhammad, were arrested on charges of sedition or draft evasion in September 1942—as well as black intellectuals.[23] Meanwhile, a continuing series of wars brought more black soldiers to Asia, binding many closer to U.S. imperial interests while baptizing others in forms of radical internationalism.[24] One strain of the interest turned toward Third Worldist politics, particularly Maoism,[25] while another manifested in pop-cultural obsessions with kung fu and in Afrofuturist explorations of outer space by musicians like Sun Ra.

But Du Bois's early transpacific analyses are not merely useful for a taxonomy of black cultural formations. More broadly, they anticipate how the subsequent course of black history may be approached through an Afro-Asian interpretation of the twentieth century, which identifies the social and political advances of black and Asian peoples as the era's defining event, and the jaggedly articulated strivings of metropolitan minorities and colonized or imperially subjugated populations of color as its indispensable condition. In the most straightforward way, this is the prophecy of the color-line thesis. Yet the cold pragmatism of Du Bois's geopolitical analyses can seem disconcerting to the liberatory spirit driving recent recuperations of black internationalism and Afro-Asian sympathies. The epochal break he saw in 1905 would be generally recognized after World War II, and while he has been rightly accused of insufficiently critiquing Japanese imperialism,[26] his larger theme, shared by Corrothers and Bruce, was actually vindicated by the war: in contesting U.S. imperialism's monopolization of the terms of racial justice, Japanese imperialism helped create unprecedented openings that were seized by black freedom movements, even if its own dubious claims proved disastrous for populations under its sway.

Put differently, what feels insufficient in the otherwise reasonable revisionist identification of an "Afro-Asian century"[27] is the seemingly unbridgeable distance between the extravagant visions of freedom it prophesied and the bitter realities it left behind, culminating in the impoverished conditions of formal national independence and formal racial equality. Moreover, the geopolitical conditions that enabled those visions no longer obtain. The color line is *not* the problem of the twenty-first century, in Du Bois's sense; even as racism persists and expands, questions of racialization no longer provide the dynamic link through the social conflicts driving global change. To understand this trajectory of the prophecy, and to understand why its radical potential is not yet exhausted, I turn to the second aspect of the Asia/Pacific interest in African American culture.

This aspect traversed the pathways of U.S. imperialism, which offered fragile opportunities for black performances of colonial privilege, most extensively in the Philippines and Hawai'i.[28] Not reducible to simple patriotism or Afro-Asian solidarity, this aspect of the Asia/Pacific interest illustrates the fraught yet generative racial, sexual, and gendered contradictions embodied by American Negro uplift emerging within transpacific imperial competition. The ambivalent participation of black soldiers in the controversial Philippine war provided the first major nexus of this history, along with debates over their conditions of service and their relationship to other nonwhite groups. Another linked post-Emancipation debates over black education to U.S. imperialism in a complex transpacific circuit, connecting white American missionary education in Hawai'i, via Samuel C. Armstrong, to the Tuskegee model of industrial education championed by his protégé, Booker T. Washington, which subsequently served as a model for U.S. officials in Manila. Meanwhile, African American educators found opportunities for professional advancement under the colonial regime, including a young Carter G. Woodson, who wrote approvingly of the experience in his 1933 *Miseducation of the Negro*.

A third nexus involved debates over colonial migration, whether by upwardly mobile individuals or en masse; the Philippines briefly served as the focus for black emigration schemes, and the U.S. government entertained proposals to import black labor to the colony. Finally, the complex global circuits of modernizing popular entertainment brought black musical culture to the colonies, returning the latter to the metropole in cultural practices, memory, and fantasy. James Weldon Johnson, with Bob Cole and his brother Rosamond Johnson, wrote a groundbreaking 1906 play, *The Shoo-Fly Regiment*, about soldiers in the Philippines, as part of a brief fad of similarly themed productions, including works by Black Patti's Troubadours and the Pekin Stock Company. As late as 1927, the New York playwright Eulalie Spence could offhandedly introduce a character as "one of these here Philippine gals" (*Her* 139). While memories of the colonial period faded quickly after the 1946 end of direct U.S. rule, traces persisted among veterans and their families: Ralph Ellison recalled his father's service in Cuba, the Philippines, and China in his 1981 introduction to *Invisible Man* (xiii), while Ann Petry helped to preserve the letters of an uncle who served in the Philippines and an aunt who taught in Hawai'i (E. Petry 2005).

If Du Bois's 1899 address sketches the contours of a future Asia/Pacific interest in African American culture, the methodological implications of its comparative spirit entail a contrapuntal narration of Afro-Asian history, which is why this book also takes up reciprocal, if uneven, interests in blackness in Japanese American and Filipino migrant cultures. As Vicente Rafael and Paul Kramer have shown, race-making under U.S. colonialism in the Philippines was contradictory: anti-insurgent warfare tended to conflate territories and populations into a singular racial enemy, while the exigencies of civilian colonial rule demanded the proliferation and classification of racial differences into a progressive hierarchy, whose heterogeneity was yet to coalesce into nationhood.[29] Intraimperial migration further complicated matters, and Filipino intellectuals frequently deployed figurations of blackness to negotiate the conjunctures of metropolitan and colonial racial formations, in the long advent of Philippine formal independence.

Japanese Americans in this period similarly relied on figurations of blackness in navigating a trajectory amid the competing claims and disavowals of Japanese and U.S. imperialisms. At times, they contrasted Negro servility to Japanese virility and militancy—persistent stereotypes in U.S. culture prior to World War II that were even employed didactically, if in a different spirit, by black intellectuals. At other times, drawing on overlapping experiences of segregation in the West, they figured blackness to imagine communal, if not necessarily nonhierarchical, relations outside of white supremacy. Through to the present, black presences in Japanese American culture typically signify the chance of multiracialism to which all imperialisms lay claim; thus, as Japanese Americans contemplated their destiny in the shadows of transpacific imperial competition, blackness came to figure histories of racial violence whose repression could be exchanged for degrees of privilege, but whose unleashing might be the condition of an unimaginable freedom.

Comparative and global inquiry, in Du Bois's color-line writings, was organized in terms of continents, in 1899, and of empires and transimperial movements, in 1924. They have rightly been cited as a precedent for transnational approaches to American studies and ethnic studies, as those fields seek to escape the geopolitical imagination of post–Cold War American exceptionalism. In drawing a methodology from Du Bois's color line, I approach the histories of black and Asian racialization in terms of *migrations,* rather than geopolitical units defined by past or present state borders, as processes in and of motion rather than geographical fixity. By "migrations," I refer to the large-scale and long-term resettlement of racialized labor, but also the transient movements of casual workers, military personnel, and displaced groups, as well as the individual journeys of students, educators, government officials, intellectuals, artists, and political activists. These bodily travels, furthermore, shaped and were shaped by proliferating modern telecommunications media. Thus, I conceptualize migrations as multidirectional and interrelated processes of physical movements and cultural circulation, rather than the unidirectional passage between fixed locations in classic U.S. narratives of *im*migration.

Through this model, you may interpret relationships between the movements of colonial Filipino workers to and along the West Coast and the deployments of African American soldiers in Asia and the Pacific, as two circuits of migrant labor within empire, articulating histories of dispersal on both sides that precede U.S. occupation by centuries. Or you might connect black urbanization in cities like Chicago and Los Angeles, accelerated by the demands of wartime production in the 1940s, with the forced removal, incarceration, and resettlement of West Coast Japanese Americans through concentration camps to Chicago and points east, before their gradual westward return over the next few decades—and then relate these "internal" migrations to the "foreign" threat their convergence invoked, from the specter of imperial Japan to a U.S. front of Third World revolution by the 1960s.

Now that the century of Du Bois's prophecy is over, the liberatory potential of a Third World front, or of previous figurations of Afro-Asian solidarity, seems thoroughly exhausted. The color line is not the problem of the twenty-first century, even if the problems associated with it remain. From this vantage, his faith in an Afro-Asian future can actually function as a constraint on the imagination of freedom—a trap you might evade by considering a contemporaneous vision that consigned an Afro-Asian century to an unrealized past before it even began. To recover this possibility, I return to the earlier suggestion that Du Bois's 1899 address is surprisingly *unoriginal* within African American discourses of its moment.

Although its central conceit, that issues of race must be viewed from a global perspective, could appear as a revelation a hundred years later, as ethnic studies and American studies undertook a transnational turn, it was hardly unconventional in 1899. For example, at the previous year's American Negro Academy meeting, Howard University professor Charles C. Cook presented "A Comparative Study of the Negro Problem." Assessing English and Japanese histories of national emergence, Cook comments, "What it took England ten centuries to accomplish, the United States has done in two hundred, and Japan in thirty years" (3). While the latter was clearly not Cook's area of expertise—at least half of his brief section on Japan was a long quote from William Elliot Griffis's popular 1876 volume, *The Mikado's Empire*—it shows that Du Bois's impulse was hardly unique.

More substantive engagements with global affairs can be found across a range of black newspapers and journals of the period, including the A.M.E. *Church Review*.[30] Indeed, the same October 1900 issue that published Du Bois's address featured a series of aphoristic "Editorials" that tartly and succinctly capture the ambivalent perspective on imperialism theorized by Du Bois. Presumably written by editor Hightower T. Kealing, an educator, lay A.M.E. church official, and A.N.A. member, they range from a sentence to several paragraphs. One item pungently captures the common-ground position between growing antiwar black popular opinion and the concerns of some black elites that challenging Republican administration policies would deliver the election to their enemies: "Imperialism seems to mean the bringing of more colored people within contact with American contempt; while anti-imperialism is saving all this contempt for the colored people already on hand"! Other items illustrate the preoccupations of uplift ideology, bemoaning American drunkenness in the Philippines and celebrating the attendance of Cuban schoolteachers at a summer program at Harvard, and speculate on the rise of China (175). A longer piece relates the Zionist Max Nordau to

A.M.E. bishop Henry M. Turner's support for African emigration, offering a sympathetic critique of both (179).

Another item puts the promise of imperialism's racial justice in stark terms. Analytically linking three ongoing imperial wars in China, South Africa, and the Philippines, it condemns the "motives" of the Western powers as "undeniably and declaredly selfish and sordid," while upholding their core justification: "the rape of Africa, Asia and the islands will open them up to Western progressiveness, invention, comfort, personal liberty and the Christian religion." The logic of uplift detaches itself from white corruption, operating providentially, for "beyond" and "in very antagonism to" their reprehensible intentions "will come the elevation and equalizing of the protesting semi-savage that is despoiled." Following the occidented logic of imperialism to the same end predicted by Du Bois, he imagines that colonial violence will leave this semisavage "fresher from the fount of rejuvenation than his late master," eventually to achieve "domination in things commercial, literary, artistic, and economic, over the Western world" (177). The bluntness of Kealing's assessment strains against the resignation of its conclusions, illustrating the severe constraints he faces as a political actor. Indeed, the next item proclaims imperialism to be the highest moral issue in the upcoming presidential election, one the incumbent gets wrong and his challenger gets right, then endorses President McKinley anyway, citing his opponent's damning reliance on anti-black Southern Democrats.

In the end, what's the difference between Du Bois's and Kealing's analytical responses to U.S. imperialism? Read together, it seems largely rhetorical, a matter of tone rather than substantive effect: the prophecy of a coming Afro-Asian world collapses into an affirmation of imperialism's own justifications, fully recognizing that its actualization is indistinguishable from violence. The limitations of their responses trace the constrained and compromised structural condition of the American Negro intellectual, whose capacity for action is given *within* relations of empire. But to identify the difference between them as rhetorical is merely to say that Du Bois's great contribution, again, is poetic. Its originality and genius lies in the unexpected way it reads, or learns to read, the positionality of the American Negro intellectual within imperial competition. Where Kealing endorses imperialism's principle of racial justice with a curse, Du Bois offers an inspirational exhortation. Both draw on rhetorical traditions of prophecy, yet only Du Bois articulates his insight in a singing phrase that would become a great watchword of antiracist and anticolonial struggle.

Yet on the far side of that prophecy, as a century's visions of Afro-Asian liberation recede in disenchanted dusk—the long-awaited rise of China, the election of an African American commander in chief—you might recover a more apposite rhetorical formulation in one additional item from Kealing's editorials. It reads: "If Aguinaldo were the statesman he is reputed to be, he would form an alliance with King Menel[i]k of Abyssinia and do something worth while" (175). Here, the fantasy of Afro-Asian liberation, joining the leader of the Philippine resistance to the hero of African opposition to Italian imperialism, can be expressed only as a sarcastic counterfactual—it comes into view only after it is deemed impossible. Kealing's conception of racial justice cannot be extricated from the imperialism against which he would turn it, and the best rhetorical figure he can find to evoke the volatility of this paradox is a bitter joke.

To appreciate the operation of this joke, I borrow a term sometimes used in English language teaching to describe the grammar of conditional sentences. In the so-called first conditional, the relation between a condition and its consequence foretells a possible future (if X occurs, Y will occur), whereas in the "second conditional," a condition represented as unfulfilled determines a potential consequence as unreal (if X were true, Y would occur). Du Bois's exhortations follow the logic of the first conditional—*if you take up the black man's burden, white supremacy will fall*; Kealing's joke takes the form of the second—*if Aguinaldo were the hero advertised, he and Menelik would form the Afro-Asian alliance you desire.* But Kealing's tone and his other editorials make it clear that he has abandoned any fantasy of a Filipino-Ethiopian alliance, and is left unable to foresee any Afro-Asian future but what is bequeathed by uplift: that the semisavage could one day ascend to the position of the master.

In other words, Kealing already occupies the place where you now stand, on the far side of despair, gazing out at an unreal possibility already consigned to the past. This is the structure of the "third conditional": *if the antiracist and anticolonial movements of the twentieth century hadn't fallen short of the extravagant hopes invested in them, they would have achieved another world*. Just as this bitter-mouthed joke is the sole rhetorical figure through which Kealing can express a desire excluded by the terms of racial uplift, it may be that this negated image of a future lost to history, this third-conditional world, offers you an apposite structure for expressing those desires for freedom that elude the epistemological and aesthetic constraints of imperialism's racial justice.

For his part, Kealing can go no further in expressing this desire, at least not in words, for what words he can find are capable only of betraying it. But where the words leave off, if there could still be music, that music would come to be called *the blues*.

resounding a red ray

If the color line serves as a tool for mapping the geopolitics of race and projecting its destiny across centuries, it also marks the site where race is produced, where bodies are given coherence and torn asunder. This is not a line to be crossed in triumph; to be crossed *by* it is to feel the violence of imperial incorporation extending itself as justice. The anecdote that began this chapter invokes such a crossing in order to evade it, in what I propose below is an improvised theoretical gesture of a radical poetics, out of which unfolded that enormous history of action—aesthetic, intellectual, political—which travels under the name Du Bois. So let me return to April 1899, to the earnest young man making his way up Mitchell Street. Eight months away from the speech in D.C., he is on the other side of a vast divide: over ten days in May, his son, Burghardt, age two, will take ill and die, in a city where white doctors would not treat black patients, and black doctors were in short supply (Lewis, W. E. B. Du Bois 227–28). For now, carrying his *reasoned statement* and his *letter of introduction* to the newspaper, he may still imagine that the violence he hopes to address reaches toward someone else.

This is a story about imperialism's racial justice and its tokens. In it, the ambitious young scientist recognizes his own tokenization: all his hard-won achievements suddenly seem meaningless before the evidence of overwhelming violence. If he's been endowed with the power to speak as a representative of his race, which he'd planned to use with the editor of the *Constitution*, it is because his achievements, his person, could be taken to justify a civilizing mission. He appears, in autobiographical caricature, as what would later be called a model minority.

This is racial incorporation in a mode of sponsored uplift, whereby the nation guides the education of its nonwhite wards in the ways of white civilization—a mode pioneered in the metropole before its extension to the Philippine colony. If this process engineers a kind of model nonwhite racial subject hybridized by internalizing white civilization, it also secures the nation's claim to whiteness via the demonstration of a racial capacity for benevolent mastery. Further, the scientific efficiency by which the United States performs the civilizing mission proliferates racial distinctions *within* whiteness, engineering a modern, hybridized yet pure variety that could be heir and successor to European empires.

But I find another form of racial token here, manufactured by another mode of racial incarnation. I refer to the gruesome trophy said to be on display at the grocer's, the dismembered knuckles of the lynched body of Sam Hose. I argue that lynching is one manifestation of a mode of imperial incorporation through overwhelming violence, and that the lynching form may be understood as a communal, narrative act of sexual violence—a sex act, whose performance establishes and secures whiteness, as well as blackness, as racial categories of violent mastery and conquest. A racialized, sexualized, invasive violence is projected, as threat, onto the body to be sacrificed, and then mastered through an overwhelming, preemptive violence.

The trophy is a token of this act, condensing its narrative into a magical object, whose display reenacts the ritual. The token on display serves as a warning to black people in its vicinity, to fix them in place in the local racial order—not to expel them, not to exterminate them, but to *fix* them, in intimate bondage, in relation to whites. It serves, too, as a celebration and a commemoration for local white audiences. But it also addresses other white audiences, who may or may not be present, who may provisionally hold a superior position in a social order, and thereby deign to condescend to the community of lynchers. It defiantly proclaims a racial difference *within* whiteness, between higher but decadent strains of whiteness whose capacity for rejuvenating violence has degraded, and a lower but more vigorous, youthful, potent, rising racial strain. At issue here is a perceived threat of overcivilization, giving rise to moral and sexual perversion, feminized men and masculinized women, and the inevitable decline of a great race in the cyclical rhythms of world-historical progress—that orientation to civilization I have been calling *occidented*.[31]

Lynching is commonly misunderstood as a strictly Southern phenomenon, exemplifying the conflict between a subordinated regional white community and a disapproving nation. I contend instead that lynching is just one of the manifestations of racial incorporation through sexualized violence crucial to the ways the United States, as a rising world power, claimed the imperial legitimacy of whiteness while asserting the exceptionality of its white racial character. Thus, one response to the spectacle of lynching, a condemnation from the perspective of some Northern or European elites, which would become dominant and shape subsequent histories of racism, takes it as evidence of the backwardness and debasement of white lynchers, of their savage or uncivilized ways— that the process, in effect, made them less than white, contaminated or blackened. Yet the danger of contamination is the necessary risk of a procedure to inoculate whiteness from overcivilized decline by infusing a sexualized, racialized savage essence, of the engineering of a hybrid modern whiteness that projects primal nature onto a nonwhite body in order to abstract and consume it in an act of sacrificial communion. As I argued in my reading of *King Kong*, this act makes white people more white, white men more manly and potent, white women more feminine and sexually desirable. Another analogy appears in the "Optic White" episode of Ralph Ellison's *Invisible Man*, where the secret ingredient of a superior white paint turns out to be ten drops of "dead black" liquid (163). In an influential analysis of this "remarkably astute parable of the production of whiteness" (74), Harryette Mullen reads it as an analogy, not to lynching, but to *passing*, taken as a model for fabricating "pure" whiteness from racial difference (72). If the social phenomenon of passing unveils the "formula" of whiteness's manufacture—not as an exception to the general rule of white reproduction, but as the exemplary case revealing the underlying principle—then the lynching form is one of its instances.

It would be tempting to narrate Du Bois's decision to turn back down Mitchell Street as a deferral or postponement, to say he reverses course because he has not yet prepared the theoretical formulation sufficient for the scene he is on the way to witnessing. For the color line, as he would shortly define it, is first and foremost the natal site of whiteness, even as Du Bois's intervention seeks to overturn this priority to herald the emergence of modern nonwhite subjects. But the lynching form does not merely instantiate the color line—it seeks to collapse that line into a single, fixed point. Du Bois is justifiably less concerned, in this instance, with elaborating the multiple strains of whiteness lynching nourishes than with its propensity to reduce all varieties of nonwhiteness to the same fate. One might say that Du Bois hesitates before or evades the embodied experience of being crossed by the color line—except that, as I will argue, you may take his deferral or hesitation, the swerve or detour from the scene of lynching that necessarily returns him to it, as itself the crucial theoretical gesture of his narrative, improvised on the spot.

What happens in the encounter that Du Bois quite prudently avoids? Something of an analogue can be found in chapter 10 of James Weldon Johnson's *Autobiography of an Ex-Colored Man*. The unnamed protagonist, whose New England boyhood is closer to Du Bois's biography than Johnson's, has come to the South after a series of adventures across the United States and Europe, determined to become a great composer by transforming the raw materials of black popular culture into a refined, concert-hall music. Following classic European models of modernizing nationalism—to reconstitute the collective accomplishments of the peasantry first into folk culture and then into the product of individual genius—his ambitions are fully worthy of Du Bois's vision of uplift. Arriving in the poor communities of the Black Belt, he begins "jotting down in my note-book themes and melodies, and trying to catch the spirit of the Negro in his relatively primitive state" (Johnson, *Writings* 105), but he is compelled to abort his initial research when he finds himself observing a lynching bee.

Jacqueline Goldsby persuasively argues for a reading of the book as a novel of lynching rather than passing, shaped by Johnson's own traumatic encounters with the violence. Indeed, it is the experience of lynching that transforms the protagonist into an ex-colored man. His representation of his decision appears disingenuous—"I would neither disclaim the black race nor claim the white race," he says, and merely "change my name, raise a mustache, and let the world take me for what it would" (115), though subsequent events reveal he must actively hide his past. He rationalizes the decision as an impossible attempt to distinguish between the putatively biological inheritance of race and its function to mark social inferiority, while leaving privilege disingenuously unmarked—"it was not necessary," he tells himself, "to go about with a label of inferiority pasted across my forehead" (115).

It is not clear, however, that there *is* a decision at all; already passing "incognegro" as a witness to the lynching bee, he becomes trapped in this condition, looking for reasons after the fact: "It was not discouragement, or fear, or search for a larger field of action and opportunity that was driving me out of the Negro race. I knew that it was shame, unbearable shame. Shame at being identified with a people that could with impunity be treated worse than animals. For certainly the law would restrain and punish the malicious burning alive of animals" (115). From within his new racial status, he distances himself from a shame he attributes to blackness, due less to the denial of its humanity than its expulsion from the protection of the law. But a few paragraphs earlier, before he's "made up his mind" (115), this shame appears first in a notably different form. Coming out of the fugue state he'd passed into during the lynching, he comes to consciousness before its material remains—"a scorched post, a smoldering fire, blackened bones, charred fragments sifting down through coils of chain, and the smell of flesh—human flesh"—and walks off to sit and "clear [his] dazed mind": "A great wave of humiliation and shame swept over me. Shame that I belonged to a race that could be so dealt with; and shame for my country, that it, the great example of democracy to the world, should be the only civilized, if not the only state on earth, where a human being would be burned alive" (113). Consciously or not, Johnson is unmistakably reproducing the structure of Du Bois's famous formulation of double consciousness, that narrative subjectivity split in two along the contradiction of nation and race, American/Negro (Du Bois, *Writings* 364–65).

In the post-multicultural present, in which the grammar and lexicon of cultural diversity supply the dominant language of racial justice, the celebration of identity abstracted from historical and social analyses of racial inequality provides affirmative pathways for inequality's continuation and expansion. Following the logic of his own rationalization, then, it is easy for present-day readers to accept the ex-colored man's severing of this formulation of doubled shame, forgetting his initial emphasis on his ethical implication as a member of a national body marked by exceptional violence, and condemn him for the sin of racial self-hatred. Yet the agony of the ex-colored man's passing, that joke which turns back onto him as tragedy, is that he never ceases to love and value black culture, even as his belief in uplift abstracts that love from the experiences of any particular black people he might know. In the logic of the narrative, the project of uplift is aborted only to be aggrandized, for the novel is a cautionary tale, staged to encourage readers to affirm the narrator's famous conclusion that he "sold [his] birthright for a mess of pottage" (127).

The shame the narrator remembers to confess—that the violence incarnates blackness, given birth as expulsion from the protection of the law—is what transforms him into the ex-colored man, driving him into whiteness. But because he confesses it, first in private, prior to marrying a beloved white woman who bears him two white children, and then, after her death, in the pages of his book, he lays open his shame to expose what Harryette Mullen explains is whiteness's own shared secret. Following Goldsby, you might read the novel as the author's own exposure of that same shame, the secret of Johnson's encounter with lynching, laid open to advance a race's transformation into *race men* dedicated to Negro uplift. In sum, if something in the ending leaves present-day readers uneasy, it cannot be attributed to the repression of a racialized shame. Rather, it's how easily the narrator toggles between his dream of uplift and his assumption of whiteness that is striking, now that uplift is no longer the dominant form of racial justice. The distinction between Negro uplift ideology and racial passing, on which the novel turns, proves troublingly difficult to maintain, and if this might seem bizarre to Johnson, it would be the very theme of Nella Larsen's 1929 novel, *Passing*.

This uncanny doubling becomes easier to understand if you recall the confession that the ex-colored man forgets to remember, the shame of membership in a political body constituted by the violence, of belonging to a state exceptionalized by lynching. This shame does not derive from an identification with whiteness, but with a civilization constituted and regenerated in the devolution of violence upon blackness. This is the shame of the American Negro as civilized subject, as the token of benevolent tutelage, which must be forgotten once *his mind is made up* to pass. It risks revealing, among other things, that what passes for freedom across the color line, the mastery of civilization white status entails, which Negro uplift would contest, is merely the illusory privilege of standing on the lee side of the violence, a trick of perception that can be maintained only by separating oneself from what the violence bears away. For the violence has no master, only servants who hope to redirect its force onto others further down its course. Here you may recast the tradition of the passing novel, running through Johnson and Larsen, to understand its continuing salience as a challenge for reading. It asks, How is it possible to perceive the difference between whiteness, or racialized privilege, and freedom?

In short, Negro uplift ideology comes to seem indistinguishable from passing because of this second shame—because it is a manifestation of U.S. civilization's gospel of violence. The unbearable encounter between the tokens of uplift's benevolence and its violence reveals, beyond the author's intention, that the protagonist's dream of *catching the spirit of the Negro in his relatively primitive state* is homologous with both passing and lynching. Each posits the internalization of a black essence—refined, consumed, secreted, but at all costs mastered—in producing a reconstituted racial subject fit for modern civilization. Lynching exposes the logic of the violence that extends uplift's loving embrace. Following Goldsby's insight that "lynching's narrative force . . . compels the narrator to tell his story backward, with the result that the novel develops according to a process akin to that of photography" (217), you may understand the relation of passing to lynching as that of a negative to a photograph: one fabricates a white body, and the other fabricates its black essence, but the process they comprise together establishes the perception of the racial image.

Returning to Du Bois, you may recognize what lies before him as the scene of perceptual training in an aesthetics of racial terror, which he evades in the movement of an improvised countertraining. In the close encounter between two varieties of the racial token, each is empowered to speak only by silencing the other; each draws power by reference to the other but can express that power only in the other's absence. But Du Bois does not risk actually coming into the presence of the lynching trophy; instead, silenced, he turns away. This is not merely prudence, the justifiable fear of being overwhelmed by the violence and mistaken for its proper target, but the unsettling premonition, on its way to surfacing as (double) consciousness, that he is already implicated in it, prior to intention or will, in his very constitution as a civilized American Negro subject. This is why he does not reschedule his appointments at the *Constitution* or submit his statement by post—why his modernizing scientific project is unsettled at its very core.

The U-turn down Mitchell Street may seem a retreat—repairing to the security of the university to theorize a response to unforeseen conditions—but retrospection identifies the detour as the opening of Du Bois's journey, an ongoing improvisation whose narration is itself the theorization it demands. The text, recall, is not an autobiography of the development of its historical subject, but *an essay toward an autobiography of a race concept*—a literary exercise marshaling the empirical facts of personal history in the service of a conceptualization. The turn away from the presence of the lynching trophy may therefore be understood as a narrative theorization of hesitation and detour. The text refuses to witness the token of lynching's violence, to represent the overwhelming sensory experience of the blackened knuckles, the char and stench, so as not to reproduce and reenact the lynching form.

This is *in some sense, illusory*, for Du Bois *swerves away from* the trophy only to *run right back to* and *through* it,[32] but the narrative introduces a kind of lag in this movement, tearing at the discrepancy in the doubled vision of uplift's twinned tokens at the site where they would be fused, in order to disrupt uplift's aesthetic protocols. An extemporaneous motion, the swerve opens Du Bois to an agency arriving from outside all that his knowledge and training has prepared him to perceive—which is to say, the act is prophetic. This is the strange *red ray*, cutting across his scientific blueprints, by which the narrative improvises the retraining of attention not on the lynching trophy but on that felt condition of insufficiency, shared by protagonist and narrator and reader, down all the decades of the violence's repetition and across the unbroken moment stretching back to the killing of the man known as Sam Hose, a problem of perception before it is ethics or epistemology.

This *red ray*, put simply, is a figure for what transforms Du Bois from a scholar to a political activist. But his activism continues to involve the production of knowledge and of writing. In "Poetry Is Not a Luxury," Audre Lorde describes a "quality of light" that has "direct bearing upon the product which we live, and upon the changes we hope to bring about through those lives," defining poetry as a practice that "forms the quality of light within which we predicate our hopes and dreams toward survival and change" (36). In this sense, the figure of the red ray captures something of the quality of light that shapes and is shaped by Du Bois's developing poetic method, his epistemology and his aesthetics, in his relentlessly polygeneric, interdisciplinary, multimedia writings from *Souls* onward. The optic is just one aspect of this, of his ongoing improvisational orchestration of what Fred Moten calls "the ensemble of the senses"—*Souls*, for example, combines not only autobiography, sociology, history, biography, and fiction, but concludes with and is constantly interrupted by inscriptions of music.

With that in mind, I want to shift from reading the red ray as a strictly visual metaphor to think of this quality of light as having a sound, and to consider how it resounds or is re-sounded, not just in the sense of an echo but of a transformation or translation, as it moves along a global color line. It may be set to work, as in Du Bois's case, on the apparently impossible task of imagining racial justice beyond the terms laid down by imperialism's own justifications, which determine what can be perceived even before they dominate what can be known and represented. For Du Bois in this period, and arguably throughout his career, the agenda remains a form of uplift, but the sound of this red ray begins to bend his vision of black modernity onto a different course.

The red ray may be perceived at any number of locations along the color line—the site where modern racial subjects were incarnated and incorporated, where uplift and violence, logically incommensurable but regularly indistinguishable in practice, converged in a kind of blind spot of racialized perception, the occasion of aesthetic training and counter-training. As preparation to hear a quality of light, you may turn to the resources of black aesthetic traditions, following the guidance of poet-theorists like Lorde, Moten, Brent Edwards, Nathaniel Mackey, and others. Attending to the ways black cultural practices work the material edges of multiple representational media simultaneously—not to privilege the oral over the literary or imagine some combination adding up to total knowledge, but to mobilize the invisible and unspeakable at the limits of any medium or sense—you may find a pedagogical function in aesthetic form.

What I call reading as learning how to read, invoking the radical theorizations of literacy characteristic of black literary traditions, submits to this improvised aesthetic training beyond the historical constraints of racialized perception. Pursuing this reading along the color line, this method seeks to activate the imaginative longings within literary resoundings of the red ray, which open up a field of political engagement even as they are effaced in the historical record of social action. Persisting in their texts as a muffled call, they await a collective response enacting as-yet unknown forms of belonging across difference, while training reading as learning the conditions of collective responsibility.

In Du Bois's anecdote, the red ray emerges from a comparative moment *within* the heterogeneity of the category "Negro," but extending comparison's range across racial categories and formations can open up the unequal relations and unpredictable possibilities subsumed within a single term. His color-line concept expresses how racial forms produced at any one location always allude to others, whose exotic distance might function in excess of their capacity to signify in a local racial order. This allusive excess, found at the intersections of black and Asian migrations, signals a fugitive trajectory. Following lessons from Du Bois, the remainder of this book examines encounters between tokens of uplift and violence along the color line. If the violence of imperial racialization at times imposed a fictive identity conflating blacks and Asians, the resounding of the red ray emitted by these encounters served to operate an articulation of and through difference. The texts I consider, emerging from within the history of imperialism, did not triumph over its violence, and largely reproduced its civilizationist grammar and lexicon; yet by attending to their translations, striving to *hear* their quality of light, you might learn to read for what is excluded by, or eludes, imperialism's racial justice.

a fugitive end

In conclusion, I take up two further translations of the red ray, as it recedes into the dimming recollections of guerrilla warfare across the Pacific. The first appears in the aforementioned Sam Hose propaganda generated by the Filipino nationalist resistance. Here is one version of the full text:

TO THE COLOURED AMERICAN SOLDIERS.

It is without honour nor profit that you shed your costly blood.

Your masters have thrown you to the most inicuous (sic) fight with double purposes.

In orders (sic) to be you the instrument of their ambition.

And also your hard work will make soon the extinction of your race.

Your friends the Philipinos (sic) give you this good warning.

You must consider your situation and your history.

And take charge that the blood of your brothers Sam Heose (sic) and Gray proclaim vengeance.[33]

The blood of the soldiers being addressed is here aligned with the blood spilled out from the body of Sam Hose, another token, if rhetorical, of lynching's violence. But in this translation, it is endowed with the agency to speak a different message, a power of speech that is also the power of action—the blood does not cry out for, plead for, or even demand justice, but *proclaims* vengeance. Who is speaking for whom? Who, or what, is speaking? As propaganda, you might read this speech as ventriloquism: if the token seems to speak, it is only the voice or the message of the *insurrecto* that is actually heard. Alternatively, you might read it as possession: the proclamation of vengeance is a call that occupies and overwhelms whatever vehicle transmits it, emanating from an agency beyond mortal reach. What *is* certain is that the translation of this sound, which is of course never literally heard, is intended by the translators to produce a response, severing the bond of duty between the Negro soldiers and the U.S. nation, not to assert a racial identity between Negroes and Filipinos, but to make possible an articulation through difference—a provisional alliance of friendship.

Yet, as Du Bois and Kealing already foresaw, any realization of such an alliance would come on terms the propaganda dearly sought to avoid—

not the military coalition of Afro-Asian soldiers against Anglo-Saxon imperialism, but an uneven correspondence of sidelong glances between Negro and Filipino elites committed to racial and national uplift under U.S. rule—and even these efforts would be fleeting and fragile. The great counterexample to this statement, of course, is the aforementioned David Fagen, the most famous of the few soldiers who switched over to the Philippine cause, a figure of myth given new life in recent decades. Yet the reading with which I conclude, from the recollections of a comrade of Aguinaldo's who eventually served as a senator under the U.S. regime, suggests that even this figure is inscribed by the hand of uplift.

My text is taken from a memoir by General José Alejandrino, Fagen's immediate commanding officer, a chemical engineering graduate of the University of Ghent and close friend of José Rizal. In *The Price of Freedom*, originally published in Spanish as *La Senda del Sacrificio*,[34] Fagen is portrayed in disturbingly racist terms that largely align with U.S. imperialism's construction of black primitivism. In this episode, Alejandrino describes his surrender to General Funston and his honorable refusal to hand over his notorious subordinate. He describes "Fagan" as "a Negro giant of more than six feet in height" (174),[35] of nearly superhuman physical endowments. For example, asked why his soldiers understand that a retreat is signaled when he dismounts his horse, he explains that he rides to save his legs, in seeking the enemy or in battle, but he descends in retreat "because his feet are faster than those of his horse" (175). But like that of a loyal servant or pet, his astounding physicality corresponds to a touching solicitude to his less robust superior. He was "very affectionate and helpful to me," Alejandrino reports, "carrying me in his arms or on his shoulders when I, weakened by fevers and poor nutrition, had to cross rivers or to ascend steep grades. The services which he rendered to me were such that they could only be expected from a brother or a son" (174).

These extraordinary qualities correspond to a lack of manly discipline—Alejandrino's Fagen is "very fond of carousals and drinking" (175), and, as a matter of policy, not allowed custody of white American prisoners, as his habit was to kill them without trial or confirmation from his superiors (174).[36] But the most bizarre anecdote Alejandrino shares involves a woman Fagen lives with in camp, who comes to him "crying and showing one cheek bitten off and saying that Fagan had done it." Summoned, Fagen explains he'd dreamed he was attacked by the enemy, and the "fury" of his resistance, down to "punches, kickings and bitings," fell upon "his woman companion" (176). You may hesitate to read too closely here—surely "bitten off" must be an exaggeration, in the original or in the translation?—but in any case, these are just old war stories, spun by an aging veteran, perhaps inured to the disbelief of younger generations. What is nonetheless clear is that "Fagan" is savage, even bestialized. His affections, however innocent and faithful, can be as dangerous as his enmity; his capacity for violence overwhelms normal men, but this physical superiority corresponds to a moral inferiority, whether in his techniques of combat (biting) or in his behavior toward captives (murder). By contrast, he illustrates the manly honor of his civilized commander, who is more suited than the duplicitous Funston for the patriarchal responsibility of civilizing love toward a darker brother or son.

To be clear, this brief reading of a distant memoir in subsequent translation allows no reliable broader assessment of Alejandrino's relationship to Fagen, much less his attitudes towards Fagen's race. Surely, the primary function of this depiction is not to inform his readers of the characteristics of American Negroes. Rather, it seems to provide the vehicle of a vicarious identification with an exaggerated violence motivated by the colonizer's racism—the "most outstanding characteristic" of this "Fagan" "was his mortal hatred of American whites" (174). Alejandrino's text comes as close as it might dare to inhabiting that terrifying savage figure in which Negro and Filipino were conflated by the totalizing imperatives of U.S. colonial warfare, pivoting away only through the operation of a racial *décalage*: it reminds his readers that it is the Negro and not the Filipino who is America's savage. And if this portrayal expresses the unspeakable desire for an overwhelming vengeance that could defeat U.S. imperialism in the name of its Filipino and Negro victims, the continuity of its representational logic with that of white imperial racism cannot be ignored.

The myth of David Fagen would rise again, during the Vietnam War and the second war in Iraq, in variations that took for granted their distance from the racist trappings of an earlier period's civilizationist preoccupations—just as uplift has itself been rendered obsolete by new configurations of imperialism's racial justice, organized by languages of development and of diversity. But I will not tarry with these later versions, where the limitations of my capacity as a reader result from the familiarity of the terrain. In the end, whatever impulse pursues Fagen into the boondocks can only be dissatisfied, as what it desires cannot be found in the positive terms by which his figure is perceived, represented, and known, but in the negative space into which he escapes—the torn page in the archive, the scratch and skip in the historical record. For he did not return from the shadows, and the world he fought for was not won.

2.

Shaming a Diaspora

One: Love Notes

In the last chapter, I argued that the transpacific rise of U.S. and Japanese imperialisms at the dawn of the twentieth century occasioned a transformation of the meanings and destinies inscribed in concepts of race, as announced in W. E. B. Du Bois's theorization of the color line. For the United States, the imperative of expansion required the incorporation of racial difference into an imperial order through intertwined processes of tutelary uplift and sexualized violence. But the convergence of these racializing processes was "re-sounded" or recast, by writers like Du Bois, to project alternative forms of racial modernity, for which a linkage between the discrepant racial categories forged by U.S. imperialism could serve as a pivot toward other horizons.

Below and in the following chapter, I explore some examples of black transpacific culture between the 1890s and 1940s, arguing that the trajectories of black political and cultural modernisms, shaped by tensions between a fragile, developing middle class and a Southern peasantry on the threshold of the Great Migrations, were conditioned by the historical effects of participation in U.S. imperialism across the Pacific. In counterpoint, I consider the emergence of a modern Filipino intellectual in the metropole, who was both provincialized and provincializing in relation to a new Anglophone elite in the colony, itself produced within the educational and cultural apparatuses of empire. In the Anglophone Filipino literature arising from these circuits of migration and tutelage, tensions between flight and return within were negotiated through figures of blackness.

To approach these histories comparatively via the question of diaspora is not simply to align a series of formal parallels—actual and speculative patterns of imperial transit by soldiers, teachers, students, and agricultural laborers, ideologies of collective development through the training of an enlightened elite—but to look out for their uneven interarticulations, those animating points of connection through difference that set them spinning in their respective trajectories. Attending to these encounters along the color line, I find that the problem of race is itself conceived and experienced as a problem of sexuality, to be resolved through normative gendering. Thus, in this chapter, I ask how a diaspora is constituted in and as a mastery of shame, while in the next I consider how a surrendering exposure of shame opens perception to lost alternative worlds.

To place transient transpacific movements and counterfactual schemes of migration within a black diaspora is both a historical and a theoretical task. How are conceptions of black diaspora transformed by the inclusion of real and imagined journeys of African American soldiers, educators, intellectuals, artists, activists, and colonial officials along the transpacific circuits of U.S. imperialism? How do these circulations complicate already elusive concepts of dispersal and reassembly, of flight and return, of (severed) past and (fugitive) future?

What holds diaspora together, in imagination and in practice? What blasts it apart? What sustains it as the echo of what it might yet become?

The preparation for these questions may call for a little music . . .

audience with Betty

You'll be / forever grateful / for all the love notes / you hear: listen, if you can hear this; Betty Carter is singing. In the apparent silence of print, of course, the words may seem drained of the greater part of their eloquence, a phenomenon all too familiar to those who have longed to record "the literature of music"—how those lyrics that sounded so eloquent may turn lifeless on the page, in much the same way that the achievements of black literature are said to pale before those of black music.[1] Taken as a whole, the words of Carter's "Love Notes" seem only to tell a simple story, of the *soothing* capacity of music in *this crazy world*, a message verging on platitude, saved only by the graceful pun in the title phrase. Yet this slightest play on words, if you can hear it, rippling lightly along the placid tension covering uncertain depths, riffs across a long, complex, and profound black intellectual and aesthetic tradition that improvises variations on the interrelation of aurality and literacy.

In Carter's phrase, the love note, a written document that is merely the ephemera of an affair—of romance in its most fleeting manifestation, however much you might hope to extend such a phase or revive such a feeling—becomes a figure for the ephemeral quality of musical sound, of the experience of hearing music that eludes capture, for example, in the words on a page.

As written document, a sweet nothing put to paper, a love note communicates not through the content of the message but through its form: the authenticity of its sentiment is expressed through the elaborateness of its artifice. As heard sound, the expression of the love note exceeds the words that may carry it, and their capacity to communicate meaning; the ease of its appearance, the seemingly effortless way it is called into hearing in improvisation, requires the most intense rigor in the musician's preparation and habitual practice. If you saw Betty Carter perform, how intensely she engaged each member of her band, you know that this rigor is first of all a training in listening, in the preparation to hear as the condition of the ability to respond. If you witnessed her interaction with each and every member of her audience, you know that the rigor of this responsibility falls on you, as well. The apparent indolence of her sound is a ruse, a seduction establishing an ethical demand, whether you recognize it or not. What, then, does she ask of you when she states with such commanding assurance, *You'll be / forever grateful / for all the love notes / you hear?*

The advice or the desire to preserve a love note is surely morbid. For a love note is not meant to be preserved, except and precisely to the extent that it measures love's loss, the disappearance of that feeling in that form, whether a lover has departed or a love has been transformed into something else—more secure, stable, and habitual, yet less novel, fleet, and elusive. But if the love note is evanescent, the song insists, the appreciation of its auditor is without end: *because* love must die, you will forever be giving thanks, a gratitude that is infinite because it can never redeem the debt it incurs. Now that Carter has herself passed on, her recordings remain, so the analogy in her elegant pun must be more complicated than it appears: the "note," after all, denotes musical sound only by reference to the long history of the material transcription of music. The invention of technologies to record and reproduce sound did not diminish the prevalence of music as a figure for ephemerality, to be sure, but if the song passes off this old trope—music's unmediated presence as a *restful*, timeless, natural tonic for the *stressful* modern world's encompassing *turmoil*—you shouldn't presume a naïveté to such passing.[2] Carter must have been aware that her recordings would survive her death, but this is not what she is after when she sings, *forever*.

Memory, too, is mortal, faulty, or changeable: I believe, though I cannot verify, that I first heard "Love Notes" in the mid-1990s, at a performance in a London jazz club. But perhaps I invented this memory, in the intervening years, while listening to a copy of Carter's *Feed the Fire*. Ironically, I was convinced the words were "*You've got to remember / all the love notes / you hear*," which is not what's on the album, recorded elsewhere in London a few years earlier. Did she sing it that way, that time? Or did I fall short of an imperative I only imagined, myself, after the fact? I may have conflated Carter and Walter Benjamin—for doesn't her song offer another way of reciting his familiar dictum, "Nothing that has ever happened should be regarded as lost for history" (254)? Or rather, might Carter's phrasing reanimate Benjamin's poor old, worn-out standard? Her rigorously refined talent for such rescue and recovery efforts—"interpretations" or "readings"—is well noted. In any case, I offer up these echoes of Carter's song to mark a historiographical challenge for inquiries into diaspora, and the transits and circulations it comprises: What kind of listening *for all the love notes*, what training of the perceptions of the senses, is indicated in her repetition of the words, *you hear / you hear*?

This challenge requires, first of all, some consideration of the peculiar problematizations of love, as a theme and trope, across the cultural traditions Carter's phrase references and refracts. In his reflections on post-Emancipation black music in *The Black Atlantic*, for example, Paul Gilroy observes, "The stories which dominate black popular culture are usually love stories or more appropriately love and loss stories. That they assume this form is all the more striking because the new genre seems to express a cultural decision not to transmit details of the ordeal of slavery openly in story and song" (201). Singing and speaking of love in this habitual, if not ritual, fashion functions like the recoding of Christian concepts of an afterlife in black religious and secular sycretisms. It becomes an occasion for creative philosophical rearticulations of any number of historically obstructed or suppressed social and political desires, and for critical commentaries on themes such as self-possession and the submission to an other, or social recognition and the pursuit of a fugitive idyll. Of particular note are the ways that this concern with "love" engages and recasts the normative categories of gender, sexuality, family, and home. Through these categories, African Americans were both excluded from national belonging at any given moment, and inducted, voluntarily and under duress, into forms of national and/or racial community promising the dissolution of imperial hierarchies in a future always just out of reach. Repeatedly worrying the figure of sexual union, "love and loss stories" provide a resource of critical reflections on desires for reunion, reassembly, and return, "systematically transcod[ing] other forms of yearning and mourning associated with histories of dispersal and exile and the remembrance of unspeakable terror" out of which diaspora is made (201).

While the romance of diaspora has been known to sweep folks away, Saidiya Hartman's *Lose Your Mother* provides an incisive critique of the fantasies of return and the ruses of love operating in its uneven terrain. Reflecting on the tense, often bitter relations between disillusioned African American expatriates and local communities in West Africa, and on the commodification of trauma in contemporary "roots tourism," Hartman exposes how ritualistic expressions of shared love occlude starkly unequal socioeconomic positions, conflicting political interests, and discrepant historical memories descending from the event of abduction and enslavement. Professions of love provide a fiction of consensual relations that enable mutual antagonism and exploitation while maintaining and securing inequalities, as she illustrates in "Come, Go Back, Child," a chapter named for the *kosanba*, the "spirit child" caught in a repetitive cycle of premature death and rebirth. It is this figure, Hartman imagines, who is addressed by the crumpled letters pressed into her hands by adolescent boys outside Ghana's Elmina Castle, protestations of love to their sister from America.

This misidentification is characteristic of a history confounded by ruses of familial love, the intimate bonds that fix people to places: "Mothers, disavowing their love, have called their children *donkor* (slave) in order to save them, while slaveowners have called their property 'beloved child' in order to protect their wealth." Just as the mothers beg the *kosanba* not to go back to the spirit world, the slave masters insist that the slave forget the land of her birth: "Come and stay, child, they both implore" (86). While these conundrums may recall Vicente Rafael's conceptualization of U.S. colonial policy in the Philippines as *white love*, Hartman pursues a history whose most distant traces may not mark a racial divide. Of the various words in Akan that refer to forms of servitude, she notes that the closest to an American concept of chattel slavery is *odonkor*—"the only derogatory and stigmatized term"—whose etymology derives from "the words 'love' (*odo*) and 'don't go' (*nti nka*). *Odo nti nka*: because of my love for you, don't go" (87). Such mystifications generate dangers for those who would deny their historical effects, or mishear their echoes, running down the centuries:

> Love encourages forgetting, which is intended to wash away the slave's past. Love makes a place for the stranger; it domesticates persons from "outside the house" and not "of the blood"; it assuages the slave's loss of family; it remakes slaveholders as mothers and fathers. Owning persons and claiming kin are one and the same; so love cannot be separated from dispossession or property in persons. . . . Love extends the cover of belonging and shrouds the slave's origins, which lie in acts of violence and exchange, but it doesn't remedy the isolation of being severed from your kin and denied ancestors. (87)

Mortified by her status as a tourist, Hartman—a confirmed New Yorker—is vigilant for a scam. "Peddlers, swindlers, and ingenious adolescents," she observes, "were the only ones in Elmina brazen enough to espouse the love of slaves." But the shtick with the letters charms her with memories of home, where the hustle "would be three-card monte or a shell game": "You'd approach the table knowing that you shouldn't, but something about these boys acting mannish, and the mix of guile and innocence, and the sharp edge of desperation would break down the protective barrier and convince you that you had a chance after all and that you were not predator and prey but somehow all in it together" (88). In Ghana, "the traffic was in redemption" and "the odds were not any better," but Hartman recognizes the boys' notes as tokens of a diasporic ritual in which love is always being exchanged for loss: "What I could salvage amounted to flattering words, make-believe brothers, and vows of love. Go, come back, I love you. The tug and pull, the advance and recoil, the longing and the disappointment: Wasn't this the dance of love?" Listen and it might sweep you away: an "indiscriminate and promiscuous love that did not differentiate between persons; it never required a name or retreated from the wretched and the loathed; it thrived in lowly places" (89). Is there anywhere in the world you can go that hasn't been enchanted by its music?

But Hartman's desire for reciprocity breaks the spell, as she pictures herself in their position—"How could these scruffy adolescents love me or anyone else like me? You could never love the foreigner whose wealth required you to inveigle a handful of coins"—and contemplates the material inequalities that fracture diaspora: "In their eyes, I must have appeared a foolish woman who acted as if slaves existed only in the past and who conducted herself as if dispossession were her inheritance alone. Looking at me, the boys imagined the wealth and riches they would possess if they lived in the States. After all, who else but a rich American could afford to travel so far to cry about her own past?" (89). With bitterness and horror, she concludes, "Looking at me, the boys wished their ancestors had been slaves. If so, they would be big men" (89).

If love is proffered as that which holds together the community of diaspora, as a network of intimate bonds, then what repulses Hartman is not the *severing* of those bonds, their exposure as mutual but conflicting exploitations on an uneven terrain of desperation and deprivation. Rather, it is the possibility of *securing* them: that the romance of diaspora might sustain unequal relations as a more intimate bondage. Interrupted in the private loneliness of her shame—that solitary condition crying out for connection, *take me, remake me*—she is presented its reflection as guilt: *your condition may be redeemed at a price; make recompense, and it will be separated from you, restoring us both to what we were.* This love falls short, to her ears, for she's heard it all before.

What blasts the community of diaspora apart? In Hartman's eyes, the boys' desire to flee to a life of riches is an ambivalent, resentful identification masquerading as love. If their identification with her as an (African) American pursues inclusion and uplift through intimate ties, its ultimate aim is to pass through and transcend this shameful familiality, dissolving those bonds in surpassing them. "They wanted to break out of this dusty four-cornered town," she imagines, nevermore "to plead for small change . . . or repeat the words 'slave trade' and 'one Africa'"

(89). This desire appears as a familiar memory, for it is also a trace of a familial history. A longing for flight, for an *elsewhere*, is nourished by fantasies of return, even as it endlessly departs from its location in an imagined past: "return and remaking, or restoration and transformation, can't be separated into tidy opposing categories. Sometimes *going back to* and *moving toward* coincide" (96). While it exposes and eludes forms of intimate bondage transacted in the image of familial belonging, it also risks severing those ties of love it deems precious, without guarantee of redemption or reunion. In the histories of black migration and dispersal, this *elsewhere* has been projected variously on an African homeland, a new home in the North, Canada, England, or the industrial towns of the Northeast, the Midwest, and the West—but the city of refuge was only ever actualized as an echo of a religious afterlife or a utopian future. In the bitterness that swells within the distance unbridged by the boys' professions of love, Hartman perceives the historical disenchantments of both flight and return, and the gap between differential forms of unfreedom.

Ultimately, Hartman finds that her desire to restore a broken lineage cannot be fulfilled by immersion in local histories descending from the slave trade, which are organized by the memory of different ancestors—those who remained, resisting, collaborating with, or eluding its murderous traffic. The trope of common ancestry, for the recuperative practices of historical knowledge, is insufficient for a liberatory diasporic politics that attends to the nonequivalent positions of its various subjects.[3] Nonetheless, she explains, "At the end of the journey, I knew that Africa wasn't dead to me, nor was it just a grave. My future was entangled with it, just as it was entangled with every other place on the globe where people were struggling to live and hoping to thrive" (233). This figure of entangled futures introduces what "return" can indicate but never encompass: "The fugitive's dream . . . was a dream of the world-house" (233). She chooses this "legacy," this "dream," this "elsewhere," claiming it in the name of *"we who become together"* (234)—an "African people" that "referred not to the past or to an extant collectivity but to a potential unleashed by struggles for autonomy and democracy" (233–34). Just as different historical circumstances require changing how this "we" is imagined, its name must also be changeable, for, she asserts, "a name is just a call for freedom" (234).

This conception of diaspora as an ongoing political imperative aligns with Brent Edwards's contention that it must be approached as a *political project*, manifested in practices that operate through difference. Elaborating Stuart Hall's theory of articulation, he apprehends difference not as a mere impediment to coordinated action or proclamations of "unity," but as the pivot point of a dynamic mobility, theorized as *décalage*—"a haunting gap or discrepancy that allows the African diaspora to 'step' and 'move' in various articulations."[4] An account of the collectivity temporally enacted in such practices can be found in the poetics of Nathaniel Mackey. In "Destination Out," he describes what others term an experimental or innovative strain in black literature as "black centrifugal writing": "In the face of a widespread fetishization of collectivity, it dislocates collectivity, flies from collectivity, wants to make flight a condition of collectivity." Resonating with Hartman's elusive diasporic "we," he recasts her exposure of the vexed interplay between flight and return, and the occluded antagonism within familial and romantic professions of intimate bonds: "not so much a war between family and flight as the familial song of one's feeling for flight." Individuation and communion, call and response: if *flight* is what pulls one out of many, by inciting an affect or sensibility, it performs the reassembling of the *we* in its organization of collective, re-membering sound. For Mackey, these insights of black centrifugal writing emerge from "the lessons it has learned from black music."

You may recall, then, that this music may provide the most extensive critical resources for the kind of fearless inquiry into love and loss Hartman's narrative undertakes. Her insights may already be encoded in its sophisticated, modest, and discerning wisdom, whose lessons, if not implied, must surely await their activation when you are capable of hearing them.

As in Carter's simple admonition: *You'll be / forever grateful / for all the love notes / you hear.*

Two: The Original Model Minority Hoboes the Empire State

In this section, I consider how U.S. transpacific imperialism appeared, to an emerging African American elite, as both a problem and a chance—providing a possible refuge from domestic white supremacy through individual or mass migration, and a stage for claiming and performing the civilizing mission through military service and tutelage. Theorizing the position of black intellectuals, soldiers, and educators on their journeys through the complex, contested racial formations of a transpacific domain, and analyzing the formal conventions of their initial fictional representations, I ask how their investment in the gendered norms of modern civilization both bound them to and severed them from racial and national communities in the metropole and beyond, and how their desires for both flight and return might point toward the fugitive's dream of diasporic collectivity.

the chance of empire

The rise of U.S. transpacific imperialism—*for us and for the nation the greatest event since the Civil War*, as Du Bois put it ("Present Outlook" 1900, 102)—transformed the politics of race and nation at the dawn of a new century, raising a series of questions that resounded across the range of black political and cultural modernisms. During the Spanish-American War and the Philippine-American War, African Americans participated in heated national controversies over imperial policy, military campaigns, and their implications for domestic questions of democracy, race, and gender, situating them within ongoing debates over black citizenship rights. Would demonstrations of patriotic loyalty, most of all through military service, suffice to prove—or seize—full citizenship? If so, how should black soldiers comport themselves, what conditions of service could be demanded, and how should their sacrifice be effectively publicized? Or was service in a segregated military foolish, demonstrably ineffective, or fundamentally demeaning? Were black soldiers degraded by complicity in suppressing the legitimate political aspirations of another nonwhite group, or in racist atrocities carried out in the Philippine campaigns? Was it more patriotic to oppose a misguided and objectionable policy—as many white anti-imperialists also argued? Or should African Americans accept that their political rights would never be recognized within a racist nation, and seek out other sites of belonging?[5]

What was the ethnological status of these newly acquired populations, in relation to African Americans and to U.S. whites? Would their incorporation into a U.S. polity increase or decrease African American influence? If colonization was predicated on a supposed Filipino incapacity for self-rule that could be rectified through tutelage, what were the implications for a black population similarly questioned, and for an African American elite invested in the pedagogical processes of uplift? Would the new territories provide greater political and economic opportunities for black migrants, individually or en masse?

For the intellectuals who carried out these debates, including such prominent figures as Henry M. Turner, Theophilus G. Steward, T. Thomas Fortune, Kelly Miller, William S. Scarborough, and Pauline E. Hopkins, the event of U.S. transpacific colonialism recast two overarching questions they confronted at the century's outset: Where did the Negro fit in the dynamic world order of modern civilization? What were the proper means of racial uplift? These were precisely the questions that concerned Du Bois in his 1899 address, in which the presumption of Philippine conquest and incorporation provided the world-historical conditions of "American Negro" racial modernity. Du Bois's gendered, Talented-Tenth collective subject thereby took up a "heavier burden" than Kipling and his Anglo-Saxon brethren could imagine, duty-bound as leaders of both their own race and the empire's darker wards in a civilizing mission aiming to transcend global white supremacy ("Present Outlook" 1900, 103).

where in the world may we go and be safe?

Given Du Bois's proclaimed opposition to conquest, the ease with which his address assimilated a Filipino population still engaged in armed resistance into the imperial polity seems peculiar, if typical of the pragmatic mode of his analyses of geopolitical competition. In any case, by 1903, after four years of bitter insurgency and widely publicized U.S. atrocities, it is not surprising that this willed optimism for Pacific colonization does not appear in *The Souls of Black Folk*. Its more famous formulation of the color-line thesis—"The problem of the twentieth century is the problem of the color-line,—the relation of the darker to the lighter races of men in Asia and Africa, in America and the islands of the sea" (*Writings* 372)—does include a kind of catchall category, favored by Du Bois and not atypical for the period, that clearly calls to mind the Philippines and Hawai'i.

Elsewhere in *Souls*, the islands surface more explicitly, at the especially sensitive moment when Du Bois turns from a historical analysis
of Booker T. Washington's emergence to his own assertion of an alternative political program. Carefully articulating it in the collective voice of
established figures "like the Grimkes, Kelly Miller, [and] J. W. E. Bowen"
(400), Du Bois disavows the intemperate militancy of a separate group
of Washington's critics, left unnamed, whom blind hatred and lack of
manly self-restraint have rendered incapable of formulating a coherent agenda. The only item they can agree upon is that "the Negro's only
hope lies in emigration"—sufficient folly, Du Bois proposes, for their
dismissal from the political stage: "nothing has more effectually made
this programme seem hopeless than the recent course of the United
States toward weaker and darker peoples in the West Indies, Hawaii,
and the Philippines,—for where in the world may we go and be safe
from lying and brute force?" (399–400). Behind this canny rhetorical
positioning is a strikingly far-reaching insight: as the wars had shown,
by 1903 it was already too late for the diasporic dream of return to be
actualized through the establishment of a homeland, for there was no
place on earth beyond imperial competition's discursive and military
reach, which colonial emigration schemes could only serve to extend.

The example was not idly chosen. According to Willard Gatewood,
between 1900 and 1903 the Philippines and Hawai'i became the focal
point of an ongoing series of emigrationist proposals that otherwise
ranged across "Africa, Puerto Rico, Cuba, and even Haiti" (*Black Americans* 295). Such schemes typically featured an odd convergence between
Southern white supremacists and militant black leaders like the A.M.E.
bishop Henry M. Turner. Gatewood's detailed study suggests that, while
the transpacific proposals never gained much traction among white or
black audiences, they generated a surprising amount of interest. Through
the determined advocacy of Alabama senator John Tyler Morgan, in
1902 the prospect of a mass relocation of Southern African Americans
to the Philippines was investigated in congressional hearings and in a
separate formal report by George W. Davis, commander of the Department of Mindanao, commissioned by the secretary of war. Neither proved
favorable to Morgan's proposals, but later that year President Theodore
Roosevelt appointed the journalist T. Thomas Fortune on a fact-finding
tour of Hawai'i and the Philippines—an ill-fated trip I examine at length

in Chapter 3. Meanwhile, Turner rejected colonization anywhere but Africa (309), and most black public opinion was justifiably suspicious of schemes tantamount to mass deportation. Just as Fortune was arriving in Manila in February 1903, for example, a detailed article rejecting Morgan's plan was published by the future union leader Rienzi Lemus, then a soldier-correspondent reporting on the Philippines for the black press.

If these visions of a black Zion across the Pacific, or of a South cleansed of its race problem, seem fanciful, their greater significance lies not in the fact but in the fancy, as Du Bois himself might have put it: the fantasy of a realizable homeland provided a discursive site for organizing a heterogeneous range of black desires for political belonging beyond the United States. Yet the more pragmatic alternatives offered by their critics are also telling. In his report, Brigadier General Davis floated a separate scheme to establish a sugar industry by importing black labor from Louisiana, under a contract system explicitly modeled on the intra-imperial traffic in labor established "for East Indies coolies" (rpt. in Baylen and Moore 73), echoing contemporaneous plans by Hawaiian planters to recruit black workers (Gatewood, *Black Americans* 298–300). Conversely, small-scale migration by ambitious professionals, rather than Southern peasants, was widely advocated by figures like Charles Steward, one of Theophilus Steward's sons, and the scholar William S. Scarborough, a key opponent of mass resettlement.[6] The class distinction pursued by uplift, in this instance, was meant to establish the difference between the reversal and reconstitution of a lineage of unfree labor descending from slavery.

After Fortune published a series of articles based on his travels in *Voice of the Negro*, one of Du Bois's star students from Atlanta University, Harry H. Pace, responded with a detailed rejection of emigration schemes in the same journal. While his essay begins with a diligent paraphrasing of some famous passages in *The Souls of Black Folk*, Pace rejects the argument that new nonwhite populations would increase black political influence already suppressed under Jim Crow. In bracingly blunt terms, he refuses to add to the black man's burden—"If we must ally ourselves as a race, with another people, in heaven's name, let that people bring some advantage; let it not add to the already heavy burden of illiteracy and thriftlessness which the intelligent portion of the race has to bear today"—and dismisses Morgan, Fortune, and Turner:

"Whether the advocate of emigration be white or black, editor or bishop, the majority of thinking people of both races have already concluded that the masses of the Negro people will, for a long time to come, live in the South, and that it is best that they should" (485).

As it happened, those masses would come to a different conclusion over the coming decades. For Alain Locke in *The New Negro*, the agency of "the migrating peasant" (7) proved epochal, even as the Southern black professional class lagged behind. Contra Pace, this agency arrives from the future to recast the significance of the emigration debates, as speculative rehearsals for what became known as the Great Migration. An entrepreneur and committed race man, Pace himself would seize the opportunities provided by black urbanization in founding the first major black-owned record company, Black Swan, noted for classical music and spirituals, along with blues and jazz sides by Ethel Waters, Alberta Hunter, and Fletcher Henderson. Over the course of its brief but influential existence, the company reportedly maintained active sales agents as far away as the Philippines, and even issued some recordings of Hawaiian music.[7]

violence and tutelage

As these debates proceeded, soldiers from several segregated black regiments played crucial roles in the conquest and occupation, and some stayed on to pursue opportunities in business and colonial administration. One key figure was Walter H. Loving, who rose from private to major in the U.S. Army and to lieutenant colonel in its Philippine counterpart, becoming a close acquaintance of Presidents Theodore Roosevelt, William Taft, and Manuel Quezon.[8] His greatest public success came in leading the Philippine Constabulary Band to acclaimed performances at the 1904 Louisiana Purchase Exposition and Taft's 1909 inaugural, but he also played a noted role in U.S. military intelligence in World War I, investigating reports of sedition by, and mistreatment of, African American soldiers.[9] Later, at Quezon's urging, he returned to his band-leading duties in the Philippines, and was killed in Manila in 1945 by a retreating Japanese military.

Within the colonial service, the most prominent African American intellectual was Theophilus G. Steward, a prolific scholar, American

Negro Academy member, and longtime A.M.E. chaplain of the 25th Infantry whose sons Charles and Frank also published notable writings
on the Philippines. His duties included serving as military superintendent of schools in Zambales Province, an experience he wrote about for
Colored American Magazine ("Two Years in Luzon"). With the transition
to civilian administration, other African American men and women
followed in the soldiers' wake to take up posts in colonial education.
Among the black "Thomasites" (nicknamed for the S.S. *Thomas*, on
which one early group of educators had arrived) was an unknown high
school teacher and principal from West Virginia, Carter G. Woodson,
who went on to fame as the leading black historian of his time.[10]

Assigned to a school in 1903 in San Isidro, Woodson quickly taught
himself Spanish, and was promoted to supervisor of schools and placed
in charge of teacher training in Pangasinan. Though he returned to the
metropole for health reasons three years later, he was still pursuing re-
employment in the Philippines as late as 1909, after beginning his PhD
at Harvard (Goggin 16–23). In his 1933 classic, *The Mis-education of the
Negro*, Woodson briefly alluded to the colonial regime, comparing it
favorably to African American schooling. He recalls a successful col-
league, an "insurance man" fortunately untrained in educational theory, who rewrites the song "Come Shake the Apple Tree" to refer to the
lomboy tree, and replaced stories about George Washington with ones
about Rizal (98–99). (Decades later, the prominent diplomat and scholar
Renato Constantino would publish an influential essay titled "The Mis-
education of the Filipino," sharing much of Woodson's trenchant critique of education while drawing directly opposed conclusions about
U.S. colonial rule.)

Even before 1899, post-Reconstruction debates over African American education had been entwined with U.S. Pacific imperialism. Booker
T. Washington's Tuskegee model of industrial education extended the
theories of his mentor at Hampton, Samuel Chapman Armstrong, which
drew on his experiences as the child of U.S. missionary educators in
the kingdom of Hawai'i. Hampton maintained its Hawaiian connections
over the years; for example, Helen James (Chisholm), an aunt of the
novelist Ann Petry, left there in 1901 to work for three years in Hawai'i
schools modeled after her alma mater, meeting both the deposed Queen
Lili'uokalani and Anna Cate Dole, the wife of the first territorial governor

(E. Petry 108). Frederick Atkinson, the first Philippine superintendent of education under the U.S. regime, wrote Washington in April 1900 seeking his recommendations, and his tour of Tuskegee and Hampton the following month rated two separate mentions in Hampton's *Southern Workman*.[11] He subsequently reported to the Philippine Commission that the institutions' model would protect against the presumed failures of Reconstruction (Kramer, "Jim Crow Science" 234–35). Meanwhile, Washington wrote to the War Department in 1901 to pursue positions for Tuskegee alumni in the new colony (Goggin 17).

Washington's theories did not go unopposed. A year later in Zambales, concerned about the scholastic qualifications of industrial school graduates, a recent arrival from North Carolina, John Henry Manning Butler, wrote discreetly to Du Bois, urging him to forward copies of his publications to the Department of Education in Manila, omitting mention of Butler's name or request (Letter from J. H. M. Butler). After serving as superintendent in the provinces of Isabela and Cagayan over a three-decade career, Butler retired in 1933 to join the education department at the National University of Manila.

The following year, he published a detailed, generally glowing account of Philippine education in the *Journal of Negro Education*, concluding with a call for comparison under the banner of uplift.[12] "Destiny has thrown the Negro and the Filipino under the tutelage of America," he wrote, praising U.S. "ideals [which] seem the purest and the best in developing manhood and womanhood." Nodding to the long history of black patriotism in wartime, and the Filipino's undiminished "gratitude for what America has done for his country," he asserts: "Greater development is rooted in self-determination. Both of the races need to know more about each other" ("New Education" 267–68).

Like Loving, Butler died during the Japanese occupation. Woodson published their obituaries one before the other in his *Journal of Negro History* in April 1945. According to a 1978 letter from his widow, Loving's defiant last words, before being beheaded by the Japanese, were: "I am an American. If I must die, I'll die like an American" (qtd. in Richardson 26). In the obituaries, Woodson described his death as "a great loss to the Philippines and the United States" ("Walter Howard Loving" 245) and praised Butler as "not only a representative Negro but a distinguished American citizen who made a contribution to the modernization of the

Philippines" ("John Henry Manning Butler" 244). Yet these formulations cannot foreclose the paradoxes of identification they raise: Did Loving and Butler die as patriotic Americans or as functionaries of an oppressive colonial regime? As patriotic Filipinos, or at least longtime Philippine residents committed to the realization of long-promised independence, or as "representative Negroes" in service to the race, whose memory would be preserved from oblivion in the pages of its journals? Or, if the echo of Claude McKay's famous sonnet, "If We Must Die," gets to the gendered heart of the matter, did they die simply, and against all odds, as *men*?

riding the blind

These paradoxes of identification illustrate the ambivalent positioning of this emerging elite at the century's dawn, seeking to stake its claim in the dynamic order of civilization, on terms set by the training of sexuality and gender. From this vantage, prevailing notions of civilization offered a narrative schema to explain and articulate natural science, geopolitical history, and cultural achievement—all within a world-picture of unilinear progress, ever upward and forward, measured out in the cyclical cadences of organic life. This "occidented" schema flattered the racial self-perception of U.S. nationalism, placing it within the family of white imperial powers and the more specific bloodlines of the Anglo-Saxon race, while implying that U.S. civilization remained demonstrably inferior to that of its European brethren. Yet such inferiority, understood as youthful vigor, could be cast as the promise of a coming ascendancy. Across the Pacific and in the South, the civilizing mission of Anglo-Saxon uplift could distinguish U.S. white men and women from both the primitive Filipino and Negro and the older imperial powers of Britain and Spain. Competing on the same terrain, Negro uplift could assert its own claim to the position of an ascendant racial subject, absorbing the lessons of its superiors while advancing the realization of their moral ideals, because this racializing discourse of "civilization," itself the dominant justification of imperialism, forecast the decline of the West as the natural outcome of an organic cycle.

Hence, the apparent lapses in the oppositional writings of an intellectual like Pauline Hopkins instead reveal the contradictions within a

historical conception of racial justice once perceived as internally consistent. In an important early essay on uplift, Kevin Gaines reads Hopkins's
1905 ethnological survey of "the darker races" in *Voice of the Negro*,
identifying a disparity between a "militant black anti-imperialism"
("Black" 437) evidenced in "claimed solidarity" with Japanese and Africans
(437), and an affirmation of the U.S. civilizing mission in the Philippines, along with distancing, dismissive representations of South Pacific
peoples. What Gaines calls "two distinct visions of imperialism" (444)
are better understood as a redirection of civilizationist ideas, differentiating between nonwhite subjects and objects of uplift, that extended
imperialism's own justifications even as it pointed toward alternatives it
could not yet envision.[13]

A transpacific arena of imperial warfare and colonial rule provided
opportunities for drawing this distinction between nonwhite groups,
juxtaposing the Filipino and the Negro to emphasize the latter's cultural
refinement and civilized ways. But the comparison was fraught with
risks: colonial tutelage tended to elevate its new pupils over its older
wards, as preferred objects of its more advanced techniques of uplift,
even as imperial violence threatened to conflate the civilized Negro and
the primitive Filipino into an undifferentiated nonwhite category. Moreover, the autonomous, self-determining character of Negro uplift could
not be definitively separated from white tutelage, requiring the incorporation of the split between primitive and civilized *within* the racial community, as a benevolent relation between the masses and a modernizing
elite.

In "Of Our Normative Strivings," Roderick Ferguson reads the
construction of this new middle class within "a discourse of sexuality
specific to African American racial formations and a genealogy of governmentality within the United States," provocatively terming it "the
original model minority" (89–90). Tracking its emergence through Du
Bois's account of postbellum education in *Souls* and Booker T. Washington's promotion of industrial education, Ferguson provocatively suggests that "a dichotomy between industrial education and humanistic
training . . . might have been fictitious because of shared moral and normative investments." The resulting "alliance between sexual normativity and citizenship . . . would refine and elaborate power through twin
processes of nationalization and normalization," calling forth "a new and

emergent moral and intellectual formation" that "would inherit modernity by adhering to gender and sexual propriety" (92). The appearance of
this model minority illustrates that "governmentality actually describes
power's activation through the constitution of agency" (95), here linking
industrial education to imperial soldiering: "As the conscripted subjects
of war, African Americans testify to the perfectibility of the state as that
system that can accommodate a previously inadmissible population
whose naturalization as citizen is dubious at best. As the conscripted
subjects of sexual normativity, African Americans swear on behalf of
the capacious embrace of the nation as that moral ideal that can aid a
group whose struggle against perversion is tenuous, to be sure. Both
war and sexual normativity claimed to be able to draft African Americans into citizenship and humanity" (96). Ferguson's analysis aligns with
the account of an occidented civilizational schema that requires sexual
regulation where violence and tutelage meet. The revitalizing effect of
conquest distinguishes a rising race from a decadent one through the
incorporation of a primal sexual force, the essence of masculine potency and feminine fertility, which must be trained into civilized gender
norms.

But inquiring into the poetics of black transpacific culture must go
beyond specifying the conscription of this new African American elite
into U.S. imperialism, as witnesses to the perfectibility of the state or
the inclusiveness of the nation, and instead attend to the ways they expressed or enacted desires that passed through or transcended, rode
with and departed from, or fell short and were excluded from the imperial
nation/state. Rather than dismissing them as complicit, or vindicating or
condemning them as unaware, you might approach them as caught in a
different location within a predicament you share, of structural complicity
within an imperialism whose power extends in the name of justice.

Let me illustrate this point by way of a somewhat fortuitous analogy,
from "Empire State Express," a recording by the great Delta blues musician Son House. Neither a form of governance nor a skyscraper upon
which one might lynch a giant ape, the title's referent is an indispensable
motif of Afro-diasporic cosmologies, surfacing as an icon of modernist cultures—a train. When it was introduced, the Empire State Express
was the fastest in the history of the world. In the song, it is an object of
intense ambivalence, of awe and admiration, hatred and longing, the

physical manifestation of the desire for flight. It's the vehicle of dispersal that severs intimate bonds, yet the recurrence of its unmistakable whistle in the soundscape, keeping and marking time, reminds you not only of the lover's absence but of the tantalizing chance of reunion—here, back home, or in some happier elsewhere. And it represents the chance of modernity, of unprecedented power and speed, from which the singer may be excluded but which he persists in seeking. Having lost his lover, he begs the depot agent to let him "ride the blind"—hitch along in the forbidding space behind the engine or in the baggage compartment—but he is denied: *I wouldn't mind it, Son / but this Empire State ain't mine.*

The depot agent's reply, whether cruel or justifiable, is surely comprehensible: *I am only an employee, I don't set the rules, I follow them to keep my job.* But this disavowal of an agency based in property rights is oddly disingenuous when opposed to the actions of the singer, who, you might imagine, will ignore this refusal and hobo along, if he can get away with it. *For myself*, the depot agent says, *I might be willing to grant your request, but I cannot claim the prerogatives of ownership and hence cannot act.* Yet this refusal is active, not passive—he does not simply look the other way, but enforces a law. If this action is not petty or ungenerous, it must be that he is acting in the name of the Empire State, *as* the Empire State, both possessing and possessed by the authority it vests in his person. The depot agent's disavowal, you might say, effaces his situated agency within the institution of the Empire State while seeking the moral comfort of an independent conscience, absolved of all complicity via its embrace of utter powerlessness. By contrast, the hobo, if he can get away with it, appropriates the Empire State, asserting an ownership that does not attain the inalienable authority of property rights but, if he can steal away with it, may be just enough to transport him to places unforeseen.

Not entirely dormant, the hobo remains a powerful figure in the blues and all those cultures of popular music sharing relations with it, but it feels somewhat incongruous to imagine an aspiring African American middle class as "hoboes" in the transpacific circuits of U.S. imperialism. This group was, justifiably, quite exercised in fighting indignities imposed upon them in the accommodations of fully paid train travel. In a 1923 essay, "The Superior Race," later reworked for *Dusk of Dawn*, Du Bois himself would go so far as to define "the black man," in a pithy and brilliant formulation, as "a person who must ride Jim Crow in Georgia" (*Writings* 666). Yet this analogy suggests a methodology for studying African Americans' ambivalent participation in imperialism, one that attends not to the good faith or clean conscience of a political program, nor to the expansion or restriction of a system of inalienable rights, but to the risky movements of desires and to actions taken without guarantee. These soldiers, educators, colonial officials, and intellectuals had a critical vantage different, but no more limited than the hindsight of future scholars. Their uplift ethic of sacrifice notwithstanding, they could not have been motivated solely by a dream of inclusion and full citizenship in some far-off future, or by the dubious prospect of equal recognition and privilege befitting their class status. In projecting modern forms of Negro identity and performing the roles of civilized race men and women, you may imagine, they aimed less to plead for acceptance than to seize and live out a tenuous, transient dream of freedom. Any pittance of recognition from whites would likely be paid, not in guilt, but in shame. In this distinction, guilt may lead to reparations (*I must make recompense for the injustice I've done to you*), but rests on the guilty party's superior position and disdain for relations (*let us be even, and go our separate ways*). Instead, shame offers a moral satisfaction (*I acknowledge your superiority, if only begrudgingly or in retreat*), even when it is not confronted through a more difficult and intimate accounting (*the injustice done to you and the harm done to me link us, if unevenly; undoing the harm to myself binds me to you in mutual responsibility for our collective transformation*).

They sought, in other words, to live not as equals to whites, but as their betters.

Yet in recasting the civilizing mission as the burden shouldered by Negro manhood and womanhood, they also incurred responsibility for its debts, whose transference onto less fortunate others only deferred their inevitable return. Ferguson's account remains useful here, revealing "a partnership between an emerging indigenous black elite and state power over the regulation of a subaltern black population," in which "African American elites learned the tactics of sexual and gender regulation from the itineraries of imperialism, imposing those tactics onto black poor and working-class folks" as well as to "their children" (98). What is this imposition, this benevolent assimilation, if not an expression of love, tough yet tender, weaving and securing a network of intimate ties? Lovers have been known to struggle against such constraints, children to bide their time until they may fly. This love seeks to bind the loved one close, only to find that what it holds has turned to loss.

spinning the bottle

For African American audiences in the period, and historians in subsequent decades, the conditions and achievements of black military service presented the primary thematic concern for writing on African Americans in the Philippines. As in other moments when white disparagement of black veracity hindered a political imperative to dispel white representations of black experience, writing on Negro military valor—reportage, historiography, or even verse—generally presented itself as nonfiction.[14] Nonetheless, literary-historical scholarship has recovered a significant body of black fiction inspired by the Philippine-American War, including three stories by Frank R. Steward, published in *Colored American Magazine* in 1902 and 1903; Sutton Griggs's 1902 novel, *Unfettered*; "In Love as in War," from James McGirt's 1907 short story collection *The Triumphs of Ephraim*; Bob Cole, Rosamond Johnson, and James Weldon Johnson's 1906 musical theater production *The Shoo-Fly Regiment*; and F. Grant Gilmore's 1915 *The Problem: A Military Novel*.[15] In each case, the danger and allure of a journey to distant, violent locales is emplotted within the trials, triumphs, and tragedies of heterosexual love. Taking the measure of dispersal and return, worrying the irresolvable puzzle of loyalty and betrayal conjured by ambition and the exotic, required narratives of romance, running through an array of racial permutations of heterosexual coupling. While these texts typically allude to historical fact in describing heroic battlefield exploits, they are largely relegated to characters' back-stories or otherwise subordinated to the development of the romance plot, suggesting a different agenda for which the epistemological status of fiction was better suited. But if the primary aim of these texts was not to publicize the accomplishments of black soldiers in the service of political claims to citizenship rights, then what were they after?

First, a brief survey of the variations on the formula is in order. In McGirt's "In Love and War" and Gilmore's *The Problem*, a black man wins a woman's favor in competition with a Southern white man. Mc-Girt's Sergeant Roberts, identified as the true hero of San Juan Hill, instantly captures the heart of Princess Quinaldo, the richest and most beautiful woman in the land, despite the efforts of Lieutenant Vaughn, scion of an elite New Orleans family. Gilmore's William Henderson, also a sergeant and hero of San Juan, competes with Henry Fairfax, a military surgeon from a wealthy Richmond family, for the love of Fairfax's foster sister, Freda Waters, who, in a climactic twist, is revealed to be the secret black child of Fairfax's father.

In Steward's "The Men Who Prey," Captain Duncan Lane, heir of a powerful Texas family, takes up with an innocent young woman of Laguna, Jacinta. Here, the triangle's third leg is Fanny, his pregnant wife back home. In the end, Lane returns to Texas and names Fanny's new baby after Jacinta, whom he leaves swooning at the wharf—also pregnant. Only a hint of the triangle remains in Steward's "Pepe's Anting-Anting," which opens with a flirtation between Chata, who works in her father's Laguna canteen, and the narrator, a captain of the occupying forces. As he learns, her true love is Pepe, an educated Filipino favored by the garrison's commanding officer who is discovered, after being shot in battle, to be a lieutenant in the resistance; a week later, Chata follows him in death. The same narrator, in "Starlik," is drawn, in even more restrained fashion, to a different Filipina, Enriqueta, the niece of a gentleman landowner. Eventually, he learns that her mother fell victim to her father, a hated Spanish friar, and that the shame of her parentage drives her from one town to another, until she ends up as a prostitute on the outskirts of Manila.

Dorlan Warthell, the brilliant hero of Griggs's *Unfettered*, falls in love with the light-skinned Morlene, trapped by pity in a loveless marriage to Harry Dalton. Here the triangle links three black characters in the South, but the action of the convoluted plot turns on Dorlan's explosive campaign to organize a third party, splitting black voters from the Republicans on the issue of full equality for Filipinos. Finally, according to Seniors's reconstruction of Cole and Johnson's *Shoo-Fly Regiment*, its central storyline followed the temporarily thwarted romance between Rose Maxwell, the principal's daughter at the fictional Lincolnville Institute, and a young graduate, Ned Jackson. Ultimately, his heroism in the Philippines convinces her father to allow the marriage. Secondary storylines involved the courtship of Lincolnville's upwardly mobile janitor and a town widow with ten children—presumably a comedic contrast to the Talented-Tenth Ned and Rose—and the romance between another black soldier and a Filipina dancer.

What can be distilled from these variations on the narrative formula of imperial romance? It may include a triangle (two men and a woman, two women and a man) or a heterosexual couple. It may span the Pacific, to separate or unite the lovers, or take place entirely on one side. Yet even when the third corner of the triangle is absent or the action is limited to the colony or the metropole, the centrifugal force of imperialism's transpacific circuit is the basis of the romance's disruption and possible resolution. An array of permutations of race (Negro, Filipino, Southern white) and gender is possible, but only within certain limits. Filipino men and black women neither travel nor take partners outside their group—in Gilmore, Freda's discovery of her blackness not only legitimizes her choice of a partner but effectively guarantees it. Running through all of these possibilities allows the narrative formula to organize a range of questions about black participation in imperialism, and about diaspora and the chance of the modern, while fixing the position of civilized manhood at the center. Because the precondition of this position was mastery through violence, imperial soldiering was seen as an opportunity even by sympathizers to the Filipino cause. But the chance to which the formula clings, in seeking to disrupt the equation of whiteness with civilized status, was that its final proof lay not in violence but in morality. And the key to this morality could be found in gendered norms.

Situating black transpacific circuits within diaspora reveals how these texts' interventions in contemporary politics were shaped by a longer historical memory. Dorlan's proposal that African Americans should break away from the Republican Party over imperial policy referenced actual debates in which Griggs had publicly participated (Gatewood, *Black Americans* 249–50). Yet setting it within the romance plot allowed him not only to compare black loyalty to the party of Lincoln to a loveless marriage, but also to connect questions of political loyalty to deeper concerns with familial and affective bonds. Where was home? Who was family? Do Dorlan's efforts on behalf of Filipinos imply that nonwhite groups were more durably linked than African Americans and white

Republicans? Does the issue's eventual disappearance from the plot—instead, winning Morlene's hand requires nothing less from Dorlan than a plan to resolve the problem of the Negro in the United States once and for all—imply, intentionally or not, that the earlier cause had been a distraction from his true loyalties?

These questions become more pointed as you draw closer to the actual historical experience of African American soldiers. For Gilmore's Sergeant Henderson, imperial military service in the Great Plains, Cuba, and the Philippines makes a disciplined man of a rambunctious boy, but the love of a good black woman settles him back home in Virginia. For McGirt's Sergeant Roberts, heroism is rewarded with an exotic beauty and vast wealth. Like W. E. B. Du Bois's better-known, more sophisticated, but no less fanciful *Dark Princess*, McGirt's story is a wish-fulfilling fantasy tethered to the historical present by a few nonfictional details, but his princess is drawn without any noticeable regard for actual Philippine society. It is significant, nonetheless, that the women are attracted to Roberts for his dark complexion as well as his heroism, and that his rival admits defeat by insisting he was joking, for marrying a Filipina would be miscegenation. While Vaughn's embarrassed attempt to fix Quinaldo within the protocols of Southern antiblack racism is clearly disingenuous, it functions to domesticate her racial difference within marriage, even if her ethnological status is unresolved.[16] Similarly, the closing description of their new household comprises a single detail—a framed record of Roberts's heroism in the parlor, with a commendation from the president himself—that marks the indeterminacy of its location, geographical, geopolitical, or generic: in an alien land that is U.S. territory or in the fictive home of full Negro citizenship, in a daydream of paradise where state authority leaves its signature on the wall.

The Philippines, you might say, was really neither here nor there for McGirt or for Gilmore, yet imaginatively valuable for precisely this reason. For Steward, whose unnamed narrator shares the author's rank and Harvard education, the Philippines was a tangible place, connected to the metropole by a network of affects and interests, memories and ambitions, and private and public histories. Brother to Charles and son of Theophilus, Frank Steward was an army captain and provost judge under the occupation. His familial status, reputation, and personal and professional relationships help explain why his fiction treats the prospect of romantic love between black men and Filipina women with such delicacy: his narrator may admit attraction to Chata or Enriqueta, but pursues nothing beyond a mild flirtation.

In each case, a crossing of linguistic borders provides occasion and cover for the exploration of romance. While he typically relies on his Harvard Spanish, the narrator surprises Chata with a "phrase-book greeting in the native vernacular" (358), leading to an impromptu, reciprocal lesson in Tagalog and English, which ends when he coyly introduces the word for "sweetheart" (359). Enriqueta comes to his attention for her reputed facility with English. Remembering Chata (388), he is dubious, but when they meet, language provides both the means and the topic of conversation. She had learned it, he discovers, from an American prisoner early in the war, and took her lessons well: her "pronunciation," he judges, is "nearly perfect" (389), but for a slight accent whose charms are orthographically and thematically marked. "I liked the way in which she lisped out 'sair,'" he comments (389), and this same lisped word allows him to recognize her at the end of the story, when he overhears a prostitute address an intoxicated soldier as his carriage is detoured through a red-light district.

More observer than protagonist, the narrator serves primarily to convey information, like the recurring character Flora, the "buyo-chewing hag" ("Pepe's" 359) whose weakness for gossip is the vehicle by which many plot elements are brought to the reader.[17] Yet this function determines or is determined by an elusive quality to the narrator's sexuality. If his desire introduces the stories of Chata and Enriqueta, bearing the reader's identification with that desire into their exotic world, that desire is purely without consequence in it. This elusiveness negotiates a twofold risk. On one hand, in 1902 or 1903, a metropolitan black audience following the exotic experiences of its favored sons would likely be more concerned with their ultimate return; a narrative like Gilmore's, in which a beloved woman back home guarantees reunion, would likely be preferred to McGirt's. On the other, actual relations between U.S. soldiers and Filipina women tended toward Lane's arrangement with Jacinta, even if white and black commentators regularly insisted that concubinage was exclusively practiced by the other race. In short, the social meaning of the category of race that was at stake in the imperial project was that of *sexuality*.[18] It is therefore impossible for Steward to avoid raising the topic, and so he does his best to make it disappear as quickly as he can.

Hence the major work of the stories is to shift the focus onto the racially marked sexuality of others. Negro manhood steps into the background, to be contrasted with what is in the foreground: the decadence of white Spanish manhood in Father Sebastian, whose sins condemn the helpless Enriqueta to corruption; the decline and fall of Southern white manhood in Duncan Lane, who brings shame to Fanny and Jacinta, and breeds it into the next generation; the misguided but honorable Filipino manhood of Pepe, doomed to defeat by more advanced races, but worthy of sympathy and firm, uplifting tutelage. Between writer and audience, an understanding may pass—left unsaid more out of modesty than fear of repercussion—that *only* Negro manhood is morally capable of bearing the burden of civilization. In this schema, the position of the Filipinos—earnest, misguided Chata and Pepe, grotesque Flora, even the doomed Enriqueta—is structurally equivalent to that of the Southern black peasantry, those benighted masses that were the primary object of uplift for Talented-Tenth achievers like Steward. Here, we return to Roderick Ferguson's claim that imperialism provided black elites with a training in "the tactics of sexual and gender regulation," which they passed on both to nonelite groups and to their own children (98).

In sum, considered as a body, these narratives run through an entire array of permutations, using race as a variable, in order to keep gender constant; and they hold gender constant so that its aspirational norms can be universalized and naturalized. It does not matter so much, in the end, if even the minority trained to this aspiration so often falls short of its ideals, only that a faith in this desire marks them, on behalf of their people, as elect. The form of the love story, by this logic, transcends history and the petty differences of race. It is true, always and everywhere, because it belongs to a cyclic temporality that comes before history, its secret engine. If "race" marks a position in this cycle, "sexuality" is its essence, "gender" the means of training it into control.

Three: The Two Faces of an American Dime

If the emergence of an African American elite in the early twentieth century, amid the transpacific rise of the United States as an imperial power, was shaped by imaginative and actual possibilities of migration, expanded opportunities in education and military service, and the normative training of gender, all these forces may be seen to operate upon another group targeted by uplift—the new colonial subjects of the Philippines. As the U.S. regime expanded across its new territories, it encountered preexisting colonial patterns of migration, shaped by chaotic processes of capitalist modernization and strong cultural associations between education and economic and political advancement. These patterns conditioned flexible, geographically dispersed family structures that could be perceived as evidence of nonnormative sexuality—a depraved condition requiring benevolent intervention, a threatening contagion demanding quarantine. As these patterns proliferated and accelerated, Filipino migrants in the metropole largely found that their hopes of education and uplift dissipated into the exploitative conditions of racialized labor within a racial order suffused with threats of sexualized violence. Yet, on both sides of the Pacific, new Anglophone intellectual types were emerging, within the empire's cultural apparatuses, to confront questions analogous to those of the African American elite: Where did the Filipino fit within the dynamic schema of modern civilization? What were the proper means of racial uplift? How did one become its autonomous, self-determining agent?

the school of empire

It begins with a brother's return from war, and ends with the departure of two more brothers to the war that followed. But where diaspora watches empires and nations come and go, home is not a place, just a running struggle of centripetal and centrifugal desire. Carlos Bulosan's 1946 *America Is in the Heart: A Personal History* hasn't always been well served by its reverential reception in Asian American studies and Filipino diasporic studies, but reading beyond its selective canonization still offers new insights into the history and poetics of Filipino colonial migration.[19] As Rick Baldoz summarizes in *The Third Asiatic Invasion*, this traffic begins with three distinct groups in the first decade of the century, drawn from different strata of colonial society—college students, the government-sponsored *pensionados* expected to return to positions in colonial administration;[20] military servicemembers, who sometimes settled in the metropole, following McKinley's 1901 order authorizing Filipino enlistment in the U.S. Navy; and laborers, recruited to plantations in colonized Hawai'i (46–47). Each group set a precedent for later streams of migration, which, as Mae Ngai explains in *Impossible Subjects*, would confront a distinctively sexualized racism in the metropole.

As Dorothy Fujita-Rony shows, many migrants came from communities already constituted by multiple circuits of labor migration under Spanish colonial rule (39–44). These ongoing, multidirectional patterns of "internal" and "external" migration across competing imperial formations date back even farther, suggesting a complex diasporic history before and beyond any manifestation in a nation/state. The oft-neglected first section of Bulosan's book, nearly a third of the text, takes place entirely in the Philippines, and sets the narrator-protagonist's early life within an analysis of his family's multigenerational engagement with this history. As it opens, his older brother Leon returns from World War I to the barrio of Mangusmana, to the plot of land Allos[21] helps his father to work. His mother lives with a sister and another brother in a nearby town, Binalonan, occasionally traveling to markets and farms to seek work, and two more brothers have left the area for school and military service. Whipsawed by modernizing social conditions, this dispersed kinship unit is held together and driven apart by two doomed imperatives—to maintain ownership of a small piece of land, a nostalgic resistance to the exploitation of tenant farming and seasonal labor, and the progressive aspiration to pay for at least one brother's education.

Alongside these changes are shifts in sexual regulation that would pathologize such a family structure, which the text instead displaces onto a representation of primitive sexuality when Leon, bringing home a wife, fails to verify her virginity. Entering a hut during a traditional wedding ritual, the groom is meant to communicate her status by sending up black smoke—or else send her back to her family in shame. When the smoke does not appear, the festive crowd turns into a mob, beating the bride, then Leon and his father, disgusted by their determination to follow through with the marriage; in the end, they flee the barrio to Manila. Horrified by these "fast-dying . . . backward customs," Allos insists that they are exogenous to their town, deriving "from the hill people who had intermarried with the villagers and had imposed their own traditions" (6–7). Strikingly, Bulosan avoids identifying these non-Christian "hill people" as "Igorot," the tribal designation he uses elsewhere, in a more celebratory primitivism that often becomes masquerade.

Leon's military service alludes to the expansion of one stream of colonial migration. As Fujita-Rony notes, Filipino employment in U.S. Navy galleys and mess halls dramatically increased in the aftermath of World War I, following the exclusion of African Americans (36). Similarly, after the racial restrictions of the 1924 immigration act, larger numbers of Filipino laborers began arriving in the metropole from Hawai'i and the Philippines, relying on their ambiguous status as U.S. "nationals" rather than aliens. Yet, as Bulosan's text demonstrates, it was education, seen as continuous across empire, which provided the governing narrative of colonial migration, and of colonialism generally. Under the Spanish, student travels in the metropole famously shaped *ilustrado* nationalists such as José Rizal, whose dissatisfaction with colonial education was central to their radicalization. The U.S. regime's emphasis on greater access to schooling responded to these lingering grievances, and was crucial to its ideological legitimacy.[22] Thus, a 1904 Bureau of Insular Affairs pamphlet asserts that "the entire governmental structure erected in the islands is itself a school" whose curriculum was "American methods of government" (United States 20), before highlighting the *pensionado* program.[23] After the latter's end in 1910, future student-travelers, known as "fountain-pen boys," found diminishing "returns on education" (Fujita-Rony 68), especially when, as with Bulosan, their class distinction from the laborers was largely aspirational.

Meanwhile, in Manila, an Anglophone intellectual class was emerging from colonial institutions, with a corresponding literature largely centered on the University of the Philippines and its U.P. Writers' Club, whose 1927 founders included José Garcia Villa. In the following decade, a vigorous debate developed between a rarefied "art for art's sake," whose dominant advocate, Villa, had moved to the metropole, and "proletarian literature," whose most articulate champion was the journalist and critic Salvador P. Lopez. These debates were complicated by a broader language politics, setting writers in English against an older, smaller Spanish-speaking elite, supporters of a Tagalog-derived national language, and popular literatures in other dialects. In 1939, the Philippine Writers' League was founded—largely, and controversially, following the proletarian position, and in 1940, under the patronage of

Commonwealth president Manuel Quezon, it offered the first (and only) annual Commonwealth Literary Awards, in English, Tagalog, and Spanish. The English prizes went to S. P. Lopez in the essay, for his elegant *Literature and Society: Essays on Life and Letters*; Manuel E. Arguilla in short fiction, for *How My Brother Leon Brought Home a Wife*, whose title story had appeared in the New York–based *Story* in 1936; and Juan C. Laya in the novel, for *His Native Soil*. Honorable mentions included R. Zulueta da Costa and Villa in poetry—with Villa, pointedly, receiving a lesser cash award. For his part, Bulosan placed a poem, "If You Want to Know What We Are," in the collection published in conjunction with the awards, demonstrating its unmistakable proletarian affiliations by concluding: "WE ARE REVOLUTION!"[24] But even if Bulosan may have downplayed the extent of his formal schooling, in narrating his education through labor activism, he lacked pedigree in U.P.-dominated circles, and his politics, forged in workers' movements along the U.S. West Coast, were decidedly more militant than the elite proletarianism associated with Lopez—whose status and interests placed him closer to the upper-class Villa.

Bulosan's complicated relationship to these writers is highlighted in Martin Joseph Ponce's brilliant essay "On Becoming Socially Articulate," which demonstrates how *America Is in the Heart*—through intertextual allusions recognizable only to readers already versed in this literature—both honors and figuratively "kills off" the author's rivals, thereby elevating him as the exceptional literary representative of the Filipino masses. The book's opening episode, Ponce explains, evokes the title of Arguilla's celebrated story ("Leon," like the names of all the narrator's brothers, is a pseudonym) to displace its pastoralism with a socialist analysis of economic modernization.

In arguably the book's most famous passage, Carlos's brother Macario delivers a stirring speech to a group of Filipino worker-intellectuals in the early 1930s. "*We are America!*" (189), he asserts, placing the Filipino migrant at the end of a series of iconic figures, culminating with the Founding Fathers. No plea for inclusion, this is a revolutionary gesture, rhetorically seizing the capacity to speak for the nation. Embodying the conditions of colonized Native Americans, uneducated immigrants, the displaced poor, and black lynching victims,[25] the Filipino is not one American among equals, but the messianic redeemer of a national history it reveals to be the story of world revolution. But as Ponce explains, this speech, along with a related one in the same chapter assigned to a dying Filipino socialist writer named Pascual, is taken nearly verbatim from a 1943 essay by Bulosan in the *New Republic*, composed as an open letter to S. P. Lopez's wife. Based on the mistaken belief that he'd been killed by the Japanese—Lopez survived to have a distinguished career as a diplomat and University of the Philippines president—Bulosan identifies him to metropolitan readers as "the most important Filipino writer in English" (*On Becoming* 210). Here, Pascual's and Macario's words appear as Bulosan's summary of Lopez's ideas, extrapolated from the position of the migrant. This entails a flexible use of the first-person plural that particularizes and reconnects the migrant struggle in the metropole and the nationalist resistance to yet another colonial occupation, articulating a transpacific Filipino "we" within the dialectical history of world revolution. Explicitly, in the essay, and implicitly, in the book, Bulosan figures the death of the conception of proletarian literature developed by Manila intellectuals to situate himself as their heir and redeemer.

For his migrant audience, Macario's reference to black lynching cited above might invoke cross-racial solidarity, but more to the point, it provided a concrete figure for their experience of sexualized racism. In *Impossible Subjects*, Mae Ngai suggests that the presumption that job competition motivated Filipino exclusion movements is demonstrably false. While they extended a long tradition of anti-Asiatic organizing and violence, Ngai argues that they were motivated by sexualized anxieties: white mobs, respectable anti-Asiatic politicians, and liberal sociologists opposed to exclusion all shared a belief in the overwhelmingly male, unmarried migrants' nonnormative heterosexuality. While other Asian immigrant communities also exhibited "abnormal sex ratios," Ngai explains that the sexuality attributed to Filipinos diverged from "Orientalist tropes" (109), and instead "derived from racial representations of African Americans, especially those that depicted black men as sexually aggressive" (110). A language of *common* derivation is more appropriate here, as both processes draw on a wider history of representations of the not-yet-civilized primitive, rather than the postcivilized decadence featured in Orientalist racialization. The larger point is that Filipinos were deemed "oversexed" in ways "linked to their primitive development": their "'childlike' nature" explained "both labor docility and

sexual promiscuity," and their tastes for "flashy clothes, cheap entertainment, and white women"—particularly blondes—marked them "as a social and sexual menace to white society" (110). Thus, media outrage and
outbreaks of violence regularly coalesced around taxi-dance halls, which
sold timed dances with women, and controversies developed over the
extension of state antimiscegenation laws to marriages between Filipino
men and white women.[26]

The sexualization of the migrant continued processes of imperial
racialization already evident in the initial encounters between U.S.
and Filipino troops. As Ngai recalls, the slur "nigger" was used in the
Philippine-American War, and in the attacks by white U.S. Marines at
the 1904 Louisiana Purchase exposition, scandalized by interactions
between Philippine Scouts and white women in segregated St. Louis.[27]
Filipinos were imagined to embody a racialized sexuality whose "blackness" was not African, but Pacific, and whose juxtaposition with an
advanced Western civilization was necessarily violent. Thus one judge
quoted in Ngai characterized Filipinos as "a race scarcely more than
savages" (114), while another described the sharp-dressing migrants as
"just ten years removed from a bolo and breechcloth" (113). In an immigrant newspaper, José Bulatao countered by recalling "thousands, tens of
thousands of fatherless children" of U.S. soldiers in the colony: "And our
people are still jungle folk and of Primitive Moral Code?" (115). Once
again, the civilizing mission requires, as its enabling condition, the imposition of a racialized primitive sexuality to be uplifted.

Not surprisingly, similar accounts of Filipino sexuality were produced, not only by "progressivists and liberals" like David Barrows, the
first colonial superintendent of education, or white Chicago School sociologists like Emory Bogardus, or even the journalist and activist Carey
McWilliams (Ngai 110–11), but also by Filipino political leaders, sociologists, educators, and other intellectuals on both sides of the Pacific.
Furthermore, as Fujita-Rony, Melinda de Jesús, and Kandice Chuh have
each pointed out, Asian American studies has continued this tradition
in accounts of exclusion-era "bachelor societies," where the tragedy of
anti-Asian racism has been identified as the obstruction of healthy heteronormative conjugal relations. Moreover, the pathologization of Filipino migrant sexuality and the desire for heteronormative uplift may be
found in Bulosan's classic narrative itself.

a love for letters

In two groundbreaking readings, de Jesús and Chuh read *America Is in the Heart* for what each describes as its resistance to heteronormativity, with specific reference to the protagonist's first experience of heterosexual intercourse at a California workers' bunkhouse. Against his will, Carlos is seized bodily and stripped by his coworker Benigno and two other Filipinos, and delivered to a "naked Mexican woman" who has already had sex with several other laborers (159). After the sex act is euphemized with a series of pastoral images, he flees, "trembling with a nameless shame . . . ." (160, ellipsis in original). For Chuh, this "eroticized violence," delivered by "his fellow Filipinos," may be read as "critiquing heteronormative masculinity and not just its white iteration" (41); the "ellipsis" signifies "a disappearance of sexual desire" (40–41). For de Jesús, the scene "implies gang rape" and hence "homosexual desire" for the narrator by his coworkers, "a desire which must be sublimated through heteronormativity—through the prostitute's body"; the ellipsis marks the narrator's "mortification as well as the novel's ambivalence in allowing [him] sexuality at all" (103).[28]

Yet what Carlos is fleeing from, here and throughout the text, is not heteronormativity, but the perverted, degraded, primitivizing condition of racially nonnormative Filipino migrant sexuality. The depravity of the bunkhouse and its denizens, characterized as overcrowded and unhygienic, repeats tropes of Oriental sexuality shared by anti-Asiatic exclusionists and liberal reformers. Throughout, the text reproduces normative assessments of the contaminated, hypersexualized spaces inhabited by Filipino migrants on the West Coast *and* in Manila (slums, vice districts, gambling dens, bordellos, labor camps) and of the contagious, excessively embodied, uncivilized practices developed within them (fornication, prostitution, sex with multiple partners, alcohol and drug abuse, card playing and cockfighting, physical violence). While the narrator assigns structural responsibility for this unhealthy sexuality to capitalist exploitation and racism, he retains a moralizing attitude toward the Filipino migrants, and white and nonwhite women, who succumb to its contamination. Like the respectability politics of Negro uplift, the text evidences a considered strategy to counter sexualized racism, going so far as attempting to normalize stigmatized interracial relations—but this strategy condemns the masses to a redemption figured by the exceptionalized protagonist.

As de Jesús and Chuh each note, the text's persistent tendency to efface the protagonist's embodied sexuality is linked to its persistent idealization of white women. For de Jesús, this "ambivalence" contrasts with "the fundamental truth which anchors this narrative . . . Bulosan's great love for his countrymen" (107). For Chuh, "the feminine ideal" indicated by these poorly characterized "shadows of women" is "dislodged from the body," such that "overcoming a particular and violent version of masculinity" becomes the precondition for the ideal's "realization" (39). More directly, Ponce notes that these "desexualized" interracial relations are explicitly contextualized by commentary on the legal and extralegal enforcement of antimiscegenation taboos (*Beyond the Nation* 96). Yet given the extravagance of the text's representations of its protagonist's relationships with white women—an extravagance that manifests an aesthetic of migrant labor possessing Bulosan's writing beyond intention—I cannot read the protagonist or his relations as asexual or desexualized. Rather, I find them so heavily eroticized that they seem contrived not to allay but rather to provoke or bait antimiscegenationist paranoia, steering into the threat of racist violence. Instead of critiquing normativity, they exceptionalize the protagonist's sexuality, prefiguring revolution as the normalization of colonial relations. In short, I contend that the text depicts scenes of a tutelary intercourse between the protagonist and a series of benevolent white women, an intercourse of books rather than bodies, as themselves sexual acts.

In one episode, for example, Carlos becomes infatuated with a white shopgirl named Judith: "I would go to the store pretending to buy something, but I wanted only to look at her. The way she moved around the room, the grace of her arms, the smile on her face. . . . But when she asked me what I wanted, I felt embarrassed and fumbled for something to say" (172, ellipsis in original). Fortunately, she knows just what he wants—"I have some books. You'd like to read, perhaps?"—and leads him through the back: "I followed her slowly, drinking in her grace, the lovely way she moved her body. In the living room, piled along the wall, were books of many sizes and colors. Books! I was enchanted when I saw them. They drew me irresistibly to them" (173). She reads to him, a pleasure that becomes a regular habit until Carlos loses his dishwashing job and leaves town—after assaulting a headwaiter who had refused service to a Filipino man and a white woman.

As the figurations of white women critique the violent, sexualized racism inherent to U.S. imperialism, they also reiterate and recast the process of tutelary uplift. White love is represented as an exchange, not between white fathers and native sons, but between white women and the Filipino male migrant—an erotic initiation transacted entirely through books. This is not to suggest that, in these scenes, books are a euphemism for the hidden "truth" of heterosexual intercourse, like the old-fashioned cinematic convention of a slow pan from a bed, cutting to the lighting of a cigarette. Literally, I am claiming that the sharing of books and their knowledge is itself represented as a sexual act. The migrant's tutelage, as the narrative progresses, will not engender a colonial-nationalist desire to return to the Philippines to fulfill the civilizing mission. Instead, it generates an internationalist proletarian literary consciousness, developed via patrons like Harriet Monroe, the editor of *Poetry* magazine, and Alice and Eileen Odell, pseudonyms for the leftist writer Sanora Babb and her sister Dorothy. This perversely normalizing drive figures the revolutionary sexual education of the Filipino migrant as exceptional, differentiating the protagonist from his brethren so he can serve as their representative literary voice. This process turns on the production of a nonnormative excess, which gets deposited in other colonial and metropolitan forms of racial difference.

This tutelage begins, not in the metropole, but in the Philippines, while Allos is in the resort town of Baguio, trying to earn enough money for passage to the United States. Homeless and jobless due to his lack of English-speaking skills, he gets the first lesson in his colonial sexual education from "an American lady tourist," who pays him to undress and be photographed. For a time, he earns a living this way, making himself "conspicuously ugly" whenever he sees "a white person with a camera," though he realizes the tourists prefer taking pictures of "Igorots" rather than "Christian Filipinos like me" (67). The best known of the so-called primitive tribes, Igorots were the subject of intense official and popular interest under the U.S. regime, including a notorious exhibit at the 1904 St. Louis exposition.

Throughout Bulosan's corpus, characters explicitly or implicitly iden-tified with the author frequently masquerade as Igorots,[29] in scenes recalling blackface or "playing Indian" in metropolitan U.S. culture. Cannily articulating parallel but discrepant imperial racial formations, these identifications position the writer as the benevolent representative of nonwhite populations placed beneath him in a social hierarchy. As Vicente Rafael observes, colonial accounts often characterized these "wild men" as "ideal colonial subjects": "free from the so-called corrupt-ing influence of Catholic Spain and lowland mestizo elites, wild men were seen to be far more receptive to the firm, straight-talking tough love of white men" (33). In Baguio, Allos recognizes the prurient desires manifested in this love, noting the tourists' preference for "Igorot girls with large breasts and robust mountain men whose genitals were nearly exposed, their G-strings bulging large and alive" (67).

At this stage of his education, Allos's knowledge of imperialism's racial and sexual orders is insufficient for him to become the subject of civilizing love. Then he meets the first in a series of white women pa-trons, Miss Mary Strandon, a librarian and aspiring painter from Iowa whose father was killed in the Philippine-American War, who hires him to carry some rice and Igorot pottery she has purchased. After paying him, she asks him about the charcoal marks on his face, which he has drawn to mimic the "natives with painted faces" preferred by tourists (68); shamed, he claims they are just dirt and complies with her demand to wash them off. She then offers him a permanent job as her houseboy. More adept than the tourists at employing the classifying white gaze, Miss Strandon thus fixes Allos in his proper racial position, even as she orders him to differentiate himself from the less civilized "natives" by cleaning his body.

While in her employ, Allos strikes up a friendship with an Igorot houseboy and pupil of the white schoolteacher next door, Dalmacio, who also aspires to go to the United States, and offers him English les-sons in exchange for occasional chores. They begin by reading a book about Abraham Lincoln, who, Dalmacio explains, "was a poor boy who became a president of the United States. . . . He was born in a log cabin and walked miles and miles to borrow a book so that he would know more about his country" (69). Captivated by this story of the overcom-ing of poverty marked by an indomitable desire to read, Allos asks Miss

Strandon about Lincoln that evening. She repeats the line about his rise from poverty, but Allos wants to hear the rest of the story:

> "Well, when he became president, he said that all men are created
>   equal," Miss Strandon said. "But some men, vicious men, who had
>   Negro slaves, did not like what he said. So a terrible war was fought
>   between the states of the United States, and the slaves were freed
>   and the nation was preserved. But one night he was murdered by an
>   assassin. . . ."
> "Why?" I asked.
> "*Why?*" she said. "He was a great man."
> "What is a Negro?" I asked.
> "A Negro is a black person," she said.
> "Abraham Lincoln died for a black person?" I asked.
> "Yes," she said. "He was a great man." (70, ellipsis in original)

While Dalmacio's lesson allows Allos to read the Lincoln myth in terms of poverty, social mobility, and education, its racial content can be revealed only by Miss Strandon. As Allos realizes that the racializing processes situating him in relation to the Igorots can be placed within a broader imperial horizon, he comes to desire the knowledge of racial and sexual orders Miss Strandon possesses—for if metropolitan history is animated by the dynamics of racial formation, their articulation to his own racialized, sexualized subordination might allow the dialectical possibility of its overcoming.

Allos's eagerness is recognized by Miss Strandon as a "passion for books," a civilized and civilizing desire, which she cultivates by arranging for him to assist her at the library, tutoring him in the pursuit of pleasures dematerialized from the body. His development into a more mature sexuality—a civilized sexuality, detached from the body, seeking an intercourse of minds—will continue in his dogged struggles for education over the next fifteen years. The chapter concludes by flashing forward to the narrator's life in the metropole, where the proof of his maturation is established by the publication of his first book. In this trajectory, he not only leaves behind his Igorot friend Dalmacio, but also symbolically befriends and then exceeds "the American Negro writer, Richard Wright." Alluding sympathetically to the latter's account of being excluded from "his local library because of his color" in *Black Boy*, the narrator savors his relatively privileged encounter with the uplifting ministrations of civilizing love (71). Returning to Miss Strandon's hometown to find she's been dead for over a decade, he inscribes her name in a copy of his book and donates it in her memory to the local library—a romantic and poignant tribute to the memory of a youthful affair.

Elsewhere in his writings, Bulosan offers divergent variations on this episode. The protagonist of "The Story of a Letter," published in the same year as *America Is in the Heart*, recounts many similar experiences, including undressing for tourists in Baguio, but in place of Miss Strandon, an unnamed painter who "claim[s]" to be from Texas takes him to Manila to work as a nude model, an "experience that made [him] roar with laughter for many years" (62–63). "As Long as the Grass Shall Grow," published three years later, sets a similar story on the U.S. West Coast, where the efforts of a young schoolteacher to tutor Filipino pea pickers at night are cut short by violent reprisals from local whites. These stories push Bulosan's tales of tutelary relations between white women and Filipino men closer to an explicit representation of sexual transgression and the racist violence it provokes. But a more striking revelation of their logic may be found by reading the closing scenes of *America Is in the Heart*, which feature a noble "Negro bootblack" named Larkin, against a related, unpublished story, "Sammy Cooke's Shoeshine Box."

the unforgiven debts of brotherhood

In three dizzying final chapters, *America Is in the Heart* depicts the chaotic combination of despair and hope loosed by the outbreak of the Pacific war. The convergence of colonial elite and migrant proletarian resistance to Japanese imperialism leads to a unified prowar front, while metropolitan opposition to Filipino civil rights wanes due to the ideological and military utility of Filipino volunteers. Carlos's literary career takes off after the fall of Bataan—a collection of his poems is solicited and published, after which he begins work on an anthology of contemporary Philippine verse (320)—but the triumph feels hollow. He brings a copy of the book to his brother Amado, who is drinking with two women, one of whom mocks and tears it, disappointed he hadn't brought liquor instead; Amado beats her, calling her a whore, and she cries to Carlos that her own ambitions had been destroyed by "this lousy street" (321). Days later, Amado leaves to join the navy, and soon Macario departs for the army, as do most of their friends.

In farewell, Macario offers a handshake, that ritual of fraternal affection, but the touch of his labor-scarred body reminds Carlos of his own weakness: "I could feel the roughness of his toil-worn hand; the toughness of his palm revealed more of himself than his words. I was ashamed of my little soft hand in his" (323–24). He muses, "It was the end of our lives in America. . . . The end of our family. . . . Our world was this one, but a new one was being born. . . . In this other world— new, bright, promising—we would be unable to meet its demands" (324). Macario leaves his brother two hundred dollars, plus a dime he solemnly asks to be delivered to a "Negro bootblack" to settle a debt. Carlos finds the man, Larkin, who takes the money, buys a glass of beer, drinks half of it, and offers him the rest. They complete the ritual with another handshake—"His hand, too, was like my brother's—tough, large, toil-scarred"—and Larkin explains that he's enlisting too: "I know I'll meet your brother again somewhere, because I got my dime without asking him. But if I don't see him again, I'll remember him every time I see the face of an American dime. Good-bye, friend!" (324–25).

When the narrator watches Larkin disappear down the block and returns to his lonely transient's room, you might expect that the book has come to the end. Yet there is one more chapter, barely a page long. Having deposited Macario's two hundred dollars in a bank, Carlos rides a bus to the Portland canneries, reflecting on his memories as he watches Filipino laborers in the fields. In a stirringly lyrical passage, which doesn't overcome despair so much as resignify it as defiance, as a feeling in excess of any political program or appeal for rights, the book concludes, "I knew that no man could destroy my faith in America that had sprung from all our hopes and aspirations, *ever*" (327). Merely the last in an unremitting series of vertiginous reversals between inconsolable despair and impossible hope that constitute the text, with only the flimsiest of motivations in the narrative action, this declaration makes sense only if you can see despair and hope as two sides of the same coin, two aspects of the same affective insight, both lyrically inflated to wildly impractical heights in accordance with the extravagant aesthetic of Filipino labor migrancy.

By appropriating the name of the empire for his third-conditional world, Bulosan caused some consternation for future readers. Certainly, the convergence of interests to which this polyvocal rhetorical strategy belonged—aligning class- and race-based revolutionary international-isms, Philippine nationalisms from the elite to the peasantry, radical and liberal metropolitan movements against racism, all in a united front against Japanese imperialism—would not survive to sponsor postwar designs on the appellation "America." Indeed, the tone of Bulosan's con-clusion suggests that he is consciously writing an epitaph. Rather than attempting to disentangle this rhetorical strategy, however, I want to pause over the figure of the bootblack, who mediates what you might call the flipping of the coin.

Appearing before the chapter break and subsequent shift from sorrow to defiant hope, Larkin's handshake emends Carlos's declaration of the end of his family. Even after Amado and Macario are gone, he can still find another outstretched hand of brotherhood—one that releases him from the shame he finally confesses with his hand in Macario's. While his book celebrates the strenuous physical labor of Filipino migrants through the figure of its protagonist, Bulosan's health in the United States was so frail that he was unable to work the jobs his narrator recounts, which is why he has the *little soft hand* of a man of letters. His shame is released because Larkin chooses to accept the dime not as payment of a debt, but as a gift, marking his own entry into the fraternal diaspora of soldiers, and promising the family's reunion within the nation's embrace, via the circulation of its common currency. This is made possible not by Larkin's own struggle against racism, his defiant decision to enlist in a military that denied him equal rights—much less by the gradualist liberal promises of benevolent white supremacy—but by the exchange of fraternal embraces from Macario to Larkin and back, via Carlos. You may not recognize this revolutionary "America," for the face on the coin is Filipino.

But you should know who this character is. Larkin is a manifestation of one of the oldest and most pernicious stereotypes in the long history of U.S. paternalism, or white love, who in the popular culture of liberal multiculturalism is often called a *magic Negro*. A hollow construct of moral purity, abstracted from historical or social context and cut loose from any generic expectations of psychological plausibility—his interiority, if there is any, is hopelessly lost behind the Veil—his job is to bestow the benediction of blackness upon the protagonist, in brief and idealized embrace. This becomes clearer if you read, as a gloss upon this character, an unpublished story by Bulosan that offers an apparent variation on the encounter, in which both the figuration's offensiveness and critical potential become more explicit.

"Sammy Cooke's Shoeshine Box" may be found in two manuscript versions, typed with handwritten revisions, in the collection of Bulosan's papers at the University of Washington.[30] Though the texts are undated, the story presents itself as a recollection of an episode that took place ten years earlier, during the war. The unnamed narrator, an aspiring young writer lifted from poverty by the sale of his first novel, is looking forward to celebrating his success on his first trip to New York City: he has a few hundred dollars in cash and a date with the blue-eyed, long-legged Merla Jackson, whose sister he'd met in a California bookstore. As he waits in reverie outside a cocktail bar for her to show, a "dark shadow" with a "rough-hewn" box asks repeatedly, "Shine, mister?" Realizing he'd ignored the young boy unnerves him, even after Merla takes him inside. As he drinks, he notices the boy's face pressed against the bar's glass wall, and suddenly sees his younger self, staring in at the affluent, beautiful world he desires. This vision ruins the ritual of seduction; in his eyes, Merla turns old and damaged, a ruined woman grasping after money, and he rebuffs her offer to fly back to California. Seeing the boy again, he waves him in, but before completing the shoeshine the boy is chased out by a waiter, smashing violently into a table—after which the narrator can recall only "the infernal siren of an ambulance." In the light of morning, he imagines finding the boy and giving him two hundred dollars, to cover medical expenses and perhaps rescue him from "the streets," but instead flies back to Los Angeles and runs through the money in a matter of days.

As the narrator's *dark shadow*, Sammy Cooke explicitly figures everything his benevolent assimilation into literary success must repress, whose return exposes that success as illusory. Ten years later, his professional triumphs have gone "sour," Merla and her sister are still chasing men, but he "remember[s] Sammy Cooke vividly"—and, a handwritten interpellation in what I take to be the later version adds, "in shame." Sammy Cooke embodies not just the specter of poverty, but a racialized threat to white womanhood, which must be met by preemptive violence. You may read the narrator as autobiographical (Bulosan also enjoyed fleeting success, but fell out of favor after the war, and was persecuted in the anti-Communist backlash) or as a white alter ego (a possibility that must be considered in light of *All the Conspirators*, a recently published manuscript recovered from the same archives), but either way, the underlying dynamic holds: violence interrupts the consummation of a love for letters, pursuing its racialized remainder embodied in the boy at the glass.

That figure is irredeemable, I contend, for any reading of a sainted Bulosan as an icon of antiracist coalitional politics. For "Sammy Cooke" is simply erased, not only by the narrator's solipsistic, mirrored identification, but by the way the text buries him under the burden of its critique of sexualized racism. In what I take to be the earlier manuscript, the narrator casually admits he invented the name "because I like the name Sammy and I have a friend named Joe Cooke," another good-hearted Negro, around the age of the boy in the story. The other version omits this line and has the boy identify himself in dialogue, but retains a conclusion in which the narrator finishes telling the story to Joe, who listens impassively, then walks away in silence. By separating the author and the narrator, you might attempt to redeem the former by reading Joe's departure as ironically critiquing the latter, but doing so requires ignoring the force of the text's exposition of anti-Filipino sexualized racism.

The shoeshine boy is, by all appearances, simply the Filipino migrant writer in blackface. He is irredeemable, then, except and to the extent it is possible that what is excluded from representation in this story also eludes capture by this story's conditions of representation. This may be the opening provided by reading Sammy Cooke as a gloss on Larkin in *America Is in the Heart*. For if the Negro bootblack and the shoeshine boy are truly interchangeable, merely the prop or wedge that holds a diasporic fraternity together, then you may see that there really are no Negroes here at all, only the agency of a blackness alien to, yet constitutive of, the Filipino migrant writer himself. The manly soldier is reduced to an abject boy; the dime that had been transformed into the gift of brotherhood disappears before the boy can see it, and the two hundred dollars is gone before anyone makes it to the bank. The narrator's reckless expenditure is fueled by a nameless shame, the negation of an extravagant fantasy of repayment, at once too much to give and never enough to purchase what it is meant to buy: the termination of guilt through benevolent uplift, a poor black boy saved from the streets.

I hold no brief for the redemption of the author of these texts, but I am not ashamed to say that it is the reckless extravagance in Bulosan that I love, which I read as characteristic of an aesthetic that conditions and exceeds the politics of his writing. It is this spirit that looks upward at the end of Bulosan's personal history, watching as its hopes ride on the other face of despair, suspended in anticipation, like a coin spinning in the air.

And then watches it fall, as it does in the story, face down. As it did for the writer, who died, the stories go, more or less broke, more or less forgotten, hounded, ignored, or, if you can forgive a little rhetorical excess, not one thin dime to his name.

But you saw that coming, didn't you?

Four: Colonial Nationalism Takes Dancing Lessons

What holds a diaspora together? What blasts it apart? In his ambition to challenge the sexualized violence of white racism, while projecting a literary persona as the most advanced Filipino intellectual of his time, Bulosan did not reject the primitivization of Filipino sexuality, even as he traced its corruption to the social conditions of capitalism. Rather, he positioned himself as the exemplary subject of an uplifting sexual education, by which the unfulfilled ideals of U.S. civilization, embodied by benevolent white women teachers, would be actualized in global proletarian revolution, with fronts on both sides of the Pacific. But the remainder of shame he could not dispel, displaced onto Igorot and Negro figures, would recirculate across empire, reconstituting the national destinies of both colony and metropole in turn.

On February 2, 1930, Filipinos in Manila, Los Angeles, and across the empire marked a "National Day of Humiliation," protesting the murder of Fermin Tobera, shot in his sleep in Watsonville, California, by white rioters incensed by the opening of a private Filipino taxi-dance hall.[31] If sexualized terror, as Ngai argues, drove anti-Filipino movements, those movements were the determining factor in the debates that declared an official end point for U.S. colonialism. As Paul Kramer explains, after failing to pass exclusion laws without giving up colonial rule,[32] anti-Filipino politicians found common cause with Filipino nationalist aspirations, leading to the 1934 Tydings-McDuffie Act, which set a ten-year time line for independence, while preserving certain economic and military privileges for the United States. At the same time, it set an annual quota for Filipino immigrants at fifty (half the minimum for any nation under existing law), and reclassified noncitizen nationals currently in the United States as aliens. Formal U.S. colonialism in the Philippines would end, not with the success of tutelary uplift, but with the anxious disavowal of an invasive sexual threat.

Following this change, anti-Asiatic politicians developed an ambitious program to encourage the permanent "repatriation" of Filipino aliens, but after several hundred thousand dollars of expenditures, only 2,190 had taken advantage of the free passage (Baldoz 193). Ngai's research suggests that most were not the poor laborers the program targeted, but more affluent families already planning their return. Filipinos' justifiable suspicions of this generous offer of expulsion were hardly allayed when the Immigration and Naturalization Service began collaborating with the California prison system to ship back "convicts, the insane, and persons with leprosy, tuberculosis, and other illnesses" (Ngai 124). Meanwhile, the interest in repatriation shown by some white wives of Filipino men caused great embarrassment for state agencies on both sides of the Pacific.

ten cents a dance

Some indication of colonial reactions to the program appears in Juan Cabreros Laya's 1940 novel *His Native Soil*, begun in a graduate program at Indiana University and published in Manila after taking a first prize in the aforementioned Commonwealth Literary Awards. The hero, Martin Romero, is the scion of a landowning Ilocano family. Though he is returning with a business degree from the University of Washington, his status as a repatriate subjects him to continual humiliation. As he approaches home, a fellow carriage passenger, Dencio, sneers, "Did you get deported, *chico*, or—or simply taking advantage of the free transportation?" (7), and relates a series of insulting tales about the "queer lot, these repatriates." One, a tough-acting criminal from LA, showed interest in a local girl and ended up "unconscious in the canal . . . his head all swollen and soft . . . his eyes gentle as a lamb's." Another is "a harmless, sexless fellow," who "slaved for an A.B. somewhere in a Bible school and now sells New Testaments to penniless villagers." If the sexuality of these repatriates is simultaneously excessive and insufficient, the target of these insults is heteromasculinity. One "little runt of a Pinoy" brought his "ferocious American wife . . . to a nipa hut to eat salted fish," but she ran off to Manila within days. Another brought back "an M.A.," but couldn't find work, and instead "married a rich spinster" and became "a gentleman of leisure" (8). That Martin is no dissolute primitive, but a painfully upright model of manly rectitude, only seems to encourage such jibes and gossip, as his headstrong efforts to uplift his community, through modern business strategies and hygienic practices, prove no match for local corruption.

Not surprisingly, perhaps, the underlying logic of the narrative is provided by a romantic triangle, which is unabashedly didactic. Martin is both repulsed by and drawn to a glamorous, ultramodern, half-white femme fatale, Virginia Fe, but he realizes the limitations of his modernizing ambitions, and the need to root them more deeply in the national soil, only as he recognizes true love in the shy Soledad, an idealized figure of traditional feminine virtue. In retrospect, this plot can be identified as a formulaic structure of anticolonial nationalist narrative. The novel concludes with renewed hope, as the idealized heterosexual coupling of the modern, educated, domineering man and the traditional, submissive, but determined woman prefigures the birth of a nation capable of self-governance.

The degraded sexuality of Filipino migrants, Laya's novel argues, can be traced back to the colony—not to a primitive racial essence, but to the perversions of imperial conquest and colonial rule. White love, both Spanish and American, has interrupted the natural reproductive lineage of Filipino civilization; its decadent progeny is embodied by Virginia Fe. But the paradoxes inherent in the anticolonial appropriation of this civilizing discourse become striking in one scene, in which the distance between the intellectual and his people, and between the people and the national ideal, floods over with uncontrollable shame.

Shortly after his return, the slippery Attorney Murcia, Dencio's uncle, invites Martin to speak at a reception for local graduates—presumably an honor, even though the event seems primarily to be an occasion for dancing and gossip. When Martin begins his speech in the local dialect, he is mortified to discover that his linguistic skills have abandoned him, and finally resorts to completing the speech in English, to open derision from the audience. Anticipating Fanon's classic analysis of the language crises of the returning colonial student in *Black Skin, White Masks* (23–25), the scene seems straightforward in its representation of the anticolonial imperative to return to the *native soil* of national culture.

But it is preceded by another humiliation, on the dance floor. Goading him to join her, Virginia Fe alludes to the migrants' reputation as "great dancers" and "lovers": "Are they, really? The boys who have come back have such interesting stories to tell about dance-hall girls in California. They aren't lily white. I like them" (103). Playing on intertwined associations of whiteness with cleanliness, sexual morality, and racial purity, Virginia Fe manages adroitly to insult Martin both for embodying and not embodying a racialized sexuality. Trying again, she asks about "college dances," imagining "those wild parties we see so often in the movies," but he scoffs, "A Pinoy with any sense does not crash into white parties" (105). In the end, he submits to a single waltz, warning her in advance that he doesn't know how to dance. But even he is surprised by his stiffness and clumsiness, and when the song is finally, mercifully over, he is surrounded by sarcastic applause, which fills him with "a desire to slap somebody—he did not care whom" (106). His inadequacy laid bare before a mocking public, Martin struggles to contain a shame that—to borrow Du Bois's description of double consciousness—would rend his *dark body, whose dogged strength alone keeps it from being torn asunder* (*Writings* 365). An overwhelming, compensatory violence rushes in through the breach, only to prolong his agony, for it can find no outlet other than the bitter, unappreciated burden of uplifting a people.

The peculiar operations of this scene bear comparison with a contemporaneous work of fiction that also contemplates the figure of repatriation. "The Man Who Played for David," by Conrado V. Pedroche, an early member of the U.P. Writers' Club who went on to a successful literary career, appeared in the *Commonwealth Advocate* in 1938.[33] Brief and sweetly melancholy, it relates the story of David, aimless and without prospects, who returns home after fifteen years in the metropole. But what's most noteworthy, for these purposes, is the title character, Joe, an equally disaffected wanderer who becomes David's drinking buddy and only friend, and who is affectionately addressed by David, the third-person narrator, and himself with the slur "nigger."

As the following chapter will show, the valences of this slur in the context of Philippine conquest and imperial racialization are complex, but there is nothing complicated about Joe. If Bulosan's bootblack is a wholesale appropriation of a favored stereotype of white paternalism, Pedroche's Joe is pure minstrel show: easygoing and charmingly irresponsible, physically imposing with long, apelike arms, apt to break into a lazy song or a wild tap dance without prompting. Inevitably, Joe is killed—run over by, of all things, a train—and David lingers over the "mutilated body," laying his fingers over the bloody breast and contemplating the mortality of "most lovely things" in a cruel world (403). Later, waiting in the next room as his father is dying, he recalls Joe's bulging white eyes, muscular, dancing legs, and a singing voice so overwhelming in memory that he covers his ears. Thinking of America and of Joe's corpse, he ignores his father, whose death is accompanied by "irreverent jungle music" blasted on a "broken-throated phonograph": "Oompha, oompah, blared the snickering demon. Oompha, oompah, sang the voice of Joe, the nigger" (403).

Like Laya's Martin, Pedroche's David returns to the colony burdened with a sexual degradation imposed by life in the metropole. Indeed, David also finds himself, initially, unable to dance—before meeting Joe, he is a wallflower at the cabaret, lost in the memory of a French taxi dancer in New Mexico. But where the doomed David embraces his degradation, via its projection onto Joe—"Ah guess Ah am but a no 'count nigger that knows nothin' else. It's all Ah am good at," Joe tells him after an impromptu performance, and David replies, "I can't even sing" (402)—Martin denies it, enduring humiliation and adversity with a dogged faith in modern progress. Yet the scene of the dance reinscribes that degradation as a characteristic inherent to the local community. What's more, by serving as the introduction to his disastrous speech, it aligns Martin's inability to dance with his inability to express himself in his native dialect, a troubling side effect of his colonial education, evidence less of moral rectitude than of his alienation from his own people.

For Laya and other emerging Filipino intellectuals, like the post-Reconstruction African American elite, the processes of "normalization and nationalization" (Ferguson 98) offered a path of autonomous uplift, which promised to reassemble the dispersed members of the racial populace and restore its collective body to vigorous health. But in the long advent of Philippine independence and African American citizenship rights, this promise must be continually deferred, and its progression regularly demands more division, separation, dispersal. At the end of Laya's novel, Martin and Soledad must leave their hometown to seek horizons more amenable to patriotic renewal, as his younger brother Rodrigo, an aspiring writer who may be a stand-in for the author, serenades them with an impromptu violin performance. His selection is "Aloha 'Oe," the deposed Hawaiian Queen Lili'uokalani's most famous composition, a melancholy song of a lover's farewell that evokes the loss of her country to white imperial rule.

In Laya's phonographic performance, a Filipino nationalist cover of an iconic song of Hawai'i, can you hear the broken-throated crackle of a diabolical laughter? Behind this allusion, you might identify a figure that bedevils colonial nationalisms, which José Rizal called the demon of comparisons[34]—appearing here as the trickster-like agency of a substitution, riding like an unaccounted passenger along the transpacific routes of U.S. imperialism. In the strains of the song you might hear a beauty that stretches the novel to its bursting, turning its normalizing nationalist vision inside out, pointing to an alternative it cannot represent. This alternative, if there is one, is less the promise of a transpacific political coalition of anticolonial nationalisms than an opening into complex circulations of globalizing popular entertainment, complicating the novel's references to the racially and sexually ambiguous music and dance culture spreading like an epidemic in West Coast dance halls and provincial Philippine towns—not to mention Delta juke joints and Harlem record companies.

If this reading is possible, it would rely not on the text's express politics, but on its prior commitment to an aesthetic preference for the failure of whatever politics it expresses, as the occasion for a song of love's loss. In any case, what you are left with is only failure, a dream of uplift in ruins, its centripetal fantasies of normalization and nationalization collapsed onto itself, leaving Martin and his Soledad fleeing to seek their chances elsewhere, leaving Bulosan's protagonists gazing out in loneliness at the receding centrifugal shadows of their unredeemed shame. It is here, staring in the face of defeat, in the occasion of loss, that the next chapter begins. Listen.

3.

Love Notes from a Third-Conditional World

One: Fortune's Correspondence

In the previous chapter, I argued that ideologies of tutelary uplift worked to constitute the Negro and the Filipino as modern subjects, securing their positions within the occidented progress of civilization by training racialized sexuality into normative gendering. Yet where that training broke down, a sexual shame was released whose centrifugal flight might displace circuits of black and Filipino migration from containment within imperial rule. In this chapter I pursue these moments of failure through a series of readings in black and Filipino transpacific culture, proceeding from ambivalence, exhaustion, and frustration to outlandish, shameless defiance of gendered respectability, listening for their fleeting recordings of other worlds lost to history.

I begin by focusing on the construction of Negro manhood in the initial phase of participation in Pacific imperialism, juxtaposing T. Thomas Fortune's account of his 1902 tour of the Philippines with an anonymous public letter addressed to Fortune by a soldier three years earlier. In doing so, I consider how the *décalage* between Negro and Filipino racialization was put to use in projecting a model, modern black subject, and how its professions of love and performances of gendered normativity sought to bind the diaspora together, even as they recirculated the debts threatening to drive it apart.

three shrugs and a collapse

Widely regarded as the leading African American journalist of his time, the *New York Age* editor T. Thomas Fortune was probably the best-known black public figure to visit the new colony. Born in slavery in 1856, he'd been touted as a potential successor to Frederick Douglass before forming a curious alliance with Booker T. Washington, playing militant agitator to the latter's accommodationism. According to his biographer, Emma Lou Thornbrough, Washington's rise brought this alliance under strain, culminating in Fortune's breakdown in 1907. Though he never recovered his former stature, he achieved late recognition as editor of Marcus Garvey's *Negro World*, from 1923 until his death in 1928. Notorious for drinking too much and making incendiary comments at public meetings, Fortune was considered intemperate—a damning flaw under uplift ideology, which upheld self-restraint as a defining characteristic of civilized manhood. In writing about his Philippine tour, however, Fortune depicts himself and his military hosts as exemplars of a Negro manhood contrasted to white corruption and Filipino primitivism.

Fortune's appointment to investigate conditions in Hawai'i and the Philippines as a special agent of President Theodore Roosevelt's Treasury Department was hardly an endorsement of the emigration schemes—Willard Gatewood interprets it as simultaneously a stalling tactic and as patronage for his support in the 1900 election (*Black Americans* 307). Even so, it was a disappointment for Fortune, whose hopes for a diplomatic post—preferably ambassador to Haiti—had been derailed by rivals (Thornbrough 222–23). News of his appointment in November 1902 drew quick criticism in the white and black presses, as did his public statements the following June, when he returned to find the prospects for emigration already dimmed.[1] He was attacked by the Manila press upon arrival, and critics on both sides of the ocean happily noted a run-in between the police, Fortune, and his guide, Captain Robert Gordon Woods (Gatewood, *Black Americans* 313). Thornbrough wearily notes that the trip, "like everything else in which he was involved, turned out to be a fiasco financially," and his threat to withhold his report until the Treasury Department fully compensated his expenses seems not to have inspired interest in either matter. Also, he had a recurrence of malaria (Thornbrough 240).

The entire enterprise was clearly disastrous for Fortune, who made no mention of migration in a September 1903 *Independent* article on Philippine politics, characterizing the colony as the South to Hawai'i's North. Finally, in 1904, he published "The Filipino," a three-part series narrating his travels, in *Voice of the Negro*, but even there the prospect of mass emigration appears, as if an afterthought, only in the final installment's last paragraph. Along lines closer to Brigadier General George

W. Davis's plans for sugar plantations than Senator John Tyler Morgan's dream of racial cleansing in the South, Fortune estimates that the unexploited agricultural potential of Luzon could accommodate up to "5,000,000 Negroes." The irony of contemplating an importation of racialized labor on a scale somewhere between the coolie trade and the Middle Passage does not trouble him, as he explicitly references the former traffic in his closing sentences before telegraphing his resigned exasperation: "The Chinese cannot be drawn upon, because American sentiment is against it and the Filipino people will have none of it. Give the American Negro a chance in the Philippine Islands, if he wants to go there" (III: 246).

Fortune's larger concern in the articles is to position himself, along with the soldiers, veterans, and businessmen he meets, as a representative specimen of black manhood, contrasted to the charmingly primitive Filipinos and decadent, dishonorable whites. He opens the series by evoking a rejuvenating tropical excursion, which both reveals and reinforces his civilized status. On the peculiar local custom of the siesta, he explains, "I, who am a bundle of nerves, restless in repose in this country, soon learned to do as the native in this respect and found that it was good, conducting [*sic*] alike to vigor of mind and body" (I: 95): primitive ways can have a tonic effect on the fashionable nervous disorders of modern life. Sympathetically reproducing tropes of the lazy native and Orientalist idyll, Fortune demonstrates both pragmatic open-mindedness and cultured refinement while presenting himself as the Filipino's champion. In one anecdote, he silences a group of white Americans bemoaning Filipino sloth by tartly commenting, "I have been in the Philippines two months and I have not seen a white man working with his hands; they were all working with their mouths. Why do you expect the Filipino to do what you will not and cannot do?" (I: 94).

If such behavior earns gratitude and respect from the Filipinos, it helps explain why, Fortune argues, "it is written on the wall that ultimately, if the American flag remains in the Philippines, the Afro-Americans will have to be drafted to hold it up" in colonial administration, military service, and labor. For now, he counts "some four hundred Afro-Americans" in the colony, reputably engaged in "civil service, . . . private service, and . . . independent business"—not a one "begging bread in the streets," he testifies (I: 97). Their exemplar, conscientiously introduced in each article, is Captain Woods, his "companion, interpreter and guide," formerly "military governor of the Province of Isabela" (III: 241), "a man of splendid physique and a military bearing acquired by eighteen years of service" (II: 200) who returned to Manila after being discharged in California "with the determination to 'grow up with the country'" (I: 96).[2] By contrast, white American men cannot be entrusted with the civilizing mission. Beset by unmanly greed for "power and the money that goes with it," unable to abide "either the climate or the people and their ways" (I: 97), they are as doomed as the decadent empire they replaced: "It is impossible for a white man, whether he be Spaniard or American, to treat an alien people on terms of equality" (I: 98). For imperialism can be justified only as a lesson in love: "The Filipino hates the white man as the devil hates holy water, and will never learn to love him, because the white man will never learn to love the Filipino" (I: 98).

The most damning proof of white incapacity for civilizing love is found in unmanly, dishonorable sexual practices. Spelling out the implications of Frank Steward's "The Men Who Prey," Fortune defines colonial concubinage as an exceptional characteristic of American whiteness: "The white American is the only white creature on earth who seems to have no abiding affection and makes no sort of provisions for his children resulting from common law relations with Negroes, Indians or Malays." By contrast, he finds "a thorough understanding between the black and brown man, in so far that they married and gave in marriage"—characterizing relationships between African American men and Filipina women as a reciprocal exchange within patriarchy (II: 200). Hence, as the subtitle of the second installment of Fortune's series succinctly puts it, "the Filipinos do not understand the prejudice of white Americans against black Americans."

This natural amity is evidence of Filipino suitability for uplift. Quoting the notorious comments by a Japanese representative at the recent Louisiana Purchase Exposition in St. Louis—"High class Japanese and Chinese desire to associate exclusively with white people. We wish the colored people would let us alone"—Fortune reminds his readers that similar attitudes were demonstrated by "Haytian and Dominican" elites, as well as by the wretchedly primitive "Red Indian" and "Hawaiian Kanakas." Behind this conflict of "dark people towards other dark people" is "the American white man," whose behavior they mimic in a deluded effort "to get out of the tabooed class" (II: 199). But even as this attitude extends to many African Americans, he asserts, he could not find it in Japan and China, nor among Filipinos (II: 200). Thus, Fortune affably defuses an affront to interracial solidarity via a distinction homologous to the white colonial preference for the unspoiled primitive—the purity of Filipinos' love for African Americans is unsullied by the failures of colonizers past. Meanwhile, he assures his readers that "the Japanese and the Chinaman are inferior to the Afro-American in the higher and nobler qualities"; even "the ignorant and poor Afro-American [is] superior to the Chinese and Japanese and Kanakas in intellect, morality and industrial force," if behind "in persistence, frugality and ethnic adhesiveness" (II: 199–200).

The contrast between Filipino primitivism and Negro manhood is rendered most starkly in several groupings of photographs. On one page, a dignified Fortune shows off the quasi-military garb of a Westerner on safari, juxtaposed to another image, captioned "The Filipino and His Rooster," showing a darker-skinned man in a loose shirt and shorts and what appears to be a cloth wrapped on his head (I: 97). The chicken in his arms references Fortune's commentary on the natives' passion for cockfighting and other forms of "small gambling, which is an Oriental disease" (I: 95). Elsewhere, another posed photograph shows Fortune, in the same outfit, sitting with an obedient dog at his boot, flanked by the stylish Captain Woods and another black veteran, Captain W. C. Wormsley (III: 245), identified in the text as a physician, proprietor of a drugstore, and owner of "several large tobacco plantations" (III: 245). The following page displays "A Fine Group of Young Filipinos"—a larger group of young men and boys, many partially or entirely naked (III: 242).

As the final article opens, Fortune's tone shifts to a comic crankiness, as if to mimic a weary traveler's eagerness to come home. Returning to the theme of climate and acclimatization with which he'd begun, he admits the "necessity" of the midday nap, but grumbles, "As for thinking, for mental effort, it is out of the question" (III: 240). This sets off a litany of complaints about life in Manila, where "it is possible that there are 3,000,000 chickens," all crowing at once. Along with chiming churches and brass bands, they keep up such a racket, from midnight until siesta, that, he opines, "it would indicate more strongly than anything else, that the Filipino has no nerves" (III: 240). This is no small insult—"People without nerves do not think much, rapidly or profoundly, and the basic elements of their character are superficiality"—nor is he reluctant to fling it about: "Eighty per cent of American negroid people are afflicted in the same way" (III: 240)!

Of course, this is only a joke, signaled by its mock-scientific language, and even so the statistic is arguably twice as generous as Du Bois's equally figurative calculation of a Talented Tenth. Nonetheless, on strictly mathematical grounds, you might note that the five million migrants Fortune contemplates transporting would necessarily include a majority of the afflicted population he casually derides. This leads to a more serious point, for Fortune's joke makes the subtext of his representation of Filipino primitivism explicit. Throughout, the series emphasizes stereotypes familiarly associated with the Southern black peasantry—impervious laziness, aversion to intellectual effort, and quickness to laughter; a predilection for chickens, gambling, knife-fighting, and music; a fanatical zeal for a religion that engenders little in the way of upright moral behavior. While the series' primary thrust projects elite Negro manhood as the civilizing mission's true heir, the doomed migration scheme Fortune was sent to investigate, and still gamely advocates, targets a distinct population of black laborers.

In positioning himself, his companions, and his presumed audience as the exceptional agents of uplift, Fortune does not go so far as to assert the primitive racial *identity* of those he'd termed "the ignorant and poor Afro-Americans" with the Filipino—a demonstrably false claim to which many readers would surely take offense. Rather, he articulates both groups through the rhetorical indeterminacy of a joke, whose meaning cannot be pinned down because it flickers across an irresolvable difference: *he means what he says / he isn't serious; if you are insulted, maybe you should be / if you can laugh, you aren't one of them.* Fortune is a canny writer, and it seems clear that the joke's function in the text is to evade an irresolvable problem, the irruption of the contradictions inherent in uplift, which might expose the corrupted figure of the trafficker in racialized labor behind the image of the benevolent race man. This evasion mimics the genre of colonial complaint Fortune had so righteously, manfully silenced earlier in the series. Yet the inherent formal instability of the joke necessarily holds open what it seeks to foreclose.

How might this rhetorical gesture, Fortune's joke, find its expression in a gesture of the body? The answer, I imagine, is a shrug. Like blues humor or blues tragedy, the message such a gesture would communicate is not resignation or despair, if you listen for not just the content of expression, but the transformation effected by its form. With this shrug, Fortune would dismiss his figuration of the primitive, thoughtless "negroid" masses, only to face their return at the article's end, when the weary race man returns from his Pacific tour and lifts up his burden, offering them a migrant's chance. The response, which the text anticipates, is another shrug, dismissing the race man to bear his lonely burden elsewhere. In fact, the Southern black peasantry would soon leave, in many millions, for a different opportunity in industrialized cities to the north. But in fancy, if you accompany the figure of the race man as he turns, you might imagine one last repetition of the gesture. In this third shrug, the race man momentarily shifts the weight of uplift's burden, a slight jostling of the muscles, loosening joints fused under the downward pressure, and making possible a pivot in another direction.

As it happened, the weight proved too much for Fortune. Within a few years, the burdens of the ideology of manhood he'd advocated in such brilliant prose would collapse upon his own intemperance, but it had long been apparent that he was going down slow. His nobler dreams and smaller ambitions proved ill-fated, and the fruits of his labors would fall to those he surely saw as lesser men. The invigorating tropical excursion he'd imagined was physically straining; his commission, as much insult as honor, neither stabilized his finances nor raised his stature, drawing mostly scorn from all sides. The grand ambitions of his desire for uplift brought him to the edge of ruin, and if there was any chance left for those desires that motivated his joke or shrug, they could find expression only in a general derision.

He wanted, you can imagine, to be free of the whole sorry business.

the war back home

For the soldiers serving in the colony, the burden of black imperial manhood was no easier to bear. Take the case of Sergeant Major John W. Calloway, a decorated veteran of the war in Cuba who occasionally wrote about the Philippines for the black press. In September 1899, after his 24th Infantry returned from its first combat expedition in the islands (Marasigan 50), he published a letter in the *Richmond Planet* alluding to his seemingly inexpressible position on the unpopular war: "If I had time I would drop you a few lines bearing on the subject. I say a few lines, but we black men are so much between the 'Devil and the deep sea' on the Philippine question, I fear I would not know what to say, should I attempt to scribble it."[3] In another article in November, he quoted "a wealthy Filipino planter," Tomas Consunji, as saying, "We want Occidental ideas, but we want them taught to us by colored people." This desire leads Calloway to encourage black professional migration along lines later promoted by W. S. Scarborough and Charles Steward, calling for "our young men who are practical scientific agriculturalists, architects, mechanical, electrical and mining engineers, business men, professors and students of the sciences and who know how to establish and manage banks, mercantile business, large plantations, sugar growing, developing and refining," as well as "missionaries and teachers." By the following autumn, however, following the celebrated defection of David Fagen, a member of his regiment whose enlistment he'd signed as a witness (Schubert 27), Calloway's correspondence with Consunji became grounds for suspicion. Significantly, he was charged not with treason, but adultery—abandoning his legal wife to live with a Filipina. Acquitted of that too, Calloway was demoted to private, dishonorably discharged, and promptly deported to the United States.[4]

In the metropole, editors like the *Planet*'s John Mitchell Jr. could honor the soldiers while openly condemning the war, but within the narrower range of discourse available to servicemen, Calloway's initial vexed dispatch went about as far as most would publicly go. A few other items from that same September 30 edition delineate the ideological concerns at stake: one enthusiastically endorses the latest volume on the history of black soldiering, *Under Fire with the Tenth U.S. Cavalry* (" 'Under Fire' "); another quotes the *Washington Post* for evidence of white soldiers' predilections for sexually assaulting Filipina women ("Heinous Crimes"); while a third approvingly cites the example of a Virginia man who gave up the status and salary of a captain in the segregated regiments to become a schoolteacher ("Deserves Much Praise").

Within this framework, another letter, reprinted in the *Planet* on October 14, 1899, under the headline "Terrible Scenes There," is exceptional.[5] Apparently written on August 11, and reproduced widely, it was addressed to the editor of the *New York Age*—T. Thomas Fortune. Since its reproduction in Willard Gatewood's invaluable *"Smoked Yankees" and the Struggle for Empire*,[6] it is probably the most widely cited text by the war's black soldier-correspondents, for the same reason, presumably, that it was published anonymously—its unusually explicit criticism of U.S. imperialism. Decrying the racist violence at the war's core, the letter exposes the debts incurred in performing civilized Negro manhood in the Philippines, which threaten to sever bonds of racial and national community, stranding the black soldier far from home.

What was he doing there, this man whose name is unrecorded, Fortune's unsigned correspondent in the Philippines? Whatever his personal reasons, the social meaning of his service was defined by uplift ideology. Enacting loyalty to the nation and sacrifice for the race, the work of soldiering was the racialized, gendered performance of a model minority aiming to secure "manhood rights" at home. But manly honor demands that he consider his adversaries' perspective, by "mingl[ing] freely with the natives" and consulting "American colored men here in business . . . who have lived here for years," and to admit the Filipinos "have a just grievance": the refusal to acknowledge *their* manhood. When the occupying army discovered that its erstwhile allies against Spain "were desirous of sharing in the glories as well as the hardships of the hard won battles," he explains, "they began to apply home treatment for colored peoples."

White soldiers engage in a variety of crimes, but the most shocking proof that they place greed above honor is rampant grave robbing: "This may seem a little tall—but I have seen with my own eyes carcasses lying bare in the boiling sun, the results of raids on the receptacles for the dead in search for diamonds." This unsettling image is quickly displaced by a different threat, an offer of fraternity to black soldiers from their white comrades, Northern and Southern, through the exchange of other tall tales, of racialized violence against women: "Thinking we would be proud to emulate their conduct, [they] have made bold of telling their exploits to us," including severing "a native woman's arm in order to get a fine inlaid bracelet." When this proposition is rejected—"colored soldiers would never countenance such conduct"—the white soldiers' response reveals the threat to black manhood it entailed: "They talk with impunity of 'niggers' to our soldiers, never once thinking that they are talking to home 'niggers' and should they be brought to remember that at home this is the same vile epithet they hurl at us, they beg pardon and make some effeminate excuse about what the Filipino is called."

Repulsing the emasculating, contagious effeminacy of fraternity with whites frees him to remember another intimate, gendered bond, and what it entails. His primary duty is to return, with his shield or on it, to the ones left behind: the heterosexual (re)union of manhood, proven in violence, with the feminized domestic space violence secures makes possible the future of the race, its regeneration and reproduction. Loyalty to the race keeps him from switching sides and calls him home: "I want to say right here, if it were not for the 10,000,000 black people in the United States God alone knows on which side of this subject I would be."

Apparently posted just weeks after the 24th and 25th regiments arrived in the Philippines, and published at least a month before Fagen's defection, this letter goes no farther in publicly reconsidering his loyalties. But because the correspondent is unwilling to sever the bonds that tie him to home,[7] to the race of which he is the token representative, he remains bound to act in the name of the nation, unable to separate himself from the white troops, and therefore incurs responsibility for their atrocities. Like the figure of the earnest scientist in Du Bois's anecdote of the Sam Hose case, he is caught between his position as a model minority and forms of violence, *home treatment for colored peoples*, he recognizes as familiar, which hail a different identification. The violence touches and marks him, doubly and incommensurably, as complicit subject and potential object, manned and unmanned. Conscripted in the dishonoring of the disinterred dead and the severing of the native woman's arm, crimes he cannot avenge without cutting all ties to home, his racialized manhood is burdened with an irremediable shame.

Yet rather than suppressing this shame, he publicizes and circulates it. Rather than forgetting the call of the dead or the wordless speech of the woman's arm, he transmits their sound back home, translating it into a request that Fortune's readers reject Republican imperial policies in the coming election. That is, in exchange for his blood sacrifice abroad, he asks those black men at home who can exercise the franchise to redeem his manly honor, assuming and discharging the debts he's incurred on behalf of the race. In re-sounding the call, he anticipates Sutton Griggs's appeal to sever the race's bond of loyalty to the party of Lincoln—"Party be damned!" he insists—not to unite Negro and Filipino in the slurred identity imposed by imperial violence, but to sever Filipinos from their own bondage to U.S. empire, allowing each group to pursue its discrepant destiny.

As it happened, despite an early outburst of opposition over the war, Fortune stayed loyal to the GOP in McKinley's 1900 campaign. The Philippine tour was repayment for his endorsement, coming after Roosevelt, successor to the assassinated McKinley, proclaimed the war over in 1902. But the occupation and its resistance would go on indefinitely, and the debts continued to pile up, circulating back and forth across the Pacific. Among those entangled were two relatives of the novelist Ann Petry, as her daughter Elisabeth reveals in a 2005 collection of family letters, *Can Anything Beat White?* Helen James (Chisholm), mentioned previously, spent three years working in schools and orphanages in Hawai'i, reveling in her role as a sophisticated, modern young woman. Her brother Willis traveled even more widely. Family legend inaccurately placed him at Roosevelt's side at San Juan Hill (Petry 42), but he served with the 48th Regiment in the Philippines and received several promotions. However, as his great-niece acknowledges, he did not fulfill the model of normative manhood Fortune celebrated. In fact, he enlisted shortly after a woman he had been courting became pregnant. Though they had more children together after his return, they may not have been married, and he would leave her again (60–61). Something of a black sheep, he hoboed across the country, working as a waiter in hotels and on trains, using aliases on occasion, borrowing money from the family without repaying it and apparently fathering other children.

Meanwhile, after Hawai'i, Helen James went on to study under Du Bois at Atlanta, and subsequently taught on the Sea Islands off South Carolina and in Florida. Eventually, however, a woman of her status was expected to get married. In Petry's account, the wedding caused her much anxiety and grief, and was delayed when Helen, whose "hypochondria" Petry elsewhere questions (189), became too ill for the necessary preparations. After the marriage, her professional life and travels came to an end, though she did manage to run "a correspondence class on reading and literature" (185).

I do not repeat these indecorous details from Petry's account to dishonor her extraordinary family, but to emphasize her courage in honoring them, not for upholding the image of an impossible ideal, but for the flawed, complex lives they actually led. The book concludes with her own letter to the family, addressed in public, a kind of prayer or poem addressing each of her subjects in turn, expressing her feelings about their accomplishments and failures. Unafraid to air family secrets, she exposes their shame in composing her own love notes—that they may be heard by her dead, releasing them from shame while securing the bonds of family beyond death.

(But what stronger tie exists than a family secret, a shame that will not be acknowledged? What else might bind you so securely, draw you back so powerfully and immediately, no matter where in the world you might go and imagine you are safe?)

Two: Queerer Still the Immaculate Conception

The constraints of normative gendering were embraced as a liberating burden by the African American strivers following uplift's call across the Pacific, but too often that call proved a siren's song, and the collapse of their ambitions released ever-outward circulations of shame. In counterpoint, this section reads a series of literary texts emerging from the sexual education of the Filipino national—the unevenly articulated processes by which elite colonial institutions trained an Anglophone intelligentsia at the same time that metropolitan Filipino labor migration was constituted as an alien sexual threat—focusing on the early short fiction of José Garcia Villa. Acknowledged by his contemporaries as the preeminent Filipino writer in English, Villa was a product of the Philippine elite who rode sexual scandal to a long, lonely career in the metropole. In contrast to Bulosan, who struggled to represent sexual normalization as the migrant's tutelary path to global revolution, Villa's idealization of erotic unfulfillment pursued the liberation of nonnormative sexuality beyond the normative domain of the political.

the effacements of a racial slur

For readers in Asian American studies, contemporary interest in Villa can largely be traced to the 1993 publication of Jessica Hagedorn's landmark *Charlie Chan Is Dead*, which announced Asian American literature's expansion beyond the perceived boundaries—ethnic, gendered, and aesthetic—of its early institutionalization.[8] Arguably the most striking selection in the anthology was Villa's sixty-year-old work of experimental prose, "Untitled Story." Not a story that declines a title, but one dramatically named for its refusal of convention (and for the metropole?), "Untitled Story" is composed of brief, numbered paragraphs, with only a sparse, elliptical relation to a narrative plot. Periodically eschewing standard syntax or punctuation, and burgeoning with rhetorically extravagant abstractions, paradoxes, and fantasies, it exploded the field's settled expectations of form and content. Furthered by Kaya Press's 1999 collection of his selected writings, *The Anchored Angel*, edited by Eileen Tabios, Villa's recuperation as an Asian American literary forefather has since accelerated. Recent developments include the Penguin Classics publication of *Doveglion: Collected Poems* and the acquisition of his papers by Harvard's Houghton Library, both through the efforts of his literary trustee, John Edwin Cowen; his reclamation for a tradition of experimental U.S. minority poetry by Timothy Yu and others; and his recontextualization as a practitioner of queer transpacific modernism by Martin Joseph Ponce and Denise Cruz.[9]

But these are just the latest chapters in the reception of a figure who has appeared in many guises. Villa has been credited, sometimes as if single-handedly, with establishing a modern Anglophone national literature from abroad, dominating Philippine literary debates from the 1930s to the 1950s as its most accomplished (if sometimes tyrannical) poet and critic, before his antipolitical aesthetic purism, deemed complicit with a neocolonial regime, was dethroned by a more socially attuned nationalism.[10] Meanwhile, he managed at least *two* celebrated debuts on the metropolitan literary scene, first as a short-story writer and protégé of the influential critic Edward J. O'Brien, and later as a young poet praised by Marianne Moore, e. e. cummings, and Edith Sitwell. After two years as an associate editor at New Directions, he spent decades as a feared, beloved leader of poetry workshops at City College, the New School, and privately, ending his career in genteel poverty in lower Manhattan. For his own part, Villa would narrate and renarrate his career as punctuated by several dramatic renunciations—turning from painting to literature as a young artist in the Philippines, abandoning prose for the more rarefied rigor of poetry in the United States, and then "graduating" in 1954 from the field of his greatest accomplishments, to spend his last decades on poetic collages adapted from found texts, and on a monumental multivolume philosophy of poetry sometimes whispered to be nonexistent.[11]

As Hagedorn surely knew, Villa was a rather disobliging conscript to the late 1980s–early 1990s multicultural wars her anthology joined. I myself can recall the excitement of discovering "Untitled Story" as an earnest undergraduate, as well as the twinge of discomfort I felt reading two early passages in which the narrator, a young fountain-pen boy making his way to the University of New Mexico, reflects unsympathetically on two less fortunate figures:

8

In California too I saw a crippled woman selling pencils on a sidewalk. It was night and she sat on the cold concrete like an old hen but she had no brood. She looked at me with dumb faithful eyes.

9

The Negro in the Pullman hummed to himself. At night he prepared our berths and he was automatic like a machine. As I looked at him I knew I did not want to be like a machine. (*Charlie* 463–64)

This is hardly the solidarity with the oppressed that students of Asian American studies thrilled to find in Bulosan. Instead, the narrator reinforces his distance from the social conditions projected in these figures: just as he is neither African American nor a woman, he hopes never to become poor and disabled, spiritually vacuous, or reduced to servitude, alienated from a body so given over to labor's automated rhythms that its music is merely the humming of a machine.

Even so, I was shocked, years later, rereading the story in Villa's 1933 collection *Footnote to Youth*, to find that the Pullman worker in paragraph 9 is not described with the historically correct if outdated term

"Negro." Instead, the word used—essentially unprintable in a 1993 anthology of Asian American fiction—is the slur "nigger" (74).[12] That a Filipino writer might use this racist epithet to characterize an African American Pullman porter in 1933 seems all the more objectionable if you recall that the same term had been applied to Filipinos, three decades earlier, by white soldiers in the Philippines. Nor is it unreasonable to imagine that a young Villa, traveling from Manila to New Mexico by way of California, would have heard it applied to himself, along with alternates such as "gu-gu," "gook," or "monkey."

But this last insight points toward another, more vexing possibility: What if the "nigger in the Pullman" was not a "Negro" after all? As Barbara Posadas's research has shown, the Pullman Company began hiring Filipinos as early as 1925, aiming to undermine the unionizing efforts of A. Philip Randolph's famed Brotherhood of Sleeping Car Porters (362) through a nominal distinction between Filipino "attendants" and black "porters," regularly blurred or disregarded in practice.[13] Like most Filipino migrants in this period, attendants typically hoped to pursue higher education in the metropole, modeling their aspirations on the *pensionados* of the early U.S. regime (352), and on the heroic *ilustrados* of the Spanish era, like José Rizal. Yet unlike Villa or his narrator, they were so inhibited by poverty and working conditions that, according to Posadas, none of the attendants completed a college degree (353–54). Her account further suggests that mechanization is no idle metaphor for their heavily surveilled and regularized working conditions—though a humming attendant could be a practitioner of *palocso*, jargon for the arts of augmenting one's wages through petty workplace deception and corruption (359), rather than a model employee satisfied with his lot. The difference, in any case, would surely mean little to Villa's narrator.

It is possible, if hardly certain, that Villa was aware Filipinos were working on Pullman cars when he composed "Untitled Story." Nonetheless, it is impossible to determine, on the evidence of the 1933 text, whether "the nigger on the Pullman" is a "Filipino attendant" or a "Negro porter." However, it is clear that Villa's mobilization of a racist slur that could be turned on himself as well as African American service workers functions to differentiate his narrator from the conditions of racialized migratory labor experienced by the overwhelming majority of Filipinos in the U.S. West. Just as Fortune's representation of Filipino primitivism worked to inscribe his class distinction from a benighted African American majority, Villa employs the slur to disavow the masses of his countrymen in the metropole. While explicit antiblack racism might be disqualifying in a 1993 anthology of Asian American literature, Villa's gesture goes even further—distancing itself, with imperious disdain, from the minimal presumption of collective identification at the basis of any ethnic, let alone panethnic, literary project.[14]

This gesture is presented as a step toward the narrator's formation as a writer in the metropole, itself a curious, polyvocal act of disavowal, as a broader reading of "Untitled Story" makes clear. The narrator, identified in one case by the nickname "Pepe" (104), is clearly autobiographical, one of many authorial personae Villa constructed over his career. The story begins by playing on the most notorious event in that career, the circumstances of his departure from the Philippines:

1

Father did not understand my love for Vi, so Father sent me to America to study away from her. I could not do anything and I left.

2

I was afraid of my father. (73)

In fact, Villa's departure had been spurred by a widely publicized literary scandal. As a student at the University of the Philippines in 1929, he published several poems in the *Philippines Herald* collectively titled "Man-Songs," whose unabashed eroticism caused an uproar. Brought to court for indecency, Villa was fined and subsequently suspended from the university. Later that year, however, his "Mir-i-nisa" won a short-story contest in the *Philippines Free Press*, and he used the cash prize to migrate to the United States, apparently of his own accord.[15] Nonetheless, Villa's tempestuous relationship with his father was also well known. Simeón Villa, a physician, had served as a colonel and aide to the revolutionary leader Emilio Aguinaldo, at whose side he was captured in 1901. According to a 1961 profile by Nick Joaquin, which bemoans "the loss to Philippine literature of a re-singing of the Revolution" (Tabios 157–58) entailed by the gulf between father and son, their relationship broke down prior to the "Man-Songs" controversy, over the son's devotion, not to a girl, but to a dog (160).[16]

Because details of Villa's life would likely be known to a Philippine audience, but not elsewhere, the text makes available a second level of reading in which the young writer's formation in the metropole must be approached as a critical transformation of biographical narrative already circulating as gossip and scandal. Villa's persistent use of this seamlessly polyvalent mode of address throughout his career, effacing prior successes in the colony to make a series of grand entrances on the metropolitan scene, has caused much consternation for some readers. His consistent, ambitious participation in Philippine literary life notwithstanding, this strategy has been read as symptomatic of racial shame—as if his role in Philippine letters were relegated to a kind of colonial closet. Yet there is evidence that this technique developed under somewhat different conditions, before he left Manila. In a pathbreaking reading, Ponce invokes "Man-Songs" as the opening gesture of Villa's "queer modernism," teasing out their carefully constructed "play with gender ambiguity" (*Beyond the Nation* 59). For example, "what constitutes a 'man-song'" is ambiguous: "some are sung by a man, while others are about or addressed to men" (62). Though the poems' erotic scenes can be read as conventionally heterosexual, if shamelessly explicit, other interpretations are available—a possibility that the text seems to endorse, as Ponce notes, in the final poem's opening lines: "I have not yet sung as I want to sing. My songs are queer songs but when I grow older they will be queerer still" (59). This declaration offers a guide to what a colonial cognoscenti would recognize as a fictional revision of Villa's scandalous biography, displacing Pepe's formation as an author to the United States, which "Untitled Story" narrates as the transformation of a flower from purple to white.

Villa's phrasing of the opening lines repays close attention. The problem with the father, corresponding to the son's powerlessness and fear, is not lack of approval, but comprehension: he *did not understand* the son's love, so he sent him away. Once in New Mexico, a series of intense relationships thematize the narrator's efforts to understand it himself. David, a boy "like a young flower," recites poetry with him on nighttime walks, but leaves before the term begins, for lack of funds; the narrator's unpunctuated reaction, the entirety of the section numbered "20," is: "I died in myself" (76). Georgia, a blonde, lets him run his fingers through her hair. In love letters, she calls him "My Lord" and "Beloved," but he calls her "just Georgia" or "sometimes . . . Georgie," which makes him smile "because it was like a boy's name" (78). After a fight, he spends nights wandering and talking to himself: "I did not know what I was saying. I called myself, 'You . . .' but the sentence did not get finished" (79, ellipsis in original). Then it does get finished, though not in any words he will report. Instead, he reports, "The finished sentence was beauteous as a dancer in the dawn"—and he and Georgia are finished too (79).

"I would be through with girls," he tells himself, "and love only the girl back home," the elusive Vi (80). This allows him to torture himself by inventing fantasies of her unfaithfulness, and to transfer this anger to his father, thereby enacting or reenacting the scene of his poetic genesis:

39

I was very angry I became a poet. In fancy my anger became a gorgeous purple flower. I made love to it with my long fingers. Then when I had won it and it shone like a resplendent gem in my hands I offered it to my father.

40

My father could not understand the meaning of the gorgeous purple flower. When I gave it to him he threw it on the floor. Then I said, "My father is not a lover." (80–81)

Once again, the father rejects the flower not because he cannot appreciate beauty—though that may be—but because he lacks understanding. So what is its meaning? Not simply that his son defies his authority, or fancies beauty, or has extravagant, unusual desires—all these he seems to recognize well enough. If the son's response is explication, then the flower must profess a love that would implicate the father if he accepted it, as the lover he is not. But if he is shamed, even threatened, by what he cannot understand, the son's love, his rejection is that love's necessary condition, for it survives on a lack of fulfillment: "I picked the flower and it lived because my father refused it" (81).

So the logic of this scene, temporal and causal, is circular, increasing in force and breadth as it spins around: centrifugal. Because his father misunderstands his love, it flowers as poetry; offered up to his father, it is again misunderstood; but because he misunderstands, the flower survives being picked. Although the scene seems to efface Villa's literary career in the colony, which it makes no effort to introduce to metropolitan readers, the narrative's elliptical form also allows you to read it as a memory, or the allegory of a memory, of an earlier spin around the circuit. In any case, the scene takes place not in New Mexico but *in fancy*, a setting spiraling off from the chronology of his metropolitan adventures, the location of his return to his father, the state in which he *becomes a poet*. And if it effaces Villa's colonial career, it does so to dupe a metropolitan audience, impoverishing their reading while courting their misunderstanding.

Immediately following this scene, the narrator tells his new friends he is leaving, not for Manila, but for New York City. Crying alone in his room, he reveals this is a lie. Then, for over a dozen paragraphs, the story recounts those experiences of "going about starving" in New York that it emphasizes are false. In one, a piece of paper blows through the window, and his "mind beg[ins] to work about it," imagining that a waiting lover has sent him a note (83). Then the wind shifts it again, and he declares: "—It is a white flower trembling with love. It is God's white flower.—It made me think of my gorgeous purple flower which my father had refused and I wanted it to become God's white flower. Make my purple flower white, God, I prayed" (83–84). In this outward turn of his fancy, the colonial family home is exchanged for a rented room in the metropolitan center, whose cold, alienating welcome he desires. Magically, a white love note appears, but *even in his fantasy*, the note is not legitimate, just a product of his fancy. If no sweetheart girl waits at its other end, this is no flaw but the chance of perfection, for the love and the magical agency at stake are only poetry, his own artifice. And the love note's whiteness opens another level of poetic transformation, exchanging the father for God, the object of a purer, more abstract and perfected relationship of supplication and struggle.

When he is done with these fancies, he leaves his room and pretends he really is leaving. One of the girls, Aurora, walks with him to a bus; as he rides, he wonders why they did not become lovers. At the station, he waits for a train and watches it leave—"Had I bidden myself goodbye?" (86)—then wanders the streets searching for himself, to no avail:

"Where had my god fled? Where was he taking my gorgeous purple flower which my father had refused?" (88). His god, who is not God, has left with his flower, which is not white. But the next morning, when he faces his friends again, he asks Aurora to let him feel her hair, which is not blonde.[17] The story concludes enigmatically: "My god was in her hair. My god was there with my purple flower pressed gently to his breast. I opened his hands and he yielded to me my flower. I pinned it to Aurora's hair. And as the purple petals kissed the soft dark of her hair, my flower turned silver, then white—became God's white flower. Then I was no longer angry with my father" (89). The purple flower sustained by his father's rejection is transformed again, into that white ideal dreamed in the metropolitan center, releasing the son from anger into relation with another Father. This turn of the cycle may not give closure, but marks a new level of poetic accomplishment—and so it is appropriate to ask, Why is this development figured as a turning-white?

Before reaching that question, you might note that, if the story revises the writer's biography, it must have advanced into the future—Villa eventually left for New York, but it's as if that phase of his career is projected back into his student days in New Mexico, displacing the story of the "I" who did leave on the train. And so you may take measure, here, of the distance the text has traveled from that other disavowed shadow in the Pullman car. There, the story violently figured blackness in a slurring that left its precise racial signification ambiguous. Yet it eliminated the primary feature linking racist representations of the Negro and the Filipino—a vigorously primitive but aggressively threatening sexuality—substituting a familiar figure of modernizing labor. The "nigger on the Pullman" is monstrous not as a sexually voracious ape, but as a contented machine.

Curiously, the same figure and formal gesture appear in an essay by S. P. Lopez, Villa's friend and chief adversary in a defining set of debates in Anglophone Philippine letters. In his prize-winning 1940 collection, *Literature and Society*, Lopez championed proletarian literature against the Villa-dominated art-for-art's-sake school. One chapter bears the title "Up from Slavery"—clearly alluding to Booker T. Washington's autobiography, which the educator John H. Manning Butler had recently complained was all an educated Filipino likely knew of African American letters ("New Education" 268). Yet Lopez's essay omits any reference to the history of racial slavery in the United States, instead favoring references to Greek slavery and to the coming liberation of human labor by the machine.

Invoking and effacing black enslavement allows him to embrace the development of a proletarian heteronormativity, graduating from colonial tutelage. Because Lopez's proletarianism is largely an abstraction, cannily negotiating the politics of a colonial elite, it does not share Bulosan's deep engagement with the lived reality of interracial sexual relations and sexualized racism. Instead, it clears space for colonial proletarian writing by appealing to its celebration in metropolitan letters. The goal, as he titles one essay, is "a red-blooded literature," foregoing not the theme of love as such, but its immature and decadent manifestations. "The Filipino writer must grow up," he proclaims. "He must be discontented with merely sniffing odorous flowers of emotion. . . . He must write of virile people winning victories towards freedom."[18]

Where Lopez's figuration of the machine effaces blackness, Villa's marks it, explicitly and violently, only to deny its sexualization. It pivots away from the dynamics of sexual racism constituting the subject of Filipino labor migration, to clear a space, in the lee of the normalizing forces of anti-Filipino violence, anticolonial nationalism, and proletarianism, where nonnormative sexual desires might achieve aesthetic transcendence. The Villa-Lopez debate, then, is less about politics than about the normative limits of the political: unlike Lopez, Villa cannot imagine freedom within them, and so spirals outward into the aesthetic.[19] But if they diverge regarding the relation between sexuality and freedom, their separate trajectories leave intact the shared gesture by which each seeks to imagine liberation from the dehumanizing forces of modern capitalism, by displacing unfreedom onto the denigrated figure of the machine. The song that neither could hear, what you might call the *black noise*[20] of that machine, is the Pullman worker's hum.

from purple to white

As Ponce notes, reading "Untitled Story" in isolation, as its repeated republication encourages, may leave "a false impression of formal closure and heterosexual resolution" (*Beyond the Nation* 68). In *Footnote to*

Youth, it is the first installment of "Wings and Blue Flame: A Trilogy," part of a cycle of five stories recirculating episodes and themes related to the narrator's experiences at the University of New Mexico. By "White Interlude," the second entry, his interest in girls has fallen away, and what plot there is involves his more intense relationships with boys—and one in particular, Jack Wicken. The third story, "Walk at Midnight: A Farewell," relates a complicated dynamic between four boys: Jack, the narrator, Dick, and Johnny. Later in the collection, "Song I Did Not Hear" revisits the trilogy's characters and stylistic peculiarities, displacing any apparent closure, and elevates a previously minor character, Joe Lieberman, whose jealousy of Jack drives him to leave school and write the narrator an accusatory love letter. Finally, the brief "Young Writer in a New Country" attempts a gloss on the trilogy, abandoning the numbered-paragraph format along with any semblance of plot.

"White Interlude" opens by reworking several familiar elements—the loss of David, the father sending the narrator away from Vi, and the trope of the machine. The latter, now detached from the figure of racialized labor, is opposed to a curiously gendered and color-coded incarnation of love. After David repeats the father's "unwholing of me" that generates a "song of hurt" (94), he imagines, "If I could know people and make them pass out of my life with the smoothness and painlessness of a machine I would always be whole"—but he is no machine: "I am like a great mother wing nourishing loves and never deserting them. I am a great white wing of love" (95). Along with further ruminations on David and his father, the story relates his experiences with Jack—the son of a "Swede" (100) who the narrator initially was sure hated him for being "a foreigner" (99)—and Johnny, whose "dark eyes" and "olive skin" lead others to say he's "Armenian," though he says he's "Welsh" (103). In the final scene, Jack receives a letter from Morgan, a boy in Philadelphia whose feelings he doesn't reciprocate. Much like the narrator's father, he "could not understand why Morgan had written him," and angrily crushes and flings the letter away. Horrified, the narrator recovers it, smoothes it out, and insists that he keep it, but Jack just laughs and crumples it once again: "and then I knew I would never be lost to Jack for Jack never could lose anything, Jack who could crush God's whisper in his hands, who could bruise my white wing of love. And the loneliness of the time when Jack was not yet in my life came a-tiptoe, a-tiptoe, to sing for me another song of hurt" (114). Recognizing his own rejection as a regret that he can't make Jack suffer from his loss, he looks forward to his own future abandonment. But this is a loss that *sings*: Is this not his true desire?

The trilogy's conclusion, "Walk at Midnight," begins by displacing the paternity of the father in a figure of immaculate conception. No less shocking for being a repeated motif in *Footnote to Youth*, it allows the narrator to imagine surpassing even *God's* understanding: "Sometimes at night I wonder if when I was born God realized the bigness of the thrust with which He was bringing me to earth. God's white arm held me to His breast where I could hear His heart beating loudly and the beating of His heart was like the beating of wings against blue flame. Then after I had breathed of the beating of His heart God passed me into my mother and in a night in August I was born" (117). Even before he enters his mother's womb, God's love makes him unwhole: "On the breast of God as I listened to His heart my own became vast and hollow so the earth could fill it with the music of mortality" (117). The drama with his father, it turns out, is merely secondary, a continuation of the cycle— "The filling of my heart that God had promised I found in the silence of my father and the sharpness of his words" (118)—even as he again questions God's omniscience: "Did God know that giving me to my mother gave me also to my father?" (119).

After recapping the previous episodes' events, the narrator summarizes the story's formulaic situation, misaligned romance: "Yet even as I liked Jack better than Johnny so did Jack like a boy Dick more than me and when I thought of it it hurt and sometimes it made me angry with Jack in silence. In these moments of anger I wanted to know if Johnny felt that way too about me but I could not know" (122). Eventually, the conflict comes to a head over those long nighttime walks the boys are so fond of taking. The narrator cries when Jack refuses his invitation one night, and he must walk alone; another night, Jack leaves him and Johnny to go walking with Dick, and he runs to his room. Unable to stop crying, he wakes up Johnny, who leads him out to the mesa, where he finds ecstasy and release among the wildflowers—picking them madly till they "drip gorgeously" from his hands, leaving him "weak . . . on the ground," where they "became unstill with dew . . . unstill with love"; he "flow[s] into flowers, filling them," until he is "perfectly still," his "heart . . . drained of love . . . vast and hollow," and he hears "the faint beating of wings," exulting, "—I am hungry for You, O God!" (129–30). Unmistakably, these walks are represented as sexual acts, but this business with the flowers isn't a euphemism for other acts too shameful to be described—rather, their abstraction and aestheticization is rendered shamelessly. Rather than assuming that the truth of the narrator's sexuality would be revealed by clearing away the artifice, recognize that the artifice is precisely what he is after, which is why he is interested only in love that is unrequited. To "decode" these representations by substituting a language supposedly more direct or accurate would not be liberation, but the unraveling of the poetic achievement of his desire: for Villa, this flowery language *is* explicitly sexual. Finished, the narrator is filled with "the rain of music"; his achievement of love is not fulfillment, but withdrawal, returning what had never been requited, forgiving a debt that had never been acknowledged: "And I knew that when I lay on the ground, with the sky wet with stars above me, I was taking Jack out of me and giving him to the earth and the sky, and the white flowers in my hands were my gifts of forgiveness" (130).

Lest you mistake this "farewell" for closure, a later story, "Song I Did Not Hear," reveals that the narrator's obsession with Jack persists after that midnight walk, while Johnny's presence in the scene is omitted. But the last word on the series is given in "Young Writer in a New Country," which is really more commentary than story, though it emphasizes—if not exaggerates—its difficulties in communicating meaning, repeatedly questioning the reader's understanding: "What I am trying to say is . . ." (299); "What I want to say is . . ." (301); "Do you get what I mean?" (302); "Do you get what I am driving you to see?" (303). Rehearsing, revising, summarizing, and glossing the events of the trilogy, the story passes from the homeland and the suffering of separation to New Mexico and David, who, he now understands, embodies what modern civilization both pursues and abandons: "Even in my country Davids are not many. Civilization does not want Davids: You got no speed, David. You must be left behind." (302). This insight releases him to achieve the destination and destiny of his migration: "Do you see America getting clearer in my mind? Do you see myself getting articulate, getting voice? Little by little calm comes to my mind. Little by little comes my white birth—a white cool birth in a new land" (302–3).

It is tempting, of course, to read this *white birth* in a reductively racializing fashion, just as it is to imagine that enlightened hindsight can
identify and thereby liberate the truth of the narrator's sexuality. Both
readings come at the cost of denying all the poetic work the stories
fashion from the language history provides. This does not mean that
the phrase bears no racial signification, as if the meaning of the word
"white" were not dynamically at stake as Villa was writing. Then as now,
whiteness, even in its more restrictive function as a racial designation,
operated through a range of distinct but articulated meanings within the
life sciences, social sciences, law, and everyday practices, interacting unpredictably across historical, local, national, and transnational contexts.
Its overriding geopolitical function was to designate civilized mastery
as a quality biologically transmissible via specified forms of sexual reproduction, yet its particular boundaries in any instance were regularly
put to debate—for example, in the racial prerequisite cases establishing the legal boundaries of U.S. whiteness. Indeed, the racial status of
Filipinos would still be contemplated by the courts over the next decade
(Haney López 167).

It may be possible, then, to read this cycle as a variation on the passing narrative, following my earlier argument that narratives of passing
press the question of discerning the difference between freedom and the
achievement of the status privileges accorded to whiteness. Here, whiteness is resignified as the natal endowment of a young Filipino writer
ascending to civilization's most rarefied altitudes of cultural achievement. For Villa, this is no appeal for inclusion or recognition from U.S.
colonial tutelage, but its overthrowing, as becomes clearer when his text
inverts the second term of the trope: "I, father of tales. Fathering tales I
became rooted to the new land. I became lover to the desert. Three tales
had healed me" (303). This queer figure of conception—of a poet, of the
tales he is healed by fathering—is the *white birth*. It is the flowering, to
be sure, of what Rafael terms "white love," whereby the subject of colonial tutelage claims autonomous agency, maturation into the position of
the father. But like any other love, it is of use to Villa only insofar as it
goes unrequited. Because this *civilizing love and love for civilization* was
not returned, the narrator may transmute it into writing, healing the
wounds left by an earlier unrequited love that precedes and surrounds

it: the greater drama was never about the love of the metropolitan white father, but that of his own father in the Philippines.

And behind this love is an even greater love, the divine eroticism he ascribes to and blasphemously desires in God, which allows you to recognize that what's paramount in Villa's resignification of whiteness is not its racial but its *sexual* meanings—its connotation of moral and sexual purity. The transformation achieved in the narrator's *white cool birth* is not from brown to white but from purple to white. It asserts that purity is not founded on the denial or normalization of sexual desires, but on a sacred fidelity to sexual desire unashamed by "civilized" morality, a love that transfigures submission or subordination and is most pure when unfulfilled and unreciprocated. Here, too, Villa presses the limit of what may be read as a passing narrative, arrogating the divine sanction of sexuality as the apotheosis of shamelessly nonnormative desire.

Because the father/son conflict in these stories exceeds both imperial inclusion and colonial nationalism, the outcome—the young writer's maturation as a creative subject—cannot resolve into either a new homeland or a return. Thus, reflecting on New Mexico from his new life in New York, having reached the metropolitan center in fact beyond fancy, he longs to return to the elsewhere that is his aesthetic terrain, "the desert of [his] white birth," to "surrender" and "never leave"—before interjecting, "in the homeland, *there* I was young," and beseeching, "Do you get what I am driving you to see?" (303). The text concludes:

> Will the native land forgive? Between your peace and the peace of a strange faraway desert—Between your two peaces——
> O tell softly, softly. Forgive softly. (303–4)

The young writer has reached his final destination, the big city where, six and a half decades later, Villa would die. His fiction enacts his imaginative return, but its destinations are doubled: the desert of his birth, where his writing is always born in the peace of love's desertion, and the land before birth, where he was young. So his address splits, hailing the native land as "you"—surely he wasn't addressing the Philippines all along?—asking its forgiveness and recalling its peace. And if his writing is what emerges in between these two peaces, then his address shifts again—unless this is the one he was addressing all along?—in an imperative directed to the creator of the stories. For the one who tells is the one who forgives, even if the recipients of this forgiveness never acknowledged, *could not understand*, the hurts they had caused.

stillbirth of the alien national

As if in response to the concluding lines of "Young Writer in a New Country," the next item in *Footnote to Youth*, "Story for My Country," enacts a return to the homeland. To understand how it recasts the previous story's assertions, a broader look at the collection is necessary. The majority of the stories are set in the Philippines, and like the New Mexico tales, they form several cycles, linked by their titles and themes, which rework three bodies of source material: precolonial folklore, Christian mythology, and nationalist legends of the U.S. colonial period.[21] The cycles are also stylistically distinct,[22] as becomes apparent if you turn, as I briefly shall, to the latter group—the Rizal stories, which contemplate the legacy of the national hero in a series of grotesques.

While their implications are finally no less blasphemous or perverse, they are conventionally formatted, narrated in a mature, measured first-person voice, which roughly corresponds to the respectable, cultured member of the colonial elite Villa was expected to become had he not migrated. In "The Son of Rizal," he is a husband and father who travels first class when closing "an important land deal" (133) or being honored as "godfather to [a friend's] firstborn" (146); in "Daughter of Rizal" he's a physician—Simeón Villa's occupation, which he'd hoped his son would follow. Each story begins with an "Author's Note" sketching the biography and martyrdom of "the national hero of the Philippines"; the former concludes, "*Doctor Rizal left no son*" (133), whereas the latter, without the emphasis, states, "Doctor Rizal had no children" (205).[23] If the title characters in each story nonetheless claim Rizal's paternity, their assertions are carefully, rationally distinguished from a scientific basis in biological reproduction. "Son" even footnotes a biography of Rizal, to assure his readers of the "veracity of facts mentioned" in the otherwise fictional tale, grounding the epistemological distinction between fact and fancy (142).

In "Son," the narrator meets the eponymous character on a train, where he gives him a spare ticket, and kindly entertains the man's claim to be Rizal's child by Josephine Bracken, the Irish woman he reputedly married prior to his execution. Some time later, passing through the area, the narrator decides to stop by to give him a plaster bust of Rizal. A friend explains that "Juan Rizal" is actually a poor shoemaker, Juan Kola—called "Juan Sirá" ("nutty") by cruel children (147)—who never recovered psychologically after his abusive biological father died when he was twelve. Too poor to attend school, he befriended a kindly woman teacher, whose answers to his questions about Rizal provided the basis of his fantasy.

The "Daughter of Rizal," meanwhile, is not crazy but blind. After her mother's death, she explains to her physician, the narrator, that she'd fallen in love with a young student, "Pepe," who had bought a notebook from a shop where she worked. As proof, the daughter displays a drawing of the mother, apparently given in lieu of payment. Later, married and heavily pregnant, she went to observe the now-famous Rizal's execution, and fainted as he was shot. Her fall, the daughter insists, caused her to be born blind: "I am not sorry that my mother loved him" or "that I am blind. . . . I am the daughter of my mother, and the daughter of my father, and the daughter of Rizal. I understand" (217).

While both claims of paternity are fanciful, the stories imply that they must be believed. But unlike the shameless mysticism of the New Mexico stories—as in the narrator's substitution of divine conception for his father's paternity—these claims are carefully measured against bourgeois rationality, upheld as that veracity it calls metaphorical, poetic license. These grotesques truly are the children of Rizal, a truth that exceeds the thwarted biological lineage of heterosexual consummation and reproduction. The irrational devotion of the poor, illiterate son and the insightful pride of the blind daughter qualify them as Rizal's legitimate heirs, an assertion that seems to critique the self-assured claims to nationalism's legacy by members of the colonial elite. Even so, the son's and daughter's stories require the narrator's mediation, and their truth is revealed only as it is weighed, measured, and finally verified by his cultured rationality. Indeed, "Juan Rizal" is so dutifully, tearfully grateful after his narrator bestows on him the plaster bust that he kisses the man's hands and makes his children kiss them, too. If the patrimony of the national hero survives not through the lineage of a civilized, respectable elite, but through the queer, blind devotion of an impoverished and irrational folk, it must be secured via the evaluation of the cultured intellectual. But it seems that Villa abandoned this responsibility, which he was being educated to assume, journeying instead to the metropole to be remade in a *white cool birth*. Is this the rejection the native land must forgive?

"Story for My Country" clarifies this misunderstanding. Set in the Philippines, it's another tale of a son separated from a cruel father, but now a younger brother is given the duty of narrating, and passing judgment: " 'Father, father—ask forgiveness! . . . My brother is good! Be as lovely as he!' " (312). Years after his brother left their home, he visits the monument to Rizal in Manila, and reaches an epiphany: "Then I knew why he was fine and good. José Rizal—was not his name, but José *Rosal*—and he changed it to José Rizal so my father should not know him" (313). This may seem a little irrational, so he acknowledges he is speaking metaphorically, captivated by the "moonlight" and "loveliness" in Rizal's eyes that recalls his brother's, but this metaphor expresses a paradoxical poetic truth: "If my brother had not run away—if I had spoken to him that night and held him to me—if I had turned to my father and wakened him up to behold this loveliness—there would be no José Rizal—my country would be without José Rizal" (313). Rizal, after all, went to the metropole to further his education, went into exile after his writing caused a scandal, and became father to the nation through his permanent separation from it, in an act of love, a martyr's death. His true heir, the incarnation of his legacy upon which that legacy's very survival depends, is, finally, the son who leaves. The exile who authors this "Story for My Country" is this son; the forgiveness the story grants is his own due.

This is Villa at his boldest, most outrageous, granting forgiveness for wrongs no one ever acknowledged, suggesting not only that he is Rizal's proper heir—he was not the only migrant writer to do this—but that there would be no Rizal without him. Yet this is also Villa at his most fervently nationalist, professing a form of love that would bind together a Filipino people divided by class and dispersed by colonial migrations. Rizal is an apt figurehead for tracing the queer, migratory lineage of this nationalism, which is at once the favored offspring of colonial uplift and the promise of its sunset: the mythologization of Rizal as father of Filipino nationalism was vigorously promoted by a U.S. regime in order

to narrate imperial conquest as national liberation, for unlike Simeón
Villa's beloved Aguinaldo, Rizal did not live long enough to resist the
Americans. Similarly, a fervent nationalism, and a faith in the long advent of formal independence, could unite conflicting and contradictory
political interests across the empire, including those effectively committed to independence's perpetual deferral. As its strange alliance with
exclusionist politicians in the passing of the Tydings-McDuffie Act demonstrated, even unabashed white supremacists in the metropole could
rally behind the cause. For Villa, then, the Rizal legend provides a way
to reconcile the centrifugal trajectory of his differentiating artistic self-
invention with the unfulfilled collective self-invention of a dispersed
nation.

But this is just the latest in a series of dramatizations of unfulfilled
love. Whether paternal or colonial, divine or national, the poet chases
unconsummated patriarchal love to achieve suffering and blissful release
in its withdrawal, as the condition of a creative act figured as music.
For better or worse, he seems to have found what he was seeking. The
1933 volume was Villa's farewell, not to youth, but to prose fiction. Nine
years later, he pulled off a second, more successful metropolitan literary debut with a book of poetry, *Have Come, Am Here*, followed seven
years later by a *Volume Two*—titles that shamelessly efface not only his
past as a short-story writer, but his ongoing literary career in the Philippines, where he published the poetry collections *Many Voices* (1939)
and *Poems by Doveglion* (1941), along with famous annual selections of
the best Philippine short stories and poems following the model established by O'Brien. Timothy Yu has hypothesized that Villa turned from
fiction to poetry in seeking "access to the modernist canon," exchanging the representational demands imposed on racialized narrative for an
Anglo-American modernist poetic whose Orientalism would be satisfied by formal peculiarity and an obscurity of content ("Asian/Ameri-
can"). That is, Villa's migration from fiction repeated his departure from
the constraints of the colony, and his disavowal of a recognizably "Filipino" identification, slipping the bonds of racial and national identity
for the divine abstraction of poetry. But Villa's turn also corresponds to
the passing of Tydings-McDuffie: although he had arrived in the United
States, in the guises of a student and an acclaimed young writer, as a
"national," he abandoned fiction for poetry as an "alien" ineligible for

citizenship, whose residence in the city of refuge had become far more tenuous.

Or again, if you consider that Tydings-McDuffie also established the Philippine Commonwealth, the provisional regime meant to prepare a ten-year transition to formal independence (that is, neocolonial rule), you might read Villa's flight from fiction as an intuitive, anticipatory postcolonial critique of the nation-form. The queer lineage of Filipino nationalism may not, in historical terms, be so exceptional, particularly if you don't consider the fate of nationalisms under post–World War II U.S. hegemony to be an aberration. But for that reason it's hard to blame a queer writer for keeping his distance; his aversion might trace the leading edge of a counterliberatory violence. In any case, with the exception of a few brief visits, Villa hung on in New York City until his death in 1997. In his contribution to *The Anchored Angel*, Luis Cabalquinto ponders the elderly Villa's reluctance to accept offers to arrange a comfortable return to the Philippines (Tabios 190); apparently, Villa never took U.S. citizenship. But that volume also reprints a 1953 contribution to a Philippine journal, titled „A Composition,„, which asserts, "My country is the Country of Doveglion"—another of his literary personae, merging the symbols of dove, eagle, and lion. The text's hyperindividualism and aesthetic disavowal of politics should be read in relation to all that was cast out from normative conceptions of the political under the conditions of its writing. "Countries," it proposes, "should learn to move" (Tabios 135).

Three: His Joke, Her Laughter

After the first decade of the century, the presence of the Philippines in the U.S. metropolitan media and the black popular imagination diminished, as the grander hopes excited by conquest, whether for U.S. power or black advancement, were tempered. Retrospectively, the differences in status established in the territories subjected to military conflict in the 1890s can be read as a formal experimentation with imperial structures of political and economic control. Here, the model of overseas territorial colonialism already looked outdated, and a shift toward neocolonialism was being engineered, as evidenced by the Tydings-McDuffie Act. Meanwhile, the chance migration represented was being taken up by many millions of black Southerners, not in the colony but in the rapidly expanding communities of the North, Midwest, and West. Shifting conceptions of gender and sexuality, taken as evidence of a globalizing modernity, began to fracture normalizing ideologies of Negro uplift, rendering their once-modernizing ideals decidedly behind the times.

Nonetheless, questions continued to surface in the press about the status, influence, and destiny of the Philippines and about the opportunities and obstacles faced by Filipino migrants. In black press coverage, a specifically racialized curiosity was taken for granted, whether that fueled a greater sympathy for Filipinos or the opposite. From governmental and global affairs, to civil rights, to popular entertainment and sports (especially boxing), the Philippines and Filipinos were an unremarkable presence in the black "current events" landscape through at least the 1950s, and the traces of black transpacific soldiering remained a familiar landmark in the cultural memory of African American communities.

In this section, I examine the circulation of these traces through emerging forms of black modernist popular culture in the 1920s and 1930s, attending to the dispersal of the history of black soldiering as its status shifted from that of a primary event, consequential in itself, to a secondary figure whose significance was oblique and referential. Put simply, if the Philippines had once appeared as the frontier of an advancing modernity, for U.S. imperial ambitions and ambitious African Americans, during the interwar period it seemed far more provincial. What uses might a modernist, modernizing culture have for a visit to these boondocks? Below, I turn to Robert Johnson's famous 1936 blues recording, "I Believe I'll Dust My Broom," and to Eulalie Spence's play *Her*, first staged by W. E. B. Du Bois's Krigwa theater company in 1927— the year their production of her *Fool's Errand* became the first play by an African American woman performed on Broadway. In juxtaposing the song's conclusion in a man's cunning joke to the play's conclusion in a woman's unsettling laughter, I consider how a transpacific *décalage* could be operated to elude, if not critique, the normative demands of uplift.

Both Johnson and Spence pursued models of upward mobility and modern sophistication through the commercial entertainment industry in tension with older pathways to social status, associated with uplift ideology's emphasis on educational attainment and performances of altruistic duty. Ironically, Johnson's premature death in 1938 facilitated his recuperation, decades later, as a primitivist icon of untutored folk genius, but Elijah Wald has persuasively reinterpreted him as a worldly professional, a technically versatile and ambitious modernizer, identified more with Northern recording stars than his older Mississippi Delta mentors, who, had he lived, might have achieved the slick commercial success across multiple popular styles deemed inauthentic by a later Delta blues revival.[24] For Johnson, the path out of a Delta-based itinerant blues circuit to the celebrity pioneered by "classic" or "women's blues" artists like Bessie Smith and Ma Rainey did not pass through genteel uplift.

By contrast, the Nevis-born, Brooklyn-raised Spence seems a paragon of Talented-Tenth virtue. The eldest daughter of a large immigrant family, she held an eminently respectable job as a schoolteacher for forty years, appeared in the society columns of the *New York Amsterdam News* and the *Pittsburgh Courier*, and earned a bachelor's degree from NYU and a master's from Columbia's Teachers College years after her successes as a playwright. Nonetheless, as in her rocky relationship with Du Bois's Krigwa group, Spence positioned herself across a generational divide separating the earnest uplift agenda of an older black elite from the modern sophistication of a younger group of artists who regularly took pleasure in scandalizing their elders. Less a dreamy aesthete or flamboyant bohemian than a technically minded professional like Johnson, Spence described her theatrical writings, usually short and satirical, as, above all, popular entertainment.

Thus, I approach Johnson's song and Spence's play as works of popular culture, folk in content but self-consciously modernist in form, that activate the historical memory of black participation in imperial warfare while detaching it from its normative conscriptions in previous varieties of uplift ideology. In the song and the play, the ambivalent memory of black soldiering in the Philippines is inscribed in a figure of traditional feminine sexual virtue, a nostalgic ideal threatened under the morally degraded conditions of modernity. This "good girl" repeats a central feature of the earlier phase of black transpacific romance narrative: traditional feminine virtue within heterosexual coupling is the figurative ground on which diaspora is domesticated. Further, she provides a specific historical referent and geographic focus to a diasporic nostalgia whose doubled sense of loss seems to sentence it to aimless, endless rambling. Yet by placing this feminine figure in inherently un-stable rhetorical forms—a bawdy joke, a ghost story—these texts subject nostalgic desire to a type of restless, exotic movement I've been calling, after Nathaniel Mackey, centrifugal. This movement opens up a worldly domain of radical, transimperial politics, even as its concentration on pleasure, sexuality, and gender does not register as political in that do-main. Rather than performing civilized gender norms to secure racial community across the divisions of class and multiple migrations, these texts finger the jagged grain of the black man's and the black woman's burden, recalling the shameful aspects of sexual relations and the un-acknowledged debts incurred by uplift.

the boondocks of the Mississippi Delta

The history of black music is a story of migration, as the old blues clas-sic, "Sweet Home Chicago," illustrates, but the greater part of that story remains to be told. First recorded in a San Antonio hotel room in 1936 by the Delta-based Robert Johnson, the song went on to become a standby of the postwar Chicago blues scene and an unavoidable cliché of subsequent blues revivals. Its cachet derives in part from its invocation of not just a place, but a narrative of the Great Migration as blues origin myth, wherein the music clambers up from the rural South to make its way up the Mississippi to be modernized and electrified in Chicago. This same narrative has shaped the posthumous career of Johnson, who has been rediscovered on several occasions as an icon of the "authentic" Delta style and is known less these days for his technical virtuosity than for the legend that he acquired it one midnight by selling his soul to the Devil at the crossroads.

But Johnson's recording of "Sweet Home Chicago" contains a minor geographical curiosity. His chorus invites its addressee to go *Back to the land of California / To my sweet home, Chicago*. This apparent inconsis-tency has unsettled a number of his devotees, anxious to disavow the possibility he didn't know his geography—one theory even proposed he had a distant relative in an obscure "Port Chicago" in California (qtd. in Scruggs 1). Such anxiety reveals not only the primitivism underly-ing Johnson's iconization, but also the developmentalist structure of a broader narrative of the Great Migration. Patterned after dominant national myths of European immigration, it turns on the distinction between a premodern past, a space of innocence and ignorance, cultural tradition and political unfreedom, here located in the rural South, and a modern present of knowledge and corruption, cultural dissolution and economic opportunity, located in the urban North. Within its logic, Johnson's ignorance of basic geographical details of the world beyond the Delta seems *less* improbable than his explicit claim to a sophisticated knowledge of unfamiliar places and a modern, worldly notion of belonging—grounded in movement, but expressed from the perspective of the South.

Placed in the South, Johnson's lyrics are simple enough to read, and remind you that the history of black urban migration was never inevitable. From this vantage, Chicago and California are as interchangeable as the Philippines and Cuba had been for advocates of colonial emigration a few decades earlier. Wald dispenses with this matter neatly enough by suggesting that you "simply imagine a gentle 'or' between the relevant phrases" (303n6), though this would undo the poetic work of Johnson's paratactic elision of the "or," which stresses the facility of the singer's substitution of locales. The very manifestation of cosmopolitan glamour—what Zora Neale Hurston's Tea Cake calls "an up-to-date man"—he is equally at home anywhere in the world you might want to go. Like the narrator of Fortune's Philippine travelogue, the singer appears as the sophisticated envoy of opportunity and adventure, and this exotic or outbound movement becomes, in his company or by his grace, a movement *back*, a return.

But another geographical oddity, in the track just preceding "Sweet Home Chicago" in that 1936 session, has largely gone unremarked. "I Believe I'll Dust My Broom" also became a staple of Chicago-based blues artists after Johnson's death, recorded most notably by Elmore James. The title's idiomatic phrase refers to the singer's intention to take leave from an unfaithful lover and go *back home* where she cannot mistreat him. This is not a song about a Great Migration to the North: migration within the South has already created a geographical split between modern, degraded sexual morality and a nostalgic image of traditional community. Meanwhile, the singer imagines another female figure, the ironic inversion of the first—his *good girl*. Initially, he seeks her in two Delta locations, West Helena and East Monroe, sometime bases of operation for Johnson himself, but in the last verse, his pursuit extends to what seem like the ends of the earth—China, the Philippines, and Ethiopia.

The standard transcription of the lyrics, credited to Stephen C. LaVere in the booklet to the 1990 issue of Johnson's complete recordings, implies that these locations are meaningless. It reads, *I'm 'on' call up Chiney / see is my good girl over there / I'm gon' call up China / see is my good girl over there / 'f I can't find her on Phillipine's Island / she must be in Ethiopia somewhere*, and a footnote explains, " 'Chiney' and 'Phillipine's Island' are not typographical errors, but simply approximations of how Johnson pronounced those place names" (25). Although there is an audible difference between his pronunciations of "China" in these two instances, the booklet does not orthographically mark similar shifts in the pronunciation of "California" in its transcription of "Sweet Home Chicago." Furthermore, while the insertion of an apostrophe in *Phillipine's*, for which there can be no definitive aural evidence, may be justifiable as a habit of black vernacular speech,[25] the repeated inclusion of an extra "l" and omission of a "p" presumably *is* a typographical error. In any case, the presumption that these places are insignificant actually betrays the ignorance of subsequent critics, contrasted with the historical and geopolitical knowledge circulating in Johnson's Delta milieu.[26]

Certainly, these locales may signify spatial and temporal distancing—the exotic fantasy of Orientalism, the transhistorical mythology of Ethiopianism—but they are also bound by a logic *within* historical time, in which the memory of black transpacific soldiering is linked to geopolitical events that black publics followed with great interest. These included the 1934 Tydings-McDuffie Act, culminating years of debates over independence and labor migration regularly reported in the black press, and more notably, the 1935 Italian invasion of Ethiopia. One subplot of the latter's extensive coverage was the disappointed hope for Japanese intervention.[27] As Ernest Allen has shown, black organizing on behalf of Ethiopia intersected with a preexisting, shadowy movement of pro-Japanese radical groups whose leadership included blacks and Asians, operating from the Eastern Seaboard through the Midwest to the Mississippi Delta, overlapping the circuits of itinerant Southern-based musicians like Johnson. One 1933 event at a St. Louis church, moderated by a newspaper editor, featured three speakers from the Pacific Movement of the Eastern World: "George Cruz" on the Philippines, "Moy Wong" on China, and, addressing "The Struggle of the Darker Races of the World," one "Dr. Ashima Takis" of Japan, who may have been a Filipino migrant named Policarpio Manansala.[28] The inclusion of China registers on-going debates over Japanese imperialism among African Americans, including Langston Hughes and W. E. B. Du Bois, who had printed an editorial on Japan and China in *The Crisis* that January, and would publish another on Japan and Ethiopia in December (Mullen and Watson 74–75). In fact, while Johnson was recording his song three years later in Texas, Du Bois was surveying conditions firsthand in Japanese-controlled Manchuria.

In order to read Johnson's knowing exposition of moral degradation as a blues critique of modernity in the South, of the social conditions of racial and economic restructuring viewed from West Helena, Arkansas, and East Monroe, Mississippi, you must recognize that these conditions may be lived most intensely in experiences of sexuality and romantic desire. The vision of organic community embodied in the nostalgic figure of the good girl, his object of desire, activates a politics of return; but this figure of return itself travels, through the media of letter writing and telecommunications, to the most exotic reaches of a modern world. Not to its glamorous capitals, Paris or London, say, but to its boondocks—a word derived from the Tagalog *bundok*, or "mountain," entering English during the Philippine war with a hidden meaning, for the boondocks were also the site of fugitivity and resistance. Thus the geographical substitution in the verse's repetition, leaping from the Delta to Asia and Africa, may be read as opening up, in an offhand, almost careless way, a political cartography connecting Southern black itinerancy to the most far-flung circuits of black internationalism. This is hardly to imply that the song endorses the agendas of these pro-Japanese groups, which I do not assess here, and which were hardly advanced by the dashed prospects of a Japanese-Ethiopian alliance. Nor would I impute any conscious political program to Johnson, his audiences, or the lyrics themselves. My point is simply that all three shared a milieu in which the historical and geopolitical knowledge to critically connect African and Asian locations was readily available.

Given the collective nature of blues authorship, it is not even clear that the lyrics are original to Johnson. Wald's meticulous effort to reconstruct the song's antecedents yields a suggestive comparison, however. He proposes James "Kokomo" Arnold as the major influence, in numerous songs recorded at this session, including "Sweet Home Chicago," which reworks Arnold's hit, "Old Original Kokomo Blues." Johnson's lyrics for "Dust My Broom" parallel Arnold's recordings of "Sagefield Woman Blues" and "Sissy Man Blues," the latter of which includes the reference to China.[29] Here, China may be read as merely a hyperbolic figure for distance, a vernacular-Orientalist "elsewhere," the other side of the world you might reach if you keep digging. The only twist, in a gesture typical to popular musics in this period, is the reference to that wonder of modern technology, telephone service: *I'm gonna ring up China, see if I can find my good gal over there.*[30] But the next line refers not to geopolitics, but to the religious source of traditional morality: *Since the good book tells me that I got a good gal in the world somewhere.*

Unlike Johnson's *good girl*, this reference is satirical. Arnold's song is not a romantic lament but a comic celebration of ubiquitous sexual immorality.[31] The most famous verse implores, *Lord, if you can't send me a woman, please send me a sissy man* (135). Deliberately scandalizing religiously grounded norms of sexual behavior, the singer is not diminishing his manhood but aggrandizing his sexual voracity, in his brazen desire for a sissy man if no good gal is available. This is hardly an identification with either subordinated position, no matter that his tone warrants the reasonable suspicion that he might prefer the former even if the latter were actually available.

If Johnson's recording revises Arnold's, then you may take his Afro-Asian good girl as a substitute for the heaven-sent sissy man, and his evocation of tragic romanticism as a substitute for Arnold's exuberantly shameless sexuality. In this reading, Johnson repeats the transpacific gesture of an earlier uplift ideology, journeying to distant racialized lands to recuperate a heteronormativity degraded in the modern metropole, a motion pivoting on the slight discrepancy between convergent figures of a sexualized primitive. Yet, while the persona of a wounded romantic was a feature of Johnson's repertoire, the larger cultural context he operated within disdained and scandalized the conventions of middle-class black respectability. His song may therefore be read as a parody of model minority manhood's transpacific tour, though it could just as easily read as a parody of radical black internationalism.

In linking the Delta to the Philippines and Ethiopia, Johnson utilizes the same ambivalent rhetorical technique via which Fortune linked the primitive Filipino to the Negro masses: he makes a joke. The joke is simultaneously a mock-tragic satire of the impossible search for a faithful lover and a mock-heroic celebration of romantic determination. The exaggeration of desire figures the extravagance of the longing for return, imagined as heterosexual (re)union, while the impossibility of fulfillment excites continued movement. If this joke opens up a political domain, it cannot be taken seriously there, for to do so would require fixing its meaning—to interpret it as merely saying, for example, that Ethiopian women are more virtuous than African American women, or that a black man in the Philippines must have lost his mind. A more sensitive reading would situate the joke in the tradition of playful sexual braggadocio common to both men's and women's blues. The joke satirizes the singer's masculine romantic prowess, playing him for a fool, while simultaneously protecting and aggrandizing it.

This is a canny performance of a damaged masculinity, calling out for redemption in the form of female desire. As in Arnold's recording, the singer's assertion of manhood's patriarchal prerogatives eludes or exceeds their normative function. He is a seducer, a sweet-talker, whose professions of love are difficult to resist, even if you know they cannot be trusted; he is an alluring stranger, inviting his listeners to imagine themselves in the role of the good girl. But she will prove to be elsewhere, and his escape is already planned.

a good girl leaves home

Placed within the history of black transpacific cultural representation, Johnson's joke may be read as a formal intervention, worrying the gendered contradictions that early repetitions of the romance plot sought to contain. On these terms, despite predating Johnson's recording by almost a decade, Spence's play suggests a kind of feminist response to his joke. *Her* is about a black veteran, John Kinney, who found his *good girl* in the Philippines, and about what happened after he took her home to Harlem. As in the song, a certain historical memory seems to be taken for granted: the title character is casually identified as "one of these here Philippine gals," whom Kinney met while "soljerin' in them parts." Her name is never revealed, but you can recognize the nostalgic feminine ideal: "pretty's a picture, with her big, black eyes an' a head uv hair lak we doan never see no more" (139).[32] Her story is recounted by Martha, a stock figure of folk matriarchy, a tenant and property manager of one of Kinney's tenements who lives with her invalid husband Pete in the rooms where the play is set. Kinney's bride never appears onstage, not because she is dead, but because she'd sworn beyond death never to leave the apartment where she killed herself. The plot turns on Kinney's decision to ignore Martha's warnings that her ghost still haunts the upstairs rooms, and to rent them to an unsuspecting young couple, Alice and Sam Smith.

As the play opens, Martha worries over Kinney's plans, while Pete expresses doubts concerning the ghost's existence. "It ain't natural—this talk 'bout Her," he mutters, to which Martha replies, " 'Course it ain't natural, but it's *real*" (134). Pete's skepticism seems to be a mere formality in the performance of their marriage, where his inevitable deference to his wife is played for laughs. In a minor bit of business, his lament for not providing for the household after becoming disabled is sharply put down by Martha, to which he replies, "*proudly*," as the directions have it, "That ain't no woman lak yuh, Martha, nowhar" (133). She dispatches his doubts about the ghost with the same firmness: "Yuh kin call it conscience, or yuh kin call it HER! 'Tis one and the same thing, Ah reckon" (134).

If the war bride's ghost manifests a repressed shame in the historical memory of black imperial soldiering, she also signifies other unacknowledged debts of uplift. As Martha explains, Kinney appropriated his wife's money, promising to buy her a "pretty house," and instead invested in real estate (139). This stolen capital provides the basis for his class position above the other characters, a distinction emphasized in his dialogue, which lacks markers of vernacular speech, and his skin tone—a haunted, haggard "*yellow*" (134) contrasted with "*black*" Martha (132), "*brown*" Alice, and her "*somewhat browner*" Sam (136). Kinney's upward mobility as businessman and landlord requires, furthermore, the violent imposition of a bourgeois patriarchal order, in which a wife, constructed in the ideal image of traditional virtue, must be protected from modernity's degradations by confinement within domestic space. She was like "a little wild bird, caught an' put in a cage in a dark room,"

Martha explains, "lonesome an' scared uv New York"—adding darkly, "scared too, uv that husban' uv hers." Overwhelmed by homesickness but unable to return to her homeland, she fixes on Kinney's idle promise of a few rooms of her own. When this promise too is broken, she resolves to reclaim her property, to occupy it permanently—an oath no one takes seriously until her body is discovered the next day, "hangin' between the parlor an' the bedroom" (139).

Between the parlor and the bedroom is the scope of her confinement, her intimate bondage, the domestic space of conjugal bliss promised by the normative migratory trajectories of uplift. But if her dream of a *sweet home* turned nightmarish, its reversal into a nostalgic fantasy of return, *back home*, was impossible. She turns, instead, to its horrible parodic substitute, the tenement apartment she appropriates as her own forever, literally binding her body to its structure to secure her claim beyond death. Yet at the end of the play, she reappears, not only thwarting her husband's plan to rent the rooms, but apparently reclaiming him, along with the ability to leave the home. As Martha reports in the play's final lines, "Pete! Pete! yuh wanted a sign! Ah jes seen John Kinney walkin' down the stairs with *Her*! She had him by the hand an' she was laughin!" (140).

The play closes with a woman's laughter. But this is not actually heard, only reported secondhand, by Martha; what is heard, in its place, is a different aural expression, in excess of language, emanating from a woman's body—from Alice, whose *"piercing scream rings through the room"* as the curtain falls (140). As a ghost story, the play shares the unstable, duplicitous formal structure of a joke. The audience is invited to experience terror, and to take pleasure in its release. The social anxieties of a black theater audience in 1927 New York, generated by upward mobility and communal experiences of migration—whether from the rural South or, like the playwright, the Caribbean—are condensed in the ghost, whose exotic origins intensify them by defamiliarizing them, projecting them onto a horrible, alien form. But the play's resolution, if it works, must be unstable, double-edged, containing these anxieties even as it teases and provokes them, leaving them to linger unsettlingly open.

While the performances of Spence's works were the highlight of the Krigwa theater group's brief existence, the personal and aesthetic differences on which it foundered were manifested most dramatically between the young schoolteacher and Du Bois. To appreciate what was at stake in this conflict, and to clarify Spence's contribution to the ongoing literary renaissance, I pause to consider a fascinating letter sent to Du Bois in November 1927 from a *Crisis* subscriber in Manila, J. W. Calloway. This is indeed the same Sergeant Major John W. Calloway who'd been railroaded from the colony decades earlier. In fact, Calloway was deported twice, enduring repeated imprisonment, but was eventually reunited with his Filipina wife and daughter, and raised a large family until his death in 1934 as a respected figure in Manila.[33]

The letter itself is a fascinating piece of transpacific theater criticism, offered from a distance of "10 000 miles" and "more than a quarter century from America," which engages debates over black representation and performance currently raging in the salons and publications of what one can hardly keep calling the *Harlem* Renaissance (Calloway 1). Calloway reports that the Negro is in vogue not only in Harlem but across the world's stages, "from Tokyo to Peking and Harbin to Batavia; from London, Paris, and Madrid to Hong-Kong and Manila": "Even Russian artists in the Orient use his mode rather than their own" (1). While he takes pride in this success, he calls for art to displace the falsifying trends of popular entertainment. His views mostly follow an older generation's concerns with respectability, decrying "the surfeit of sordid city alley life which the silly jazz ditties of the present pour out to the world as a reflection of the Negro self" (2), though there are traces of Filipino aesthetic sensibilities—for example, he asserts, "a people so gifted in bringing to one *joy* must also possess the gift to make one *cry*" (2).[34]

Thus Calloway comes to the purpose of his letter, a detailed and ambitious proposal for Du Bois to write a serious opera treating all of African American history. Set in three acts, it would begin by contrasting "the humble romances of the young slaves" (2) with the coercive relationships between masters and enslaved women, to illuminate "the present day psychology of American race relations, largely influenced by sex" (3). Act 2 would cover the period from Reconstruction to Booker T. Washington, showing "the thorny path the black man in the western world has trod to civilization" (3). The final act would come up to the present, dramatizing "the hope . . . for full recognition as Men by all the world instead of a kind of JOKE which is tolerated because of his ability to please by surprise and sooth[e] by r[h]ythm," grounded in "the deep, touching, soul scourging music of the Negro. Even some of our light music could be used—but dirty, suggestive alley ditties, never!" (3).

Calloway's attempt to pass the burden of uplifting representation onto Du Bois may seem grandiose and impractical, though Du Bois was never one to be cowed by grand ambition. Presumably, he was too busy, already deeply engaged in theorizing the relations between politics and aesthetics. In 1926, he'd famously declared, "All Art is propaganda and ever must be" (*Writings* 1000), and in 1927, he was finishing the massive novel *Dark Princess*. Meanwhile, he was struggling to guide the Krigwa group, which would soon collapse, just after its greatest successes, when he abruptly withdrew from it. He was getting it from both sides of the debate, perhaps, for if there was an aesthetic principle on which the group foundered, it was the refusal by Spence and her supporters to accept the version of the burden Du Bois tried to pass on to them.

In the year following Krigwa's production of *Her*, at the pinnacle of her career as a dramatist, Spence published an article in *Opportunity* that came out boldly against the aesthetic politics advocated by Du Bois. "A Criticism of the Negro Drama, As It Relates to the Negro Dramatist and Artist" opens by contrasting the recognition achieved by black stage performers to the obscurity of "the Negro dramatist," and estimates that dramatic writing in the United States is "from twenty to thirty years behind" prose fiction in its freedom of content, alluding to a recent example that famously made Du Bois feel in want of a bath: "There is almost no subject to-day that cannot be discussed with the most revolting detail between the covers of a book. If there are any who doubt this, let them read *Home to Harlem* by Claude McKay. Not so with our drama." Happy to leave McKay's shameless excesses to the page, she wants instead to emphasize the formal advances of modern drama—"a new technique, new ways and means, a new genius of mechanism and a new direction." Triangulating McKay and Du Bois, she advocates a Negro modernist movement emphasizing technique and sober professionalism over a hazy romanticism wallowing in obscenity or a moralizing criticism that privileges politics over craft.

Given such attitudes, she complains, "almost everyone thinks he can write a play," thoughtlessly dismissing the fundamentals of generic form, and leading aspiring playwrights with "no eye for the box-office" astray: "May I advise those earnest few—those seekers after light—white

lights—to avoid the drama of propaganda if they would not meet with
certain disaster? Many a serious aspirant for dramatic honors has fallen
by the wayside because he would insist on his lynchings or his rape. The
white man is cold and unresponsive to this subject and the Negro, himself, is hurt and humiliated by it. We go to the theatre for entertainment,
not to have old fires and hates rekindled." Her prescriptions are not
limiting, she insists. The Negro dramatist, grounded in modern technique, may "portray the life of his people," all "their foibles," "sorrows,"
"ambition and defeats," but a prudent appreciation for what "white and
colored" audiences want requires avoiding "the old subjects." She concludes, with a flourish: "A little more laughter, if you please, and fewer
spirituals!"

What may seem a conservative rejection of politically committed art,
this caricature of the playwright clinging to "*his* lynchings or *his* rape,"
takes on a different cast if you can hear, in Spence's concluding request
for "a little more laughter," the absent sound of the war bride's unsettling
triumph.[35] Drawing on the insights of black feminist cultural history,
you may recognize Spence's dismissal of politics as a defiant response to
the dismissal from the realm of the political of her interest in women's
freedom from intimate bondage. Spence's modernist aesthetic is deeply
antisentimental, unromantic, and satirical—satire is her preferred
mode—but in this play the figure of the war bride, as a linked but discrepant nonwhite racial form, allows her to explore the desire for return
engendered by diaspora, a desire bound up in nostalgic, sentimental,
romantic, patriarchal fantasy, in order to pursue its centrifugal travels.

The key, if you can learn how to read it, is the shift from the laughter
of the Filipina's triumph, which goes unrepresented, to the sound that
is heard, the black woman's scream. This is Spence's artful translation,
her resounding of the red ray, an expression that turns on difference
rather than identity—the racial difference between the war bride and
the prospective tenant, and the rhetorical instability animating the joke
and the ghost story. It may be possible to collapse this instability into a
reading that says the message is that black men shouldn't marry Asian
women, or that a woman who leaves her proper place becomes monstrous. But this sound calls out for other readings, other readers. Emerging within the gendered constraints of an apparently self-determining
mode of Negro racial uplift, it exposes the sexualized violence inscribed

within it, the violence it has studied and internalized and upon which its racial project depends. This re-sounding severs an idealized figure of traditional feminine virtue from its function as a fantasy of modernizing patriarchy, mobilizing a patriarchal fear of the feminine to serve as a warning against women's confinement. This is not yet a unifying identity of sisterhood, not even in the name of women of color; this is still a long way from any political program, feminist or antiracist or antiimperialist, that you might endorse. Whatever it might become, the play surely offers no guarantee.

Not yet, perhaps, no promises. For now, there is only this: one woman, Filipina, dead, walks away from the space of her bondage. Another woman, African American, still living, will not be installed in her place.

Four: Love Notes (Reprise)

In 1944, with African American soldiers again participating in imperial warfare across the Pacific, a young woman in Chicago gathered a few of their letters and fashioned them into a sequence of sonnets, published the following year in her collection, *A Street in Bronzeville*. The dedication to Gwendolyn Brooks's "Gay Chaps at the Bar" identifies it as a token of their historical memory, a "souvenir for Staff Sergeant Raymond Brooks"—her brother—"and every other soldier" (64).[36] The epigraph to the opening poem, also titled "gay chaps at the bar," credits the phrase to "Lt. William Couch in the South Pacific": "and guys I knew in the States, young officers, return from the front crying and trembling. Gay chaps at the bar in Los Angeles, Chicago, New York" (64).

William Couch was also a poet of some note. In George Kent's biography of Brooks, he's a dashing figure, much admired by the women in prewar Chicago's young black literati, and the model for two characters she satirizes in *Maud Martha*: a "first beau" whose stylish ways the protagonist both sees through and succumbs to, and a "second beau" whose resentful desire for class status manifests as intellectual snobbery.[37] Susan Schweik adds that Brooks's sonnet first appeared in *Negro Story*, which had recently published Couch's "To a Soldier" (123). Readers familiar with that poem might have recalled its soldier-narrator stoically declaring that "we shall not shed tears / home from the bar in silence—"

(Couch). Countering his public performance of black manhood, Brooks exposes Couch's own words from a private letter, signifying ferociously on his production of masculine authority through linguistic prowess. Her sonnet, narrated in the soldiers' collective voice, begins by celebrating the potency and allure of their arts of expression: "We knew how to order," they assert, "knew beautifully how to give to women / The summer spread, the tropics, of our love." But all this talk proves useless in those other tropics, where the terrors of battle find them without a "brass fortissimo" (64). It is a devastating lesson, in art and love and the arts of love, that Brooks delivers to her friend and fellow poet, though not without mercy, for naming the shame hidden by his performance of manhood might allow him release.

As the sequence continues, Brooks pushes further into the sorrows behind those tears. In the fifth and sixth sonnets, "piano after war" (68) and "mentors" (69), she dramatizes the impossibility of return for a veteran, stateside with his beloved, who knows his "best allegiances are to the dead" (69). While this alternative collectivity, the fraternity of the dead, is constructed through the soldiers' specifically racialized experience, it is nonetheless expansive, as implied by the seventh sonnet, "the white troops had their orders but the Negroes looked like men" (70). In a gruesome allusion to the careless sorting of dismembered corpses, the sonnet suggests that the soldiers neglect or even disregard racial markers in the otherworldly South Pacific "weather": "Who really gave two figs?" (70).

The linked titles of sonnets ten and eleven repeat the generic motif of black transpacific writing: "love note / I: surely" (73) and "love note / II: flags" (74). More reverie than letter, they are addressed in the second person by the soldier in theater to his good girl back home. The first lingers over the rhetorical ambiguity, or structural ambivalence, of the subtitle—to say *surely* is to betray your lack of assurance, knowing the guarantee you make or request may fail—but closes with exhaustion, "I doubt all. You. Or a violet" (73). Love's purple flower is displaced, in the next subtitle, by a figure of politics, *flags*, evoking the tumultuous romance of black patriotism, but the poem's irony resignifies it from noun to verb. His agonies of doubt dissolve into erotic fantasy, whose release allows him to recall that her love's allure consisted in being "changeful"

(74). If the sonnets' primary concern is the black male soldier's dislocation and the impossible longing for return it engenders, these love notes
consider how desire fractures and exceeds any reunion.

In these poems, the debts of black manhood in imperial warfare return, threatening to sever the intimate and communal bonds the soldier
must traverse to come home, leaving him stranded, in the Pacific or the
metropole. Yet Brooks refuses the stock image of heterosexual (re)union,
the veteran's return to his loyal mother or lover or nation, to practice or
enact diasporic reassembly differently, extending a tender and trenchant
lesson in love, from a sister to a brother, a disillusioned admirer to a first
beau, a poet to a poet, friend to friend. If there is love here, it is a kind
of grace in the art of writing, in the act of rewriting, by which the poet
takes up, resounds, offers her arts of expression to the soldiers' letters.
For finally it is love that holds diaspora together, love that blasts it apart,
love that may sustain it as an intangible grace, the echo of a divine note
borne by the poet's art.

Two other sonnets, the eighth and ninth, contemplate the divine, addressed directly as "Thee," aligning the loss of religious faith with that
in a nation or lover. If divine intervention never arrives, the latter poem
concludes, faith must be abandoned, leaving mortals to whatever "sov-
ereignty" (72) they may claim on earth, where love cannot bridge the
living and the dead. "Expression," the poet's dream, and the connection
it promises, of a "touch or look or word" tangible as the "chew" of "an
apple," cannot rescue or restore the beloved, an earlier sonnet in a maternal voice admits (67), even as this dream is pursued in the act of reading.
This must be why the only soldiers given voice in the sequence are the
survivors, why only secondhand, through them, do you hear of the cry
of the dead. Like the laughter of Spence's war bride, that cry is never
fully present in the text. The sonnets only make it possible, perhaps, for
readers to try and strain to learn to hear this call. Could these readers
or potential readers, strangers who might find these notes long after the
original correspondents have passed, yet be bound together, constituted
as a community, in responding to and taking responsibility for the call
of the dead across the Pacific?

Such a dream is too extravagant to be borne by poetry alone. History tells you so: the dead have not been saved, and all the rituals by
which a proud nation commemorates their sacrifice may only repeat

it, training citizens to perceive unending violence as the liberating arm of justice. And the poet herself tells you this, in the final sonnet, which anticipates the terrifying aftermath of war: not defeat, but victory. Narrated in their collective voice, the soldiers of "the progress" compulsively repeat the patriotic rituals of military life, until they remember that what they are celebrating is the death of soldiers like them, other members of that fraternity imperial warfare has left them to gather indiscriminately into boxes in the godforsaken seas. It is not the call of the dead, nor the sound of a love note, that the sonnet sequence ends upon, but only war's endless return: "Listen, listen. The step / Of iron feet again. And again   wild" (75).

But didn't they win that good war? Didn't they answer the call of uplift, of normalization and nationalization, earning through manly and dutiful sacrifice the privileges of citizenship in a free nation, a nation reconstituted in accordance with its founding principles? Double victory would take some time to resolve itself, granted, like a drunkard's blurred vision, but surely they have bequeathed a freedom to their children and their children's children, down through the generations? Why cry, why tremble? Didn't they help liberate the Philippines, to receive its formal independence and stand on its own within the ever-expanding circle of free nations? Weren't these freedoms, worth the price?

If you want more than this, the poem tells you, you are left in the *deepening hollow* on the inside of victory, where the rhythm of *iron feet* portends the death of all those other worlds imagined by the failures of uplift. And if this is not despair, if your desire leads you onward to further inquiry, you might begin by seeking a lesson or two from those gay chaps living that lush life at the bar. Is it possible to constitute alternative forms of social life in gathering before the performances of nostalgia, failed romance, the loss of a love that you knew when you dreamed it was asking too much from this world? Go anywhere the music is and see.

4.

What Comes after a Chance

Races and cultures die—it has always been so—but civilization lives on.
—Robert Park, "Our Racial Frontier in the Pacific"

Because something is after them, Black Herman adds.
But what is after them?
They are after themselves. They call it destiny. Progress.
We call it Haints.
—Ishmael Reed, *Mumbo Jumbo*

One: Occasion

Can you think of every occasion as a kind of falling, a fall that is merely fortuitous and, at the same time, that is fortuity itself? How might you prepare for such unpredictability? Is it possible to position yourself in anticipation of the unforeseeable[1]—would you term this an orientation or a disorientation, or both, or neither? And if you could maintain such a sensibility, what would happen to your sense of time?

My questions take off from Brent Edwards's musings on the word "occasion" in his essay "Louis Armstrong and the Syntax of Scat." Recalling its Latin etymology, he translates "occasion" as a "falling toward" or, following the *OED*, a "falling together or juncture of circumstances favourable or suitable to an end or purpose" (620). The occasion that concerns Edwards is a well-worn tale about the origin of scat singing,[2] and specifically its "seeming need to narrate scat as a fall" (620): once upon a time, in the middle of recording a forgettable number called "The Heebie Jeebies Dance," Louis Armstrong dropped his lyric sheet to the floor. Rather than interrupting the tune, he blithely improvised a combination of seemingly nonsensical words and sounds. This anecdote occasions a remarkable series of insights in Edwards's essay, but for now,

I am concerned only with his description of the "occasion" as a kind of fortuitous falling, a chance or ghost of a chance, on which everything rides. To be more precise, Edwards's occasion is a *pair* of falls, which fall together: "the lyric sheet drifts down to the floor," while the "new sound" is "itself falling away from the word" (620).

This chapter is something of a meditation on this notion of "occasion," and on its etymological associations with a few other words deriving from the Latin *cadere*, "to fall": "occident," "cadence," and "chance." More specifically, it stakes its chances on the occasion of some curious formal parallels between a pair of novels, Nella Larsen's *Passing* and Toshio Mori's *The Brothers Murata*, including aspects of narrative voice, character, pacing, and plot—as well as climactic scenes involving a fatal fall from a window. These parallels seem purely coincidental, for they appear to be historically ungrounded: What might one novel written by a black woman in 1920s Harlem and another by a Japanese American man in a World War II concentration camp possibly have to do with each other?

In asking this question, I open an inquiry, continued in Chapter 5, into the circuits of twentieth-century black and Japanese American migrations, as they were produced by and responded to conditions of warfare, economic restructuring, and racialization, within a horizon of global imperial competition. These circuits have come to be recognized, for or against U.S. national history, as organized by the founding events of urbanization ("the Great Migration") and mass incarceration ("the Internment"), which in turn have organized the separate historical narratives of each group. In comparing these novels, then, I am asking after the relations, intersections, or correspondences between two apparently discrete histories: What might these two circuits of migration possibly have to do with each other?

Passing tells the story of Irene, wife of the Harlem physician Brian Redfield and mother of his two young sons, whose cosmopolitan tastes, refined etiquette, charitable activities, and light skin mark her seemingly secure position in a 1920s Negro elite—until she encounters a childhood friend, Clare Kendry, who is passing as white in her marriage to a glibly racist international banker, John Bellew. As Irene becomes the reluctant vehicle for her friend's increasingly risky forays back into Harlem society, she comes to see Clare as a threat that might expose and demolish the hollow constructs of her racialized, classed, gendered identity. *The

Brothers Murata tells the story of Hiro, a young Nisei volunteer for the U.S. Army, and his brother Frank, the influential strategist of a movement of draft resisters in their Topaz, Utah, concentration camp. As the conflict between their factions becomes increasingly violent, Hiro engages in a series of desperate, frustrated attempts to convince his brother to abandon his cause.

As I argue in section two of this chapter, the novels may be read as parallel engagements, at the level of form, with the problem of the color line—not merely as the border between white and nonwhite but as the threshold of a modernity characterized as specifically American and urban. The new black and Asian racial subjects appearing at this threshold embodied the contradictory imperatives of U.S. imperialism. Hybrid products of an apprenticeship in civilization, the New Negro, most famously heralded by Alain Locke, and the Nisei, theorized by Robert E. Park's Chicago School of sociology, were hailed as evidence of U.S. modernity's updating of the imperial mission, whose commitment to self-determination converged with its insistence on establishing and reproducing the racial segregation of social life. Through an occidented narrative schema, which presumed the objectively superior status of Western civilization, these new subjects' potential for political conflict was deferred. Yet if the decline of Europe was foretold by the organic rhythms of world history, the question of its successor remained. For the United States to claim this legacy required a revitalization of decadent Western civilization, in the form of a hybrid modern whiteness engineered through the infusion of a primal, sexualized racial difference. The New Negro and the Nisei thus mirrored another aspect of the civilizing mission: its production of whiteness through the violent incorporation of nonwhiteness.

Read together, the novels present an exercise in formal parallelism, which mimics and subverts the commonsense mode of racial comparison that severs links between histories of racialization, setting diverse racial subjects on separate but parallel tracks of development that can converge only in the liberatory telos of the nation. This mode, central to the successive dominant conceptions of racial justice imposed by U.S. imperialism since World War II, traces its lineage to the liberal pluralisms pioneered by Locke and Park, whose theories thus provide the most readily available comparative reading of these texts. Yet taken together, the novels read this parallelism as a narrative form whose inevitable outcome is not liberation, but tragedy.

But if the novels' engagement with their shared formal problem takes the shape of a tragic narrative, they share another feature in their fleeting references to an alternative nonwhite racial form, whose incorporation in the stylization of embodiment might elude tragedy. These references come into view when the novels' resolute focus on the construction of nationally bounded racial identities is reconsidered within the horizon of imperial competition. My discussion of what I term New Negro Orientalism and Nisei swing thus places these broader cultural phenomena, referenced by the novels, within the context of a "darker races" internationalism, while foregrounding the gendered limitations of the latter's sexual politics. For if black *and* Japanese racial difference, in these texts, is incorporated by an individual body, that body does not stand in for the subject of a mass political movement, let alone for an imperial nation or an uplifted race. Instead, the novels perform a flight from what can be represented, staging the traces of such incorporation as misread or unreadable. In these scenes, the visual and the written are critiqued and augmented by way of the aural and the kinesthetic. They do not supplant "passing," and the ensemble of representational practices that secure racial identification, but rather *swing* it, in something akin to the "structural effect . . . that can be applied . . . to a linguistic medium" that Edwards finds in "scat aesthetics," in order to indicate "something outside the sayable, something seen [or heard, or felt in the rhythm and posture of the body] where it collapses" ("Louis Armstrong" 648–49).

performance and preparation

To set the stage for this reading, it is fitting to begin with a collapse. The occasion—*perversely festive*, by its own lights—is drawn from Wallace Thurman's satirical roman à clef of the Harlem Renaissance, *Infants of the Spring* (1932). In its last pages, Thurman's stand-in, Raymond Taylor, arrives upon the remains of the suicide of his friend Paul Arbian, in a scene taken as exemplary of an enduring historical narrative of that movement's fatal prematurity and its inevitable tragic fall.

Arbian's careful orchestration of the tableau of his death is a characteristically flamboyant juxtaposition of bohemian poverty and outlandish exoticism. In a "dingy" bathroom fragrant with "scented joss-sticks," papered with his "spirit portraits" and carpeted with pages of his unpublished novel, he lies "crumpled" in a bloody bathtub, dressed in "a crimson mandarin robe" and "batik scarf," having "slashed his wrists with a highly ornamented Chinese dirk" (174). Unfortunately, the over-flowing water has left the novel a "sodden mass," obliterating everything but the dedication page and title, "WU SING: THE GEISHA MAN": "Be-neath this inscription, he had drawn a distorted, inky black skyscraper, modeled after Niggeratti Manor, and on which were focused an array of blindingly white beams of light. The foundation of this building was composed of crumbling stone. At first glance it could be ascertained that the skyscraper would soon crumple and fall, leaving the dominat-ing white lights in full possession of the sky" (175). What, if not noth-ing, could you make of this novel's ridiculous title, of its ostentatiously perverse overloading of gendered, sexualized, Orientalist tropes, ampli-fied by the sensory excesses of the tableau, which seems to overshoot all possible signification? Its text, in any case, is unreadable, literally washed away in the flood. You may set it aside, to be arrested by the image: a skyscraper falling, or rather, suspended in the moment before a fall. Made certain in a *first glance*, the collapse is apparent not only from the foundation's weakness or decay, but as a visual aspect of building's power, its aggressive capacity to draw attention to itself, its glory. The play of blinding white light on distorted, inky blackness, in such dra-matic position in the heights of the sky, suggests what the crumbling stone confirms: this is both the apex and the promise of decline.

It must be noted that "Niggeratti Manor," both in Thurman's novel and in all the historical accounts to which it alludes, was never in any strict sense a skyscraper. The building at 267 West 136th Street was merely a boardinghouse, the stage for a wild social scene, whose members in-cluded many of Harlem's most dazzling personalities. Its name, generally attributed to Zora Neale Hurston, signifies a polyvalent extravagance of ambition and disdain, signifying upon the desires and pretensions of both the "new" generation of Negro artists and their more established, respectable sponsors.[3] Their diminished material circumstances made their ambitions stand out in stark contrast; Paul's image makes sense, *at first glance*, because it precisely inverts this logic. On the landscape or skyline of modernist culture, "Niggeratti Manor" imagined itself, in an aspirational self-projection, as a skyscraper. The building, more than any character, is the hero of the novel, which is the story of its dreams and downfall.

What, finally, has happened here? The novel has ended, with the death of a man, an artist, and the disappearance of his words, his novel, and with the image of a skyscraper about to fall. If you read it again, the ending will not change, of course: you will remain suspended between the death and disappearance to which you arrive too late, and the fall that never quite arrives, that is merely a promise, even if its certainty is given in the flash of a vision. It may be anticipated, however, that you would reread the novel, or at least turn back a few pages and retrace the ending.

And so you find that the novel has prepared you for this surprise, commenting in advance on both death and the fall. On the night of Paul's suicide, Raymond has been drinking with his friend Stephen Jorgenson, a Canadian-born "Nordic" who has been called home to Denmark in anticipation of his mother's death. "Dying," Raymond tells him, is "a perversely festive occasion. . . . Let's drink to the day when a person's death will be the cue for a wild gin party rather than a signal for well meant but purely exhibitionistic grief." Is this meant as preparation for Raymond himself, or for the reader, in advance of Paul's death? Or is it merely clever, pointless talk? Stephen suggests the latter, after conceding the end of his migratory, bohemian life: "I will be prevailed upon to stay at home and become a respectable schoolmaster. Now, let's finish that bottle of gin. . . . It's after three and as usual we've been talking for hours and saying nothing." Raymond offers a farewell toast, "to the fall of Niggeratti Manor and all within": like Stephen, the building is about to surrender to a lethal condition of respectability, becoming a dormitory for decent, not-yet-married young women. Then, just as he is on the threshold of sleep, Raymond's phone begins ringing and refuses to stop: "What fool could be calling at this hour of the morning? In the old days it might have been expected, but now Niggeratti Manor was no more. There was nothing left of the old régime except reminiscences and gossip" (172).

But Paul, he is informed, has killed himself.

Unprepared, Raymond's mind lags as he "mechanically" takes down Paul's address. Yet when the journey from Harlem to the Village grants him time to catch up, he disregards the gift and longs for speed. Now the awakening of his consciousness seems itself to emerge from the operation of machines, or their pervasive sonic by-product, the subterranean rhythms emblematic of the modern city, which ventriloquize his thoughts, sustaining them in antiphony:

> The subway ride was long and tedious. Only local trains were in operation, local trains which blundered along slowly, stopping at every station, droning noisily: Paul is dead. Paul is dead.
>
> Had Paul the debonair, Paul the poseur, Paul the irresponsible romanticist, finally faced reality and seen himself and the world as they actually were? Or was this merely another act, the final stanza in his drama of beautiful gestures? . . . Now perhaps he had decided that there was nothing left for him to do except execute self-murder in some bizarre manner. Raymond found himself interested not so much in the fact that Paul was dead as he was in wanting to know how death had been accomplished. The train trundled along clamoring: What did he do? What did he do? (173)

What does it mean—the death of a friend, a fellow artist, an ally? Is it the victory of a way of seeing—seeing self and world as they actually are—over an aesthete's irresponsible visions? Or is it the triumph, defiantly empty, of artifice for artifice's sake? Self-creation, taken to its limit, logically concludes in self-murder: Paul's "self" in this case is nothing but the performance of artifice. So the question is not one of intention and interiority but of action—not *why*, what he hoped to achieve, but *how*.

Yet when Raymond comes upon Paul's tableau, he deduces an intention, an ambition and a plan, which has been betrayed or has betrayed itself—passing judgment, it seems, on all the aspirations of self-imagining whose passing Thurman's novel narrates. *Why*, "What delightful publicity to precede the posthumous publication of his novel, which novel, however, had been rendered illegible when the overflow of water had inundated the floor, and soaked the sheets strewn over its surface. Paul had not foreseen the possible inundation, nor had he taken into consideration the impermanency of penciled transcriptions" (174–75). What emerges here is an enduring narrative of the Renaissance, of its fatal prematurity or narcissistic precocity—this empty *drama of beautiful gestures* lacking in authentic substance, mere *delightful publicity* which, when seen as things actually were, left behind little but *reminiscences and gossip*. Apparently.

But another narrative possibility also emerges in this passage. If there is an ironic discrepancy between the message the artist intended and the message the narrative consciousness receives, where does the second come from? For to read, from the illegible text, a lesson about *the impermanency of penciled transcriptions*, or to see in the illustration, *at first glance*, a forecast of imminent collapse, is to infer an agency immanent in the artist's performance, even if it runs counter to his conscious intentions. He is betrayed by his own poor planning, betraying a truth about himself that he cannot see, as if his performance expresses his possession by an interior yet alien consciousness. The artist's blindness is the condition of his text's prophetic insight, recalling Fred Moten's description of improvisation: "That which is without foresight is nothing other than foresight" (63).

If you flip back even further, to the unnumbered page before the novel begins, you find two epigraphs. The first, from *Hamlet*, provides the title, which refers to the inherent vulnerability of precocity. In David Levering Lewis's confident reading, the "canker" that "galls the infants of the spring" is "race consciousness," the respectable ideal of uplift that was the crux of contention between Thurman's rebellious younger generation of artists and their more decorous sponsors (*When Harlem* 280). Yet the second epigraph, from Maxim Gorky, suggests that the force dooming Thurman's generation, that flaw particular to their precocity, was at once intrinsic and alien—inspiring his affection and intellectual interest:

> The people I am most fond of are those who are not quite achieved, who are not very wise, a little mad, "possessed."
>
> A man slightly possessed is not only more agreeable to me; he is altogether more plausible, more in harmony with the general tune of life, a phenomenon unfathomed yet, and fantastic, which makes it at the same time so confoundedly interesting.

If "possession" is inextricable from a fatal prematurity, it is also a condition of one's merging with the music of one's times, and is to be preferred to the achievement of self-creation.

My presentation of this reading as an opening tableau introduces a number of this chapter's thematic concerns. On one hand, its trope of the skyscraper, representing a rising generation's destiny, is aligned with other accounts of race, culture, and modernity to which Larsen's and Mori's novels respond. Like Locke's more famous proposition of a "New Negro" as the hero of a cultural renaissance, as well as the "Second-Generation Japanese Problem" theorized by liberal sociologists, Thurman's novel imagines a characteristically American, urban modernity as an unprecedented chance. Rising to this opportunity, a new racial/cultural hybrid seeks to enter the historical movement of civilization, via an act of creative self-projection. But this is a risky ambition, a matter of precise timing. An age-old problem of merging the cyclical rhythms of generation with the linear movement of civilization is compounded by the dizzying acceleration of modern life, which leaves behind those who arrive too soon or too late. This is the irreducibly narrative conception of civilization that I term *occidented*, recalling that word's etymological association with the setting sun—positioned, as in Arbian's illustration, before an ideal whose occupation of the greatest heights forecasts an inevitable decline.

If this reading of Thurman generates a narrative measuring the distance from innocence to tragedy, it repeats a romantic ideal that is characteristically American—hardly exceptional to U.S. nationalism, but central to accounts of American exceptionalism. Canonical narratives of the national character, attached to youth as an aesthetic and political category of modernity, remain within the limits of this measure, running a course from blessed naïveté to tragic downfall. In the end—say, in F. Scott Fitzgerald's *The Great Gatsby*—it seems as if the beauty of the innocent's fall is what desire is after, averting perception from whatever knowledge of complicity and responsibility might arrive beyond it. This same structure appears in accounts of twentieth-century African American and Japanese American history centered upon the Great Migration and the Internment, whose critique of U.S. nationalism remains confined within the measure between the nation's pluralist ideal and its tragic reality. In these stories, hardworking and loyal Americans, who seek not a gift, but only a chance, are betrayed by their nation only because of the color of their skin—even as their faith in the innocence of its ideal preserves the chance of the nation's redemption.

Yet an alternative narrative possibility is signaled in Thurman's implied preference for being *slightly possessed* over the proper achievement of self-creation. If his roman à clef invites a reading from the security of retrospection, with the enticing clarity of hindsight, it withholds that position from its narrative time, suspending the reader before the visionary uncertainties of foresight. From this vantage, what comes after the chance of American modernity are not only those determined, striving New Negroes and Nisei, but also what PaPa LaBas, in Ishmael Reed's fictional exploration of the era, would identify as "haints"—from which the former might not and perhaps ought not to be differentiated. Taking these shades as clues, this chapter seeks to recast the historical narration of black and Japanese American migrations without the teleological assurances of hindsight, to ask what might yet elude a fall.

If Arbian's Orientalist stylings, like their less flamboyant analogues in Larsen's novels discussed below, are staged as unreadable (mumbo jumbo), they betray a kind of excess of signification in the practices of embodiment by which the identity of a modern self is produced. Edwards terms this a "telling inarticulacy" ("Louis Armstrong" 625); like what he generally describes of a "scat aesthetics," it "involve[s] an augmentation of expressive potential rather than an evacuation or reduction of signification" (649). Thurman's *fond* embrace of this *confoundedly interesting* condition, the embodied condition of everyday aesthetic performance, leads back to the Louis Armstrong recording with which I began: "The Heebie Jeebies Dance."

As Edwards demonstrates, the "heebie-jeebies" refers to "an inherently modern state of bodily unease, anxiety, or trembling, perhaps in the wake of an excess of stimulation . . . , that causes a loss of control, a nervous loss of articulacy that expresses itself as incommodious physical movement" (621). It may be understood as "a kind of premonition or haunting: the 'apprehension' that intuits an invasive presence" (622). Pervasive and infectious, frightening yet fashionable,[4] this condition marked its carriers as modern subjects—a distinction to be desired, even as its excesses must be exorcized. Accompanying the arrival of the New Negro and the Nisei in the modern American metropolis, it threatened to topple their vertiginous aspirations. Still, as Armstrong and Reed suggest, the chance remained that the dis-ease might also be the cure.

Two: The Modern Racial Self as a Problem of Form

Though the "trope of a New Negro" recurred in a variety of efforts to reconstruct "a new racial self" between 1895 and 1925 (Gates 133), its canonical formulation derives from Alain Locke's eponymous 1925 anthology, expanded from a previous "special Harlem number" of the *Survey Graphic*.[5] Although I share a broader interest in provincializing its status, it is Locke's restricted sense of the term that concerns this parallelist reading of the New Negro and the Nisei.[6] In his introduction, Locke locates the New Negro within a "tide of Negro migration, northward and city-ward," whose essence can be found not in extrinsic sociological phenomena, but in "a mass movement toward the larger and more democratic chance" (6). What his masses intuit, and Locke takes as self-evident, is the exceptional status of the industrial U.S. city, at the crest of world history's acceleration into the future; the chance they pursue is modernity itself, which is characteristically *American* and *urban*.

For the arrival of black migrants in "the American metropolis" (xxvi) to provide both evidence and condition for a "Negro Renaissance" (xxvii), Locke must recast the epistemological conditions under which they appear, heralding a shift from the objectification of a race "problem" to the subjective agency of a "task" (4). This shift draws on the social-scientific drive toward a singular, knowable reality, or "truest social portraiture," while insisting on the "essential" primacy of a "folk-spirit" (xxv). But in seeking to displace a social problem with a celebration of artistic achievement, Locke relies on a civilizationist epistemology in which to be "representative" is to exemplify not a demographic mean, but a cultural ideal. "So far as he is culturally articulate," he qualifies, "we shall let the Negro speak for himself" (xxv). "No sane observer," he cautions, "would contend that the great masses are articulate as yet," but the agency of "the 'man farthest down' who is most active in getting up" (7) finds its proper expression via a new generation of intellectuals: "The migrant masses, shifting from countryside to city, hurdle several generations of experience at a leap, but more important, the same thing happens spiritually in the life-attitudes and self-expression of the Young Negro, in his poetry, his art, his education and his new outlook, with the additional advantage, of course, of the poise and greater certainty of knowing what it is all about. From this comes the promise and warrant of a new leadership" (4–5). The "migrating peasant" and the young intelligentsia share a trajectory of progressive ascent along the hierarchy of civilizational time. They converge in Harlem, "laboratory of a great race-welding," redefining race from "a common condition" to "a common consciousness" through "group expression and self-determination," an unprecedented creative act of self-projection (7). This is experienced as a dizzying juxtaposition or telescoping of temporalities and tempi, "a deliberate flight not only from countryside to city, but from medieval America to modern" (6). Taken together, ascent, tempo, and self-projection may be seen as three aspects of a *formal* problem—the problem of constructing a modern racial subject—which, as you will see, were not unique to Locke's New Negro.

eyes faced toward sunset

In May 1926, fourteen months after publishing Locke's Harlem issue, *Survey Graphic* issued another "special number," on "the Oriental." *East by West: Our Windows on the Pacific* was compiled with the help of the sociologist Robert E. Park, drawing on the research he oversaw in the massive "Survey of Race Relations on the Pacific Coast of the United States." Multiethnic and transpacific in scope, it did not herald a Nisei Renaissance, but the issue reveals how the outlines of a "second-generation Japanese problem" or "Nisei problem" had already emerged across a range of discursive locations.

The second-generation Japanese problem, as Stanford University's Edward Strong succinctly defines it in his 1934 volume by that name, "is adjustment to their environment" (1). For social scientists like Strong, this subcategory of a larger "Oriental Problem" was constituted within a general theory of "race relations," developed primarily by Park, in which racism was understood fundamentally as a matter of individual prejudices, whose rise and ultimate disappearance were both inevitable phases of historical development.[7] While presumptively antiracist, this theory displaced questions of structural inequality and collective action to focus on the ability of minorities to "adjust" to social processes, within a gradualism measuring out teleological progress in the rhythm of generations.[8]

But the question of the second generation was not merely a construction of social science. As Eiichiro Azuma has shown, community organizations, intellectuals, and other elites within Japanese communities in the United States, while actively supporting the efforts of liberal social scientists, had already developed their own conception of the "Nisei Problem (*Dai-Nisei mondai*)," which operated on different assumptions and served different interests. Rather than a particular case of a universal theory, this construct was "unique to American-born Japanese, not ubiquitous to all second-generation Japanese abroad" (113). Azuma summarizes the Issei elites' definition of the Nisei problem as "the post-1924 challenges to racial development" (112). Emerging in response to a wave of juridical events by which the interests of the immigrant community became bound to the birthright citizenship of their children—the expansion and tightening of alien land laws, the 1922 *Ozawa* case excluding Japanese immigrants from naturalization, and the 1924 immigration act—this second generation is a *political* category.

More broadly, Azuma's research on pre–World War II Japanese immigrant communities shows how a corporate identity of "the Japanese in America" or *zaibei doho* emerged among the conflicting forces of state-centered Japanese expansionism, U.S. interests in the Pacific, and the racial orders of the U.S. West. Despite the increasing tension between Japan and the United States, Issei elites' ideology of racial development admitted no contradiction between their interests, offering proper and dutiful service to each—while selectively supporting or contesting either's demands, depending on the effects on the local community. What Azuma calls the "eclecticism" of "immigrant internationalism" actually intensified with the rise of Japanese militarism in the 1930s, raising the stakes on Issei constructs of dual patriotism. Only when war became unavoidable was the pro-Japan aspect of this ideology dropped—quickly and unambiguously.

The basis of this compatibility, as articulated by post-1924 immigrant intellectuals, was a convergence between the dominant racial categories of Japanese and U.S. imperialism within a civilizationist teleology. According to what Azuma terms "the Issei pioneer thesis" (91), the Issei advancing on the U.S. West, like the Anglo-Saxons coming from the east, were racially endowed with a capacity for benevolent conquest, as shown by their role in civilizing that "frontier." "This notion of *develop-ment* came to have a double meaning" (97), posing the Issei as precursors to Japanese imperial settlements in Asia and as the leaders of the Oriental races against global white supremacy. This duality remained coherent so long as an insistence on the dominant races' converging objectives, harmonizing in the inevitable progress of civilization, could be maintained.[9] These were the world-historical stakes of the Nisei problem: the progress of the Issei pioneers may have been temporarily stalled by the Asiatic exclusion movement, but the Nisei, empowered by birthright citizenship, could serve as a *bridge* between the Pacific powers, bearing the legacy of Japanese development forward and upward.

Liberal social scientists shared this goal of harmonious U.S.-Japanese relations, along with a dependence on civilizationist teleology and frontier mythology. Robert Park's unsigned preface[10] to the Oriental number opens with a play on "the new orientation—in both meanings of the word" confronting "Americans," constituted by memories of "the covered wagon" and "that stream . . . moving westward since the Pilgrims . . . and . . . Jamestown": "Once we actually reach the Pacific, however, something quite different happens to us. . . . It is not a change of position: it is rather a change of attitude. We look to the Pacific because there the future lies. It is around the Pacific that things are happening; it is from the Pacific that the news comes" (*East by West* 133). A kind of Hegelian world-historical spirit, traveling inexorably westward from the ancient Orient through Europe and the United States, is extended to its perplexing limit, "the seam of the hemispheres" (133). Ascending to its manifest destiny as the preeminent civilizing power, the United States must shift its gaze from Europe toward awakening Asia.

This civilizationist theory of history derives, fundamentally, from an Orientalist distinction—imagined as passive, closed, homogeneous, and static, the Orient defines the Occident as active, expansive, heterogeneous, and dynamic. The East is tradition, a land of stifling custom in inevitable decline; the West, especially the United States, is the home of modernity, the motor of irreversible progress. Yet, because the process is inevitable, irreversible, and universal, this Orientalism also portends the end of Western supremacy. Modernity, for Park, is no longer exclusively a Euro-American phenomenon.[11] Indeed, it is this temporal disjuncture in his Orientalism, by which the Oriental belongs to both a premodern past and an ultramodern future, that allows him to mark out the modern as an interval and instantiation of historical time.

The archetypal figure of Park's modernity is "the marginal man": "one whom fate has condemned to live in two societies and in two, not merely different but antagonistic, cultures."[12] A modification of Georg Simmel's concept of "the stranger" via Park's studies of European immigrants and the Negro and Oriental problems, the marginal man's exemplars are such cultural and racial "hybrids" as "the Jew" and "the Mulatto."[13] Typically a migrant and a city dweller, a "cosmopolite and citizen of the world" (Race and Culture 354), the marginal man is modernity's tragic hero. Formed at the leading edge of the emancipating and individualizing forces of civilization, his "personality type" tends to "spiritual instability, intensified self-consciousness, restlessness, and malaise" (356)—something like a permanent case of the heebie-jeebies. His greatest value, finally, is as an object of science: "It is in the mind of the marginal man—where the changes and fusions of culture are going on—that we can best study the processes of civilization and of progress" (356).

Yet, as Henry Yu has shown, a number of Asian American protégés of Chicago School sociologists embraced and recast the role to enable and explain their own social mobility.[14] Among them was Kazuo Kawai, one of two Asian American contributors to the Survey Graphic issue.[15] Anticipating Edward Strong, Kawai introduces the second-generation problem as one of restricted job opportunity, leading to a broader question of social adjustment. He identifies three general patterns of response: one group resigns themselves to limited prospects, disdaining education and mobility; a second tries migrating to Japan, only to struggle against their own foreignness; and a small third group, committed to slow advance through hard work, is just "beginning to find their proper places in society" (166).

This gradualist approach to social adjustment retains the assertive race pride of Issei "racial development." In an opening anecdote, a college-educated Negro Pullman porter explains that whites recognize black people only as servants, whereupon Kawai's narrator gives thanks that "we Japanese in America are not like the Negroes. We are not a servile race" (164). Although the essay immediately challenges this presumption, wondering if educated Nisei face "the same problem" (164), this very similarity motivates Kawai's rejection of the "docile servitude" (166) of "the new shiftless, pleasure-seeking second-generation element" (165) in his first group of maladjusted Nisei.

For himself, Kawai predictably chooses the third path. Recognizing that "the white and colored races [are] clashing all over the world, but particularly over the Pacific Basin," where the expansions of "the occidental culture" and "the oriental culture" meet, he spots an opportunity "for interpreters who can bridge the gap." "Culturally a child of the Occident" yet "racially a child of the Orient," he is "constituted" for a "mission in life, to interpret the East to the West, and to contribute to America the knowledge accruing from a proper interpretation" (166).[16] Like Locke's young artists, Kawai is presented as the exceptional representative of a new modern racial self, whose identity is constituted by his self-determined aspirational mission. Exemplifying Azuma's "eclecticism," he synthesizes the Issei's "bridge" concept and Park's "marginal man," locating the Nisei's chance in the United States.

Because this chance is modern, it is not merely American but *urban*. Park predicts that the Nisei will abandon farming, for marginal men "cannot endure the isolation of a rural community. The same forces that have driven the Jew into the freer air of the city, are making of the Japanese farmer a city man" (*East by West* 138). While the Issei elite, protective of their fragile niche in the agricultural economy, organized a "Back-to-the-Farm movement" in the mid-1930s, their ambitions were not so limited for exemplary figures like Kawai, or for their own children (Azuma 114–19; Strong 8–10).

In sum, the heterogeneous constructions of the Nisei Problem, like Locke's New Negro, operated through civilizationist ideologies whose progressive teleology followed on a metaphor of ascent: both "racial development" and "social adjustment" imagined a movement simultaneously upward and forward. Finding one's proper place within this teleology required the negotiation of multiple temporalities at the levels of racial and national history and of embodied experience. Where Locke's urban migrants and new cultural elites *hurdled several generations of experience* in a flight *from medieval America to modern*, the same accelerated process occurred within the *personality type* of the second-generation Japanese. Furthermore, the exemplar of this leap was the very nation their parents had left behind. As another *Survey Graphic* writer explained, in a trope already a half-century old, this leap suggested an inherent racial characteristic. Just as Japan had once "leaped from barbarism to Chinese culture in a single generation," its recent modernization compressed half a millennium of Western development into five decades: "No other such dizzy progress is recorded in the annals of peoples."[17] The vertiginous interiority of this new racial self was, finally, the stage of a world-historical drama. The subject's task was to model the resolution of social conflict, finding the position allowing proper ascent and adjusting the production of a self to its terms, and securing this inner and outer harmonization in self-expression, the successful transmission of a message from the inside to the outside.

the sway of the skyscraper

Taken together, the shared formal features of *Passing* and *The Brothers Murata* suggest a common narrative problem. Approaching literary form as an open process of creation rather than a stock of predetermined types, I organize parallels between the novels in three sets, centered on questions of *verticality*, *tempo*, and *interiority*, which correspond to the shared formal problem of the New Negro and the Nisei discussed earlier.

The first set, organized by a question of verticality, is defined by the novels' most striking similarity—the climactic scene of the antagonist's fatal fall from a window. Clare Kendry's fall occurs after her husband, John Bellew, discovers her at a party in the apartment of Felise and Dave Freeland, confirming his suspicions of her black ancestry. Though the fall's cause is ambiguous, it is set in narrative motion by Irene, who fears that a spurned Clare might run off with her own husband, Brian. Irene rushes toward her friend, standing calmly at the open window with "a faint smile," "possessed" by "one thought": "She couldn't have her free" (111).

Readers have understandably disagreed over whether Clare's death is a murder, accident, or suicide, for the action itself is not represented—it is explicitly removed from the text's narrative time. Indeed, the absenting of the action is repeated, in a stutter that calls to mind the skipping of a phonograph needle. The relevant passage directly follows the previous quote:

Before them stood John Bellew, speechless now in his hurt and anger. Beyond them the little huddle of other people, and Brian stepping out from among them.

What happened next, Irene never afterwards allowed herself to remember. Never clearly.

One moment Clare had been there, a vital glowing thing, like a flame of red and gold. The next she was gone. (111)

What is *not* ambiguous, within Irene's interior consciousness, is her sensation of guilt, and her terror of discovery. That is, on the narrative *inside*, Irene is, unambiguously, a murderer, even if this assertion cannot be expressed directly, but only through the *externalization* of its negation, in the speech of a character to herself, now alone in the room: "'It was an accident, a terrible accident,' she muttered fiercely. 'It *was*'" (112).

Frank Murata's fall, by contrast, is explicitly represented as a murder. Indeed, it is premeditated, as implied by a series of narrative clues leading up to the decisive act. Nonetheless, despite the narration's apparently untroubled access to the workings of Hiro's mind, the nature of this act—that it will be a murder—is kept secret until it occurs. As they await Frank's imminent arrest for draft evasion, Hiro arranges a weekend pass from camp for the brothers to visit nearby Salt Lake City. Meeting up to enjoy the view from the top floor of the Alta Building, they peer out into the mist, recalling their foggy San Francisco hometown, and share a nostalgic fantasy of a future return. But after one last attempt at conversion fails, Hiro entices Frank to lean out to ogle a girl, and shoves him to his death.

While these scenes of a fatal fall appear archetypal, their historical, geographical, and geopolitical specificity is indicated by their most aggressively prominent motif—the skyscraper. Granted, both the ten-story Alta Building and the Freelands' sixth-floor apartment seem modest, if not puny, by contrast with the modernist grandeur evoked by the term. But as in Arbian's illustration of "Niggeratti Manor," this is precisely the point. Just as the Alta Building, for Hiro and Frank, recalls the more spectacular towers of the Pacific metropolis from which they have been "evacuated," the Freelands' walk-up is explicitly contrasted with John Bellew's loftier high-rise. The material and metaphorical connections between racialization and elevation are underscored in a bantering exchange between Brian and Clare, arriving at the Freelands' with Irene in tow:

> "Ever go up to the sixth floor, Clare?" Brian asked as he stopped the car and got out to open the door for them.
>
> "Why, of course! We're on the seventeenth."
>
> "I mean, did you ever go up by nigger-power?"
>
> "That's good!" Clare laughed. "Ask 'Rene. My father was a janitor, you know, in the good old days before every ramshackle flat had its elevator. But you can't mean we've got to walk up? Not here!" (108)

The skyscraper, in both novels, is invoked as the privileged motif of a specifically *urban* modernity, a historically particular figure for lofty modernist aspirations, which are aggrandized by contrast with the diminished forms Irene and Hiro may access. This conception of modernity is, furthermore, characteristically *American*; thus Irene, whose fears about Brian's restlessness fixate on his frustrated desire to immigrate to Brazil, resolves: "She belonged in this land of rising towers. She was an American" (107).

The questions of verticality organized by the trope are as much historical as spatial. The geographical space of the industrial metropolis and the geopolitical space of the globally ascendant nation define the new racial self's imagined entry into world history's forward, upward progress. The nation's necessary role in mediating this movement is explicitly raised in *The Brothers Murata*'s debates over military service—for example, when Frank's argument for universal pacifism, redeeming the empty promises of post–World War I Wilsonian internationalism, is challenged by Hiro's ally, Tad: "We will have war until we reach the zenith of our process. You'd have to wait, Frank. Now isn't the time—you're way ahead of time" (189).

A second set of formal parallels centers on a question of tempo. Arguably classifiable as novellas rather than novels, both *Passing* and *The Brothers Murata* are short, overall and in the length of individual chapters. The brevity of the narrative generates a brisk pace, further heightened by a suspenseful plot—where suspense is produced not by the progressive accretion of consequential developments, but by the persistent deferral of decisive action, of an anticipated violence. Early in *Passing*, Irene repeatedly decides to be done with Clare, yet never manages to keep her resolve. Later, she vacillates between contradictory schemes for dealing with the threat Clare poses, then proves unable to act even when the occasion presents itself—as when, after deciding to reveal Clare's secret to Bellew, he shows up "as if in answer to her wish, the very next day" (99). Similarly, up until the climax of *The Brothers Murata*, the conflict between the volunteers and draft resisters always hangs on the verge of a decisive confrontation, only to be deferred when Hiro engages Frank in yet another round of inconclusive debate.

This suspense is effected as a tension between two distinct experiences of time: in one, everything moves forward at breakneck speed; in the other, everything remains still, or circles, in an unbearable waiting. The latter, for Irene, is the time of bourgeois domesticity, imagined as idyllic routine but experienced as an anxious tedium, cut here and there by the sophisticated but unsatisfying stimulations of consumption and an active social life. As she tells herself, "security was the most important and desired thing in life," the ideal that defines her gendered role, and the agency it allows: "She wanted only to be tranquil. Only, unmolested, to be allowed to direct for their own best good the lives of her sons and her husband" (107). Yet it is her friend's apparent scorn for this ideal, and for the moral constraints it imposes upon women as wives and mothers—"It was as if Clare Kendry had said to her, for whom safety, security, were all-important: 'Safe! Damn being safe!' and meant it" (66)—along with her contrary orientation towards danger, flight, and a self-conception scandalously severed from familial duty, that constitutes "Clare" as the projection of Irene's own unspeakable desires.

To say Irene is caught between an image of self, as ideal wife and mother ("Irene"), and its reversed double ("Clare"), is also to say that she is caught between two temporalities: one of a "tranquil," cyclical domesticity, the other of a wildly accelerated, open-ended risk taking. In relation to each other, they appear as a gendered opposition of "tradition" to "modernity." Even so, "Irene's" respectable pursuit of proper womanhood within the bourgeois patriarchal family and "Clare's" scandalous quest for individual pleasure within elite urban milieus are *both* attempts to seize historically specific, relatively unprecedented opportunities for African American women. That is, *both* modes negotiate *modern* conjunctions of race, gender, class, and nationality.

In *The Brothers Murata*, the dominant temporality, always in the background but suffusing the narrative, inferable only from its ironic tension with the plot's accelerated pacing, is given by mass incarceration. It is the time of imprisonment, of indefinite detention: the experience of "time itself" as torture, where "time" stands in for what fills it when what fills it is said to be "nothing"; the experience of linear time, of "homogeneous, empty time," without teleology—the timing of everyday routine calibrated to gradual progress towards an end that has been utterly excluded.[18] The urgency of this question increases if you can let go of retrospection's faith in the subsequent determinations of history, and learn to read within the historical present that the narrative action apparently shares with its own production—the novel was, according to Lawson Inada's introduction, written *in* camp (6). What will happen to the inmates is not yet decided: Will they be deported to Japan? Exchanged as prisoners of war? Liquidated? What will happen if Japan invades, or if U.S. defeat seems imminent?

That such life-and-death questions must be decided elsewhere, in a time and place beyond the reach of the detainees' conscious agency, proves excruciating for Hiro.[19] The temporality of incarceration, this sense of overwhelming vulnerability dissipated into the inconsequential business of daily routine, contrasts unbearably with the temporality of history, of world-political events, into which he would leap. This tension, too, is gendered; for Hiro, there is the time of immaturity, of the mother needing protection and the wife and children to be gained, and the time of manhood, to be established through the violence and sacrifice of soldiering. As his arguments with Frank range grandly from their father's quasi-Hegelian Buddhist theories of universal "harmony," to the issue of national compliance with international law, to their concerns for their mother's safety, their stakes ultimately turn on a question of time and action. Frank explains, "The right time will never come unless you go out and meet it. . . . Why should I wait now? If I wait I'll have time on my hands" (189).

Thus, the plot of each novel seems to hurtle towards its inevitable climax, an anticipated violence that promises to resolve two temporalities in a single decisive act. The question of tempo organizing the narrative form is thus a question of the balancing of two cadences or rhythms—one represented as modern, historical, linear, and accelerated; the other as traditional, ahistorical, and cyclical or still. Yet it is more accurate to say that what is *inherently modern* is the question of conflicting temporalities itself, whose accompanying *state of bodily unease, anxiety*, and nervousness Edwards termed the *heebie-jeebies* (621). Its resolution through a decisive act would require, the novels suggest, the stabilization of the racializing and gendering forces articulating as identity; but in their abrupt, unsatisfying conclusions, the promised resolution is withdrawn as quickly as it arrives, leaving the question unsettlingly open—a matter to which I will return.

The third set of parallels centers on a question of interiority, given, first of all, in the limited third-person form of the novels' narration. Unlike omniscient third-person narration, this voice is located within the consciousness of the protagonist, Irene or Hiro, and generally seems to lack independent access to the outside world. But unlike first-person narration, it does not issue from the protagonist's "I," introducing a potential fault line within her/his psyche, exacerbated by the use of irony to trouble the protagonist's interpretation of external reality—as when Irene's first, disapproving encounter with a passing Clare is situated in an elegant hotel where she herself must pass to receive service; or when Hiro's insistence that he is volunteering to protect his mother is countered by clear evidence that he is endangering her in the camp.

Like unreliable first-person narration, however, the prospect of a misrepresentation of external reality can only be implied. Since the narrator has no independent access to that reality, any implication of error is undecidable. Thus, for example, Larsen's readers have debated the validity of Irene's suspicions of an affair between Brian and Clare,[20] or whether Clare's ultimate death is an accident, suicide, or murder—issues whose definitive resolution requires an objective basis that the narration does not provide. Even so, the third-person narrative voice allows a more explicit irony, so long as its evidence is drawn from within the protagonist's consciousness. Consider this passage analyzing Irene's relationship with Brian—emphases added: "It was only that she wanted him to be happy, resenting, however, his inability to be so with things as they were, and *never acknowledging* that though she did want him to be happy, it was only in her own way and by some plan of hers for him that she truly desired him to be so. *Nor did she admit* that all other plans, all other ways, she regarded as menaces, more or less indirect, to that security of place and substance which she insisted upon for her sons and *in a lesser degree for herself*" (61). Note how the narrative voice suggests a kind of splitting *interior* to the protagonist's psyche, implying a site of interpretive agency distinct from, and critical of, Irene's consciousness, able to express what she cannot *acknowledge* or *admit*. Yet, by the end of the passage, this alternate interpretation falls back into Irene's, in a strikingly sympathetic, or mildly delusional, or wryly signifying representation of her proper maternal priorities. While explicitly critical interpretive commentary is largely avoided in *The Brothers Murata*, a more dramatic splitting effect occurs within its narration. At several key moments, the narrative voice splits away from the third-person to address Hiro directly, as "you" or in the imperative. This other voice may be associated with Hiro's own thought processes (186) or his image reflected in a mirror (164), or left without attribution (205), but it never takes quotation marks, remaining indistinguishable from the third-person narrator. Even more oddly, this second-person voice is sometimes interrupted, as if in response, by a first-person voice, indicated by italics!

The question of interiority further arises in the developing relationship between the novels' protagonists and antagonists. Introduced as polar opposites—Irene as the proper race woman versus Clare as the scandalous passer, Hiro as the loyal volunteer versus Frank as the dissident draft resister—they come to appear, from the protagonist's perspective, as uncanny doubles. For Irene, Clare becomes the projection of an inner desire that transgresses all the constraints of her racialized, classed, gendered social identity, threatening to usurp or destroy it. Thus, she becomes fixated on the possibility of an affair, fearing her marriage has been a sham—one she is nevertheless determined to protect at all costs. Hiro's failure to win Frank over reveals his inability to logically distinguish between their motives and goals. Just like his brother, if with greater confidence and rhetorical facility, Frank justifies his position as filial duty, to the words of their late father and the care of their mother; as service to the racial community in camp; as loyal patriotism, defending what is essential to the nation; and as commitment to an ideal of universal humanity, progressively actualized in historical time. Yet even as he remains steadfast in his plans of action, Hiro is unable to properly express how Frank's argument differs from his own, let alone overcome it. This failure threatens to paralyze him just as he prepares the leap into the gendered social agency of manhood that volunteering entails. In both novels, the logic of the plot ultimately demands the elimination of the double in order for the protagonist to survive.

The question of interiority, as it organizes these features of narrative form, can thus be understood as an engagement with identity—that concept meant to unify the "authentic" self, apparent to interior consciousness, with the conjunction of exterior social categories (race, gender, class, nationality, and so on) by which that self is distinguished from others. In facing its contradictions—identity is both inner authenticity and social legibility, demanding both the securing and severing of intimate and communal bonds—Irene and Hiro arrive at a logical limit where loyalty and betrayal become interchangeable or indistinguishable, whether in terms of race or nation, family or self. Interiority, in this sense, may expand to include the "inner" domains of gendered bourgeois domesticity, of a race constituted by uplift ideology, of family constituted by the cyclical time of generations, or of a community enclosed within the barbed wire of a concentration camp. This question can also be understood as one of self-consciousness, of a subject's struggle for awareness of the psychological drives and social or historical forces that produce and position it, in order to wrest control over its own destiny. Finally, it can be understood as a question of self-expression, where consciousness and agency are conceptualized through the metaphor of language—that which crosses and bridges the division between inside and outside, the medium that secures both speaking self and represented world. But because language takes social and historical precedence over the conscious or agential self, a contradiction inheres in this securing, revealed in the very form of the novels' narration: a voice emerges from within the protagonist's consciousness *that is not her own*.

The three sets of questions that constitute the novels' problem of narrative form come together notably in the scene that sets the stage for Irene's very first encounter with an adult Clare. Positioned at the opposite end of the narrative from the fall at the Freelands', this meeting is set on the elegant rooftop garden of Chicago's Drayton Hotel, a space the women can access only by passing as white. What drives the narrative to these heights, however, is instructive. It is an unbearably hot August day, and Irene's habitual tardiness ("I always seem to keep C.P. time," she confesses elsewhere [105]) has put her in a rush, frantically shopping for gifts promised to her sons back in New York. Her hurried condition is unhappily mirrored by the city's own rush, portrayed as a jumble of cars, streets, trolley rails, sidewalks, and crowding pedestrians, assaulting her senses with a combination of the heat, glare, noise, and stinging dust. And then, "right before her smarting eyes," is a fall: "a man toppled over and became an inert heap on the scorching cement." A crowd gathers, surrounding her, intensifying the sensory assault: she feels "disagreeably damp and sticky and soiled from contact with so many sweating bodies." All at once, she is overwhelmed, as "the whole street [takes] a wobbly look," and on the verge of fainting she waves feebly for a taxi (12). Dutifully taking note of her gendered, classed vulnerability to urban danger, the driver whisks her gallantly away to the elegant oasis of the hotel. Put simply, what sets the entire narrative in motion is nothing other than a spell of the heebie-jeebies: an attack of vertigo, brought on by excessive acceleration, which threatens a loss of consciousness as the metropolis swells up around Irene, effacing the sensory boundaries of her body, absorbing her precarious identity into its own, unsettling, relentless motion.

the faces we know have no secrets for us

The question of interiority points to a persistent instability in efforts to delineate modern racial subjects. To define a self, a border between inside and outside needed to be drawn and secured, by an expression or action that crossed it. This line would balance the two sides of identity, self-perception and social recognition, and expand outward across nesting levels of subjectivity, aligning different temporalities. Once questioned, this border never seemed to hold, but attending to the ways it was conceived shows how theorizations of the New Negro and the Nisei negotiated the conflicting geopolitics of race, nation, and empire.

For Locke, this question of a "new psychology" (3), at once collective and individual, initiates repeated tracings of inside and outside. Thus, if he is centrally concerned with defining the nascent "objectives" of the New Negro's "inner life," the ideals of "his outer life" are already established, "none other than the ideals of American institutions and democracy" (10). Racial particularity—or the active reconstruction of "tradition" that would retain particularity, while aligning traditional morality with a dominant bourgeois ethic and transmuting folk materials into the higher forms of universal "culture"—belongs in the inner domain. The outer domain of "modern" political forms is one of generality, whose highest development to date in Western civilization, and specifically American democracy, is unquestioned. And crucially, for Locke, it is the U.S. *nation* that necessarily mediates the New Negro's entry into the civilizational time, as the proper site of pluralism, of the incorporation of racial difference into unity.

For Locke, this figure would resolve Du Bois's infamous "double consciousness." As formulated in *Souls*, this "two-ness" in which "American" and "Negro" exist as "two warring ideals in one dark body" generates a desire "for a man to be both a Negro and an American," a "striving" whose ultimate "end" is "to be a co-worker in the kingdom of culture" (*Writings* 365). Locke argues that the New Negro *achieves* this status, as "a collaborator and participant in American civilization" (15), wherein the national term, "American," is a pluralist synthesis of "inner" racial particularity and "outer" generality, at the crest of historical progress.

He further insists that its national specificity is not in conflict with its "new internationalism" (14–15), but is its *chance*: as an American, the New Negro is "the advance-guard of the African peoples in their contact with Twentieth Century civilization," with "a mission of rehabilitating the race in world esteem," both beacon and mechanism of uplift for the entire "Negro world" (14). Anticipating and perhaps influencing dominant forms of American exceptionalism after World War II, this American Negro exceptionalism is more akin to that of Du Bois in 1899—and here the deferred contradiction between racial and national identity reemerges, as a duplicity that situates the Negro both inside the U.S. nation, in a domestic sense, and outside it, as the leader of the diaspora. Like the Nisei "bridge" concept, Locke's internationalism professes a facile faith in the necessary harmony between discrete racial and national geopolitical interests. In the event, Locke relies on a characteristic deferral of pluralism's realization within a national teleology, while reconciling the linear time of progress with the cyclical rhythm of generations: "if in our lifetime the Negro should not be able to celebrate his full initiation into American democracy, he can at least . . . celebrate the attainment of a significant and satisfying new phase of group development, and a spiritual Coming of Age" (16).

The question of inside and outside is also manifested in perhaps the most common trope of the second-generation Japanese problem, which appears in Mori's initial description of Hiro and his friends: "They were representative Americans but for their Oriental facial features—they were Nisei from Topaz" (139). Kawai's description of himself as "culturally" Occidental but "racially" Oriental (166) repeats the figure, neatly illustrating the theories of Park, for whom the second-generation Oriental, American on the inside, was shrouded in a "racial uniform." This visible exterior difference, in turn, explained away the lag in the inevitable progression of the race relations cycle toward assimilation, as it did for the Negro.[21] Yet even Park found this figure's inability to fully resolve beguiling. In his introductory essay in the *Survey Graphic*—illustrated with exotic, unsettling photographs of Japanese Noh masks—he describes his encounter with a young Nisei woman, whom he scrutinizes minutely, searching for "some slight accent, some gesture or intonation that would betray her racial origin." Despite himself, he is haunted by the "impression that I was listening to an American woman in a Japanese disguise." Yet, a few months later, after a trip to Japan, she reports that her appearance was so "scandalous, almost uncanny," to the locals that she drew crowds in the street, resentful of "the appearance of a Japanese woman in the masquerade of an American lady" (*East by West* 136). The uncanny effect, of a mismatch between inner and outer, is doubled as it is reversed.

In this essay, "Behind Our Masks," Park follows what would become generic conventions of racial liberalism, reducing racism to a problem of individual prejudices that inevitably disappears. Ultimately, his inquiry aims beyond the particularity of the second-generation Oriental—whose mildly pathologized psychological dilemmas lie behind the immutable "physical characteristics" of the "racial uniform" (138)—to a general theory of the relation between individual and society, aligned with a universal theory of history. If the inside/outside split is primordial—"It is probably no mere historical accident that the word person, in its first meaning, is a mask," he muses—then it is possible for him to state, "Orientals live more completely behind the mask than the rest of us," while consigning this Orientalist premise to superficial cultural differences that fade before civilization's universalizing march (137). The associated dissolution of racism through personal contact—"It is, in fact, only as faces become expressive that the persons behind those living masks assume for us the character of human beings" (138)—becomes a universal theory of unmediated "expressiveness" as the basis of human belonging, a figure of community as both origin and telos of modern, telecommunicative society:

> It is curious and interesting that this character that we call human should be so intimately connected with expressiveness. Human interest . . . attaches to anything that is "expressive"; . . . anything that suggests, symbolizes, or reveals sentiments and passions in others of which we are immediately conscious in ourselves. The faces we know have no secrets for us. . . . We feel secure and at home with them as we do not among less familiar faces. Probably the most expressive, the most human face we ever know, is that of a mother; or it may be that of an old nurse, even that of an old black mammy. (138)

Certainly Park could not have anticipated the jolt felt by future readers, for whom the primary connotation of the *mammy* is that of a discredited stereotype, a mask for secrets untold. Yet the twinge of irony in his trope, his muted jibe at the interracial intimacies underlying white supremacy, points to his inquiry's ultimate stakes. What all these proliferating, unstable figures of mismatched insides and outsides reveal is the problem of incorporating racial difference: of American civilization within the body of a Negro or Nisei, of Nisei and Negroes within the national body of a rising imperial power. This is the dangerous allure of the marginal man, the dilemma of the Americanized Oriental, the unsettling satirical charge a passing figure inserts into the celebration of a New Negro. As Park's simultaneously nostalgic and uncanny invocation of the *mammy* reveals, this problem struck at the intimate core of a *white* identity no less in flux.

The questions raised are no less urgent today than in that earlier period: How has whiteness, as an attribute of bodies both "human" and national, been produced through the incorporation of racial difference? How might one expose this process? Why, to what end, with what result? In the aftermath of multiculturalism, it has become common to claim that what the world knows as "American culture" is a product of black/white interracial relations—that U.S. national identity should be understood as "mulatto" or "mixed-race," or perhaps more accurately, as merely passing for white. This argument follows a dominant theme in black intellectual history, expounded in various ways by such thinkers as Du Bois, Locke, Ralph Ellison, James Baldwin, Albert Murray, and Toni Morrison, but its present influence may have more to do with an interracial tradition of liberal pluralism exemplified by Park and Locke, which has shaped a number of impressive, varied scholarly works on 1920s and 1930s U.S. culture by George Hutchinson, Ann Douglas, Joel Dinerstein, and others.

Accepting this argument, and recognizing the value of its empirical demonstration, I am not convinced that it is, *necessarily*, antiracist—that to expose an intercourse with blackness at the core of white identity is, of itself, to make whiteness less powerful. Because the "nation" is not merely the hegemonic emblem of a domestic social order, but also an ideological signifier of an aspiring imperial subject in a global field of competition, I contend that the whiteness of an imperial nation is grounded not on purity but on a demonstrated capacity for the hierarchical incorporation of racial difference. Put differently, for "America" was to ascend to its destined status as a world power, the question was not whether it would be homogeneous or heterogeneous, pure or pluralized; imperialism, aspiring to universality, must always expand across and internalize racial differences. Because whiteness in this context signified both universality and the right and capacity to rule over inferior races, the question was whether "America" could engineer a new, more advanced form of whiteness in succeeding to the imperial project of Western civilization.

But the falls of Clare and Frank in *Passing* and *The Brothers Murata* do not stand in for the decline of a Western civilization requiring the rejuvenating infusion of savage racial difference, nor do they herald a world-historical subject—American, Negro, or Oriental—rising triumphantly anew from such a sacrifice. Rather, these falls expose how a movement across the color line, into U.S. imperial nationality, is necessarily haunted by what it must deny. In their critical approach to the chance of an American modernity, the novels reveal what might be called its *entrancing terrors*, the heebie-jeebies, or, following PaPa LaBas, the *haints* that are always coming after it—the vertigo generated by verticality, the dizziness accompanying acceleration, the uncanny inkling of possession inhering in the act of self-expression.

This brings me back to a formal concern with the peculiar endings of the two novels. While their plots seem to hurtle inevitably to a violent end, their conclusions nonetheless manage to be simultaneously shocking and unsatisfying, ending with a dizzying abruptness, with disjuncture or dissonance. One character falls to the street; a moment later, the other follows, collapses, but only to the floor. The harmonization between interior consciousness and social time promised by the decisive act is lost; the body is immobile, the mind racing. In the interval or lag that Irene and Hiro take to compose themselves, to align their inside and outside at the face, the decisive resolution promised by violence is withdrawn as quickly as it arrives. And the novels end, run out of time, or, you might say, remain suspended within the time of a question, which they insist upon but cannot answer. The question may be phrased so: What is the difference between passing and freedom?

If the figure of racial passing, in the black literary tradition to which Larsen responds, traditionally serves to critique the potential for betrayal within racial uplift, *Passing* provocatively poses this figure as the New Negro race woman's uncanny double. Indeed, it is not Clare's passing for white that terrifies Irene, but the possibility that she might pass *back* into the Harlem elite. In *The Brothers Murata*, meanwhile, both Hiro and Frank seek to pass not as "white" but as "American," proliferating an instability of surface and interior. The text thereby critiques not just the compulsory hyperpatriotism of the volunteers, but the general violence of duty and loyalty by which imperial chains of inner and outer identities are secured. Both novels suggest that a movement *across* the color line, an ascent into an American modernity, turns out to be a trap. But is all flight impossible? Is there no other way out? The rest of this chapter takes up this question, following the traces of a movement not across the color line, but *along* it.

Three: Swinging Passing

At the climax of Larsen's novel, just after Clare disappears out the window and everyone rushes down to the street, Irene remains behind:

"She sat down and remained quite still, staring at *a ridiculous Japanese print* on the wall across the room" (111, emphasis added). At the corresponding moment in Mori's novel, after shoving Frank off the Alta Building, Hiro collapses to the floor, "his eyes unseeing and staring," and the narrative voice interrupts or ventriloquizes Hiro's "mind racing with thoughts," counseling: "Take a cut. Follow through. Go all the way" (205). Elsewhere, this running interior commentary on embodied timing typically makes recourse to sports, but one previous instance references a different area of popular culture. In that scene, having fled from an unexpected insult, the narrative shift to the second person calms Hiro's fantasies of violence by advising him, "You must jive with time" (186). Each novel here alludes to a set of popular-cultural practices—the consumption of Orientalist decorative objects and swing music and dance—whose modern allure relied on an appropriation of an alternative racial difference. Yet these references are merely fleeting and unstressed. Indeed, in the first, the possibility of reading the Japanese print is explicitly dismissed, while in the second, the appearance of jazz slang is clearly an error—surely the intended expression was not to "jive," but to "*jibe* with time."

By elaborating their contexts of production, I argue below that these corresponding sets of popular-cultural practices, which I term New Negro Orientalism and Nisei swing, are not as insignificant as the ephemeral quality of their textual appearances suggests. Indeed, their staging, as unreadable or misread, may occasion a contemporaneous critique of the discourses of Afro-Asian internationalism that this study aims to recover. Ultimately, I contend that these fleeting allusions may be taken as artful (if not necessarily intentional) operations of a structural effect in the aesthetic representation of nonwhite racial subjects, indicating, beyond the constraints of racist aesthetics and through the incorporative citation of different nonwhite racial forms, a possibility that eludes tragedy, waiting after what reading is yet able to approach.

fads jokes and errors

As this book has argued, an Asia/Pacific interest manifested in diverse ways across a range of modern African American discourses, frequently drawing on the racist lexicon of European and U.S. Orientalisms. More specifically, this chapter focuses on a "New Negro Orientalism" exemplified by the appropriation of transatlantic high- and popular-cultural practices of exchanging, displaying, and appreciating Oriental aesthetic commodities, as one element of early twentieth-century African Americans' aspirational self-imagining as modern, sophisticated, and elite.[22] For example, a nationwide fad in Japanese-themed social events among black philanthropic organizations in the first decade of the century coincided with a fashion for exchanging expensive Japanese housewares as high-status gifts (Kearney, *African American* Views 14–16). Such trends participated in an ongoing tradition of Western consumption of *chinoiserie* and *japonaiserie*, which became particularly prominent in the United States from the end of the nineteenth century through the 1920s, mediating anxieties about consumerism and modernization.[23] African American interest was further catalyzed by a racialized fascination with the rise of Japan as a nonwhite world power. The meanings circulating in the cultural practices of New Negro Orientalism may be therefore seen as discrete but overlapping with a speculative interest in imperial Japan as a threat to white world supremacy.

For the young artists of 1920s Harlem, a taste for Orientalia might connote a sophisticated appreciation for European high modernist aesthetics. In this sense, New Negro Orientalism is similar to the better-known, still controversial primitivist strain in New Negro aesthetics, influenced by European modernist appreciation for African craft and design. Thus, when Locke discusses African art's relation to transatlantic modernism in *The New Negro*, he feels compelled to assert, "It has been the most influential exotic art of our era, *Chinese and Japanese art not excepted*" (258, emphasis added). Indeed, scholars such as Cherene Sherrard-Johnson, Julia Lee, and Fiona Ngô have increasingly begun to consider the Orientalist strain in Renaissance writings by Larsen, Thurman, Bruce Nugent, Marita Bonner, and others.

In Edward Said's classic resignification of the term, Orientalism functions to consolidate a superior, Western racial self against an inferior racialized other. This function is necessarily modified in black Orientalisms, regardless of their explicit or implicit politics, as any racial self they constitute as Western and/or superior must also be differentiated from the subject of white Orientalisms. For example, where white Orientalisms celebrated the achievements of ancient nonwhite civilizations, they did so to establish superiority over the decadent, degraded conditions of latter-day nonwhite societies, on the evidence of taste manifested in practices of appreciation, preservation, and consumption. Black appropriations of such Orientalisms, however, might take evidence of ancient Oriental superiority as a prophecy of the inevitable sunset of white civilization, following the precedent of similar appropriations of Western Africanist scholarship. Meanwhile, emerging networks of race- and class-based radical internationalisms in this period allowed an articulation of New Negro Orientalism to a more robust politics of correspondence between black and Asian political movements understood as *coeval*.

In conceptualizing New Negro Orientalism as an appropriation of an appropriation of racial difference for the purpose of projecting a racial self, I align it with the widespread Nisei fascination with a jazz culture that, in the swing era, intruded upon the dialectic of racial appropriation that motors the history of American popular music. Beginning well before the 1940s, this fascination bordered on an obsession for the Nisei, serving as a touchstone of their social and historical self-imagining, with changing valences in different periods. Participating in the cultural practices of swing allowed Nisei to negotiate conflicting identifications with their parents, the distant land of their parents' birth, a segregated U.S. society, and an international youth culture. Distinctively American but promiscuously cosmopolitan, admittedly "black" in origin but arguably "white" in its most popular and supposedly "refined" manifestations, swing culture's ambiguous, polyvalent racial and national significations contributed to its exotic and modern allure. For white Americans, the appropriation of black cultural practices by national popular culture that could crown the aptly named Paul Whiteman "King of Jazz" at the same time that, as Michael Rogin and others have argued, it allowed a Jewish performer, Al Jolson, to secure whiteness by performing in blackface in *The Jazz Singer*.

The possibility of a similar transformation may have attracted some Nisei to swing music, as suggested by one informant in George Yoshida's oral history, *Reminiscing in Swingtime*:

> We Nisei all wanted to be blond and blue-eyed Americans; hated to be Japanese. Michio Ito, an internationally known Japanese exponent of

modern Western dance, criticized us young Nisei for our short hairdos—
thought we should be proud of our long, black hair. But we didn't care.
We changed our Japanese names into American names. Went to movies,
were crazy about Clara Bow and Joan Crawford! Loved jazz . . . listened
to the exciting sounds of Red Nichols and his Five Pennies, Paul Whiteman, "The King of Jazz," and clarinet-playing Ted Lewis. Loved the vocal
styles of Connie Boswell and Ruth Etting. Hawaiian music, also, was in.
(71, ellipsis in original)

While these recollections initially suggest an internalized hatred of the
speaker's Japanese phenotype, the target of her rebellion is itself represented as an Orientalist ideal of traditional femininity, espoused by a
Japanese promoter of Western high modernism, and rejected for the
scandalously liberated sexuality of a flapper. Her love for popular
music and movies asserts membership in a youth culture whose "American" status was the sign of a globalizing modernity, and whose exotic
glamour was rather free-floating—a California Nisei might, for example,
associate her taste for Hawaiian music with family connections to the
islands.

If, as the passage suggests, the musical preferences of the Nisei tended
toward popular white appropriations of swing often distinguished from
jazz proper by later critics, the cultural practices of Nisei swing were
racially complex, including the consumption of recordings by white and
black musicians, as well as participation in segregated dances and in
musical groups that included Filipinos, Chinese, and African Americans. Indeed, segregation forced many Nisei interested in careers in jazz
to pursue professional opportunities in Japan and its Asian imperial
domains.[24] During the war, swing was central to a remarkably vibrant
popular culture in the camps, usually read as a resistant assertion of the
Nisei's Americanness, and is still commemorated in two nostalgic Japanese American theater productions that reenact wartime favorites, *A
Jive Bomber's Christmas* and *The Camp Dance*. The original cast recording for the latter includes hits by Ellington, Johnny Mercer, and Hoagy
Carmichael, as well as "Go for Broke (The 442nd Fight Song)"—but
also a notorious Japanese-language number, "Shina no Yoru," evoking
Japanese imperialism in China![25] Like black connoisseurs of Orientalia,
Nisei swing aficionados may not have explained their tastes in terms of

a racial affinity, much less a radical politics of Afro-Asian solidarity, yet these practices necessarily reconfigure the white/nonwhite dynamic of incorporation underlying them.

These sets of practices seem to converge in a negative, parodic image in Shannon Steen's analysis of competing productions of *The Mikado*, reimagined with black performers in a swing style, in New York at the end of the 1930s. For white audiences, Steen argues, the juxtaposition of black popular entertainers, situated in a tradition of minstrelsy, and Japanese characters, settings, and costumes, drawn from an Orientalist imagination, was a grand joke. Just as one tendency in Nisei swing evokes ethnic whites' use of blackface to become American, Steen argues that the "swing *Mikados*" offered black performers a similar option via yellowface. Yet in each case, the color of the skin is not actually masked, presenting a dark hybrid that signifies polyvalently, if not excessively. Furthermore, African American organizations had staged versions of *The Mikado* as early as 1905 (Kearney, *African American Views* 15), and the ongoing black fascination with Japan was taken seriously enough by state officials to warrant concerted repression. The anxious joke staged by the swing *Mikados*, in other words, underscores the increasing repression of nationalizing racial processes in the advent of imperial war, constraining both New Negro Orientalism and Nisei swing, as well as the real and fantasized pervasiveness of Afro-Asian political desires emerging transimperially.

In Mori's novel, the possibility of Japanese American interest in Afro-Asian geopolitics is acknowledged only briefly. Visiting his brother's group, Hiro encounters a pro-Japanese Issei, known since their time in the preliminary detention camp at the Tanforan horse-racing track as "General" Mita ("the easy-chair strategist who talked nothing but war to everybody"), holding forth in the racialist, "Asia-for-Asiatics" terms shared by Japanese imperial propagandists and pro-Japanese black agitators (192). Though Frank is quick to correct the General's assumption that he opposes the United States, he amiably entertains the elderly man's talk, even as Hiro views him disdainfully: "You were once a janitor in San Francisco. You were once humble and weak . . . a has-been, he thought coldly" (192, ellipsis in original). Whether or not Mori was familiar with the case, his character curiously echoes one of the African Americans arrested for pro-Japanese sedition in September 1942, identified in the press as a St. Louis janitor and president of the Pacific Movement of the Eastern World by the name of General Lee Butler (Allen, "Waiting for Tojo" 48–51).

Yet when Hiro pities Mita's identification with Japan—"That gives you a lift, doesn't it? It makes you feel great and big, as if you accomplished something yourself, as if, after all, your life was not in vain. It makes you feel like a new man" (192–93)—his reasoning ironically characterizes his own aspirations. Like Mita, Hiro aggrandizes the geopolitical, even world-historical stakes of his own agency, rather than admitting he is trapped: caught between two warring imperial nations that maintain a claim on his loyalty, while disdaining him as an aberrant racial and cultural hybrid. Only Hiro's youth distinguishes him from the Issei, whose fantasy of redemption, of identification with the future—*a new man*—is an embarrassment.

A similar logic underlies Hiro's arguments to Jean, who must choose between joining her parents among the "repatriates" being segregated to the camp at Tule Lake, and staying behind, siding with him and her brother Jack in the 442nd. Though he refrains from calling them traitors, Hiro accuses her parents of disregarding their obligation to the next generation in a "selfish" attachment to their past: "Do you think they had any regards for your happiness? . . . They wanted to see their old folks; they wanted to meet their friends again. How could they leave if they love you and Jack more than anything else?" (161). Like his decision to volunteer for war, and inseparable from it, Hiro's claim on Jean would establish its own precondition—his gendered maturity, his ascent to manhood—as the old man must yield his daughter to the young man.

Perhaps anxious over her resolve, Hiro goes in secret to watch Jean see her parents off on the bus to Tule Lake, silently "gloating" despite the sorrow of the crowd—"I shall have her all to myself"—before he is suddenly discovered:

> Then swiftly, in a moment, he saw the face. It was the face of her father filled with such vicious hatred and venom, he backed away as if to ward off the fangs.
>
> "Devil! Sucker of human blood!" the man screamed.
>
> As he fled, weaving and bobbing through the mob, he heard the cry.
>
> "Thief! Devil of this earth! Devil with two horns!" (185)

As if looking in a mirror, the old man and the young man recognize each other in the same instant, demons joined in patriarchal struggle over possession of the daughter. But a *boy* runs away:

> This is hell. Why do I run? Am I the sonofabitch? You are running away, Murata. Is that the way of a volunteer? Where are your guts?
>
> Slowly, then, his color returned to his face. His ears turned pink and his eyes smarted. His nose ran. The goddam bastard, he cried, his anger rising slowly, strongly. I could wring his neck! I could exterminate him. But why should I? Why? (185–86).

The narration's shift from first to second to third person, and back to first again, weaving in and out of his consciousness, enacts the splintering of Hiro's identity as an adult man; humiliated and infantilized, he bursts out with a fantasy of overwhelming violence.

Peeking out from hiding as the bus departs, he attempts to compose himself, to restore his jittering consciousness to the rhythm of maturity, a process represented by a further splitting of the narrative voice. It is here that the allusion to jive makes its appearance:

> You could be violent and get no place, he thought. You must be smart like Frank. You must time yourself. Timing counts a lot, my boy. You must work with time. You must be ready; you must be at the peak of efficiency at the momentous time. You must jive with time. Okay. Patience, my boy. Remember that night at your apartment? You have not forgotten, have you? *Boy, if I could only trace those hoodlums!* Remember that other time when they meant to sack you? Remember? Remember well. You are the butt now. You are the receiver of foul names. They spite you for what you have done. *What have I done?* You have accomplished nothing and yet they have you on the rug. They remember you well now. *Remember me well tomorrow.* You're finished, though, according to them. They know you. They sized you. Not by a long shot, eh? They do not know you, bub. You will take knocks; you will take jibes; you will absorb beatings. They do not know this in you: You will not stand for it when they come to crush your spirit. *Yep, I am the bub who takes his spirit straight.* You need spirit. Spirit is you. Without spirit you are not you. (186)

The second-person voice, attributed to Hiro's thoughts, consoles and counsels him, rationalizing his cowardly avoidance of violence while deferring his childish fantasies of revenge, flattering his presumption of manhood while teasing him with the repeated epithet, *boy*. The first-person voice responding in italics, which must also be Hiro, continues to interject anxious boasts and complaints that betray the immaturity they disavow, falling short of the measured assurance of the second-person voice, which it mimics and mishears—turning *boy* into a slangy intensifier of determination, and *spirit* into the stiff liquor he brags about drinking *straight* like a man. To be a man, the second-person voice explains, involves self-mastery, a conservation of one's potency, a sense of embodied timing that must be trained and developed—for example, in sports. Like Frank, Hiro must save himself for the *momentous* occasion, a thought that displaces the monstrous image of Jean's father with the memory of being assaulted by Frank's allies, merging both into an indeterminate *they*: the enemy who will receive the ultimate expression of his violence.

But another message surfaces in the words of the second-person voice, perhaps inadvertently or without the author's conscious intention, seemingly resulting from a mishearing or misunderstanding.[26] To "jive with" is a variant of the phrase to "jibe with," meaning to match, to align perfectly, to be perfectly in step. This usage, not uncommon in the period, is listed in the *OED* as an alternate, "American" form. Adding to the confusion, the homonym "jibe," meaning insult, appears a few lines later. Undoubtedly, swing culture provides the context for Mori's use of the phrase—he was writing in a camp with at least four active dance bands: the Topaz Tooters, the Savoy Four, the Rhythm Kings, and the Jivesters.[27]

In his insightful and erudite study, *Swinging the Machine*, Joel Dinerstein argues that big-band swing was a momentous response to the emergence of urban modernity in the United States, understood as an experience of disrupted temporality, an unbalanced acceleration, in a soundscape dominated by machine noise. Drawing on work on Afro-diasporic aesthetics that emphasizes the primacy of music with dance in producing communal experience, Dinerstein demonstrates that big-band swing, collaboratively invented by musicians and dancing audiences, worked over this machine-dominated soundscape, providing a set of cultural practices, or "survival technology," that made modern temporality livable. Engagingly celebratory, this account ultimately rehearses a narrative of the accomplishments of a collective, multicultural subject, whose inclusive nationalism sounds the call to which the passage in Mori's novel would seem to respond: in its reference to "jive," as in the more frequent allusions to sports, popular culture provides a lesson in timing through which Hiro might commune, in time, with the nation.

But the implications of this argument are disturbing. In Hiro's understanding, to "jive with time" means to follow the logic of national loyalty through to its bitter consequences, proving it in action, committing himself not only to die for the nation, but to kill its enemies, "foreign or domestic." There is an irony, presumably unintentional, in the way that this reading shifts the meaning of the term "jive" from one of linguistic play, of the productive ambiguity of meaning, to one of fixity and precision—a direct inversion of the shift that Henry Louis Gates and others have identified in the meaning of "signifying" as it passed from so-called standard English to the black vernacular. To "jive with time," in a jazz context, *should* imply a certain flexibility or freedom with the beat, what Ralph Ellison's *Invisible Man* describes as the ability "to slip into the breaks and look around" (11), rather than the sense of absolute precision, of a *martial* cadence, that passes from the second-person voice to Hiro. And this corresponds to another irony, perhaps intended: it is a desire for fixed meaning, a desire to be absolutely in step with the martial demands of the nation, that condemns Hiro to tragedy—he isn't wise to Uncle Sam's jive; he's being jived. For by this point in the narrative, Hiro is strung up so tight that, as the old jive jibe goes, *he wouldn't swing if you hung him.*

Analyses of the Orientalist strain in Larsen's work have generally focused on its greater prominence in her first novel, *Quicksand* (1928). Like *Passing, Quicksand* considers a modern, cultured African American woman's pursuit of an identity that would balance inner desires and social recognition. For its heroine, Helga Crane, this incites a repetitive cycle of migration that may be understood as centrifugal, although her urban origins, complex itinerary, biracial heritage, and gendered class aspirations shape an individualistic trajectory that does not conform to the canonical narratives of the Great Migration. Drawing on Cherene Sherrard-Johnson's analyses of primitivism and Orientalism in *Quicksand*, I contend that, if the former scripts a role for Helga whose promise of liberated sexual agency turns out to be a trap, this promise remains open in the latter, an elusive and fugitive chance.[28]

Sherrard-Johnson offers a persuasive "painterly rather than writerly reading" (836) of Larsen's novels, juxtaposed with portraits by the influential painter Archibald Motley, which delineates an "iconography of the mulatta" incorporating Orientalist visual codes. Helga's pursuit of a socially and psychologically livable self negotiates between the positive and negative poles of New Negro womanhood that Sherrard-Johnson identifies as the "race woman" and the "Jezebel" (838)—which split, in *Passing*, into Irene Redfield and Clare Kendry. Manifested as centrifugal migration, her "desire to escape the Jezebel–race woman dilemma" is already marked in her textual-visual representation through "tableaux [that] establish Helga as exotic" (841). A "first tableau," opening the novel, modifies an older tradition of mulatta iconography by placing Helga "within a modern setting saturated with Orientalist motifs," thereby contrasting her sensuality with the repressive air of Naxos, the fictional black women's college where she teaches (841). Setting off the portrait of a beautiful, finely featured woman "with skin like yellow satin," dressed in a "vivid green and gold negligee and glistening brocaded mules," is an elegant room "furnished with rare and intensely personal taste": "Only a single reading lamp, dimmed by a great black and red shade, made a pool of light on the blue Chinese carpet, on the bright covers of the books which she had taken down from their long shelves, on the white pages of the opened one selected, on the shining brass bowl crowded with many-colored nasturtiums beside her on the low table, and on the oriental silk which covered the stool at her slim feet" (*Quicksand* 5). As Sherrard-Johnson explains, these elements "label the unique, exotic nature of Helga's beauty as Oriental" (844). The book in question, Marmaduke Pickthall's *Saïd the Fisherman*, extends the Orientalist theme, yet it only exacerbates her centrifugal desires. Setting it aside, longing for "an even more soothing darkness" (7), she instead decides, impulsively but firmly, to leave Naxos, abandoning her engagement to a fellow teacher, whose privileged background might have secured her position in African American society.

Beneath the seeming frivolity of the novel's association of extravagant commodity consumption with Helga's dramatic resolve lies a
deeper connection between her rebellion and her aesthetic sensibility,
which feminist critics have read as a frustrated artistic creativity and
sexual agency.[29] Indeed, her intuitive disillusionment with Naxos, the
exemplary institution of a previous generation's ideal and ideology of
uplift, finds its most confident expression in aesthetic terms. Reflecting
"contemptuously" on her coworkers' "dull attire," she recalls the dean of
women's stern decree—"Bright colors are vulgar" (20). Yet even though
the well-born dean is "a great 'race' woman" and she is but "a despised
mulatto," Helga realizes "something intuitive": "some unanalyzed driving
spirit of loyalty to the inherent racial need for gorgeousness told her that
bright colours *were* fitting and that dark-complexioned people *should*
wear yellow, green, and red" (20–21). "Why, she wondered"—with as much
sincerity as sarcasm—"didn't someone write *A Plea for Color*?" (21).

Helga's aesthetic sensibility here ventures into the notoriously overlapping territory between New Negro conceptions "of race, of race consciousness, of race pride" and transatlantic modernist celebrations of
a primitive African essence, celebrating "its most delightful manifestations, love of color, joy of rhythmic motion, naïve, spontaneous laughter" (21), as expressions of the healthy, rejuvenating vitality of Negro
folk character. Yet if that character is expressed in a *despised mulatto*
who "loved clothes, elaborate ones," but "nevertheless tried not to of-
fend," its embodiment is not properly performed. For "the hawk eyes
of dean and matrons had detected the subtle difference from their
own irreproachably conventional garments," evidencing not so much a
primitivist irrepressibility as a dubious masquerade that signifies in an
exotic, decadent, deviant manner: "Too, they felt that the colors were
queer; dark purples, royal blues, deep reds, in soft, luxurious woolens,
or heavy, clinging silks" (21).

Helga's escape from Naxos leads through her Chicago hometown and
a decidedly modern Harlem, but it is not until a further flight to Europe
that she is finally free to indulge her taste for brightly colored, sensual
clothing. In Copenhagen, she is taken in by her aunt Katrina, who indulges her desire for luxury and encourages her to wear extravagant,
sexually provocative clothes. Eventually, she realizes with disgust that
she is being exhibited and commodified, according to the aesthetic

codes of European primitivist fascination with African sexuality, in a calculated scheme to marry her off to a celebrated painter, Axel Olson.[30] Connecting her revulsion at a Danish audience's wildly enthusiastic response to a minstrel act to Olson's portrait of "some disgusting sensual creature with her features" (91), she rejects his proposal. A different performance of blackness convinces her to return to the United States. Recognizing the "wailing undertones" of a spiritual in Dvořák's *New World* Symphony, which suggests the kind of modernist transmutation of racialized "folk" content into high art imagined by Locke or James Weldon Johnson's ex-colored man, she responds with a profound desiring identification: "I'm homesick, not for America, but for Negroes. That's the trouble" (94).

Back in Harlem, she turns her Danish experience to account, which has an invigorating effect on her social life: "Her courageous clothes attracted attention, and her deliberate lure—as Olson had called it—held it" (99). As Sherrard-Johnson argues, Helga's "eroticized, mulatta body is seen as primitive by the middle-class African American community," particularly her old friend Anne Grey and Anne's new husband, the former Naxos principal Dr. Anderson (848–49). Playing the primitive—or being played or possessed by the role—comes at a price, setting in motion the narrative's climactic turn. In an unguarded moment, Anderson and Helga kiss; following his subsequent disavowal of desire, she tactfully accepts his apology, then suddenly slaps him. Here, Sherrard-Johnson suggests that the novel's language and action seem "ironically" to validate Olson's representation of Helga (849)—and indeed, when she stumbles into a storefront church, dazed and depressed, the congregants take her for the "scarlet 'oman. . . . Pore los' Jezebel!" (113). Thereafter, in quick succession, she submits herself to religious ecstasy, sexual pleasure, and an uncharacteristic practicality, only to find herself in Alabama, having secured her marriage to a preacher—"the grandiloquent Reverend Mr. Pleasant Green, that rattish yellow man" (119)—she'd allowed to escort her home from the church. This fateful decision is only the slightest misstep, the result of a moment's exhaustion, centrifugal desire slipping into the quicksand of domestic security in the bondage of patriarchal marriage.

Helga is released from the role scripted by primitivism, in *Quicksand*'s final sequence, via a contrast with its apparently more authentic performers in the rural South. Most notable is her rival, Clementine Richards, whom the churchwomen all agree would have made a more suitable pastor's wife: "a strapping black beauty of magnificent Amazon proportions and bold shining eyes of jet-like hardness. A person of awesome appearance. All chains, strings of beads, jingling bracelets, flying ribbons, feathery neck-pieces, and flowery hats" (120). Her simple, uncalculating, vigorous sincerity makes it impossible to resent her unabashed adoration of the preacher or the "only partially concealed contemptuousness" with which she treats Helga, whom she sees as "a poor thing without style" (120). In her initial happiness, Helga takes no notice of the churchwomen's resentment of her earnest attempts to uplift their sense of décor and decorum. Instead, she amuses herself with the novelty of a pastoral idyll, days ruled by "a glittering gold sun" whose fall brings "silver buds sprout[ing] in a Chinese blue sky": "Here, she had found, she was sure, the intangible thing for which, indefinitely, always she had craved. It had received embodiment" (121).

After giving birth to twin boys and a girl in rapid succession, a difficult third pregnancy produces a short-lived child of unrevealed gender, casting Helga into a bout of depression and ill health. At the same time, it cures her of romantic attachment to rural tradition, restores her to a coldly modern atheism, and frees her to detest her backward neighbors, most of all that "jangling Clementine Richards" whose thwarted affections could have spared Helga the "crowning idiocy" of her marriage (135). Reprising the novel's opening scene, Helga's centrifugal desires— modern, sophisticated, exotic—are figured in a taste for Orientalist literature. During her recuperation, she is overseen by the "brusquely efficient" Miss Hartley (129), and asks the nurse to read aloud to her, selecting Anatole France's story "The Procurator of Judea" (132). As in Naxos, the act of reading is ultimately cut short: somewhere around the line "Africa and Asia have already enriched us with a considerable number of gods" she falls asleep, "the superbly ironic ending which she had so desired to hear [still] yet a long way off" (133). Bored and impatient, Miss Hartley skips to the final line; "puzzled," she dismisses it as "silly," and shuts the book (133).

While Helga Crane embraces her role in a primitivist aesthetics only to pass through and reject it, her relation to Orientalism remains open, beyond the elusiveness of embodiment and the ongoing incompleteness of reading. Set alongside other, contemporary literary performances of New Negro Orientalism, however, Larsen's aesthetics may appear insufficiently political, if not frivolous. Most famously, W. E. B. Du Bois's 1928 "romance," *Dark Princess*, consummates its fantasy of a unified global movement of the "darker races" through the union of its African American protagonist and the title character, Kautilya. Arguably, appropriating Orientalism frees Du Bois to explore broader erotic possibilities than he would approach elsewhere, even as it forecloses some potential for feminist development of his thought.[31] Meanwhile, in Claude McKay's 1929 *Banjo*, the redemption of anticolonial and proletarian internationalisms is imagined via the partnership between Ray, a Haitian radical writer and authorial stand-in, and Banjo, an African American vagabond in Marseilles who both embraces and revises a primitivist stereotype. Their union is figuratively consummated across the body of Latnah, an Orientalized prostitute of uncertain lineage who takes each as her lover, but this function makes her expendable: as the two prepare to take their leave from the novel, seeking adventure in other ports, Banjo dispenses with Ray's half-hearted notion of bringing her along by explaining, "A woman is a conjunction" (326). If, as both novels suggest, the gender and sexual politics of 1920s radical internationalisms could not register Larsen's central concern with black women's freedom, then Orientalism might serve not as an entry into the political but as a liberation from its constraints.

passing: jibe jived eye = "I"

Returning to the appearance of the Freelands' Japanese print in *Passing*, it is possible to read its dismissal as "ridiculous" by the narrative voice as a critique of speculative fantasies of a messianic Japanese "champion of the darker races." Perhaps the implication is that such hopes are irrelevant to the lived experiences of black women in the United States, caught between the classed and gendered proscriptions of uplift ideology and the seductive modernist allure of sexual liberation through primitivism. Or is it the reduction of grandiose political desires to ephemeral practices of luxury consumption that is being satirized? Perhaps the print is simply ugly, in poor taste, evidence of the Freelands' inability to master the aesthetic codes by which a sophisticated viewer would evaluate an artistic commodity? Or is the investment of the Freelands in such mastery itself ridiculous, given the racist structures of Western imperial power in which both the Oriental commodity and the Negro consumer are positioned? Or are the supremacist pretensions of Western Oriental-ism, presuming mastery of Japanese aesthetics, what is laughable? Be-cause *all* of these readings are available, they cancel each other out, for the excessive signifying capacity of the print functions indistinguishably from a lack. The print simply fails to signify; it is unreadable, *ridiculous* and nothing more. Like the sodden mass of Arbian's manuscript, the novel Helga Crane lays aside in Naxos, and the story that puts her to sleep on her sickbed, the Freelands' print merely teases the prospect of a New Negro reading of Orientalism, which its readers—like Miss Hartley, puzzled, bored, or impatient—are unprepared to complete.

Yet if you attend to the staging of the scene, to its tableau, what emerges is a complex analysis of the workings of aesthetic perception in the representation of race—not simply "writerly" or "painterly" but "interartistic," in Sherrard-Johnson's terms; an orchestration of what Moten calls "the ensemble of the senses." Here is the passage in full:

> She sat down and remained quite still, staring at a ridiculous Japanese print on the wall across the room.
>
> Gone! The soft white face, the bright hair, the disturbing scarlet mouth, the dreaming eyes, the caressing smile, the whole torturing loveliness that had been Clare Kendry. That beauty that had torn at Irene's placid life. Gone! The mocking daring, the gallantry of her pose, the ringing bells of her laughter. (111)

Irene's eyes are fixed, staring, upon the Japanese print, but the vision that flashes before her is that of Clare, as if the unreadable Orientalist image is the condition or medium of its appearance. It is a vision, first of all, of absence (*Gone!*), which moves through a succession of disconnected, eroticized physiognomic details—*the soft white face, the bright hair, the disturbing scarlet mouth, the dreaming eyes, the caressing smile*—to a fig-ure of totality given in aesthetic rather than physiognomic unity: *the whole torturing loveliness that had been Clare Kendry. That beauty that had torn at Irene's placid life.* What Irene re-members is not an embod-ied subjectivity, complete unto itself, but the impression of an aesthetic *whole* that is cohered or made whole by desire, even as it tortures her and tears her own life apart.

Gone! tolls the refrain, and the vision of absence draws back, allowing the perception of a bodily figure. This appears not as the reassembling of visual details but in the apprehension or imputation of an attitude—that transmission of a felt sensation, of the kinesthetic, that occurs, for example, in observing dance performance: *the mocking daring, the gallantry of her pose.* Then the passage concludes with a sound, a characteristic aural expression in excess of language or words, *the ringing bells of her laughter.* Clare thereby takes her leave from Irene's life in the very manner in which she'd first reappeared. For in their reunion at the rooftop café, despite Irene's anxious, methodical cataloguing of all the phenotypic clues to the identity of the strange white woman who claimed her acquaintance, it was only this sound—"a lovely laugh, a small sequence of notes that was like a trill and also like the ringing of a delicate bell fashioned of a precious metal, a tinkling"—that revealed to her, in a flash, Clare's identity (18).

What are you to make of Irene's strange, final vision, this elusive perception of identity flashing up in its absence, emerging from the comic illegibility of the Orientalist commodity and vanishing in the music of mocking laughter? As contrast, the text provides an alternate take, a moment earlier, rising up from the sonic confusion that followed Clare's disappearance: "There was a gasp of horror, and above it a sound not quite human, like a beast in agony. 'Nig! My God! Nig!'" (111). John Bellew's uncontrollable exclamation, repeating the word Larsen had initially proposed as a more provocative title for the novel, may be taken as another trace or afterimage of Clare's elusive, performed identity. *Nig* is the intimate name, the identity of the beloved, that Bellew had bestowed upon Clare in happier times and that escapes him in the instant of loss, betraying the force of a desire which both contradicts and constitutes the masochistic, violently volatile racism that drove him to follow her to the Freelands'. And his last words to his wife—"a snarl and a moan, an expression of rage and of pain" before he is rendered "speechless"—are "So you're a nigger, a damned dirty nigger!" (111). This is as magnificent, dark, and bitter as any retelling of the old, dirty joke that is passing in African American literary and cultural traditions. Bellew's cry betrays the racist, sexist constitution of his desire, a desire he had repressed, not

by hiding or obscuring it, but by flaunting it, making it visible and calling it to attention. *Nig,* he called her, and not only in private; as it happens, it is the second word that comes out of his mouth when he arrives
on the novel's stage.

In an early scene in Chicago, Irene visits Clare—as usual, against her
better judgment—and is disconcerted by the presence of Gertrude, another woman from her past who passes on occasion. But she is utterly
mortified when Clare's husband walks in, and greets his wife with a careless "Hello, Nig" (39). Furious, and perceiving "a queer gleam" in Clare's
eyes, she is forced to sit through an old routine in the couple's performance of domestic bliss, as Bellew, cued to explain, chuckles, "When
we were first married, she was as white as—as—well as white as a lily.
But I declare she's gettin' darker and darker. I tell her if she don't look
out, she'll wake up one of these days and find she's turned into a nigger"
(39). He's the first to laugh at the joke, but he is quickly joined by Clare
and Gertrude, and finally by an uncontrollable explosion from Irene,
accompanied by tears and physical pain, which goes on after the others
have stopped.

Then Clare continues the skit:

> "My goodness, Jack! What difference would it make if, after all these
> years, you were to find out that I was one or two per cent coloured?"
>
> Bellew put out his hand in a repudiating fling, definite and final.
> "Oh, no, Nig," he declared, "nothing like that with me. I know you're no
> nigger, so it's all right. You can get as black as you please as far as I'm
> concerned, since I know you're no nigger. I draw the line at that. No nig-
> gers in my family. Never have been and never will be." (40)

Restraining the impulse to laugh again, Irene tries to join in the joke,
"humorously" asking, "So you dislike Negroes, Mr. Bellew?" (40). But
his reply "wasn't funny": "I don't dislike them, I hate them. And so does
Nig, for all she's trying to turn into one. . . . They give me the creeps.
The black scrimy devils" (40). Pressing further, she asks if he has any
actual acquaintance with Negroes. He clarifies: " 'Thank the Lord, no!
And never expect to! But I know people who've known them, better
than they know their black selves. And I read in the papers about them.
Always robbing and killing people. And,' he added darkly, 'worse'" (41).

Darkly moves Bellew's explication of race into the unspoken implications of what is *worse* than criminality and murder: the unspeakable knowledge of sexual violence, the shadowy realm of erotic fantasy and comic release bound to the extremes of pain and suffering. If the presence of *black scrimy devils*, or the mere suggestion of it, gives Bellew the heebie-jeebies, he clearly takes pleasure in this sensation, and further pleasure in exhibiting his enjoyment before an audience of respectable women, a mundane act of transgression sanctioned by nervous laughter. He flaunts his advice to his wife to become *as black as she pleases* because such pleasure, scripted by his desire, would only increase his own. Such blackness would always threaten yet never falsify her whiteness; her blackness only intensifies her whiteness, updates and improves it, makes it exceptional. This blackness is the primitive sexual essence that rejuvenates civilized modernity, making his wife more desirably feminine while demonstrating his own superior virility. Irene's first take on Bellew found "nothing unusual about him, unless it was an impression of latent physical power" (39), but this potency, cultivated in sexual performance, is linked to his characterization as a successful international banker, one of a rising breed of white American men ascending to global power amid the decline of Europe.

Bellew's own whiteness, in other words, is hybrid, the product of an incorporation of racialized sexual difference into gendered imperial nationality, enacted in relations with his feminine counterpart, his *Nig*. Her sudden loss wrenches from his body a cry *not quite human, like a beast in agony*: an expression of the inner primal savage he can no longer master, a voice from within he would not recognize as his own. That this expression bears and propels an entire history of racist and sexist violence does not, however, disqualify it as an expression of love. No matter how much you or I might wish for a realm in which intimacy and desire, individuation and communion, would be free from the violence of subjugation and commodification, this utopia will never arrive in the textual reality in which Clare lives. And so, too, it must be admitted that Bellew's perception of her identity, as the beloved white woman he calls "Nig," is not, in absolute terms, less "authentic" than any of the other personae she inhabits in the novel, including the identity perceived by Irene.[32]

But the difference between them matters. If Clare's death, like Frank's, and Irene's guilt, like Hiro's, is tragic, if the desire of a New Negro or Nisei self for its double is murderous, what flies or flees from the occasion of a fall is the negated chance of an alternative subjectivity, whose stylized embodiment of racial difference and exotic (centrifugal) desire mockingly eludes the tragedy it accompanies. Bellew's "Nig" is the perceptual object of a primitivist aesthetics that invites and incites patriarchal mastery, in the sexual performance of his rejuvenated white manhood. Similarly, as Irene obsessively intuits, the "Jezebel" that lures and seduces elite, civilized New Negro men—like, say, her husband[33]—is constructed by an analogous primitivism. It, too, occasions patriarchal mastery, invigorating a black manhood rising to its modern destiny, even when the Jezebel's primal sexuality is recast, say, in the celebrated fertility of Du Bois's "black all-Mother." This primitivist identity is the self that Irene must find and then kill,[34] a racialized sexual essence whose absence makes the civilized ideal of the "race woman" appear less feminine and less black, decadent and desiccated, transformed into a demonic, murderous caricature. Trapped between the contradictory demands that primitivism and civilization place on the New Negro woman, Irene, like Helga, appropriates Orientalist aesthetics to project an image of fugitive, uncontrollable erotic subjectivity, a nonwhite racial hybridity embodied in the form of a black woman freely pursuing her own desire.

This chance emerges only in the passing of desire *between* women, a desire that, in Larsen, can more easily find expression in narcissistic violence and murder than in any dimly perceptible social form that subsequent readers could name a lesbian relationship.[35] A similar passage may be found in Mori, reading perhaps more strongly against the grain, by rephrasing a comment of James Baldwin's on Richard Wright: "there is a great space [in *The Brothers Murata*] where sex ought to be; and what usually fills this space is violence" ("Alas" 188). For Hiro, tragically, violence is the only imaginable expression of his desire for manhood. Certainly, his obsession with violence and constant struggle to restrain its premature expression occupy him far more than any thoughts of Jean. Those appear primarily as a reminder to repress his longing for violent communion with other men, to save himself in order to possess her: "Keep her eyes; keep her legs; keep her lovely face; keep her personality; keep her spirit; keep her goodness, he vowed fervently. Keep her laughter; keep her smile; keep her love" (159). His love for a future wife aligns her with his mother and with the incarcerated community, an erotic agony for the virginal condition he would both escape and preserve: "Keep these people; keep their appetite and spirit, he thought pitiably. Keep them innocent though cruel they may be" (161–62). And even as he reminds himself that this is specifically a love for one girl, he loses himself in the most grandiose abstractions: "Keep you; keep you above all, he said to himself. Keep this that you possess now; keep that which you are seeking. Keep me in your world; keep you in my love; keep us in oneness; keep oneness for us all" (162). But to earn this love and assert this possession, merging into the cyclical rhythms of organic community, he must go to war, to kill or be killed by the enemy. And, thrilled and repulsed by the demonic reflection of his own possessive desires, an image that so excites him that he forgets to remember his beloved, Hiro is driven, by a mad martial cadence, from innocence to tragedy, destroying the enemy with which he longs to merge.

Perhaps this tragedy might have been averted if he'd attended fewer political meetings and more camp dances. The latter, of course, would bring their own risks for painfully serious adolescent male types like Hiro. He might have become one of those suspicious, zoot-suit-sporting Nisei delinquents respectable Japanese Americans dismissed as *yogore*, dirty, an epithet linking hygiene to sexuality and Japanese American racist stereotypes of African Americans, Chicanos, and especially Filipinos and Chinese.[36] His temperament might even have led him to those new forms of jazz attracting serious-minded young cognoscenti, which became known as bebop—or what Ellington once described as "the Marcus Garvey extension" (qtd. in Mackey, *Discrepant Engagement* 274). Ellington's gloss signals the obscured, if not esoteric, political significances of wartime jazz culture, which scholars such as Robin Kelley, Eric Lott, George Lipsitz, and Moten have recently begun to explicate. Compared with their more momentous political choices—volunteering or resisting the draft, asserting loyalty to the United States or Japan, advocating liberal pluralism, Asia-for-the-Asiatics, pacifist universalism, or unquestioning patriotism—Nisei musical tastes may seem inconsequential. Yet it should be recognized that *all* of the political options debated by Mori's Nisei function, for the most part, as mystifications of their agency. And all their conceptions of politics, in whatever permutations of race, nationalism, and internationalism, collude in imagining a racialized, sexualized subjectivity engendered by violence.[37] To kill the enemy or to die is, alike, to sacrifice oneself, communing with the collective subject of one's identity: this, so far as Hiro can see, is what is required to become a man.

What might Hiro have made of the story of an avowedly apolitical, zoot-suited young African American, who sought to evade the draft by insincerely spreading rumors of his desire to volunteer for the Japanese military? As Lipsitz's insightful analysis of this anecdote shows, the young man's jive, drawing on the prevalence of pro-Japanese sentiment in black communities, would prefigure his association with a more serious-minded Afro-Asian internationalism—after he became known as Malcolm X ("'Frantic to Join . . .'" 325). There is no direct correspondence in this anecdote, of course, no simple model a Hiro could follow. For a young Nisei incarcerated with his family at Topaz, any expression of a political commitment to Japan, or to violent resistance to global white supremacy, would have unambiguous consequences; even an assertion of black/Japanese solidarity that did not explicitly submit to the priority of wartime patriotism would invite suspicions of sedition. Nonetheless, this anecdote signals the subversive potentials lurking in the more unsettled, unsettling shadows of racist representations. Appropriating and embodying those features that give others the heebie-jeebies might allow a nonwhite subject to slip into the breaks of history in its forward rush, to improvise an escape. As I argued in Chapter 1, if racializing processes at any single location along the color line, within the horizon of global imperial competition, always allude to other racial formations—including those whose historical and/or geographical distance and exoticism function in excess of their capacity to signify properly in the local racial order—this allusive excess signals a fugitive trajectory. Indeed, the phenomenon of racial passing has historically depended on precisely this point, as Irene trusts while she is herself passing on the roof of the Drayton, confident that white people "always took her for an Italian, a Spaniard, a Mexican, or a gipsy" (16).

Four: Cadenza

Writing in 1980, Claudia Tate challenged critics of *Passing* to reject a dismissive consensus that Larsen's novel merely rehashed "the tragic plight of the mulatto" (142)—thereby inspiring several decades of feminist reevaluations. Nonetheless, the recuperation of Larsen's reputation has tended to cast her biography in tragic form: the narrative of the betrayed foremother whose frustrated literary aspirations must be redeemed by her descendants, fortunate to live in more enlightened times. Larsen, it appears, abandoned her literary career, after a plagiarism scandal and a bitter divorce, and avoided those glamorous ex-friends and patrons who seemed content, for their part, to forget her. A similar narrative shapes Mori's recuperation by Asian American writers in the 1970s, and his subsequent, gradual ascent into a multicultural U.S. literary canon, though Mori survived long enough to experience some of this late acclaim.

Although I, their devoted reader, must confess my own sense of loss in imagining what they might have produced under more amenable conditions, I must question the presumption that a life of obscurity was necessarily worse than one filled with literary accolades. According to Mori's fiction, the life of a nurseryman and aging flower salesman need not be tragic. In Larsen's, the life of a divorced nurse, of a self-sufficient professional woman free from the petty hypocrisies of Negro society, could well be triumphant. If, as a reader, I long for the redemption of some poor soul abandoned by the graces of literature, just whose redemption am I actually pursuing?

The story of Wallace Thurman's life is also told as a tragedy. Unable, by most accounts, to live up to the hopes invested in his prodigious talents, he died young; given the nature of his passing—he drank himself to death—it is hard to muster the rigorous determination to celebrate the occasion, as his stand-in Raymond Taylor suggests, with a wild gin party. Strangely enough, however, the life of Paul Arbian's model turned out differently. Richard Bruce Nugent ("RBN") outlived virtually all of his better-known colleagues. One of the Renaissance's few openly and unapologetically gay members, he survived to see the emergence of new social movements that articulated desires for racial, gender, and sexual liberation in explicitly political ways. What's more, the novel he wrote under the title *Geisha Man* is extant, excerpted in a 2002 collection of his writings and visual art edited by Thomas H. Wirth, and has begun to receive critical attention.

If, in Thurman's and Larsen's novels, the aspirations ascribed to a cultural renaissance of New Negroes conform to a tragic narrative, this tragedy may be understood as an effect of the movement's inability to articulate contradictory desires for gender and sexual liberation within a more politically recognizable racial project. But perhaps what appears as tragic, in literary representation, might correspond with other cultural practices, including New Negro Orientalism, that managed to elude such a downfall.

5.

The Rainbow Sign and the Fire, Every Time
Los Angeles Burns

But white Americans do not believe in death, and this is why
the darkness of my skin so intimidates them.
—James Baldwin, *The Fire Next Time*

One: Segregation's Death

In 1936, when Robert Johnson recorded his seductive call to a new life in
California or that *sweet home Chicago*, he could hardly have anticipated
how a future wave of the Great Migrations, set in motion by World War
II, would dramatically expand its scope from the industrial Midwest to
the West Coast. Even less foreseeable were its unpredictable intersections with the circuits of forced relocation shuttling Japanese Americans
from the West Coast to makeshift concentration camps, engineered resettlement programs in the Midwest and on the East Coast, and back
to their homelands along the Pacific. This chapter takes up those intersections, with a particular focus on their uneasy convergence in Los
Angeles after the war, as a new racial order was still under construction.

Yet this inquiry will proceed from what may seem a curious vantage,
established within a reading of a brief 1985 memoir by the Japanese
American writer Hisaye Yamamoto. Written in the midst of the redress
movement, the narrator's memories of the postwar period are further
mediated by a narrative device situating the 1965 Watts riots as the occasion for their recovery. Journeying backward along this circuitous chronology, this chapter aims to work through the present-day obstacles to
understanding this moment imposed by the epistemological and aesthetic training of imperialism's racial justice, whose perceptual protocols were reconstituted in the postwar era by the ideals of formal racial
equality and national independence.

(not) necessarily not-there

So long as the promises of integration remain unfulfilled, it is premature to inquire after segregation as if it were over. If anything, it's the former whose time may have passed, for these promises, in all their deliberate speed, are so rarely encountered these days outside the refuge of a museum. Perhaps it would be better to speak of segregation's death, if you are prepared to think of death as other than the end, for segregation haunts an officially antiracist and multicultural society in undeniably material forms. And so long as segregation's death defies its ending, so too do all the forms of death by which segregation has been manifested, whether metaphorical or literal, spiritual or corporeal.

For students of African American culture, to undertake a historical inquiry from such haunted premises should recall a familiar precedent, which Saidiya Hartman terms "the time of slavery." Reading an inscription outside Ghana's Elmina Castle celebrating "the redressive capacities of memory," Hartman is troubled by "the confidence it betrays in the founding distinction or break between then and now," and asks, "Can one mourn what has yet ceased happening?" ("Time" 758). Yet it is necessary, somehow, to take measure of the distance between then and now—a point Octavia Butler makes in dramatic fashion in her novel Kindred. As her protagonist Dana is repeatedly dragged back in time to her ancestors' slave plantation, she learns that the vanishing of this distance would, quite literally, demand her death.

To take measure of the distance from segregation's death, following Hartman, is not "to assert the continuity or identity of racism over the course of centuries" ("Time" 758), but to consider its transformations. This task is not only historical, but political and epistemological, and, as I have argued, aesthetic. You may recall Angela Davis's query: Why think of racism as formerly "overt," as if it is somehow "hidden" in the post–civil rights era? What instructs you to do so? For some, this training suffices to make racism imperceptible, as in the successful police defense in the Rodney King case, which Patricia Williams describes as a painstaking lesson in an "aesthetics of rationality" (54). The assertion that segregation actually is over, after all, is not uncommon, but symptomatic of a peculiar epidemic of blindness—not to be confused with those gifts of special sight to which the visionaries of black political movements have regularly aspired. In current ideological terms, this condition is diagnosed as "color-blindness," but it may also be understood within a longer tradition of racism's aesthetics—its activation of a set of enabling constraints on the perceptions of the senses.

In speaking of segregation's death, I refer simultaneously to its displacement, from World War II through the mid-1960s, as the dominant ideology of a racial regime, one that corresponded with Asiatic "exclusion" and Philippine colonial rule; its ongoing manifestation as the capacity to constrict life;[1] and its termination of a field of representation—how it sets the perceptual limits that enable knowledge and expression. In the post–civil rights period, U.S. national community has been constituted through the celebration of this death, in all three senses. The passing of this ideology is reconciled with its material presence through rituals of commemoration that train the nation to perceive segregation's death as the negative image of its cherished freedoms. These rituals transmit two messages, logically contradictory but mutually reinforcing, which work in tandem to construct the racial order as natural and inevitable.

On one hand, these rituals celebrate the death of segregation as a national triumph, envisioning racism as a thing of the past, a corpse safely buried. The supposed death of segregation *in law* is merely the consequence of a deeper historical law of progress, in which racism must recede before freedom's inexorable advance. If, *in fact*, segregation still here and there survives, it can only be an anachronism, doomed to extinction; more likely, it is a misperception, to be rationalized away by market or individual freedom, or the necessity of securing the domestic spaces of the national homeland and the private home. On the other hand, they transmit a message logically irreconcilable with the first, which vanishes under its own conditions of representation. It might be approximately translated by recalling a voice from beyond the grave, proclaiming *segregation today . . . segregation tomorrow . . . segregation forever*. This message is a promise that could never actually be kept, an anxious boast of the capacity to stop or transcend historical time, which betrays its weakness as soon as it is put into words. But it is only put into words as an excludable speech, in the shadows of national discourse— rumors, jokes, and other private talk to be publicly disavowed, or the loud provocations of political actors exploiting the margins of white resentment. Nevertheless, this message is received, across the duplicitous talk of color-blindness, as a verifiable description of the experience of life and death, and as a promise of the violence by which its boasts would be defended.

These two messages are reconciled not through rational explanation but through the experience of terror, as an aesthetic training that conditions rationality. The rituals commemorating segregation's death re-stage the birth of an exceptional nation: as racism disappears, the nation emerges, its destiny manifested as a beacon of freedom, beset on all sides by darkness. But this darkness aligns the innocent victims of past racism with the spectral figures of present-day racial threat—the criminal, the alien, the terrorist—who must be subjected to incarceration, banishment, and preemptive violence, to every possible form of death. To peer into this darkness, in what Fred Moten calls a "glancing [that] is the aversion of the gaze" (*In the Break* 233), is to experience a transfixing terror, which keeps the nation's subjects in their separate and unequal places by marking unfreedom as vulnerability to violence, while envisioning the degrees of privilege secured by violence as freedom's only possible form.

In this chapter, I consider a representation of segregation's death from what may appear a distant location, Yamamoto's memoir. Read alongside other historical and cultural texts, including a novel by Chester Himes, the memoir demonstrates how the passing of segregation as an official ideology, and the broader transformation of the racial order this entailed, turned on a series of links between African American and Japanese American racialization. While these processes incorporated nonwhite subjects into a national community by distinguishing between tokens and threats, they pivoted on a point of divergence or severing external to the nation. Here I again recall Brent Edwards's theorization of such haunted connections outside a national or imperial structure as an articulation through difference, which he terms *décalage*. If the racial subjects in the memoir are bound together, as differential forms of unfreedom, through their relation to segregation's death, the links between them, understood as *décalage*, point to a domain outside and opposed to an imperial nation, something it excludes or that eludes it.

Once again, the technical resources of black cultural traditions help to conceptualize a perceptual retraining beyond the limits of what can be represented. While their engagement with racism's aesthetics has most often been analyzed as a paradox of hypervisibility and invisibility, they cannot be reduced to the visual, or to any single sense. If they have challenged racism in the name of a reality beyond shared delusions, that reality is never self-evident or unmediated, but merely postulated, as nagging doubt or longed-for prize, at the point of struggle where politics and poetics converge. "We can agree, I think," writes Toni Morrison, "that invisible things are not necessarily 'not-there'" ("Unspeakable" 11)—beyond the limits of what can be rationally known, of what can be perceived by the senses, which is another way of saying beyond death.

Two: Commemoration

First published in the Japanese American newspaper *Rafu Shimpo* in 1985, Hisaye Yamamoto's "A Fire in Fontana" considers the deaths, forty years earlier, of an African American family who had recently moved into an all-white neighborhood outside Los Angeles. Just days before the fire that claims their lives, the father, a man named Short, seeks protection from the threats on his family by contacting the local black press. But although the fire causes a minor uproar, an official investigation concludes it was accidental, and further protest is ignored or suppressed; an unnamed "White priest" who writes a play about the murders, for example, is abruptly reassigned to a distant parish in Arizona (154).

For the narrator, the task of representing segregation is first encountered in her failure to defend the family from death. Then a young employee of a small black newspaper, the *LA Tribune*, she'd taken down Short's account, but the inadequacy of her response haunts her for decades. Reading the memoir in the wake of the 1992 LA riots, however, King-Kok Cheung celebrates it for "effectively expos[ing] a long-forgotten crime," comparing it to both the priest's play and the Rodney King video ("Dream" 127). Equating justice and representation, Cheung contends that the memoir triumphs by "writing/righting the wrong" (128). Redeeming her earlier failure, Yamamoto "has vindicated and reclaimed her own voice" and permanently engraved the crime into the historical record, "ensur[ing] that this disturbing event will never be forgotten as mere 'news'" ("Dream" 128). But if the crime was effaced in the proceedings of the law, it was indeed entered into the historical record, both as "news" and as literary art. O'Day Short's publicity campaign brought attention from a number of journalists, including a report in the national edition of the *Chicago Defender* within days of the fire, prior to O'Day Short's death ("3 Die"). Within California, his advocates included the local branch of the NAACP; the renowned journalist Charlotta A. Bass, who took up the case prior to the fire in her *California Eagle*, a much older and more prominent competitor to the *Tribune*; and the Socialist Workers Party, which published a twenty-page pamphlet, *Vigilante Terror in Fontana*, by organizer Myra Tanner Weiss, with an introduction by Short's sister-in-law, Carrie Stokes Morrison.[2] Following Cheung's argument, it seems necessary either to collapse these acts of representation into a single, repeated event or to presume some decisive historical shift in the conditions of representation, which endows Yamamoto's memoir with a greater, retroactive power. In challenging this argument, I turn to a reading of the aforementioned play.

the aesthetics of racial terror

Trial by Fire was written in the immediate aftermath of the Fontana murders by Reverend George H. Dunne, a noted Irish American Jesuit and political activist, and performed nationally over the next several years, with productions in California, New York, Chicago, and elsewhere in the Midwest receiving significant attention.[3] Its most enthusiastic reviewer appears to have been Langston Hughes, who first wrote about a California production of the play in a 1948 *Chicago Defender* column ("Here to Yonder"), and cited it again, five years later, as an exemplary "problem play" ("Writer Laments" 11). Based on Dunne's original investigative reporting for the Catholic magazine *Commonweal*, *Trial by Fire* was promoted as a "documentary play based on actual court records"; although the names of the characters and the locations were changed, the connection to the Short case was explicit.[4] Indeed, when the *Defender* reported on the lifting of housing restrictions in Fontana in September 1954, it implied that its readers would recall the town *because* of the play.[5] On the terms of Cheung's argument, Dunne's work should have been a greater success than Yamamoto's memoir.

In its central conceit, *Trial by Fire* presents itself as a coroner's inquest, with the audience addressed as the jury. The primary action follows these proceedings, run by a district attorney, John Applegate, determined to dispel "certain rumors and statements . . . circulated by people outside of this community which tend to reflect discredit upon the people and the authorities of both Acacia and Hooper City" (act 1-1). The mendacity of Applegate's account is established by interspersed flashbacks to the series of events leading up to the fire and the hearing. The conflict between the two sequences reaches a climax when Applegate himself takes the witness stand. After he testifies that the father of the family, Roy Johnson, had acknowledged the fire's accidental nature in a deathbed statement, the action immediately shifts to the hospital, to show how this statement was extracted. Over a nurse's objections, Applegate surprises Roy with the news of his family's deaths, then rejects his protests that he is neither free from duress nor physically capable of an interview. Finally, "utterly exhausted," Roy ceases challenging the DA's leading questions, desperate to be left alone—at which point, it is implied, he dies (act 2-22).

Strikingly, Dunne opts against a more economical account of Applegate's villainy and Roy's heroism in order to demonstrate how the epistemological mechanisms of law may be manipulated to transform untruth into truth. But this is the central concern of the play. It does not purport to depict, much less identify, the individuals who set the fire; rather, it indicts a larger system of segregation, and particularly the officials tasked with the administration of justice, as complicit in the killings. In other words, if the play takes up a task of representation, in response to the murdered family's call for justice, to "report a crime" (Cheung, "Dream" 128), this crime does not end with murder but, more crucially, continues in its orchestrated disappearance, as crime, from the domain of the law.

The play thus reveals how this crime both repeats and erases the form of an older tradition of lynching. Where lynching had once, in what might be termed its modernist phase, been formalized as a public ritual, performed before a defiant audience, and recirculated in photographic and phonographic reproductions and the gruesome display of trophies, now the event takes place at night, in the absence of witnesses, and must be vehemently denied by its very defenders. Yet even in supposedly more "overt" lynching cases, the identities of the killers had to be concealed from the perceptual mechanisms of legal investigation, in order to establish the convergence of "lynch law" and justice. Dunne's DA is placed in a paradoxical position, named by Jacqueline Goldsby's theorization of lynching's cultural logic as "a spectacular secret." While he seeks to defend the community against the charge of racism, circulating beyond control as rumor, he also seeks to perpetuate a system whose survival requires the ritual performance of the violence. As such, he must not succeed in utterly erasing the memory of the crime, which was after all intended to be a spectacle, to circulate in public and especially as rumor. Word of this violence must haunt the community if it is to serve the purpose of upholding segregation.

For Applegate, this community is racially inclusive, proudly and justly so, comprising those blacks and whites who know and stay in their places. Indeed, on his visit to Roy's hospital bed, he'd taken care to bring both a court reporter and a token black witness—Thomas Lawson, identified at the beginning of the script as "president of the Negro Chamber and Commerce, a Negro Uncle Tom," who had earlier accompanied the "real estate man" and "white Uncle Tom" Martin Jenkins on a mission to buy back the Johnsons' property. Applegate's community is tolerant of rumors, provided they are contained within the community and dispelled by the speech of the law, which speaks in the name of both blacks and whites. But when rumor forgets its place, intruding into the legitimate field of political representation, it appears, like a family in the wrong neighborhood, as a threat to the entire community which must surely come from outside, from outsiders. It, too, must be disappeared.

The DA's performance, as a perceptual training in an aesthetics of rationality, casts the violence that claims the lives of the Johnsons as the inevitable outcome of residential integration—as, in effect, motivated by nothing other than their invasion of white domestic space. This "effect" collapses the narrative operation of crime/cover-up, spectacle/secret, *now you see it/now you don't*: the phantasm of an alien violence, projected onto racialized bodies, must be met by a greater, preemptive violence. Just as the threat, bodies dwelling out of place or words spoken out of turn, must originate from an external agency, its destruction must be a necessary accident, an act without actors, the natural(ized) consequence of the community's underlying logic, and of the rationality to which its authorities make recourse in seeing justice done. As this logic's extension, the violence does not contradict the community's proclamation of racial inclusion as its own ideal of justice. Rather, it secures the domestic space in which that ideal may be realized, constituting a community of free whites and nonwhite tokens through their mutual, if unequal, submission to racialized terror. In the aesthetics of this rationality, perception is organized around, possessed by, that which cannot be represented upon fear of death.

to speak for free men everywhere

When the jury reaches its verdict, that the death was caused by "a fire of accidental origin," the DA commends them for their civic duty in restoring the community's reputation and silencing criticisms from outside: "I trust that there will be no more irresponsible talk by people outside our communities and that the newspapers which have cast aspersions on the fair names of Acacia and Hooper County will in the future show a greater sense of responsibility and restraint" (act 2-24). These words cannot be trusted, for they make a promise that could never be kept. The civil rights strategy the playwright follows does indeed call upon outsiders, circulating the news of the crime beyond the borders of town and county to national and international audiences, following the transatlantic and transpacific paths of earlier antilynching campaigns by Ida B. Wells and others, and the abolitionist movements preceding them. This strategy would mobilize new publics, binding those outside the local jurisdiction to the unfree subjects of various races within it, improvising new forms of collectivity through a different aesthetic of *responsibility* that prophesy a *community* constituted, not in submission to racialized terror, but in response to the murdered family's call for justice.

Yet *this* justice is in excess of any actual jurisdiction, for the call reaches beyond law and language to address an agency alien to the material world, even as response would actualize its domain in collective performance. The most familiar prototype for this form of address, as Stephen Best and Saidiya Hartman demonstrate in a reading of Ottobah Cugoano's 1787 *Thoughts and Sentiments on the Evils of Slavery*, lies in the appropriation of a Christian model of redemption. For Best and Hartman, Cugoano's brief for redressing the *already irreparable* harm of slavery models a sophisticated negotiation "between the unavoidable form of the 'appeal' and its ultimate illegibility and insufficiency" (3). Cugoano carefully acknowledges that his attempts to make it possible to see and hear "black suffering . . . may be of no practical value for those abandoned before the law," for in his words, "the deep sounding groans of thousands . . . can only be distinctly known to the ears of Jehovah Saboath" (2).

Improvised out of the traditions of Christian social action and Anglo-American jurisprudence, this form of address has a more specific history, which Best and Hartman invoke in the phrase "black noise"—what activates and is activated by Cugoano's text, even as it can never be contained within the actual relations between the text and any possible living audiences. Such "political aspirations" or "yearnings," they explain, "are inaudible and illegible within the prevailing formulas of political rationality . . . because they are so wildly utopian and derelict to capitalism": "Black noise is always already barred from the court" (9). Yet in straining to hear what cannot be heard, in a kind of improvised training of perception, Cugoano activates the authority of black noise to herald the arrival of an otherworldly justice, seeking in political action—the materialization of a community of response—to build the kingdom of God among living men and women. The animating risk of such political action is found in translation, in the process by which an alien justice comes to dwell within a living community, prepared by the text's artful movement "between the complaint that is audible to 'noble Britons' and the extralinguistic mode of black noise that exists outside the parameters of any strategy or plan for remedy" (3).

On these terms, it is possible to assess Dunne's literary response to the deaths in Fontana beyond Cheung's equation of representation and justice. Under its historical conditions of production, it is surely appropriate to deem this response courageous. Written and performed in those years when the movement to challenge segregation, negotiating the repressive climate of the Cold War, had yet to achieve its greatest legal victories, Dunne's play has largely been forgotten since. Nonetheless, its participation in those victories can be discerned at the very moment where a subsequent reading must lodge its critique—the point where the authority of *black noise* conjuring the arrival of justice from outside is domesticated by the community of an imperial nation. For in securing the exposure of the crime of segregation to its defeat in the forward march of history, the play gives way to a now-dominant narrative of antiracism on which the reconstitution of imperialism's racial justice was grounded: racism, in the form of segregation, disappears into the shadows of history precisely as the nation comes into view and into its voice, speaking for freedom.

Recall that the play indicts its villain for, most dramatically, appropriating Roy's voice. Once he gives up his statement, he dies; it is as if, in giving up his capacity for speech, he has already surrendered to death. The DA rests his case, the action shifts to the Johnsons' funeral, and suddenly, briefly, the play abandons documentary conventions to take on a deliberately artificial, nonnaturalistic mode, opening itself to charges of artistic failure.[6] As if to imply the DA's success in setting the terms of perception, the audience observes the funeral through the perspective of two unnamed white racists, who offer commentary on the service and the words of the officiating priest, which occasionally break through in counterpoint. But just as they bemoan the integration of the cemetery, another "Voice," confident and caustic, emerges through a loudspeaker, reminding them that they will share the same end, in the grave, and that justice will arrive beyond death: "No restrictive covenants in heaven, mister" (act 2-24). This Voice is not audible to the racists; only the audience, apparently, can hear it. It does not actually judge the men, but illustrates how they are condemned by their own words; thus, the first concludes, "Well, I'll . . . be . . . damned" (act 2-24, ellipses in original).

Whose Voice is this? Where does it come from? Whence does it derive its authority? It goes too far, I think, to say that Father Dunne is putting words in the mouth of God, though the Voice surely carries the force of divine prophecy. But if he leaves himself open to the more mundane charge of authorial overreach, I read this device, unabashedly artificial and didactic, as the playwright's great aesthetic accomplishment. A utopian impulse intruding from offstage, outside of the scene of representation, the Voice speaks from the dominion of freedom—a space literally nowhere even as its call is present everywhere to those who would hear. Strikingly, its authority does not derive from the playwright himself, nor from his theological writings (Dunne was already famous for a controversial 1945 *Commonweal* article, "The Sin of Segregation," condemning segregation on theological grounds).

Rather, it emanates from music. The scene opens in darkness, with the sound of a spiritual, sung solo; the lights rise, but only to a dim silhouette of the mourners, who join in the song and continue through a single verse; then, as the two racists appear at the side of the stage, also under muted light, the voices trail off into "a very soft hum" over which the rest of the scene is played (act 2-23). If the two men focalize the DA's orchestration of racialized perception, it seems that the entire scene, comprising racists, mourners, priest and prophecy, is itself conjured forth by the sound of the song, by the *materiality* of its sound, falling away from words. As the aural medium of the scene, this hum is what authorizes the disruption of documentary realism, sustaining its suspension before the speculative and fantastic. This music of grief, lingering beyond the surrender of speech, prepares and performs the aesthetic conditions within which the Voice can become audible as the herald of justice. If there is a flaw in this scene, aesthetically, if you would fault the playwright, perhaps, for forcing a conclusion, going too far, it would be a failing of translation: training or tuning his ear to the music, possessed by the visionary capacities of a black noise that precedes and exceeds his own religious tradition, he strains, risks overreaching, in seeking to transcribe the Voice it beckons, to carry over its message into the words of a mortal language.

Perhaps. What is more certain is that the price of this risk is exacted, moments after the play is over, in a scene the script tersely identifies as an "ALTERNATIVE ENDING" (act 2-25). This is a concession, apparently, to conditions of reception not foreseen in an original draft, preempting a desire that emerges from the audience under such conditions, in the form of a more mundane deus ex machina. The play ends with the jury's verdict, delivered from the audience by the foreman, and the DA's proclamation that the case is closed. But then, in this alternative ending, an unnamed Man springs up from within the audience to rebuke the court, and before he can be hauled away he proclaims the final word: "the case is NOT closed!" (act 2-25).

How is it that he speaks, that he claims the authority to speak, as the herald of justice—an authority that, in the intricate artifice of the funeral sequence, could not be located in the mortal world? Applegate poses this very question to him, which was left unstated in the earlier scene: "Who are you and whom do you represent?" (act 2-25). The Man replies, "I'm a citizen of this commonwealth of free men and I speak for free men everywhere. . . . I speak for millions" (act 2-25). His authority, in the anonymity of citizenship, derives from a nation that inherits its legacy of freedom as an imperative of justice, which it is destined to expand infinitely. The otherworldly authority of the Voice, conjured by the wordless music of black grief, is appropriated as the emblem of the exceptional nation. This is the world-grasping narrative of racial justice familiar to a post–civil rights nation, the figure in which its citizens may identify. Arriving after segregation's death to commemorate victory, in *triumphal procession*, they gaze upon the dead—the murdered victims, the anachronistic villains—*only* to see what they are *not*.[7] This community, constituted negatively, mistakes its access to degrees of racial privilege for its liberation. For, like the unnamed Man, *the sight is enough to convince them that they are free.*

shades of militancy and helplessness

In 1946, the case may not yet have been closed—a vibrant, heterogeneous range of antiracist, anti-imperialist, and socialist projects still dreamed of seizing the rhetoric of wartime U.S. nationalism for radical ends—but it was closing fast. Father Dunne, among others, would pay the price of Cold War repression. While Yamamoto's memoir implies that it was the play, and his antisegregationist activism, that brought about his removal from a prominent position in Los Angeles to nearly a decade of relative obscurity in Arizona, Dunne's own memoir offers a different account. While he was willing to sacrifice professional status to oppose racism—two years earlier, during the war, he'd been forced from the faculty of St. Louis University in a controversy over the school's desegregation—his postwar exile from California, as he tells it, came after he interceded in a Hollywood labor dispute. By arguing, prominently and publicly, that a discourse of Communist infiltration was providing cynical cover for union busting, Dunne earned the enmity of powerful movie producers and their allies, including the president of the Screen Actors Guild, Ronald Reagan (Dunne, *King's Pawn* 147–66).

Four decades later, when Yamamoto finally published her memoir, exposing the deaths of the Short family as a racist crime no longer required any appreciable moral courage, perceptual acuity, or rhetorical art. This historical distance does not facilitate the transit between representation and justice but impedes it; if Yamamoto is tasked with any political or aesthetic challenge, it arises from the familiarity of a story her readers know too well. Her autobiographical "voice" is not triumphant but strained: nowhere in the memoir does she represent herself speaking confidently and effectively against racism. Indeed, the memoir carefully obscures details of Yamamoto's biography that might attest to her literary and political agency.[8]

In the event, the memoir acknowledges the failure of representation to achieve justice for the Short family. The inadequacy of her initial response, "a calm, impartial story, using 'alleged' and 'claimed' and other cautious journalese," haunts her for decades, for, she explains, "anyone noticing the story about the unwanted family in Fontana would have taken it with a grain of salt" (154).[9] That the more courageous efforts of writers like Dunne did not, finally, change the outcome does not assuage her shame, nor does her characterization of her condition as a *lack* of agency. Her statement is framed by a recollection of two neighborhood characters from prewar Little Tokyo, a streetcorner preacher and a disabled boy: "I should have been an evangelist at Seventh and Broadway, shouting out the name of the Short family and their predicament in Fontana. But I had been as handicapped as the boy in the wheelchair, as helpless" (155). While the boy's disability represents his deficiency as a political subject, the preacher's speech is compared to that of a beast: "from a distance, it sounded like the sharp barking of a dog" (154). They are further linked by the boy's "Japanese military-style" haircut and the man's "uniform" and "military-type cap" (154), underscoring the condition of helplessness with heavy irony, for this desperate, pathetic militancy alludes to a prewar history of racial identification that became virtually unspeakable in the aftermath of wartime incarceration.

Finally, by the end of the text, after decades of repression, the narrator finds a way to fashion a different representation of the scene of the fire. This is made possible through a narrative operation whereby the memory of Fontana reappears as the precursor to a later event: the 1965 Watts riots. Note that it is the violent revelation of segregation's afterlife in the geography of urban abandonment that enables representation, not a celebration of the civil rights movement's triumph over Jim Crow. And yet the narrator experiences Watts only through the medium of television, from within the security of a home in a neighborhood that restricts African Americans: her recollection is conditioned by the distance between her middle-class domesticity and urban racial violence.

James Lee reads this as a "cynical distance" that rationalizes the writer's disavowal of political agency, diagnosing Yamamoto's irony as a disabling intellectualism that blinds her to "ideology's control" (91). Yamamoto's narrator does rigorously expose not only the racist hypocrisy of her white and Asian American neighbors, but her own complicity in resegregation through suburban flight ("Fire" 156–57)—the very movement denied to the Short family twenty years earlier. As Lee notes, however, her greater awareness does not correspond to any change in her actions, which he sees as evidence of a politically debilitating limit to literary representation. I will return to this scene below, to consider how the distance between subjects racialized as token and as threat enables narrative representation, arguing that the memoir's political task is not to portray transformative action, but to project a call, seeking to gather and bind a collectivity in the act of response. Thus, I read the effacement of the narrator's agency and the emphasis on her distance from African Americans as part of a representational strategy negotiating the perceptual limits established upon segregation's death. But in order to avoid reifying this distance, blinding yourself to the ways that structural disparities in a racial regime are naturalized as "common sense," it is necessary first to ask, How was this distance *historically* produced?

Three: History

Yamamoto's memoir begins: "Something weird happened to me not long after the end of the Second World War. I wouldn't go so far as to say that I, a Japanese American, became Black, because that's a pretty melodramatic statement. But some kind of transformation did take place, the effects of which are with me still" (150). Her account is swiftly contrasted with two tales from the realm of black music. First, she recalls a novel about a white trumpeter's tragic association with "Negroes" ("in 1985," she adds, "how odd the word has become!"); next, she recalls a "real life" figure, Johnny Otis, a musician who became "the pastor of a church in Watts" (150). To the narrator, Otis's life "represents a triumph"—an assessment she will not make of her own story: "Because when I realized something was happening to me, I scrambled to backtrack for awhile. I continued to look like the Nisei I was, with my height remaining at slightly over four feet ten, my hair straight, my vision myopic. Yet I know that this event transpired within me; sometimes I see it as my inward self being burnt black in a certain fire" (150). Given the text's emphasis on the historical specificity of racial naming, it is curious that otherwise sensitive readers have ignored the lowercase "b" of the word "black" here, disregarding her caution that this is *not* a story of how a Japanese American became "Black."[10] Strikingly, the narrator does not explicitly mention Otis's own persistent (if not *melodramatic*) claim to have indeed become "Black," instead noting that he was once named "Veliot[e]s—he is of Greek heritage" (150).[11] She thereby contrasts the trajectory of his biography with the familiar mythic narrative his changing name implies, the story of an upwardly mobile son of poor, swarthy European immigrants who abandons ethnic markers and passes into unmarked American whiteness. This narrative, of course, provided a model for the racial projects of sympathetic social scientists, government officials, and Nisei liberals who sought to engineer a story of Japanese American success over racism.

Rather than celebrating or decrying a Japanese American who claims to have become "Black," if you simply take Yamamoto's narrator at her word, the memoir's pursuit of some mysterious "event" or "transformation," in recounting a series of pivotal *differentiations* between Japanese Americans and African Americans, takes measure of the historically dynamic distance between racial subjects. This distance, furthermore, provides a history of Japanese American racialization as such. In other words, her memoir is not about how she became "Black," but about how she became *Japanese American*.

of wars, weddings, and other flops

The task of representing this *weird* event in narrative is impeded by its causal and chronological instability. She continues, "Perhaps the process, unbeknownst to me, had begun even earlier," recalling a wartime trip on a Greyhound bus out of Chicago (150), along which she encounters Jim Crow, not directly, but through a chatty white woman's "glee" over the refusal of service to a black passenger at an Illinois restaurant (151). She is unable to reciprocate the sentiment, associating it with her incarceration—she is, it happens, on her way to rejoin her family in an

Arizona concentration camp. Unsure how to respond, she somehow manages to indicate a dissent that surprises her previously friendly seat-mate. But as the bus swings through the South, she decides to try using the "White" toilets herself, and is unchallenged—except for the "long look" she is given by a black cleaning woman, which haunts her (151).

This anecdote, initiating a motif of transport that links circuits of migration and movement from local to national levels, alludes to a historical detail that Yamamoto does not stress: What is she doing on a Greyhound bus *headed back* to a concentration camp? Accounts of Japanese American incarceration generally feature a different journey—the forced removal of entire West Coast communities to makeshift detention centers like the Santa Anita racetrack, or the subsequent voyage on shuttered trains to remote interior locations. But the bus trip recalls a later migration—the resettlement programs by which the War Relocation Authority (WRA) sought to reintroduce inmates into society, to empty camps that increasingly embarrassed a nation aspiring to postwar hegemony in Asia. Like the better-known efforts to draft Nisei into segregated military units, resettlement demanded the careful processing of an incarcerated population, most notoriously through a so-called loyalty questionnaire, to identify model subjects of Japanese American rehabilitation. Qualifying inmates were encouraged to depart for colleges and jobs in the Midwest and on the East Coast, and discouraged from "self-segregating" into Little Tokyo communities. Despite this advice, resettlers generally concentrated in a few areas, particularly Chicago, where they encountered another wave of migrants—African Americans from the Jim Crow South. Jacalyn Harden has estimated that "as many as thirty thousand Japanese Americans passed through Chicago or lived there at some point in the 1940s" (56), adding that "for about twenty years after World War II, Chicago had the largest concentration of Japanese Americans in the country" (57). As Harden demonstrates in her book *Double Cross: Japanese Americans in Black and White Chicago*, the sponsors of resettlement saw a rigorous differentiation between the two groups as crucial to their assimilationist project.[12]

Returning to the anecdote, it becomes clear that what is novel and disturbing to the narrator is not the experience of antiblack racism, but the neighborly invitation to a shared pleasure in its observation, which seems incommensurate with her own incarceration. The liberal engineers of resettlement gambled on just such ignorant hospitality in dispersing resettlers into regions where everyday racism was not shaped against a significant Asian population. Rather than taking it for granted, however, the narrator poses it as a puzzle, a missed omen of the weird transformation she seeks to understand. Confessing her rationalization of the bathroom encounter with dismaying irony—"I decided, for the sake of my conscience, that the Negro woman had never seen a Japanese before" (151)—she alludes to the prior, ongoing histories of race with which she was freighted, which resettlement could not dispel.

Despite the WRA's efforts, most incarcerated Japanese Americans returned to their West Coast communities after the war, where they were reintroduced to forms of segregation that were not simply self-induced, but rigorously enforced, through restrictive covenants and less formal, sometimes violent means. As in Chicago, black and Japanese migrations intersected in Los Angeles, but this time a massive increase in the African American population took up residence in a "race problem" previously mapped as Japanese. In a segregated housing market, the influx of black war workers was largely absorbed by areas emptied by mass incarceration. Little Tokyo was reborn as Bronzeville, but the new name did nothing to improve housing conditions, particularly after Japanese Americans began to return. Surveying the situation, and perhaps dazzled by the Southern California sunshine, a 1946 *Ebony* spread titled "The Race War That Flopped" proclaimed "a miracle in race relations": "the wedding of Little Tokyo and Bronzeville" (3). Behind this cheeriness lay a more sober agenda, promoting a postwar "Negro-Nisei" interracialism forged in a shared struggle against segregation, whether "Jim Crow" or "Jap Crow" (7). As evidenced by a photo of earnest young "Negro and Nisei vets" planning a "Fair Employment Practice Committee" (9), the idea was to draw on the ideological capital wartime loyalty was supposed to provide.

This postwar liberal project explains why the narrator's first job out of camp is at a black newspaper. As the narrator explains, she was hired to "attract some Japanese readership," so that "maybe there would be the beginnings of an intercultural community" (Yamamoto 152). She tersely dismisses the project's failure, concluding, "It didn't work out that way at all, because I'm not one of your go-getters or anything" (152).[13] But the friction Negro-Nisei interracialism entailed is demonstrated in her initial discomfort with the "inexhaustible" conversations about race that now surrounded her: "I got a snootful of it. Sometimes I got to wondering whether Negroes talked about anything else. . . . More than once I was easily put down with a casual, 'That's mighty White of you,' the connotations of which were devastating" (152).

a Nisei is nothing if not a good sport

As on her trip from Chicago, the narrator finds herself situated on the privileged side of a white/black binary. Following the deaths in Fontana, however, she finds discomfort in a different context of race talk, with nonblack friends and family; now she's the one who seems to be "a curmudgeon, a real pill" (155). But chronology and causality remain uncertain: "It was around this time that I felt something happening to me, but I couldn't put my finger on it. It was something like an itch I couldn't locate, or like food not being cooked enough, or something undone which should have been done, or something forgotten which should have been remembered. Anyway, something was unsettling my innards" (154). This confusion persists as the narrative stumbles from one recollection to another, organized instead by the continuing motif of transport. On a bus, she witnesses an incident of racist name-calling that shakes her deeply; some time later, also on a streetcar, she is overwhelmed by a desire to keep riding, recalling the feeling she'd had years earlier driving to her mother's funeral; weeks afterward, she quits the paper with a vague "excuse about planning to go back to school" (156). Instead, "after a time," she gets "on trains and buses that carried me several thousand miles across the country and back. I guess you could say I was realizing my dream of travelling forever (escaping responsibility forever)" (156).[14] But what she figures here as aimless wandering, flight without destination, she glossed at the beginning of the text as *scrambling to backtrack*: to retrace her steps, to return to a past or a path she was on before getting lost. The past she is seeking, back before the mysterious event that transformed her, is, in fact, a past that never was.

In February 1943, authorizing the creation of a segregated Nisei military unit, Franklin Roosevelt proclaimed: "The principle on which this country was founded and by which it has always been governed is that Americanism is a matter of the mind and heart; Americanism is not, and never was, a matter of race or ancestry" (qtd. in Fujitani, "*Go*" 244). This retroactive insistence, on what *never was*, neatly captures the temporal confusion or contradiction of loyalty for the Japanese American subject who, as soldier or resettler, is called to prove what has supposedly *always been*—the antiracist ideal that predestines the nation to spread the gospel of justice. Perhaps knowing better, but no doubt aware that as a loyal Nisei she is nothing if not a good sport, the narrator goes gamely off in search of this *never was*. Instead, she finds it *is not*: in Massachusetts, New York, New Jersey, Maryland, just as she had on the bus to Arizona, she comes across supposedly obsolete forms of antiblack racism that are traveling too.

Settling back in LA to raise "a passel of children" (156), she finds these forms of racism again in the dynamic of desegregation and resegregation that motors local development. According to Daniel Widener, between 1946 and 1952, the year of her departure, Japanese American "inroads" into white areas served as "a wedge subsequently broadened" by black families, while desegregation efforts were often coordinated by groups like the Japanese American Citizens League (JACL) and the NAACP ("Perhaps" 170). But by 1965, as the narrator discovers, this wedge looked more like a buffer. Thus, just as she achieves a facsimile of that American Dream where domestic bliss is a litany of gendered labor—"in between putting another load of clothes into the automatic washer, ironing, maybe whipping up some tacos for supper"—the Watts riots appear on her TV set (157). She watches, "sitting safely in a house which was located on a street where panic would be the order of the day if a Black family should happen to move in—I had come there on sufferance myself, on the coattails of a pale husband" (157): the distance she's traveled in twenty years, from her days at the *Tribune*, is dramatic. Why does it seem so natural to contemporary readers?

on sufferance

Looking back, one clue appears in a January 1966 *New York Times* article by the sociologist William Petersen, published in the wake of the riots. Frequently cited in Asian American studies as a key text in the popularization of the notorious "model minority" thesis, "Success Story, Japanese-American Style" is a surprisingly vigorous exposé of the racist history endured by Japanese Americans. Petersen insists that they suffered "the most discrimination and the worst injustices," limiting the question to "persons alive today" (20)—thereby differentiating them from "problem minorities," whose unfortunate reaction to "well-meaning programs" is "either self-defeating apathy or a hatred so all-consuming as to be self-destructive" (21). Rehabilitated as the model minority by signifying the repudiation of black protest, the Japanese American is welcomed into the racial community of the nation. This is racial comparison as a severing or disarticulation, following the logic of resettlement, though Petersen crucially revises assimilation theory to celebrate a reified Japanese cultural difference. In setting the terms of a post–civil rights racial regime, the distance between Watts and the Nisei home is naturalized.

But for Yamamoto's narrator, to be released, *on sufferance*, from urban segregation is not triumph but continued defeat, not freedom but its substitution by degrees of racial privilege.[15] This entails, first of all, the privilege of being terrorized—of sharing in the communal "panic" by which her neighborhood is consolidated against black incursion. Hence her first reaction to the televised scene: "Appalled, inwardly cowering, I watched the burning and looting on the screen and heard the reports of the dead and wounded" (157). By locating this fear as "inward," the text demonstrates the disciplinary function of racism's aesthetics of terror. The vision of an alien violence intruding upon domestic security threatens to betray other forms of difference rendered invisible by the dominant racialized form of community. If the token (Nisei) secures racial privilege by displacing the image of threat onto others (blacks), the risk of being recognized in that alien image and made vulnerable to the community's retaliatory violence keeps her in her place. Nonetheless, underneath her internalized terror, the narrator discovers and exposes the very evidence of her identification with the violence from outside: "But beneath all my distress, I felt something else, a tiny trickle of warmth which I finally recognized as an undercurrent of exultation" (157). It is this confession that generates, in the text's final lines, the narrative representation of the fire *last time* in Fontana.

This recasting of racial comparison corresponds with a parallel gesture in an earlier literary exploration of racialized terror in Los Angeles, Chester Himes's *If He Hollers Let Him Go* (1945).[16] The novel begins with the anxious dreams of Bob Jones, a migrant from Cleveland, who awakens to a state of pervasive, visceral fear: "Every day now I'd been waking up that way, ever since the war began. And since I'd been made a leaderman out at the Atlas Shipyard it was really getting me" (3). Something weird has transpired inside him, scrambling chronology and causality. But this fear, he reasons, didn't bother him in his prewar experiences with racism: "Maybe it wasn't until I'd seen them send the Japanese away that I'd noticed it. Little Riki Oyana singing 'God Bless America' and going to Santa Anita with his parents the next day. It was taking a man up by the roots and locking him up without a chance. Without a trial. Without even giving him a chance to say one word. It was thinking about if they ever did that to me, Robert Jones, Mrs. Jones's dark son, that started me to getting scared" (3). Like Yamamoto's narrator, Jones can only narrate his experience of a shift in racism by reflecting upon a differently racialized figure. "After that it was everything," he adds, "It was that crazy, wild-eyed, unleashed hatred that the first Jap bomb on Pearl Harbour let loose in a flood" (4): this incursion of racialized violence into the domestic space of the nation generates a panicked desire for retaliation. On one hand, the racial crisis of war with Japan allows African Americans access to previously unprecedented degrees of privilege, of inclusion in a community constituted by terror. On the other, this privilege depends on an unstable distinction between a model minority and a racial threat: "I was the same colour as the Japanese and I couldn't tell the difference. 'A yeller-bellied Jap' coulda meant me too" (4). Indeed, when Jones loses his token position as the first black leaderman at the shipyard, he immediately thinks of the incarcerated Japanese (30).

In making this interracial articulation, Jones, like Yamamoto's narrator, is *not* proclaiming an identity; he is locating a site of substitution, a switching point. Their metaphors of visual indistinguishability (*I was the same colour and couldn't tell the difference, a yeller-bellied Jap coulda meant me, my inward self was burnt black*) turn precisely on *décalage*, the articulation of difference—of the discrepant histories that racism renders invisible. For Yamamoto's narrator, the deaths of African Americans in racialized violence conjure the suppressed history of Japanese American racialization and the vulnerability to the same violence by which it marks her. For Jones, the incarceration of little Riki reminds him of his own, overwhelmingly gendered and sexualized racialization, that fraught history of black maternity and masculinity condensed in the phrase *Mrs. Jones's dark son*. While the figure of the incarcerated Japanese is largely absent in the rest of the novel, it initiates a remarkable inquiry into the crisis of the U.S. racial order in the cauldron of wartime LA, demonstrating Himes's acute awareness of the particular, dynamic racialized conditions of Filipinos, Chicanos, Jews, poor white Southerners and "okies," and a local black elite anxious to distinguish themselves from the migrants of Little Tokyo.[17]

Himes was writing in the wake of the unprecedented commercial success of Richard Wright's *Native Son* (1940), which transposed an older lynching narrative from the rural South to the urban North. In a 1943 *Crisis* article, "Zoot Suit Riots Are Race Riots," Himes makes a similar point in his dramatic final sentence: "But the outcome simply is that the South has won Los Angeles" (225). The novel, however, makes a different argument. If the plot rehearses the lynching narrative, as Madge, a white migrant from Texas, accuses Jones of rape, its conclusion is strikingly revised: instead of being killed by a mob or by the state, he is released by a judge on the condition that he enlist in the army. Rather than asserting the continuity of Jim Crow, the novel identifies wartime desegregation not as a false or faltering step toward freedom that ends in failure, but as a crucial transformation in the racial regime. Against the optimistic liberalism of FDR and the WRA, *Ebony* and the JACL, it represents military service not as the proof of loyalty that will secure inclusion into an antiracist nation, but as a new manifestation of racial coercion, of the nation's boundless appetite for terror and violence.[18]

Four: Witness

As Yamamoto's narrator gazes at her TV in 1965, what she perceives is not an image that threatens her freedom from outside, but an internal sensation that longs for its release. To understand this alien agency emerging from within, whose movement makes the narration of a memory possible, it may help to locate the text in its moment of production. Grace Hong persuasively situates the memoir in the context of the

Japanese American redress movement, which in 1985 was approaching its greatest triumph—an official federal apology for forced removal and mass incarceration, along with financial reparations ("Something" 307).

Taken as a critique of redress, which banked on the equation of representation and justice, the memoir's scattered references to an "inward self" may be read as an allusion to a subject redress could never recover. Neither a patriotic Nisei nor an alien saboteur, this subject's *indeterminate* loyalty was the effect of state action. You might call her the "non-alien," recalling the now-iconic Civilian Exclusion Orders posted in West Coast communities, demanding the appearance of all "persons of Japanese ancestry, both alien and non-alien." A euphemism for U.S. citizens subsumed within the enemy Japanese, the *non-alien* is a double negative (*no-no*), a liminal category whose ambiguity threatened domestic security.[19] She is terrifying not because her race conclusively proves disloyalty, but because her race simultaneously invokes a threat and conceals it from perception.[20] Neither expelled beyond state borders nor included within a national community constituted against her, she was internally segregated, held in indefinite detention while her fate would be determined elsewhere. From her perspective, the WRA questionnaire—and *all* those subsequent processes of interrogation by which the loyalty of Japanese Americans has come to be established as historical fact—may be understood as the repression of wartime incarceration itself, along with the history of anti-Japanese racism that produced it. To be called to prove her loyalty is to deny the very state action that demanded her appearance; her only possible response is to vanish.

Banished from sight, she continues to haunt the rehabilitated Japanese American, most of all in the latter's possession by an inkling of vulnerability, a racialized terror that keeps her in her place. But the narrator's references to an "inward self" may indicate a different manifestation of haunting. The quavering or quickening of the shade, as an unlocatable *itch*, a misplaced memory or duty, like undigested food, *anyway something was unsettling my innards*, rises from beneath a *cowering* as *a tiny trickle of warmth, an undercurrent of exultation*. These phrases may be read as a "flickering interiority," akin to the twinge of a phantom limb stirring to life after being severed above the joint.[21] Her vision of *an inward self burnt black in a certain fire* does not represent a Japanese American freely choosing to forego or disavow her privilege, but a non-alien emerging from the grave, whose desire for revenge binds her to those other figures of death that conjured her forth.

The word "certain," paradoxically, renders uncertain just which fire is being referred to; but what distinguishes Fontana from Watts is the measure of a narrative, which shifts identification from the object to the subject of violence. In postwar Japanese American culture, the trope of consuming flames is most frequently associated with scenes of immolation, set between Pearl Harbor and incarceration.[22] What is burned, by parents and their children, are the irreplaceable traces of an immigrant past—letters and books in Japanese, photographs, toys, heirlooms—that might be misperceived or threateningly unreadable in the eyes of state officials. You might read this as an act of commemoration against all hope, secreting what is precious in a domain beyond perception. Generally, though, these scenes stage a desire for recovery through representation by the children or their descendants, who hope to redeem their inheritance by producing cultural texts. But in linking this trope both to the immolation in Fontana and the conflagration in Watts, Yamamoto's memoir critiques this desire, turning it back toward risk and destruction, gambling the legacy redress sought to recover against the chance, beyond hope, of justice.

into a burning house

While this justice cannot arrive in the text, across the measure taken by narrative, it may be useful to consider some of the forms by which its fugitive, utopian domain has been imagined. One stock of figures foresees an intervention from the realm of the afterlife. Not surprisingly, perhaps, this is the strategy taken by Father Dunne in the funeral scene discussed earlier, but it has a long, rich, and varied history across the syncretic range of black religious traditions. Put differently, Hartman's insistence that "we are coeval with the dead" ("Time" 759) expresses the insight of such prophetic desires: in the realm of freedom, the claims of the dead will be heard.

Another stock of figures awaits the arrival of justice from across earthly borders. While James Baldwin staked his faith on a radical demand for national integration, in *The Fire Next Time* he considered the perspective of the Nation of Islam, in phrasing that famous question of the 1960s: "Do I really *want* to be integrated into a burning house?" (127). This house is inhabited by an imperial nation, heir to a Western civilization understood as white supremacy; *outside* it waits a different figure of interracialism, the rising specter of a Third World. In his 1966 article, Petersen dismisses the "anomalous delinquency" of a young Sansei charged with attempted murder by invoking his association with Black Muslims (40), which he finds so self-evidently bizarre and irrational that it requires no explanation. In doing so, he rehearses the epistemological inaccessibility not merely of the long and shadowed history of the influence of pro-Japanese sentiment on African American Islam, but of the living memory of the black sedition scares of two decades earlier, which included the 1942 arrest of Elijah Muhammad in Chicago. Indeed, countering the more common tendencies by black intellectuals to suppress or belittle poor and working-class pro-Japanese attitudes during the war, Himes allows his Bob Jones to remark offhandedly that "at first" he "wanted Japan to win" (38).

These apparitions of *disloyal* interracialism, of a black-Asian convergence outside and against a white nation, haunted each of those projects that sought to exclude it—resettlement assimilationism in Chicago, Negro-Nisei liberalism in LA, model minority theory after Watts. While they do not appear in Yamamoto's account, they are positioned, just offstage, at both ends. Guarding both wings is the figure of S. I. Hayakawa, whom she invokes as a kind of precedent for her job at the *Tribune* (152). The Canadian-born Nisei had been hired by the *Chicago Defender* in 1942 in the wake of the sedition trials, and served as a reliably loyal columnist, going on to achieve prominence as a semanticist, political liberal, and jazz critic for several decades. By 1985, however, Yamamoto's readers would remember him as a Republican senator from California, flamboyantly opposed to redress, whose sharp rightward turn began when Governor Ronald Reagan named him president of San Francisco State to put down the Third World students' strike.[23] My point here is not to endorse, or even evaluate, the specific political programs enumerated in the name of the "darker races" or "Third World," but to emphasize how these figures point to a range of utopian desires outside the representational field of imperial nationalism.

In any case, the memoir does not portray a promise of Paradise or a call for Third World revolution. It does not foreclose these desires, but it cannot translate, or carry over into representation, what waits beyond the measure of its narrative. In the end, it seeks only to accept the task that the narrator had been given by the man named Short: not to depict an ethical or political triumph, but to publicize a call for help. As an individual, a Nisei woman might have been no less *helpless* before the forces of segregation than a Negro man, but his appeal is addressed to a power beyond her, in the collectivity that might gather in response to the call. The writer's task is to mediate and amplify this call under conditions that threaten to render it inaudible, to fashion a representation whose material form might gather into itself both sides of an antiphonal structure. The task remains, decades later, complicated not only by the family's death but by the transformation of the field of representation, thronged by images of similar deaths whose ritual commemoration would absolve a nation's guilt and silence the claims of the dead. The task thus involves a kind of improvised training of perception. For to pursue responsibility, to be capable of response, requires first of all, as in the biblical exhortation, that you have the ears to hear.

This training is performed, in the memoir's final depiction of the fire, as a straining against the material limits of multiple media at once, foregrounding the artificiality and insufficiency of representation to point to what lies beyond its borders.[24] Like the hum of grief interrupting Dunne's play, this passage might be understood, borrowing Nathaniel Mackey's phrase, as "eroding witness." Brent Edwards glosses the term as responding to "an aesthetic imperative to test and break the limits of what can be said," describing a "fascination with edges, with extremes, with erosion, with modes of expression that strain against themselves" that is "ultimately less involved with the particularities of the media involved" than "with the task of pressing or distending elements of those mediums . . . to bear witness—'eroding witness'" ("Notes" 572). Here is the final passage of the memoir: "To me, the tumult in the city was the long-awaited, gratifying next chapter of an old movie that had flickered about in the back of my mind for years. In the film, shot in the dark of about three o'clock in the morning, there was this modest house out in the country. Suddenly the house was in flames and there were the sound effects of the fire roaring and leaping skyward. Then there could be heard the voices of a man and woman screaming, and the voices of two small children as well" (157). The stumbling, mixed-media metaphors that frame the memory, from the spectacle of televised news, to the linearity of a novel or history book, to the flickering of a film screened only in the interiority of misplaced consciousness, are underscored with a peculiar rigor. No actors are visible, neither criminals nor victims, much less the belated agents of local law or the triumphant cavalry of national justice, only the stolid nighttime exterior of a house suddenly consumed by flames. The impediments to vision are joined to the artificiality of *sound effects*. Then something crosses over: the sound of four specific voices, which have fallen away from or exceeded speech—for if words could be discerned, they are not recorded. This sound was never actually heard by anyone who lived, yet it is phonographically reproduced on the page, beckoning the reader to follow, into and through the burning house, to cross the threshold of death. It is the sound of a man, a woman, and two children being killed.

If this is all that can be achieved in the text, if the inadequacy of representation only marks the deferral of justice, you must remember that no one has been saved. But Yamamoto's literary recording of the sonic materiality of segregation's death, what Fred Moten might term her "terribly beautiful music" (*In the Break* 5), improvises a different training or dissonant tuning of perception, in preparation to hear a call. Response—and responsibility—still waits.

Afterthought

The Passing of Multiculturalism

No one has been saved. This is the point at which all that this book has tried to explain must end. To say as much is not to diminish the material accomplishments of antiracist and anticolonial movements, nor to suppose a moral autonomy to my critiques of their pursuits of uplift, citizenship, national inclusion, and national independence. If, in seeking to imagine and actualize freedom and justice, black and Asian movements on both sides of the Pacific drew momentum from U.S. and Japanese imperialisms and the putative universality of occidented civilizationism, and borrowed freely from since-discredited grammars and lexicons of race, you should not presume that they lie on the other side of a historical divide—that perceiving their unfreedom will reveal you to be free. What desire to universalize freedom, what politics that enacts such desires, might finally be released from its inheritance of the long history of imperialism's justifications, its animating claims to justice, without a willed and disingenuous blindness? Perhaps nowhere has this book's inquiry been more continuous with the incorporative logics of U.S. imperialism than in its insistence on the task of learning: the occasion of education in reading, knowledge, and action, of tutelage in racial and sexual subjectivity, of training or countertraining of aesthetic and ethical perception, is both a problem and a chance. And this chance may always appear as foreclosed, as lost, in the historical explanations that come after it.

In calling this book's closing entry an Afterthought, I once again allude to the poetic endeavors of W. E. B. Du Bois, who sometimes used this term as a generic designation for the concluding flights of poetic prose by which he liked to frame his longer works. However, the usage that particularly interests me here pertains not to literary form, but to epistemology, or, more precisely, to the formal conditions by which rationality appears. It is taken from chapter 6 of *The Souls of Black Folk*, which opens with his musings on "three streams of thinking" running down to the present from that "shimmering swirl of waters" in which "the slave-ship first saw the square tower of Jamestown" (Du Bois, *Writings* 424). Behind each "thought," each collection of beliefs and theories, attitudes and structures of feeling, he says, "lurks the afterthought," which directly opposes it and which it cannot shake.

The second thought, in this series, is that "of the older South," the idea of black subhumanity—"the sincere and passionate belief that somewhere between men and cattle, God created a *tertium quid*, and called it a Negro." Yet its afterthought, that "some of them with favoring chance might become men," becomes evident in all the elaborate defensive structures and practices built up against even the exceptional controversion of black inferiority (424). Last in the series is "that third and darker thought,—the thought of the things themselves": before it is an assertion of equal humanity, it is merely a "shriek in the night for freedom," a cry for opportunity, for "the chance of living men," itself haunted by the afterthought of racialized self-doubt: "suppose, after all, the World is right and we are less than men?" (425).

But the first thought in the series, the most encompassing, is the most relevant for the purposes of this book. It is the thought of "a new human unity, pulling the ends of the earth nearer, and all men, black, yellow, and white," a thought "swollen from the larger world here and overseas," proclaiming that "the multiplying of human wants in culture-lands calls for the world-wide coöperation of men in satisfying them" (424). Its afterthought is the expression of this dream of unity via "conquest and slavery" (425), "force and dominion,—the making of brown men to delve when the temptation of beads and red calico cloys" (424). In the structure of this thought and afterthought you may recognize what I have attempted in this book to understand as *imperialism's racial justice*.

Meditating on this contradictory legacy, "the tangle of thought and afterthought" that he receives as the historical condition of his striving, Du Bois turns soberly to take up the task of uplift given to him as an educator: "to solve the problem of training men for life" (425).

No one has been saved.

alternative ending

But *some people manage to stay free*. Listen, if you can hear this: Mosquito is speaking.

Mosquito is one of the names of the eponymous narrator of Gayl Jones's gigantic 1999 novel, an African American woman truck driver in South Texas who becomes involved in the Sanctuary movement, or "new Underground Railroad," transporting refugees from Latin America. Through her relationships with Father Ray, a radical priest of mixed African American and Filipino heritage who becomes her lover, and others, she becomes connected to a dizzying range of international revolutionary networks that draw on pan-Africanism, Afrocentrism, black feminism, Marxism, and liberation theology—but she always remains resolutely independent.

Among the characters she encounters are two women who, as she puts it, always seem to be in the middle of the same conversation, even as the novel's action leaps forward and back, months and years at a time. This conversation is nothing serious, no report or plan or coded message, just the gossip and rumor rumbling like an underground current below the serious talk of political action. In a fragment of that conversation set in a scene years after the book's major events, one woman comments, "You talk that shit when you're in school, then you join the system" (276). To this offhand allusion to the question of co-optation and complicity, within the normative life-rhythms of radical intellectuals who misperceive their freedom in the sheltering embrace of an institution of class privilege—Mosquito interjects, "Some people manage to stay free" (276).

This sentence is relatively unstressed in the novel, and indeed there isn't really any sign that the women are listening to what she says, as their conversation continues on its course. Nor does Mosquito appear to find their inattention troubling. Yet I have tried to hold on to these words as a continual interruption, heard or unheard, to every sentence I have written here, less in the sense of either call or response than of a rumbling undercurrent or walking bass, accompanying and sustaining my text even as it gazes off in another direction. Freedom, in this formulation, cannot be mistaken for privilege, though it has material conditions; it is not an object to be possessed or a space to be secured—*You can't spend what you ain't got / You can't lose what you ain't never had*, as Muddy

Waters puts it—but a kind of disposition to be *managed*, sustained in mortal temporality, a preparation and performance opening up to the unforeseen. It is surely fugitive, if not maroon then at least transitory, symbolized in the truck of which Mosquito is so proud and steadfastly refuses to describe to the reader, and enacted in her book's form, whose long digressions, joking asides, and dizzying shifts in setting that defy simplistic notions of plot or narrative translate the temporality of oral storytelling and conversation within the generic constraints of print. Mosquito, you see, is Jones's written figuration of oral tradition's ideal chronicler, for she is endowed with the capacity to remember everything she has ever heard. She is the ideal auditor, say, of what I imagined earlier as Betty Carter's revelatory interpretation of Walter Benjamin.

The word "stay," as Brent Edwards has shown, bears a crucial charge in Claude McKay's *Banjo: A Story without a Plot*—one of the many books read and passed around in Jones's novel. For McKay's title character, an African American vagabond in interwar Marseilles, the word "stay" gives rise to a scene that is as close as he will come to the "aesthetic realization of [the] orchestra" he dreams of leading. In it, Banjo's loose crew of African Americans, Afro-Caribbeans, and Africans perform a West African song made up entirely of slight variations on a verse that concludes, " 'Stay, Carolina, stay.' " The novel observes, "The whole song—the words of it, the lilt, the pattern, the color of it—seemed to be built up from that one word," and Edwards further glosses it as "the Nigerian coast calling out to the American Carolinas like a distant lover with an endless complaint," "a gendered representation of desire," "an exilic desire for a home that is ever-receding," "an expression of desire for the music itself, a desire to continue and even to perpetuate the state of collaboration and communion it orchestrates" (Edwards, *Practice* 221). Reading McKay's "vagabond internationalism" as an instructive variation on "the practice of diaspora," Edwards finds its only ground in the music, playing on the novel's subtitle—"music is the only place the black boys stand—there is no other 'plot' " but this resonating longing: "only the music sings 'Stay, Stay' " (240).

A further gloss on the word's complex valences in diasporic translation appears in Saidiya Hartman's reflections on the *kosanba*, or spirit child, and the vexed history of the intimate bonds fixing people to places. As discussed earlier, Hartman juxtaposes the figures of mothers, who call their children slaves to trick spirits into thinking such valueless life is not worth taking, and slave owners, who call "their property 'beloved child' in order to protect their wealth." Each seeks to forestall a return, whether to the "spirit mother" or "the mother country": "Come and stay, child, they both implore" (86). But the same words may have discrepant meanings, if you can learn how to read them: "The slave and the master understand differently what staying implies." The history of slavery persists in the ways black people imagine and speak of home: "We may have forgotten our country, but we haven't forgotten our dispossession. It's why we never tire of dreaming of a place that we can call home, a place better than here, wherever here may be. It's why one hundred square blocks of Los Angeles can be destroyed in a single evening. We stay there, but we don't live there" (87). This meaning is embedded in everyday vernacular usage, as Hartman explicates: "Two people meeting on the avenue will ask, 'Is this where you stay?' Not, 'Is this your house?' 'I stayed here all my life' is the reply. Staying is living in a country without making any claims on its resources. It is the perilous condition of existing in a world in which you have no investments. It is never having resided in a place that you can say is yours. It is being 'of the house' but not having a stake in it. Staying implies transient quarters, a makeshift domicile, a temporary shelter, but no attachment or affiliation" (88).

No one has been saved. But some people manage to stay free.

what felt like the end of the world

With Mosquito's interruption in mind, I turn to one last text engaging the complexities of love and staying, of flight and return, amid the conflagration of racialized urban violence—Cynthia Kadohata's second novel, *In the Heart of the Valley of Love*. Kadohata's earlier, semiautobiographical *The Floating World* told the story of a young Japanese American girl growing up in a family of migrant workers in the 1950s, and the second book picks up the life of a similar narrator roughly where the first left off. But now the setting has shifted to 2052 Los Angeles, and the character, now named Francie, is racially mixed, the orphaned child of a Japanese American mother and a "Chinese-black" father. Her aimless adventures—she ponders the disappearance of her aunt Annie's boyfriend Rohn into a widely known but inaccessible system of "secret" prisons; she gets her own apartment and begins attending community college; she joins the school newspaper, acquiring a group of friends and a boyfriend, Mark; she indulges her impractical habit of caring for too many houseplants—are set against impending social collapse, as a tiny "richtown" elite rapidly sheds its members into a vast nonwhite multi-racial underclass.

Like Yamamoto's memoir, the novel displaces the trope of immola-tion in the service of historical recovery with a trope of conflagration invoking the recurrence of racialized urban violence. After the novel was completed, but shortly before it was published, Los Angeles again burst into flame, less than three decades after Watts. In a postpublication interview, Kadohata disavowed any claim to special sight—"It seemed to me that there was going to come a time when there would be riots, but I was as amazed as anyone when they came. I guess I should have set the book just three years ahead" (See 48)—and certainly, in 1992, one's ear did not need to have to be that close to the ground to predict the response to the police acquittal in the Rodney King case. Her decision to set the novel in the future, occurring after much of the original draft had been written (See 48), corresponds to a moment of popular media debates over U.S. Census projections that predicted the end of a white majority in the middle of the twenty-first century (Udansky). But her representation of the structure of feeling of U.S. urban life in the early days of the New World Order critiques the narratives of multicultur-alism produced by both its advocates and its opponents. The end of a white-majority nation corresponds to the collapse of its pluralist ideal rather than its utopian fulfillment, a fall neither tragic nor triumphant.

This ending is evocatively figured in the novel's opening scene, in which Francie, Rohn, and Annie, fighting traffic off "in the cool black desert" beyond LA, take a casual detour on an unfinished highway over-pass: "Before everything ran out of money, back at the beginning of the century, the government had started to build something in Southern California called the Sunshine System, an ambitious series of highways and freeways that would link the whole area and eliminate traffic jams. They never finished the Sunshine, though, and the truncated roads arched over the landscape like half of concrete rainbows" (2).[1] Already delayed, they indulge a long-standing desire: "We snuck up an aban-doned rainbow and leaned over the edge where a road abruptly stopped. We felt as if we'd reached the end of the world" (3).

In this image of a half-finished rainbow, a relic of imperial vanity—an ambition of total interconnection, unimpeded circulation, and free exchange—Kadohata's novel projects its vantage forward from multiculturalism's violent, triumphal rise to look back at its inevitable collapse. This image captures what I term *the passing of multiculturalism*, evoking a historical conjuncture whose conditions and forces have become clearer over the decades since, in a phrase I hope to resonate in at least three ways. First, it refers to the closure of a phase of debates in the so-called culture wars, as not a settled resolution but a gradual shifting of terms and positions, by which a language of racial justice developed by insurgent multiculturalism became dominant.[2] Second, it describes the unexpected way these post–civil rights era critiques, derived from the remnants of a revolutionary Third Worldism, crossed over to provide the ideological grammar and lexicon for resurgent U.S. global power in the various iterations of a New World Order.

But a third sense of the phrase is suggested by the revived fascination over the past two decades with phenomena of racial passing and its cultural representations, itself sponsored by multiculturalist curricula. As it did in the aftermath of World War I, this fascination expresses anxieties over the transformation of a racial order. Where the phenomenon of racial passing may be understood as an attempt to claim the prerogatives of a freedom whose social conditions are unrealized, its representation in the African American passing novel can be read as an inquiry into the difference between the acquisition of the status privileges accorded to whiteness and the actualization of black ideals of freedom. Similarly, "the passing of multiculturalism" might signify both a kind of overreaching in excess of its established social grounds and an unresolved questioning of the difference between privileges gained and freedom yet elusive.

Here the response by Kadohata's characters, gazing out from the ruins of a past era's doomed and unfinished aspirations, is salutary. Rohn clowns around, mugging and drooling and limping, pretending to be an animal and exaggerating the grotesque features of his fat, hairy body, as Francie eggs him on and Annie scolds him in mock annoyance, a joking ritual of familial affection. From there, the novel goes on to depict Francie's changing awareness of her position in the decaying social order, and the implications of its imminent collapse, as a developing critique of the misrecognition of privilege as freedom.

Joining the student newspaper at her community college, she notices, in her fellow staffers, "a cunning that I both envied and feared,
and eventually realized that I, too, possessed. The cunning was a sword
against the world, the way wealth was a shield for the people of richtown."
Underlying this cunning is a "hope" that distinguishes them from "students at universities [who] held expectations of the world": "Sometimes
I longed to have that ease, to be a person who expected, but I couldn't. I
felt I didn't have rights so much as hopes" (34). Because this hope swells
in the absence of achievable goals, she and her colleagues throw themselves into the newspaper rather than their studies, without any concrete ambitions: "When someone from the 'real world,' some richtown
journalist, came to talk to us, it didn't really matter much. We knew we
would never hold jobs like they held." They hesitate, not so much in
self-doubt as in Du Bois's structure of thought and afterthought—"We
hated these journalists because they condescended to us and because,
deep down, we weren't sure whether we deserved to be condescended
to. They would tell us what would happen if we ever made it in the real
world. But what made one world real and another not?"—in a condition
that would be familiar to the model minority of Negro uplift: "We didn't
always want to be us, but we never wanted to be them. That's what they
didn't understand" (82).

This still inchoate distinction between the privilege she is encouraged to desire and an alternative Francie cannot articulate is reinforced
by a developing social analysis, starting from the insight that "someday it would be our children who would be inheriting the country, if
there was a country left to inherit" (82). But as conditions deteriorate,
she sees only the work of negation, whether in her succinct and incisive parody of "political liberalism among the affluent"—"I could still
remember a time when some people in richtowns spoke out in favor of
some of the changes they thought the rioters wanted. Let's have more
richtowns, they said"—or in her diagnosis of its opposition: "It became
clear that the rioters had long ago stopped rioting for change. Now they
rioted for destruction" (190). Though she identifies with the social and
political forces driving the increasing urban unrest, her primary concern
is with more mundane questions of survival. As her fellow Angelenos
begin planning to escape the city, Francie resists making a decision to
leave, observing, "I didn't think conflagration was coming; conflagration

was doomed to fail. Collapse was coming" (117). This formulation is too evasive to be logically consistent—is she saying that conflagration won't happen, or that one mustn't put one's hopes in it?—but this very evasiveness may be her survival instinct.

For Francie, the question of staying or leaving remains undecided at the novel's conclusion. Nonetheless—and despite her awareness that the coming violence will take the lives of many people she loves, and perhaps her own—it ends on an upbeat note. In the final chapter, she heads to the Pasadena arroyo with Mark and their friends Lucas and Jewel, to search for a secluded spot mentioned in a story told by Jewel's father, Hank, which held a mystery he'd never resolved. Jewel's own decision about staying has become dependent on learning this secret. Eventually they find the spot and dig up a box buried a half-century earlier by Hank's father, which contains a pair of rings. One is inscribed with his name, also Hank, and the other with the name Maria—a woman Jewel has never heard of, but who is *not* the wife her grandfather always hated but never left.

This excursion turns out to be the last time the friends are all together. Later, after Jewel, who is probably dying, has moved east, Francie and Mark return to the arroyo, intending to dig up the rings to send her as a gift. Instead, they discover that she's already taken them, leaving in their place a note with her name and the date, July 2052. Francie impulsively adds their names to the paper, along with those of Lucas, Annie, Rohn, and a mentally disabled man named Pyle, whose late mother Francie had admired. They each add a good luck charm—a bracelet that was Mark's first independent purchase after leaving an abusive home at fourteen, and a pair of rocks Francie identifies with her dead parents—and bury it all again before heading back to LA. The novel closes: "In the months to come, the sky [where Francie senses the souls of the recently deceased watching the living] would get even more crowded, but I would take my inspiration from right here" (224).

This act of burial recalls an alternative form of the immolation trope in Japanese American narratives, in which the heirlooms abandoned prior to wartime incarceration are not burned but buried—a less extreme act, but one that also invokes the ritual disposal of the dead. While the names on this list are of the (for-now) living, they will never again be together in one place, so their material registration on Jewel's note binds them across absence. The odd name out, Pyle, is "an after-thought" (224)—another orphan with whom Francie identifies, whom she symbolically adopts. The rocks are, for her, the material presence of her parents, who, in a chronologically ambiguous earlier passage, have already disappeared from the sky (192).

The buried items betoken a network of affective ties constituting what the orphaned Francie can conceive of as family. Though such a queer familial arrangement would be unrecognizable in the eyes of the state, it may be read as a figure for mutual belonging in a diasporic collectivity that cannot be founded on common ancestry. The secure lo-cation in which this family is bound is not a house or private home, but a grave with no marker. It is hidden in a spot folded within the land-scape of "domestic" spaces invisible to the state's ruling gaze—a geog-raphy of abandonment the novel traverses between the twin poles of the city and the desert. *Right here*, for Francie, provides the *inspiration* she needs to keep moving through a falling world, not by securing her against violence, but as a relation across distance, a reworking of alien-ation: because this "home" is *not* where she stays, it might establish her belonging-in-movement.

Like *Trial by Fire*, however, the novel is also supplied with an alterna-tive ending. Father Dunne's revision, you may recall, seemed to respond to his audience's desire for some promise of justice's triumphal fulfill-ment. But Kadohata's changes, silently amending the 1997 reprint of her novel—after she had herself lived through the riots her novel seemed to foretell—withdraw the upbeat note of the original's conclusion, sub-stituting figures of terror, violence, and death. According to her editor at the University of California Press, when Kadohata was approached regarding the reissuing of the novel, she asked if she could make a few changes—an unusual request for a work of fiction, but one that did not seem to pose any difficulties.[3] These revisions, never explicitly marked, all occur in the final chapter. I present them below in the order that they appear in the text.

In this version, Jewel *is* able to identify the mysterious woman named on the second ring buried by her grandfather in the Pasadena Arroyo: Maria is her great-aunt, the sister of her grandfather's wife. Further-more, she now reveals that her grandfather *did* love her grandmother at one point—but that she married him only because she was poor and he was making a lot of money at the time. Francie then wonders aloud whom Maria may have loved. Later, when Francie and Mark find Jewel's note on their return to the arroyo, Francie adds only her own name and Mark's to the paper, along with a phrase that looks like graffiti or an epitaph: "In Love, August 2052" (224).

As before, they bury their keepsakes, but now when they prepare to head back, they discover their car has been stolen. In this version, the strangers roaming the area are more menacing; where previously they threw trash into the arroyo, now they also fling a howling dog, in a meaningless act of ill will. Horrifically, the dog does not die a quick or quiet death. Francie also reveals that the gangs reportedly frequenting the area do not simply target richtowners, as in the earlier edition, but also include pro-government vigilantes. The new ending leaves Francie here, having spent the entire night cowering with Mark in the brush, blood from a scratch drying on her cheek, beset by the stench of garbage and the cries of the dying dog. The concluding sentences draw back sharply in fierce, anguished closure—one in which the question of staying or fleeing is now definitively revealed:

> Los Angeles was the only home either of us had ever known, and maybe this would be the only love we would ever know. For these reasons, I knew I would never leave Los Angeles.
> I could not. (225)

In this alternative ending, the hopeful representations of an affiliative family of orphans and of home as the condition of mobility are replaced by a diminished insistence on romantic love between a woman and a man, and on the fixed location it seems to demand—both of which necessitate a tone of failure and loss. Indeed, the original contexts of the buried box no longer represent an idealized, reciprocal romantic connection. Meanwhile, home, in the final passage, comes into focus only in proximity to catastrophic violence certain to overwhelm it. It is only by admitting its imminent destruction that Francie finds an answer to the question of staying, and is able to identify LA not as the only place she has lived in more or less happily, but as the only home she has ever known. This recalls a passage from the very first chapter, in which Francie, just back from the desert after searching vainly with her aunt for a disappeared Rohn, sits alone, wondering if Annie is crying, and reflects, "I thought then that there were two reasons in the world to cry—because you *were* at home, with people you were more or less attached to; or because you weren't at home" (17).

Given Francie's earlier comments on the persistence and sufficiency of hope, the despairing turn of this alternative ending may seem tragic. In stories one often speaks of hope as life-giving, as that which gives future, apportioning time; the loss of hope, conversely, is equated with death, as if despair halts and concludes time's passing. I am tempted to call this a purely literary conceit—a claim literary criticism could hardly disprove—but the literatures I seek to learn to read do not conclude here. It would be more accurate to say this is where they begin, where they take form and flight in narrative. As hopelessness, despair, and death coincide with the mundane temporality of everyday life, what continues to come after a chance, to make a way out of no way? For Francie, hope is not so much a feeling she experiences as a quality she intuits from the evidence of *cunning*—the characteristic weapon of all those whose condition is defined less as exploitation, dispossession, or disenfranchisement than as a kind of waste product of a self-destructive order. As a *sword against the world*, cunning bears the potential of destructive violence in the pursuit of an unimaginable freedom. This is contrasted with the *shield* wealth provides to the inhabitants of richtown—terrorized privilege as freedom's profane substitute—who, she imagines, have *expectations* and *rights* rather than hopes. In the alternative ending, Francie seems to pass beyond hope to despair, but in imagining the destruction of home and the death of love, her narrative gives future beyond despair, on the far side of despair. This is its blue note, which is other than tragic.

It is even grateful, if you can hear this, and *forever* so, if Betty Carter is right. To say this may seem morbid. The note Francie buries in the arroyo surely appears as such, commemorating the love between her and Mark from the perspective of its certain death; but how else can a love note be preserved? It is only from the vantage of its destruction that Francie can perceive her home in Los Angeles, and that she can assert, in anguish, she will stay, so long as she can manage. This is a lesson for which she must be grateful, in the fragile temporality of love, its irremediable exposure to irreparable loss. For it is the mortality of love, she learns, that makes it *binding*.

NOTES

1 On the limitations of oceanic frames, see Edwards, "Uses" 63.

2 For an example referencing black sympathies for Japan, see "Our Monthly Review" 125; in a discussion of Filipino preferences for African American colonial tutelage, see Scarborough, "The Negro" 345.

3 See, among others, A. Jones and Singh; Prashad; B. Mullen; Ho and Mullen; Jun; Onishi.

4 For appropriately playful and theoretically unstressed usage, see George Lipsitz's excellent 1997 essay, " 'Frantic to Join . . .' " (327).

5 Taketani continues this line of argument in "Colored Empires" as well as in *The Black Pacific Narrative*, which was published too late for me to fully engage with in this study.

6 This places the island in the Indian rather than Pacific Ocean, a distinction that would justify situating Kong within other historical circuits between Asia and Africa. Nonetheless, within the fields of U.S. racial signification in which Kong appears, the island falls within a territory of racialization better described as Pacific.

7 See Ignacio et al.

8 Entry 1a in the *OED*'s definition of "amok" reads: "A name for a frenzied Malay."

9 For a classic account of lynching as ritual, see Harris. On the ethical limitations of studies of "lynching," see Goldsby.

10 Holiday's autobiography is often treated as a fabrication of its coauthor, William Dufty, but Griffin provides grounds for recognizing Holiday's creative agency in shaping the narrative through its basis in original and published interviews (*If You Can't* 51).

11 Anecdotes of this cruelty are legion. Irene Kitchings recalls "a white man from Georgia" who summoned Holiday to his table at Café Society to, in his words, "show [her] some 'strange fruit' . . . this very obscene picture on a napkin." Kitchings adds, "She picked up the chair and hit him on the head, and before it was over, she showed him, honey. . . . I mean that she was wiping the floor with this man" (qtd. in Margolick 55).

12 See N. Baker 45–54. While Holiday's memoir falsely claims she and an accompanist wrote the music, it is indisputable that the song as now known came into being through her artistry.

13 The artists Kerry James Marshall (in *Heirlooms and Accessories*) and Shawn Michelle Smith ("In the Crowd") each attempt to intervene in the aesthetic training enacted by this fascination, in responses to the same 1930 Indiana photograph.

14 See also Nicholson 113.

15 In a brief sociological lesson in her memoir, Holiday admits to hearing her "first good jazz in a whorehouse," as did "a lot of white people [who] helped label jazz 'whorehouse music,'" explaining that this "was about the only place where black and white folks could meet in any natural way," being "the only joints fancy enough to have a victrola and for real enough to pick up on the best records" (10).

16 On "black women's vocality," see Griffin, "When Malindy Sings."

17 This claim is appropriately dismantled by A. Davis (*Blues Legacies* 184–87) and Griffin (*If You Can't* 130–32).

18 For a discussion of this and related blues and jazz songs, usually written by men but sung by black women, see A. Davis, *Blues Legacies* 26–33, 177–79.

19 On scat, meaning, and this anecdote, see Edwards, "Louis Armstrong," esp. 624.

20 *Lady Sings the Blues* notoriously opens: "Mom and Pop were just a couple of kids when they got married. He was eighteen, she was sixteen, and I was three" (3). Nicholson establishes that there was no marriage, that the text cut six years from Sadie's age, making her younger than the father Holiday claimed, who wasn't recorded on her birth certificate. But Griffin persuasively argues that these details in the autobiography aim to defend Sadie from moralizing criticism (51–52).

21 Cf. Dove's gloss on her eponymous songbird, musician's slang for a female vocalist, as the canary in the coal mine, in the audio clip on the poem's *Poetry Foundation* webpage.

22 But see Shilliam, published too late for me to engage substantively in this book.

1. THE VIOLENCE AND THE MUSIC, APRIL–DECEMBER 1899

1 This appears to be an editorial error, as Du Bois accurately described the case in earlier and later accounts. See the 1938 speech that was the basis for *Dusk*, "A Pageant in Seven Decades" (254); typescripts of the speech in the University of Massachusetts's online Du Bois archive; the May 14, 1938, installment of his "Autobiography of William E. B. Du Bois" in the *New York Amsterdam News* (13); and his 1961 recorded interview with Moses Asch, *W. E. B. Du Bois: A Recorded Autobiography*. The error recurs in his 1968 *Autobiography* (222). Meanwhile, the facts of the case are still disputed over a century later by local white communities; see Arnold.

2 Du Bois's famous dictum in "Criteria of Negro Art" that "all Art is propaganda and ever must be" (*Writings* 1000) seems to contradict his indictment of antiscientific uses of propaganda in U.S. historiography in "The Propaganda of History." However, that text crucially distinguishes between history as "a science" and "an art using the results of science" (*Writings* 1029); the latter has pride of place for Du Bois within a hierarchy of culture. Du Bois's literary project can thus be understood,

roughly, as art (propaganda) using the results of science. Even so, the error is regrettable.

3 See Brown [as Ngozi-Brown], "African-American" 45; Balce, esp. 52–58.

4 Marasigan 62, 67. For more on the placards, see ["A placard"](*Richmond Planet*, November 11, 1899); "Negro Troops Are Asked to Revolt" (*Atlanta Constitution*, November 2, 1899); Ontal 125; Gatewood, "*Smoked Yankees*" 258–59n2. "Gray" is presumably Edward Gray, lynched in Louisiana in June ("Latest Louisiana Lynching," *Chicago Daily Tribune*, June 16, 1899). Gray is mentioned in at least one account of a presentation by Louis P. Le Vin, the detective hired by Wells, describing a follow-up visit to Georgia after his initial report became public ("Detective L. P. Le Vin Makes a 2nd Trip," *Afro-American Advance*, July 1, 1899).

5 On Fagen, Robinson and Schubert's 1975 article remains essential, as is Schubert's 2008 essay. See also San Juan, "An African American Soldier," and Ontal.

6 Robinson and Schubert 75; "American Deserter a Filipino General," *New York Times*, October 29, 1900. Also in the *Times*, see "Negro Deserter Beheaded," December 9, 1901, and "Lieut. Alstaetter Talks of David Fagin," December 10, 1901.

7 Robinson and Schubert 78. According to Russell, the accused man, Rube Thompson, had worked for the U.S. Army in the Philippines (219).

8 Robinson and Schubert 76–77. Fagen's end is shrouded in myth; despite questionable reports that he was ambushed and beheaded in December 1901 or "hacked to death with a bolo" in late 1902 (80–81), rumors that he survived, possibly faking his own death, continued to circulate.

9 For important readings of the 1900 text, see Edwards, *Practice* 1–2, and Shepperson 307.

10 Except where indicated, all references are to its subsequent publication in the A.M.E. *Church Review* in October 1900, which Herbert Aptheker lists as the source for his reprint in *Writings of W. E. B. Du Bois*.

11 The *Church Review* version is apparently the only extant text, so it may be impossible to determine if changes were made for publication. A growing but still limited scholarship on the address occasionally misdates it to March 1900. However, an American Negro Academy (A.N.A.) program in the Du Bois Papers at the University of Massachusetts has the speech scheduled for 7:30 P.M. on December 27, 1899 (American Negro Academy), corresponding to the text's statement, "We stand to-night on the edge of the year 1900" (104). A contemporary account in H. T. Johnson's A.M.E. *Christian Recorder* praises the speech effusively, expressing the intention to reproduce it in the future ("The Negro Academy"); see also coverage of the meeting in the *Colored American* ("National Negro Academy") and a subsequent *Church Review* article that quotes Du Bois's text, referencing the A.N.A. (Mossell 223, 224). Curiously, Alfred Moss's history of the A.N.A. reports that Du Bois neither appeared at the meeting nor submitted his speech to be read (65), only to contradict itself in the same chapter (92, citing the *Colored American*). Finally, the December 1899 date is accepted by the most assiduous reader of Du Bois's early work, Nahum Chandler, in an annotated

reprinting of the speech in his invaluable new collection of Du Bois's essays in this period (Chandler 125–26n1).

12 I follow Aptheker ("Present Outlook," ed. Aptheker, 77–78) in correcting two errors in the *Church Review* text: "period" for "peroid," and, more aggressively, "Hawaii" for an otherwise redundant "Havana," thereby tracking references to "Hawaiians" in the same paragraph, quoted below.

13 Cf. Du Bois, "Negro Mind" 397–406.

14 On black responses to Kipling, see Gatewood, *Black Americans* 183–85, as well as H. T. Johnson's 1899 lecture, *The Black Man's Burden*, which reprints his widely cited poem of the same name.

15 An earlier version of this article appeared in *Foreign Affairs* ("Worlds of Color").

16 See Du Bois, *Writings* 359, 372, 391. The word "world," whose elision improves the rhythm and makes the phrase easier to repeat, is effectively redundant—for Du Bois, a "century" is self-evidently a category of *world-historical* time.

17 That is, you might say that the radical desires of this project are staked on the chance that what appears in the historical record as *mimicry* might be read, recalling Zora Neale Hurston, for and as *improvisation*, following Fred Moten's meditations on the term in *In the Break*.

18 In "Souls of White Folk" (339), later collected in his 1920 volume, *Darkwater*.

19 "Atlanta University" 197. These paragraphs are virtually identical to a 1906 standalone essay in *Collier's*, "The Color Line Belts the World," which is better known (see, e.g., Mullen and Watson). While Du Bois's enthusiasm suggests a growing radicalism, the political agenda here is still to preserve alignment with *the greater ideals of white civilization*.

20 Since the rise of a post-Soviet New World Order, interest in Afro-Asian connections has steadily increased, including a growing body of scholarship on African American interest in Japan and Japanese Americans. Joining early contributions by Hellwig and Shankman, important work was begun by Allen, Kearney, Gallicchio, and Lipsitz, and subsequently extended by Horne, Widener, Taketani, and Onishi, among others.

21 The novel's depiction of the relationships between nonwhite characters dramatizes a complex reading of geopolitics, in which Japanese guidance ultimately gives way to a messianic child, born to the hero and an Indian princess.

22 See Allen, "When Japan" and "Waiting for Tojo," and Hill.

23 See Allen, "When Japan," and Ottley 327–42.

24 See Peery, *Black Fire* and *Black Radical*, and Green.

25 See Kelley and Esch.

26 For an extensive but generally sympathetic accounting, see Kearney, "Pro-Japanese Utterances."

27 See A. Jones and Singh.

28 Scholarship on black/Filipino connections has also expanded in recent years, driven both by American studies' critiques of empire and by the growth of Filipino American/diasporic studies. The essential works of Gatewood, along with

articles by M. Robinson and Schubert, Payne, Brown, and San Buenaventura, have since been joined by Ontal, Murphy, Gruesser, San Juan Jr., Marasigan, Y. Cho, Puente, Mendoza, and others.

29 See Rafael; Kramer, *Blood*; and also Salman.

30 For an extensive discussion of the A.M.E. Church and imperialism, see Little.

31 On the threat of overcivilization, see Bederman. On lynching's *modern* "cultural logic," see Goldsby.

32 These italicized phrases come from Moten's gloss (*In the Break* 4) on Saidiya Hartman's instructive refusal, in *Scenes of Subjection*, to reproduce Frederick Douglass's account of the beating of Aunt Hester.

33 Reproduced as quoted in Marasigan (67) from U.S. military records. See also note 4 above.

34 Translated by Alejandrino's son, this English version appeared in 1949, under quite different historical conditions than the 1933 original.

35 Robinson and Schubert list him as five foot six (73), though Ontal, apparently reviewing the same U.S. military records, has five foot ten (119).

36 For contemporary testimonials to the contrary, including an interview with one of his prisoners in the *New York Times* ("Lieut. Alstaetter"), see Robinson and Schubert 78.

2. SHAMING A DIASPORA

1 But see Brent Edwards's provocative consideration of Duke Ellington's phrase "the literature of music" in "The Literary Ellington" (2).

2 See Alexander Weheliye's transformative reading of this tension between the ephemerality of music and technologies of sound recording, *Phonographies*.

3 This is not to imply a conclusive dismissal of the trope, whose multivalent, esoteric force exceeds its deployment within the epistemological constraints of any particular mode of knowledge.

4 Edwards, "Uses," 66; cf. Edwards, *Practice* 11–15.

5 The work of Willard Gatewood remains the best introduction to these debates; see *Black Americans* and *"Smoked Yankees."*

6 See Charles Steward, "Manila and Its Opportunities," and Scarborough, "The Negro and Our New Possessions" and "Our New Possessions—An Open Door."

7 See Suisman. Despite its policy of using black musicians exclusively—per its famous slogan, "The only genuine colored record. Others are only passing for colored"—the company eventually reissued some records by white musicians under pseudonyms. Yet if these sides were among them, this still suggests some hope of an audience for black-performed Hawaiian music.

8 For more on Loving, see Richardson; Kornweibel; Woodson, "Walter Howard Loving."

9 David Levering Lewis credits Loving with the "coup de grace" to the controversial military ambitions of Du Bois and NAACP president Joel Spingarn, but praises the nuance and integrity of his reports, noting his subsequent friendship with Du

Bois (*W. E. B Du Bois: Biography* 559–60). Kornweibel provides a more detailed account of Loving's activities, including efforts to quiet wartime critics of crimes against black soldiers like Kelly Miller, but comes to similar conclusions about his competence and character.

10 On Woodson and the black Thomasites, see San Buenaventura, "The Colors of Manifest Destiny" 18–20.

11 "Training" 390, "Hampton Incidents" 491. The latter issue also featured an article on Hawaiian education.

12 Complaining that Filipinos know little beyond Washington's *Up from Slavery*, Butler suggests a course of "Wheatley, Douglass, Elliott, Tanner, Scarborough, Du Bois, Pinchback, Braithwaite, Bruce, Dunbar, Meta Warrick Fuller, Carver, [and] Woodson," and reciprocally, "Gomez, Zamora, Burgos, Rizal, Mabini, the Lunas, Bonifacio, del Pilar, Aguinaldo, also Quezon, Osmeña, Roxas, and others" (268).

13 For more recent reconsiderations of Hopkins's transpacific writings, see Colleen O'Brien, "'Blacks,'" and especially Yu-Fang Cho, "Cultural Nationalism."

14 Notable here is the controversy over Theodore Roosevelt's accounts of black soldiers at San Juan Hill; see, e.g., Gatewood, *Black Americans*, and Kaplan, "Black and Blue."

15 The earliest survey appears to be James Robert Payne's 1983 "Afro-American Literature of the Spanish-American War." Gretchen Murphy and John Cullen Gruesser recently reprinted Frank Steward's stories in *PMLA*; see also Gruesser, *Empire Abroad*; Murphy, *Shadowing*; Jennifer James, *Freedom*. Paula Moore Seniors diligently reconstructed the story of *The Shoo-Fly Regiment*, whose script is not extant, in *Beyond "Lift Every Voice and Sing."* I have found evidence of a minor fad in Philippine-themed productions by black musical theater troupes in the same period as *Shoo-Fly*.

16 As it happens, communities of Filipinos in Vaughn's Louisiana date back to the mid-eighteenth century and have had a complicated history of racial classification (see, e.g., Cordova 1–7).

17 Because the key action in "The Men Who Prey" takes place in settings inaccessible to a black officer or an older native woman, the narrator mostly disappears there into an omniscient third person.

18 Gretchen Murphy has boldly proposed reading the narrator as deliberately "de-raced," not "black or white" or "raceless": "a de-raced character has [a race] that must be deliberately left unspoken and negated, only seemingly forgotten" (98). By contrast, I read the narrator's unmarked racial status as a privilege entailed by Steward's presumption of a predominantly black audience; lacking explicit contradictory evidence, the reader may fairly expect that the narrator is a Negro (and that the drunken soldier addressed by Enriqueta is white). Yet what Murphy's provocative claim touches on, I contend, is the delicacy of Steward's representation of the narrator's sexuality, which is the crux of the text's representation of race.

19 Bulosan's habit of fabulating his own life story has caused much grief for scholars, who have debated the text's proper generic classification, given its divergence from what is known of his biography—it understates the extent of his formal education in the Philippines, wildly exaggerates his personal experiences of labor in the United States, and places him at key events in Filipino migrant history where he could not have been present. But it may be sufficient to simply accept the text's subtitle—*A Personal History*—while recognizing that Bulosan consistently disregards any epistemological distinction between fiction and nonfiction in telling stories about himself.

20 For a reading of *pensionado* literature, including a reference to black soldiers' supposed criminal degeneracy and sexual violence, see Mendoza.

21 The protagonist goes by a series of names in the text—"Allos" in his early years in the Philippines, "Carlos" after arrival in the metropole, and then "Carl" (after Marx) among his comrades in the labor movement. In one instance, he is even referred to as "*Mr.* Bulosan" by the educated Filipina wife of a successful migrant (273, emphasis in original), a designation of normative masculine maturity that the text both privileges and turns away from. While some critics refer to the protagonist as "Allos" throughout, sometimes reserving "Carlos" for the narrator's retrospective consciousness, I prefer to follow the text's own shifting conventions.

22 For a succinct critique of these promises, see Bulosan, "The Story of a Letter."

23 The eminent black librarian Daniel Murray included this document in his collection, which eventually found its way to the Library of Congress's American Memory website, whose editors appear to have been mystified by its inclusion.

24 Bulosan's poem is omitted from Alberto S. Florentino's more widely available 1973 reprint of *Literature under the Commonwealth* (Arguilla, Nedruda, and Agoncillo, eds.) but is reprinted in E. San Juan's invaluable selection of Bulosan's writings, *On Becoming Filipino* (166–68).

25 Here, lynching is meant to resonate with Filipino experiences of sexualized racism, a connection made more explicit elsewhere in the text. See also "I Would Remember," a story published in *Amerasia Journal* in 1979 (in Hagedorn 27–32), also appearing under the title "Life and Death of a Filipino in America" in the posthumous collection *On Becoming Filipino* (85–89).

26 On antimiscegenation laws and Filipinos, see Volpp.

27 Ngai 110; see also Kramer, *Blood* 276–79.

28 But see Ponce's more cautious reading of the scene in *Beyond the Nation*, linking this "language of 'shame'" (94) to its more critical manifestation in Bulosan's *The Cry and the Dedication*, a later work based on the Hukbalahap rebellion.

29 For an opening to this aspect of Bulosan's writing, see Slotkin.

30 See Box 3, Folders 2 and 15, under Accession No. 0581-012, Carlos Bulosan Papers, Special Collections, University of Washington Libraries, Seattle. I have not found any other versions of this story. Variations in the texts suggest that the version in

Folder 15 may be a later draft, though it is unclear if Bulosan saw either draft as preferable or near completion.

31 Ngai 114; Kramer, *Blood* 428–30. National days of humiliation have also been proclaimed in U.S. history, from 1776 through at least 1863.

32 Ngai 116–120; Kramer, *Blood* chap. 6.

33 The story appears in Leopoldo Yabes's important anthology, *Philippine Short Stories, 1925–1940*, which was begun before the war, reassembled in 1946 in an aborted collaboration with Bulosan, and finally published in the Philippines in 1975, with a second printing in 1997. Bulosan's version of the manuscript is in his papers at the University of Washington.

34 Rizal, *Noli* 51. See Benedict Anderson, *Spectre* 2, and *Under* 32–33.

3. LOVE NOTES FROM A THIRD-CONDITIONAL WORLD

1 Gatewood, *Black* Americans 307–8; Thornbrough 235; "T. Thomas Fortune's Philippine Appointment," *New York Times*, 30 November 1902; "Labor Problems in Hawaii," *Washington Post*, 26 December 1902; Gatewood, *Black* Americans 316–17.

2 According to a 1945 profile (Loeb), Woods served with distinction in the Philippine military for four decades and survived incarceration by the Japanese.

3 Included in "Colored Troops in the Philippines"; like "Voices from the Philippines," the November article cited immediately below, it also included a contribution by Rienzi Lemus.

4 See Brown, "White Backlash"; Russell; Boehringer.

5 The issue's cover story reproduces Louis P. Le Vin's complete first report to Ida B. Wells on the lynching of Sam Hose.

6 Gatewood transcribes the letter from the May 17, 1900, *Wisconsin Weekly Advocate* (279); a slightly longer set of excerpts ("From a Colored Soldier") appears in *The Public* (Chicago), edited by the white anti-imperialist Louis Freeland Post, on October 14, 1899, citing the October 5 New York *Age* but retaining the August 11 date of the letter. I have been unable to locate extant archives of the *Age* for this period.

7 For Fagen's part, according to Robinson and Schubert, his father died shortly before he left for the Philippines, and his mother was long deceased (73).

8 A much-needed reconsideration of 1970s Asian American literary history might include recognition of important early research on Filipino migrant writers, including Villa, by student activists and by professional scholars such as E. San Juan Jr. and S. E. Solberg.

9 I am particularly indebted to Ponce, especially for his analysis of Villa's "reconstitution of the 'artist self' as the outcome of lost homolove" (*Beyond the Nation* 74) and of his figuring of artistic creation through homoerotic penetration rather than heterosexual procreation.

10 On Villa's influence in Philippine circles, see Chua's introduction to 2002's *The Critical Villa* (1–31), itself a landmark in his contemporary reconsideration in the Philippines. Villa's relationship with the Marcos regime is a matter of some

debate; he was named a "Presidential Adviser on Cultural Affairs" in 1968 and a "Philippines National Artist" in 1974. Francia provides some choice gossip on his "falling out" with Imelda Marcos ("In private, he would refer to her as Queen Kong, an epithet that delighted us as much as it delighted him"), explaining that Villa kept quiet because he was employed by the Philippine Consulate, and feared retribution by the eminent politician and writer, Carlos Romulo (Tabios 175).

11 See Tabios. A preliminary box list for his papers at Harvard indicates a body of material on the latter project.

12 Along with the two linked stories discussed below, "Untitled Story" was first published in *Clay*, a university-based mimeographed journal edited by Villa; reprinted in *Story* magazine, it was selected for O'Brien's *Best Short Stories of 1932*. Later appearances include 1962's *Selected Stories*, a Philippine volume drawn from *Footnote to Youth*, and *Anchored Angel*. In each case, the original slur is retained (Villa, *Story* 46; E. O'Brien 254; Villa, *Selected* 16; Tabios 107). This and all subsequent references to "Untitled Story" are to *Footnote to Youth*.

13 Though, as a point of pride, Randolph's Brotherhood eventually succeeded in establishing an interracial union, Posadas argues that it was not an unqualified success, involving episodes of antagonism on both sides.

14 Luis Francia credibly notes that Villa "would have hated the tag 'Asian American.'" (Tabios 171).

15 While Villa pled guilty to the legal charges, he penned a passionate letter of defense to the university, reprinted in Chua, *Critical Villa*; see also Ponce, *Beyond the Nation* 58–66.

16 A similar episode is recounted in *Footnote to Youth* (106).

17 In a separate story in *Footnote to Youth*, a University of New Mexico student proposes to a white-skinned, black-haired "Spanish" woman named Aurora, who becomes frustrated when he tells her she looks like Christ because she is being compared to a man (231).

18 Lopez 231; see also Ponce, *Beyond the Nation* 75–76.

19 Villa insisted that their specifically political views were closer than Philippine audiences expected (see, e.g., Ponce, *Beyond the Nation* 77).

20 See Best and Hartman 9, as well as chapter 5 in this book.

21 For a more comprehensive reading of the collection, see Cruz.

22 The book was subtitled *Tales of the Philippines and Others*, and contemporary metropolitan reviewers tended to prefer the former to the latter—Philippine settings to the experimental forms—as, essentially, the reliable provision of exoticism. See T. Yu, "Asian/American," and the 1933 *New York Times* review, "Philippine Stories." By contrast, O'Brien's introduction—no less exoticizing— reserves special praise for the New Mexico stories. For a fine recounting of the book's publication history, see Chua, "Making."

23 The variation on the note in "The Man Who Looked Like Rizal" adds that he was "educated in Europe [and] became doctor, linguist, painter, sculptor, poet and novelist" (265).

24 The valuable revisionism of Wald's *Escaping the Delta* is somewhat diminished by his excessive penitence. Eager to forswear his own earlier primitivism as an offensive white romanticization, he unwittingly erases the intellectually complex, aesthetically rich, and politically multivalent traditions of primitivism in black culture that contributed to Johnson's iconization.

25 I thank Joycelyn Moody for this observation. Growing up, I had assumed it was a Chicago thing.

26 One noteworthy exception is Wald, who acknowledges the "topical touch" of the reference to the Italian invasion of Ethiopia. He makes no mention of the Philippine-American War, though he at least corrects the spelling to "Philippine's" (136).

27 See Taketani, "Colored Empires."

28 Allen, "Waiting for Tojo" (42–43). Manansala eventually turned government informant in the World War II sedition cases against these groups.

29 If Johnson learned the lyrics live rather than from records, they might have been combined, following a blues convention of adding or subtracting "floating" verses to vary a song's length in performance (Wald 135). However, Wald suggests that the Philippine and Ethiopian references are Johnson's own (136). For an exhaustive effort to reconstruct the song's history, see Obrecht.

30 Qtd. in Wald 136. For more on the song's lyrics and performance history, see Doyle.

31 After the Bible reference, the next verse attributes the ringing of the church bell to a *dirty deacon* who absconds with the singer's female lover (Doyle).

32 According to a 1930s account by a veteran of the Philippine war, the racist slur "gu-gu," later shortened to "gook," originated in a popular minstrel song extolling a lover's "goo-goo eyes." U.S. soldiers' fascination with the eyes of Filipina women, he reports, gave offense to local men, upon which "it stuck, and became a veritable taunt" (qtd. in Kramer, *Blood* 127).

33 See Boerhinger. Many of Calloway's descendants ended up in the United States, including a daughter who danced professionally in Manila and Shanghai, and a grandson, his namesake, who teaches Latin jazz in his native San Francisco.

34 This claim runs counter to a tradition of critiquing inauthentic racial representations that considers the audience's tears no less demeaning than their laughter—-e.g., James Weldon Johnson's famous dismissal of dialect poetry in his 1921 *Book of American Negro Poetry* as "an instrument with but two full stops, humor and pathos" (*Writings* 713).

35 Later, Spence came around to the topic of white supremacist violence, in a thinly fictionalized portrayal of the KKK's putative defense of feminine purity. Yet *The Whipping* (1933), adapted from a novel by the white journalist Roy Flannagan and optioned by a major studio, is a wild satire, in which the Klan is incited not by a black man but by a sexually shameless white woman!

36 Citations are from Brooks's 1987 collection, *Blacks*.

37 Kent 48, 72; see the chapters "first beau," "second beau," and "an encounter" in *Maud Martha*, also reprinted in *Blacks*.

4. WHAT COMES AFTER A CHANCE

1 For Moten, this preparation and performance may be termed *improvisation* (*In the Break* 63).

2 The credible challengers to this myth Edwards notes include "Gene Green's half-chorus of imitation-Chinese scat in his 1917 recording of 'From Here to Shanghai'" (619) and the recordings and performances of "Cliff 'Ukulele Ike' Edwards" (620). Edwards also relates scat to what Nathaniel Mackey describes as an "unspeakable history" of sexualized racial violence (624; see also Mackey, *Bedouin* 83).

3 According to Thomas Wirth, the double T in "Niggeratti" signals another layer of the pun—it should be pronounced not as "rahh-tea" but as "ratty" (273n7). Characteristically excessive and even crude, dependent on a sonic difference hard to fix orthographically, the joke is commonly elided when the term is "corrected" to "Niggerati."

4 Cf. the discussion of "neurasthenia" and "the blues" in Lutz.

5 Citations that follow are to the anthology.

6 Similarly, I largely retain the restrictive term, Harlem Renaissance, whose canonical narratives have been challenged from feminist, interracialist, leftist, and internationalist perspectives by Cheryl Wall, George Hutchinson, Jeffrey Perry, Edwards, and others. As Wall has shown, the promotion of Locke's leadership marginalized Jessie Fauset, while Wirth, following Nugent, suggests Thurman or Langston Hughes as a more appropriate central figure.

7 See Yu's pathbreaking study, *Thinking Orientals*.

8 As Strong puts it: "As a group, the second generation have no right to expect more than that a few will accomplish great things. . . . Their success will be measured by the distance they progress from where the first generation stop" (269).

9 Azuma notes that this elite ideology was taken up variously by the heterogeneous elements of the Japanese community in the United States, and publicly opposed by a minority—most notably, leftists critical of Japanese militarism and imperialism (95, 133).

10 Yu (81) attributes the preface to *Survey* editor Paul Kellogg, but the previous issue, promoting the special number, credits a quote from this preface to Park.

11 See especially "The Problem of Cultural Differences" (1931; *Race and Culture* 3–14).

12 "Cultural Conflict and the Marginal Man" (1937; *Race and Culture* 373). See also "Human Migration and the Marginal Man" (1928; *Race and Culture* 345–56).

13 Though Park's major essays on the concept primarily refer to the Jew and the Mulatto, the concept is clearly shaped by his extensive work on the Oriental problem, particularly on the second generation; see Yu 109, 234n21.

14 See Yu, especially chaps. 5–7.

15 Like the Chinese American Flora Belle Jan, who contributed two poems, Kawai was a college student; Yu discusses them at length (96–102). Though Kawai immigrated at a young age (Modell 164–66), the title of his article certifies him as an "American-born Japanese."

16 More specifically, his goal—later achieved—is to teach Asian history at a U.S. university.

17 Rowell, "Western Windows to the East," in Park, *East by West* 175.

18 I thank Vicente Rafael for his suggestive comments on the time of incarceration.

19 By contrast, the eponymous Issei laborer of Hisaye Yamamoto's "Las Vegas Charley" characterizes this temporality as a reprieve—"As for himself, he would be quite content to remain in this camp the rest of his life—free food, free housing, friends, flower cards; what more could life offer?" (80). This is no apology for a benign incarceration regime—the implication is that his prior conditions weren't better, even though he goes deaf in one ear working by hot stoves in the desert. What distinguishes camp life is a reprieve from the impossible struggle to escape poverty, via hard work and thrift or compulsive gambling—the image and parody of the American Dream. Without teleology to give it meaning, the timing of camp routine allows Charley not happiness, but contentment. Or it *would*, if he could *remain in this camp the rest of his life*: if this timing perfectly coincided with the measure of time before death, the *rest* for and in which he would be *quite content*. Instead, as waiting, the timing of camp routine anticipates an irrevocable decision occurring elsewhere.

20 E.g., where Deborah McDowell sees Irene "projecting" (89), Thadious Davis draws on Larsen's biography in taking the suspicions more seriously (324).

21 Park, "Racial Assimilation in Secondary Groups" (1913), in *Race and Culture* 208–9.

22 By contrast with, e.g., Bill Mullen's "Afro-Orientalism" or Helen Jun's "black Orientalism," the term "New Negro Orientalism" is merely a heuristic continuation of this chapter's engagement with Locke, recognizing that the phenomena precede his formulation by several decades. These practices might be named and contextualized differently were Locke displaced.

23 Thomas Kim situates Orientalist consumer culture within a historically specific conception of American modernity, rather than as its "'outside' or alternative" (386). His analysis is especially relevant to Larsen, though it does not account for the racialized status of a black consumer. Rather than serving "a fascination with the primitive," fashionable "Oriental objects" promised "an education in beauty, an appreciation of 'nature,' and a training of the aesthetic sense" to both women and children, within "a project of education and even uplift" (387).

24 See Yoshida; Atkins.

25 I thank Stephen Sumida for this information and context.

26 Debates over Mori's facility with English have been prominent in his reception. In his foreword to *Yokohama, California*, William Saroyan, Mori's major early

champion, notoriously asserted, "Any high-school teacher of English would flunk him in grammar and punctuation" (1). Infuriated, Frank Chin and the other 1970s Asian American writers who rediscovered Mori claimed him as a model of authentic Japanese American linguistic difference. But in her introduction to Mori's *The Chauvinist*, his younger Nisei contemporary, Hisaye Yamamoto, takes the new generation to school: "I happen not to agree with the young ones on this one point of language. I think Toshio, just as I, was trying to use the very best English of which he was capable, and we have both run aground on occasion. Probably this was because we both spent the pre-kindergarten years speaking only Japanese, and, in such cases, *Sprachgefühl* is hard to come by" (2). I thank the Sansei Stephen Sumida for explaining to this Yonsei what *Sprachgefühl* means!

27 See Yoshida 183–88; Waseda 197–99.

28 But cf. Julia H. Lee's extended reading of *Quicksand*'s Orientalism in *Interracial Encounters*, chap. 5.

29 Sherrard-Johnson quotes Thadious Davis's description of the novel as a "portrait of the failed artist as a woman of color" (837) and adds, "Each time she suppresses a sexual desire, she suppresses a creative impulse" (838).

30 See Sherrard-Johnson's instructive analysis of primitivism and *Quicksand*'s Danish sequence (845–48), as well as duCille's related reading (94–96).

31 Cf. Weinbaum.

32 If the revelation of her racial heritage arguably renders this persona inoperable, one might even speculate that she could have reconciled with Bellew if some mutually self-serving arrangement, however hateful or horrific, preserved their secret before white society. Denial isn't just a river in Egypt, as they say.

33 This reading needn't presume Brian's actual infidelity, any more than it presumes Irene's sensation of guilt proves she murdered Clare. However, it does suggest a surprisingly sympathetic reading of Brian's daydreams of a racial utopia in Brazil, a centrifugal fantasyland in which freedom from racism could be distinguished from the acquisition of white racial privileges.

34 Cf. Nathaniel Mackey's reading of Amiri Baraka's statement, "New Black Music is this: Find the self, then kill it" (*Discrepant Engagement* 275).

35 See McDowell's provocative reading of hidden lesbian eroticism, as well as her reconsideration, appended to the reprint of her 1986 essay (95–97), after duCille's detailed challenge (103–9).

36 See Charlotte Brooks's discussion of zoot-suiters as *yogore* in Nisei resettlement in Chicago (1682–83).

37 Even Frank's avowed pacifism tolerates (if not manipulates) the violent actions of his allies, while inviting and inciting the violence of his opponents (if not his own martyrdom).

5. THE RAINBOW SIGN AND THE FIRE, EVERY TIME LOS ANGELES BURNS

1 Cf. Ruth Gilmore's influential definition of racism as "the state-sanctioned or extralegal production and exploitation of group-differentiated vulnerability to premature death" (28).

2 For more on the case, see Bass 135–36 and M. Davis 399–401, as well as Briones's important study of Yamamoto's wartime journalism.

3 See Dunne's memoir, *King's Pawn* 132–36, 171–74.

4 The quote, apparently from the program of one performance, is found in Hughes, "Here to Yonder"; notices in the *New York Times* ("'Trial'") and the *Chicago Defender* (Monroe) also describe the play as a "documentary," and *Phylon* mentions the Short family by name (Jefferson 103).

5 The first report, on September 4, appeared in a Hollywood gossip column, explicitly referencing the play (Levette); one week later, it received front page coverage, between articles on resistance to school and housing desegregation, with a headline alluding to the play's title: "Lynch by Fire Town Reforms."

6 See the reviews by Jefferson and Monroe.

7 On the "triumphal procession" of the victors, see Benjamin (256).

8 For example, in an obituary, the historian Greg Robinson revealed that Yamamoto helped organize the LA chapter of the Congress of Racial Equality the year after Short's death and used her column to publicize a subsequent sit-in campaign, against opposition from her editor.

9 Cf. Grace Hong's reading of this passage, a critique of a "journalistic objectivity" that trains perception in accordance with "the language of the state" ("Something" 305).

10 See, e.g., Cheung, introduction to *Seventeen Syllables*, xii, and James Lee 69, 77. Both Cheung ("Dream") and Lee then read this figure as exemplifying a variety of multiculturalism—a matter of celebration for the former and dismay for the latter.

11 Otis's claim is nuanced and grounded, though I cannot evaluate it here. Yamamoto may well have expected *Rafu Shimpo* readers to recall it. See Lipsitz, *Midnight,* and Otis's memoirs, *Listen to the Lambs* and *Upside Your Head!,* which double as analyses of LA racial conflagration in 1965 and 1992.

12 On resettlement in Chicago, see also C. Brooks and *REgenerations.*

13 In the 1940s, a Nisei "go-getter" might be a leader in the Japanese American Citizens League, whose controversial ascent was enabled by its collaboration with mass incarceration. On the ambivalence toward liberal antiracism in the postwar Japanese American community, and Yamamoto's own acid critique of the JACL in one of her *Tribune* articles, see Kurashige 193–94. For Yamamoto's comments on the paper in a 1987 interview, see Crow 77.

14 A contrast between the memoir's representation of these events and available biographical materials is instructive. On Yamamoto's civil rights and social justice activism, see G. Robinson. She did not leave the *Tribune* until 1948, remaining

in LA through 1953 to pursue a career in fiction, winning a John Hay Whitney
Opportunity Fellowship in 1950 and placing stories in *Partisan Review, Kenyon
Review, Furioso, Harper's Bazaar,* and *The Best American Short Stories of 1952.*
Prior to her rediscovery by the 1970s Asian American literary movement and
women of color feminism, this was the period of her greatest professional success.
One prominent admirer, the poet Yvor Winters, sought her out and attempted
to arrange a prestigious Stanford Writing Fellowship; instead, she moved to New
York to join Dorothy Day's Catholic Worker community (see Crow 77). Winters's
letters to Yamamoto have been published, including his dismissive response to her
comments on race (*Selected Letters* 320; see also Elliott, chap. 4) alluded to in her
memoir (155).

15 While Yamamoto's "pale husband," Anthony DeSoto, was Latino, the text allows
him to pass as white to underscore, rather than disavow, the narrator's distance
from African Americans.

16 For another reading of interracialism in Himes, see Itagaki.

17 James Lee, who also juxtaposes Himes and Yamamoto, reads the former's "deliberate" use of "Little Tokyo" rather than "Bronzeville" as "a reminder of the ghost
of Asian American presence in the midst of real Japanese American absence"
(67). I'd add that the newer term might also be read as a defiant response to "Little
Tokyo's" reputation as a slum. That is, in mid-1940s LA, the "Oriental" term might
connote a "race problem" that the "Negro" term seeks to displace. Himes includes
a scene satirizing a group of elite black women holding forth on "the problems
that confront the social worker in Little Tokyo" (83).

18 I am grateful to Ji-Young Um for her insights on imperial wars and the figure of
the racialized soldier in Himes.

19 The term "no-no boy" refers to incarcerated Japanese Americans deemed disloyal on the basis of their responses to numbers 27 and 28 of the WRA loyalty
questionnaire.

20 Arguing against the return of incarcerated Japanese Americans to California,
Governor Earl Warren warned, "No one will be able to tell a saboteur from any
other Jap," explaining that his position "isn't an appeal to race hatred" but "an
appeal to safety." See S. Cho for the quotes (118) and an analysis of their relation to
his later career as Chief Justice.

21 The phrase "flickering interiority" and its relation to the figure of a phantom limb
is borrowed from Wagner 123.

22 For an early, canonical example, see Sone 154–56. At other times, these scenes
involve a related trope of burial—the other way that U.S. society typically disposes
of its dead.

23 Hayakawa's late-1960s turn was not inconsistent with his wartime liberalism. For
example, his June 16, 1945, *Defender* column offered a sympathetic but deeply
condescending portrait of black pro-Japanese sentiment before advising his readers that well-intentioned white liberals "will ultimately do more for the American
Negro than the whole Ethiopian Army or Japanese Navy" (17).

24 In his memoir, *King's Pawn*, Dunne reports being persuaded to drop the elaborate special effects devised for his play's representation of the fire by none other than Charlie Chaplin, who "know[s] more about [the theater] than any man in this country" (141): by tacitly acknowledging the limits of theatrical representation in refusing to enact the event onstage, the playwright could call upon a more powerful effect in the audience's imaginative response.

AFTERTHOUGHT

1 Citations are to the 1992 Viking first edition until otherwise indicated.
2 While the phrase does not name a terminal point for this dominance, you might find one in the 2014 protests in Ferguson, Missouri.
3 Charlene Woodcock, e-mail to the author, April 22, 2003.

WORKS CITED

Alejandrino, Gen. José M. *The Price of Freedom: Episodes and Anecdotes of Our Struggles for Freedom*. 1933. Trans. Atty. José M. Alejandrino. 1949. Filipiniana Reprint Series, Book 18. Manila: Solar Publishing, 1987.

Allen, Ernest V. "Waiting for Tojo: The Pro-Japan Vigil of Black Missourians, 1932–1943." *Gateway Heritage* (Fall 1995): 38–55.

———. "When Japan Was 'Champion of the Darker Races': Satokata Takahashi and the Flowering of Black Messianic Nationalism." *Black Scholar* 24.1 (Winter 1994): 23–46.

"American Deserter a Filipino General." *New York Times*, October 29, 1900: 1.

American Negro Academy. "The Third Annual Meeting of the American Negro Academy." 1899. Program. W. E. B. Du Bois Papers (MS 312). Spec. Coll. and University Archives, University of Massachusetts, Amherst Library. Web, September 9, 2011.

Anderson, Benedict. *The Spectre of Comparisons: Nationalism, Southeast Asia, and the World*. London: Verso, 1998.

———. *Under Three Flags: Anarchism and the Anti-Colonial Imagination*. London: Verso, 2005.

Arguilla, Manuel E. *How My Brother Leon Brought Home a Wife and Other Stories*. Westport, CT: Greenwood Press, 1970.

Arguilla, Manuel E., Esteban Nedruda, and Teodoro A. Agoncillo, eds. *Literature under the Commonwealth*. Manila: Philippine Writers' League, 1940.

Arnold, Edwin. *What Virtue There Is in Fire: Cultural Memory and the Lynching of Sam Hose*. Athens: University of Georgia Press, 2009.

Atkins, E. Taylor. *Blue Nippon: Authenticating Jazz in Japan*. Durham, NC: Duke University Press, 2001.

Azuma, Eiichiro. *Between Two Empires: Race, History, and Transnationalism in Japanese America*. New York: Oxford University Press, 2005.

Baker, Nancy Kovaleff. "Abel Meeropol (a.k.a. Lewis Allan): Political Commentator and Social Conscience," *American Music* 20.1 (Spring 2002): 25–79.

Balce, Nerissa S. "Filipino Bodies, Lynching, and the Language of Empire." In *Positively No Filipinos Allowed: Building Communities and Discourse*, ed. Antonio T. Tiongson Jr., Edgardo V. Gutierrez, and Ricardo V. Gutierrez. Philadelphia: Temple University Press, 2006. 43–60.

Baldoz, Rick. *The Third Asiatic Invasion: Empire and Migration in Filipino America, 1898–1946*. New York: New York University Press, 2011.

Baldwin, James. "Alas, Poor Richard." In *Nobody Knows My Name: More Notes of a Native Son*. New York: Dell, 1962. 181–215.

————. *The Fire Next Time.* 1963. New York: Dell, 1964.

Bass, Charlotta A. *Forty Years: Memoirs from the Pages of a Newspaper.* Los Angeles: Charlotta A. Bass, 1960.

Baylen, Joseph O., and John Hammond Moore. "Senator John Tyler Morgan and Negro Colonization in the Philippines, 1901 to 1902." *Phylon* 29.1 (1st Qtr. 1968): 65–75.

Bederman, Gail. *Manliness and Civilization: A Cultural History of Gender and Race in the United States, 1880–1917.* Chicago: University of Chicago Press, 1995.

Benjamin, Walter. "Theses on the Philosophy of History." In *Illuminations.* Trans. Harry Zohn. New York: Schocken, 1969. 253–64.

Best, Stephen, and Saidiya Hartman. "Fugitive Justice." *Representations* 92 (Fall 2005): 1–15.

Blackburn, Julia. *With Billie.* New York: Pantheon, 2005.

Boehringer, Gill H. "Imperialist Paranoia and Military Injustice: The Persecution and Redemption of Sergeant Calloway." *www.atD21.com/Boehringer,* May 22, 2013. Web, July 31, 2015.

Bonner, Marita. "On Being Young—a Woman—and Colored." In *Frye Street and Environs: The Collected Works of Marita Bonner,* ed. Joyce Flynn and Joyce Occomy Stricklin. Boston: Beacon, 1987. 3–8.

Briones, Matthew M. "Hardly 'Small Talk': Discussing Race in the Writing of Hisaye Yamamoto." *Prospects: An Annual of American Cultural Studies* 29 (2005): 435–72.

Brooks, Charlotte. "In the Twilight Zone between Black and White: Japanese American Resettlement and Community in Chicago, 1942–1945." *Journal of American History* 86.4 (March 2000): 1655–1687.

Brooks, Gwendolyn. *Blacks.* Chicago: Third World Press, 1987.

Brown, Scot. "White Backlash and the Aftermath of Fagen's Rebellion: The Fates of Three African-American Soldiers in the Philippines, 1901–1902." *Contributions in Black Studies* 13.5 (1995/1996): 165–73.

———— [as Scot Ngozi-Brown]. "African-American Soldiers and Filipinos: Racial Imperialism, Jim Crow and Social Relations." *Journal of Negro History* 82.1 (Winter 1997): 42–53.

Bruce, John Edward. "The Call of a Nation." In *The Selected Writings of John Edward Bruce: Militant Black Journalist,* ed. Peter Gilbert. New York: Arno, 1971. 99–100.

Bulosan, Carlos. *All the Conspirators.* Seattle: University of Washington Press, 2005.

————. *America Is in the Heart: A Personal History.* 1946. Seattle: University of Washington Press, 1973.

————. *On Becoming Filipino: Selected Writings of Carlos Bulosan,* ed. E. San Juan Jr. Philadelphia: Temple University Press, 1995.

————. "Sammy Cooke's Shoeshine Box." N.d. MS, Box 3, Folders 2 and 3, Carlos Bulosan Papers 0581–012, University of Washington Library, Seattle, WA.

————. "The Story of a Letter." In *On Becoming Filipino: Selected Writings of Carlos Bulosan,* ed. E. San Juan Jr. Philadelphia: Temple University Press, 1995. 60–65.

Butler, John H. Manning. Letter from J. H. M. Butler to W. E. B. Du Bois, August 28, 1902. MS, W. E. B. Du Bois Papers 312. Spec. Coll. and University Archives, University of Massachusetts Amherst Library. *Credo, SCUA UMass.* Web, July 1, 2013.

———. "New Education in the Philippines." *Journal of Negro Education* 3.2 (April 1934): 257–68.

Butler, Octavia E. *Kindred.* 1979. Boston: Beacon, 1988.

Calloway, J. Letter from J. Calloway to W. E. B. Du Bois, November 14, 1927. MS, W. E. B. Du Bois Papers 312. Spec. Coll. and University Archives, University of Massachusetts Amherst Library, *Credo, SCUA UMass.* Web, July 1, 2013.

The Camp Dance: The Music and the Memories, Original Cast Recording. Grateful Crane Ensemble, 2004.

Carter, Betty. "Love Notes." *Feed the Fire.* Audiocassette. Verve, 1994.

Chandler, Nahum Dmitri, ed. *The Problem of the Color Line at the Turn of the Twentieth Century: The Essential Early Essays,* by W. E. B. Du Bois. New York: Fordham University Press, 2015.

Cheung, King-Kok. "The Dream in Flames: Hisaye Yamamoto, Multiculturalism, and the Los Angeles Uprising." In *Having Our Way: Women Rewriting Tradition in Twentieth-Century America,* ed. Harriet Pollack. Lewisburg, PA: Bucknell University Press, 1995. 118–30.

———. Introduction to *Seventeen Syllables and Other Stories,* by Hisaye Yamamoto. Rev. and expanded ed. New Brunswick, NJ: Rutgers University Press, 2001. ix–xxi.

Cho, Sumi. "Redeeming Whiteness in the Shadow of Internment: Earl Warren, *Brown,* and a Theory of Racial Redemption." *Boston College Third World Law Journal* 19 (1998–1999): 73–170.

Cho, Yu-Fang. "Cultural Nationalism, Orientalism, Imperial Ambivalence: *The Colored American Magazine* and Pauline Elizabeth Hopkins." *Journal of Transnational American Studies* 3.2 (October 2011). Web, June 6, 2013.

Chua, Jonathan, ed. *The Critical Villa: Essays in Literary Criticism by José Garcia Villa.* Manila: Ateneo de Manila University Press, 2002.

———. "The Making of Jose Garcia Villa's *Footnote to Youth.*" *Kritika Kultura* 21/22 (2013–2014): 9–39.

Chuh, Kandice. *Imagine Otherwise: On Asian Americanist Critique.* Durham, NC: Duke University Press, 2003.

"Colored Troops in the Philippines: Virginia Soldiers Write to Us." *Richmond Planet,* September 9, 1899: 1.

Constantino, Renato. "The Miseducation of the Filipino." In *Vestiges of War: The Philippine-American War and the Aftermath of an Imperial Dream, 1899–1999,* ed. Angel Velasco Shaw and Luis H. Francia. New York: New York University Press, 2002. 177–92.

"Contemporary Artists and Lynching: A Portfolio." *Nka* 20 (Fall 2006): 134–36.

Cook, Charles C. "A Comparative Study of the Negro Problem." American Negro Academy, Occasional Papers No. 4. *American Negro Academy, Occasional Papers 1–22.* New York: Arno, 1969. 1–11 [73–83].

Cordova, Fred. *Filipinos: Forgotten Asian Americans, A Pictorial Essay/1763–circa 1963.* Dubuque, IA: Kendall/Hunt, 1983.

Corrothers, James D. "A Man They Didn't Know" (Part I). *The Crisis* 7.2 (December 1913): 85–87.

——. "A Man They Didn't Know" (Part II). *The Crisis* 7.3 (January 1914): 136–38.

Couch, Lt. William. "To a Soldier." *Negro Story* 1.1 (May–June 1944): 60.

Crow, Charles. "A *MELUS* Interview: Hisaye Yamamoto." *MELUS* 14.1 (Spring 1987): 73–84.

Cruz, Denise. "José Garcia Villa's Collection of 'Others': Irreconcilabilities of a Queer Transpacific Modernism." *MFS: Modern Fiction Studies* 55.1 (Spring 2009): 11–41.

Davis, Angela Y. *Blues Legacies and Black Feminism: Gertrude "Ma" Rainey, Bessie Smith, and Billie Holiday*. New York: Pantheon, 1998.

——. "Civil Rights and Human Rights: Future Trajectories." Lecture, University of Washington, Seattle, April 17, 2007. "Angela Davis on Racism." *KUOW Speakers' Forum*, September 27, 2007. Web, July 1, 2013.

Davis, Mike. *City of Quartz: Excavating the Future in Los Angeles*. New York: Vintage, 1990.

Davis, Thadious M. *Nella Larsen, Novelist of the Harlem Renaissance: A Woman's Life Unveiled*. Baton Rouge: Louisiana State University Press, 1994.

de Jesús, Melinda L. "Rereading History, Rewriting Desire: Reclaiming Queerness in Carlos Bulosan's *America Is in the Heart* and Bienvenido Santos' *Scent of Apples*." *Journal of Asian American Studies* 5.2 (June 2002): 91–111.

"Deserves Much Praise." *Richmond Planet*, November 30, 1899: 4.

"Detective L. P. Le Vin Makes a 2nd Trip to Georgia to Investigate the Recent Burning of Sam Hose." *Afro-American Advance* (Minneapolis and St. Paul), July 1, 1899: 1.

Dinerstein, Joel. *Swinging the Machine: Modernity, Technology, and African American Culture between the World Wars*. Amherst: University of Massachusetts Press, 2003.

Douglas, Ann. *Terrible Honesty: Mongrel Manhattan in the 1920s*. New York: Farrar, Straus and Giroux, 1995.

Dove, Rita. "Canary." *Poetry Foundation*, n.d. Web, May 30, 2013.

Doyle, J. D. "Sissy Man Blues." *Queer Music Heritage*. February 2004. Web, July 1, 2013.

Du Bois, W. E. B. "Atlanta University." In *From Servitude to Service: Being the Old South Lectures on the History and Work of Southern Institutions for the Education of the Negro*. Boston: American Unitarian Association, 1905. 155–97.

——. "Autobiography of William E. B. Du Bois" [eighth installment]. *New York Amsterdam News*, May 14, 1938: 13.

——. *The Autobiography of W. E. B. Du Bois: A Soliloquy on Viewing My Life from the Last Decade of Its First Century*. New York: International Publishers, 1968.

——. *Dark Princess: A Romance*. Jackson: University Press of Mississippi, 1995.

——. "The Negro Mind Reaches Out." In *The New Negro*, ed. Alain Locke. New York: Atheneum, 1992. 385–414.

——. "A Pageant in Seven Decades: 1868–1938." In *Pamphlets and Leaflets by W. E. B. Du Bois*, ed. Herbert Aptheker. White Plains, NY: Kraus-Thomson, 1986. 244–74.

——. "The Present Outlook for the Dark Races of Mankind." *Church Review* 17.2 (October 1900): 95–110.

———. "The Present Outlook for the Dark Races of Mankind." In *Writings by W. E. B. Du Bois in Periodicals Edited by Others*, ed. Herbert Aptheker, vol.1. Millwood, NY: Kraus-Thomson, 1982. 73–82.

———. "The Souls of White Folk." *The Independent* 18 August 1910: 339–42.

———. "The Superior Race." *Smart Set* 10.4 (April 1923): 55–60.

———. "To the Nations of the World." In *Writings by W. E. B. Du Bois in Non-Periodical Literature Edited by Others*, ed. Herbert Aptheker. Millwood, NY: Kraus-Thomson Organization, 1982. 11–12.

———. *W. E. B. Du Bois: A Recorded Autobiography; Interview by Moses Asch*. Folkways Records FH 5511. 1961.

———. "Worlds of Color." *Foreign Affairs* 3.3 (April 1925): 423–44.

———. *Writings*. Library of America 34. New York: Viking, 1986.

duCille, Ann. *The Coupling Convention: Sex, Text, and Tradition in Black Women's Fiction*. New York: Oxford University Press, 1993.

Dunne, George H. *King's Pawn: The Memoirs of George H. Dunne, S.J.* Chicago: Loyola University Press, 1990.

———. "The Sin of Segregation." *Commonweal*, September 21, 1945: 542–45.

———. *Trial by Fire*. Washington, DC: National Theatre Conference, 1946.

Eady, Cornelius. *Brutal Imagination*. New York: Putnam, 2001.

Edwards, Brent Hayes. "The Literary Ellington." *Representations* 77 (Winter 2002): 1–29.

———. "Louis Armstrong and the Syntax of Scat." *Critical Inquiry* 28 (Spring 2002): 618–49.

———. "Notes on Poetics Regarding Mackey's *Song*." *Callaloo* 23.2 (2000): 572–91.

———. *The Practice of Diaspora: Literature, Translation, and the Rise of Black Internationalism*. Cambridge, MA: Harvard University Press, 2003.

———. "The Uses of Diaspora." *Social Text* 19.1 (Spring 2001): 45–73.

Elliott, Matthew Edwin. "Erasure and Reform: Los Angeles Literature and the Reconstruction of the Past." PhD diss., University of Maryland, College Park, 2004.

Ellison, Ralph. *Invisible Man*. 1952. New York: Vintage, 1995.

Fanon, Frantz. *Black Skin, White Masks*. New York: Grove Weidenfeld, 1967.

Ferguson, Roderick A. "Of Our Normative Strivings: African American Studies and the Histories of Sexuality." *Social Text* 84–85 (Fall–Winter 2005): 85–100.

Fortune, T. Thomas. "The Filipino [I]: A Social Study in Three Parts." *Voice of the Negro* 1.3 (March 1904): 93–99.

———. "The Filipino [II]: The Filipinos Do Not Understand the Prejudice of White Americans against Black Americans." *Voice of the Negro* 1.5 (June 1904): 199–203.

———. "The Filipino [III]: Some Incidents of a Trip through the Island of Luzon." *Voice of the Negro* 1.6 (July 1904): 240–46.

———. "Politics in the Philippine Islands." *Independent* 55 (September 24, 1903): 2266–68.

"From a Colored Soldier in Manila." *The Public* 80 (October 14, 1899): 12–13.

Fujitani, T. "*Go for Broke*, the Movie: Japanese American Soldiers in U.S. National, Military, and Racial Discourses." In Fujitani, White, and Yoneyama, *Perilous Memories* 239–66.

Fujitani, T., Geoffrey M. White, and Lisa Yoneyama, eds. *Perilous Memories: The Asia-Pacific War(s)*. Durham, NC: Duke University Press, 2001.

Fujita-Rony, Dorothy. *American Workers, Colonial Power: Philippine Seattle and the Transpacific West, 1919–1941*. Berkeley: University of California Press, 2003.

Gaines, Kevin K. "Black Americans' Uplift Ideology as 'Civilizing Mission': Pauline E. Hopkins on Race and Imperialism." In Kaplan and Pease, *Cultures of United States Imperialism* 433–55.

———. *Uplifting the Race: Black Leadership, Politics, and Culture in the Twentieth Century*. Chapel Hill: University of North Carolina Press, 1996.

Gallicchio, Marc. *The African American Encounter with Japan and China: Black Internationalism in Asia, 1895–1945*. Chapel Hill: University of North Carolina Press, 2000.

Gates, Henry Louis, Jr. "The Trope of a New Negro and the Reconstruction of the Image of the Black." *Representations* 24 (Autumn 1988): 129–55.

Gatewood, Willard B., Jr. *Black Americans and the White Man's Burden, 1898–1903*. Urbana: University of Illinois Press, 1975.

———. *"Smoked Yankees" and the Struggle for Empire: Letters from Black Soldiers, 1898–1902*. Fayetteville: University of Arkansas Press, 1987.

Gilmore, F. Grant. *"The Problem": A Military Novel*. 1915. College Park, MD: McGrath, 1969.

Gilmore, Ruth Wilson. *Golden Gulag: Prisons, Surplus, Crisis, and Opposition in Globalizing California*. Berkeley: University of California Press, 2007.

Gilroy, Paul. *The Black Atlantic: Modernity and Double Consciousness*. London: Verso, 1993.

Goggin, Jacqueline. *Carter G. Woodson: A Life in Black History*. Baton Rouge: Louisiana State University Press, 1993.

Goldsby, Jacqueline. *A Spectacular Secret: Lynching in American Life and Literature*. Chicago: University of Chicago Press, 2006.

Gooding-Williams, Robert, ed. *Reading Rodney King/Reading Urban Uprising*. New York: Routledge, 1993.

Green, Michael Cullen. *Black Yanks in the Pacific: Race in the Making of American Military Empire after World War II*. Ithaca, NY: Cornell University Press, 2010.

Griffin, Farah Jasmine. *If You Can't Be Free, Be a Mystery: In Search of Billie Holiday*. New York: Free Press, 2001.

———. "When Malindy Sings: A Meditation on Black Women's Vocality." In *Uptown Conversation: The New Jazz Studies*, ed. Robert G. O'Meally, Brent Hayes Edwards, and Farah Jasmine Griffin. New York: Columbia University Press, 2004. 102–25.

Griggs, Sutton E. *Unfettered*. Nashville, TN: Orion, 1902.

Gruesser, John Cullen. *The Empire abroad and the Empire at Home: African American Literature and the Era of Overseas Expansion*. Athens: University of Georgia Press, 2012.

Gruesser, John Cullen, and Gretchen Murphy. "Introduction to Three Stories by Frank R. Steward." *PMLA* 126.3 (May 2011): 780–83.

Hagedorn, Jessica, ed. *Charlie Chan Is Dead: An Anthology of Contemporary Asian American Fiction*. New York: Penguin, 1993.

"Hampton Incidents." *Southern Workman* 29.8 (August 1900): 490–92.

Haney López, Ian. *White by Law: The Legal Construction of Race*. 10th Anniversary ed. New York: New York University Press, 2006.

Harden, Jacalyn D. *Double Cross: Japanese Americans in Black and White Chicago*. Minneapolis: University of Minnesota Press, 2003.

Harney, Stefano, and Fred Moten. *The Undercommons: Fugitive Planning and Black Study*. Brooklyn, NY: Minor Compositions, 2013.

Harris, Trudier. *Exorcising Blackness: Historical and Literary Lynching and Burning Rituals*. Bloomington: Indiana University Press, 1984.

Hartman, Saidiya V. *Lose Your Mother: A Journey along the Atlantic Slave Route*. New York: Farrar, Straus and Giroux, 2007.

———. *Scenes of Subjection: Terror, Slavery, and Self-Making in Nineteenth-Century America*. New York: Oxford University Press, 1997.

———. "The Time of Slavery." *South Atlantic Quarterly* 101.4 (Fall 2002): 757–77.

Hayakawa, S. I. "Second Thoughts." *Chicago Defender*, June 15, 1945: 17.

"Heinous Crimes in the Philippines." *Richmond Planet*, November 30, 1899: 4.

Hellwig, David J. "Afro-American Reactions to the Japanese and the Anti-Japanese Movement, 1906–1924." *Phylon* 38.1 (1st Qtr. 1977): 93–104.

Hill, Robert A. *The FBI's RACON: Racial Conditions in the United States during World War II*. Boston: Northeastern University Press, 1995.

Himes, Chester. *If He Hollers Let Him Go*. 1945. New York: Thunder's Mouth, 2002.

———. "Zoot Suit Riots Are Race Riots." 1943. In *Black on Black: Baby Sister and Selected Writings*. New York: Doubleday, 1973. 220–25.

Ho, Fred and Bill V. Mullen, eds. *Afro Asia: Revolutionary Political and Cultural Connections between African Americans and Asian Americans*. Durham, N.C.: Duke University Press, 2008.

Holiday, Billie. *Lady Sings the Blues*. 50th anniversary ed. With William Dufty. New York: Harlem Moon, 2006.

Hong, Grace Kyungwon. "'Something Forgotten Which Should Have Been Remembered': Private Property and Cross-Racial Solidarity in the Work of Hisaye Yamamoto." *American Literature* 71.2 (June 1999): 291–310.

Horne, Gerald. "Tokyo Bound: African Americans and Japan Confront White Supremacy." *Souls* 3.3 (Summer 2001): 16–28.

House, Son. "Empire State Express." Rec. 1965. *Son House, Father of the Delta Blues: The Complete 1965 Sessions*. Audiocassette. Columbia, 1992.

Hughes, Langston. "Here to Yonder." *Chicago Defender*, May 22, 1948: 14.

———. "Writer Laments Non-existence of Permanent Negro Theater in America." *Chicago Defender*, April 11, 1953: 11.

Hutchinson, George. *In Search of Nella Larsen: A Biography of the Color Line*. Cambridge, MA: Harvard University Press, 2006.

Ignacio, Abe, et al. *The Forbidden Book: The Philippine American War in Political Cartoons*. San Francisco: T'Boli Press, 2004.

Itagaki, Lynn M. "Transgressing Race and Community in Chester Himes's *If He Hollers Let Him Go*." *African American Review* 37.1 (Spring 2003): 65–80.

James, Jennifer C. *A Freedom Bought with Blood: African American War Literature from the Civil War to World War II.* Chapel Hill: University of North Carolina Press, 2007.

Jefferson, Miles M. "The Negro on Broadway, 1947–1948." *Phylon* 9.2 (2nd Qtr. 1948): 99–107.

Johnson, H. T. *The Black Man's Burden.* N.p., n.d. [1899]. *Internet Archive.* Web, July 1, 2013.

Johnson, James Weldon. *Writings.* New York: Library of America, 2004.

Johnson, Robert. *Robert Johnson: The Complete Recordings.* Prod. Stephen LaVere and Frank Driggs. Columbia, 1990.

Jones, Andrew F., and Nikhil Pal Singh, eds. *The Afro-Asian Century.* Special issue, *positions* 11.1 (Spring 2003): 1–260.

Jones, Gayl. *Mosquito.* Boston: Beacon Press, 1999.

Jun, Helen H. *Race for Citizenship: Black Orientalism and Asian Uplift from Pre-Emancipation to Neoliberal America.* New York: New York University Press, 2011.

Kadohata, Cynthia. *The Floating World.* New York: Viking, 1989.

———. *In the Heart of the Valley of Love.* New York: Viking, 1992.

———. *In the Heart of the Valley of Love.* Berkeley: University of California Press, 1997.

Kaplan, Amy. "Black and Blue on San Juan Hill." In Kaplan and Pease, *Cultures of United States Imperialism* 219–36.

Kaplan, Amy, and Donald Pease, eds. *Cultures of United States Imperialism.* Durham, NC: Duke University Press, 1993.

Kawai, Kazuo. "Three Roads and None Easy: An American-Born Japanese Looks at Life." In Park, *East by West* 164–66.

[Kealing, Hightower Theodore.] "Editorials." *Church Review* 17.2 (October 1900): 175–81.

Kearney, Reginald. *African American Views of the Japanese: Solidarity or Sedition?* Albany: State University of New York Press, 1998.

———. "The Pro-Japanese Utterances of W. E. B. Du Bois." *Contributions in Black Studies* 13/14 (1995–96): 201–17.

Kelley, Robin D. G., and Betsy Esch. "Black Like Mao: Red China and Black Revolution." *Souls* 1.4 (Fall 1999): 6–41.

Kent, George E. *A Life of Gwendolyn Brooks.* Lexington: University Press of Kentucky, 1990.

Kim, Thomas W. "Being Modern: The Circulation of Oriental Objects." *American Quarterly* 58.2 (2006): 379–406.

King Kong. Shooting script. Screenplay by Ruth Rose and James Ashmore Creelman. Story by Merian C. Cooper and Edgar Wallace. 1933. *American Film Scripts Online.* Web, May 31, 2008.

King Kong. Two-disc collector's ed. Prod. and dir. Merian C. Cooper and Ernest B. Schoedsack. 1933. Warner Bros., 2005. DVD.

Kipling, Rudyard. "The White Man's Burden." *McClure's* 12.4 (February 1899): 290–91.

Kornweibel, Theodore, Jr. *"Investigate Everything": Federal Efforts to Compel Black Loyalty during World War I.* Bloomington: Indiana University Press, 2002.

Kramer, Paul A. *The Blood of Government: Race, Empire, the United States, and the Philippines.* Chapel Hill: University of North Carolina Press, 2006.

———. "Jim Crow Science and the 'Negro Problem' in the Occupied Philippines, 1898–1914." *Race Consciousness: African-American Studies for the New Century*, ed. Judith Jackson Fossett and Jeffrey A. Tucker. New York: New York University Press, 1997. 227–46.

Kurashige, Scott. "The Many Facets of *Brown*: Integration in a Multiracial Society." *Journal of American History* 91.1 (June 2004): 56–68.

"Labor Problems in Hawaii." *Washington Post*, December 26, 1902: 6.

Larsen, Nella. *Passing.* Ed. Thadious M. Davis. New York: Penguin, 1997.

———. *Quicksand.* Ed. Thadious M. Davis. New York: Penguin, 2002.

"Latest Louisiana Lynching." *Chicago Daily Tribune*, June 16, 1899: 6.

Laya, Juan Cabreros. *His Native Soil.* 1940. Quezon City: Kayumanggi, 1972.

Lee, James Kyung-Jin. *Urban Triage: Race and the Fictions of Multiculturalism.* Minneapolis: University of Minnesota Press, 2004.

Lee, Julia H. *Interracial Encounters: Reciprocal Representations in African and Asian American Literatures, 1896–1937.* New York: New York University Press, 2011.

Lemus, Rienzi B. "The Negro and the Philippines." *Colored American Magazine* 6.2 (February 1904): 314–18.

Levette, Harry. "This Is Hollywood." *Chicago Defender*, September 4, 1954: 21.

Lewis, David Levering. *W. E. B. Du Bois: The Biography of a Race, 1868–1919.* New York: Henry Holt, 1993.

———. *When Harlem Was in Vogue.* New York: Penguin, 1997.

"Lieut. Alstaetter Talks of David Fagin." *New York Times*, December 10, 1901: 2.

Lipsitz, George. "'Frantic to Join . . . the Japanese Army': The Asia Pacific War in the Lives of African American Soldiers and Civilians." In *The Politics of Culture in the Shadow of Capital*, ed. Lisa Lowe and David Lloyd. Durham, NC: Duke University Press, 1997. 324–53.

———. *Midnight at the Barrelhouse: The Johnny Otis Story.* Minneapolis: University of Minnesota Press, 2010.

Little, Lawrence S. *Disciples of Liberty: The African Methodist Episcopal Church in the Age of Imperialism, 1884–1916.* Knoxville: University of Tennessee Press, 2000.

Locke, Alain, ed. *Harlem: Mecca of the New Negro.* Special issue, *Survey Graphic* 6.6 (March 1925): 622–724.

———, ed. *The New Negro.* 1925. New York: Atheneum, 1992.

Loeb, Charles H. "Victim of Japs Has Given Life to Army: Capt. Robert G. Woods, 72, Was Key Man When Nips Entered Manila." *Afro-American* (Baltimore), May 12, 1945: 11.

Lopez, Salvador P. *Literature and Society: Essays on Life and Letters.* Manila: University Publishing, 1940.

Lorde, Audre. "Poetry Is Not a Luxury." In *Sister Outsider: Essays and Speeches.* Freedom, CA: Crossing Press, 1984.

Lutz, Tom. "Curing the Blues: W. E. B. Du Bois, Fashionable Diseases, and Degraded Music." *Black Music Research Journal* 11.2 (Autumn 1991): 137–56.

"Lynch by Fire Town Reforms." *Chicago Defender*, September 11, 1954: 1.

Mackey, Nathaniel. *Bedouin Hornbook*. Los Angeles: Sun and Moon, 1997.

———. "Destination Out." *Callaloo* 23.2 (2000): 814.

———. *Discrepant Engagement: Dissonance, Cross-Culturality, and Experimental Writing*. Tuscaloosa: University of Alabama Press, 1993.

Marasigan, Cynthia L. "'Between the Devil and the Deep Sea': Ambivalence, Violence, and African American Soldiers in the Philippine-American War and Its Aftermath." PhD diss., University of Michigan, 2010.

Margolick, David. *Strange Fruit: Billie Holiday, Café Society, and an Early Cry for Civil Rights*. Philadelphia: Running, 2000.

McDowell, Deborah E. "The 'Nameless . . . Shameful Impulse': Sexuality in Nella Larsen's *Quicksand* and *Passing*." In *"The Changing Same": Black Women's Literature, Criticism, and Theory*. Bloomington: Indiana University Press, 1995. 78–97.

McGirt, James. "In Love as in War." In *The Triumphs of Ephraim*. Philadelphia: McGirt, 1907. 63–76.

McKay, Claude. *Banjo: A Story without a Plot*. 1929. New York: Harcourt Brace, 1957.

Mendoza, Victor. "Little Brown Students and the Homoerotics of 'White Love.'" *Genre* 39 (Winter 2006): 65–83.

Modell, John. *The Economics and Politics of Racial Accommodation: The Japanese of Los Angeles, 1900–1942*. Urbana: University of Illinois Press, 1977.

Monroe, Al. "Scribe Sees 'Trial by Fire' but Escapes the House Crying Brigade." *Chicago Defender*, December 11, 1948: 16.

Mori, Toshio. *The Brothers Murata*. In *Unfinished Message: Selected Works of Toshio Mori*. Berkeley: Heyday, 2000. 137–205.

Morrison, Toni. "Unspeakable Things Unspoken: The Afro-American Presence in American Literature." *Michigan Quarterly Review* 28.1 (Winter 1989): 1–34.

Moss, Alfred A., Jr. *The American Negro Academy: Voice of the Talented Tenth*. Baton Rouge: Louisiana State University Press, 1981.

Mossell, Mrs. N. F. [Gertrude Bustill]. "The Afro-American's Council from an Absentee's Point of View." *Church Review* 17.3 (January 1901): 222–25.

Moten, Fred. *In the Break: The Aesthetics of the Black Radical Tradition*. Minneapolis: University of Minnesota Press, 2003.

———. "test." *Ploughshares* 39.1 (Spring 2013): 95–97.

Mullen, Bill V. *Afro-Orientalism*. Minneapolis: University of Minnesota Press, 2004.

Mullen, Bill V., and Cathryn Watson. *W. E. B. Du Bois on Asia: Crossing the World Color Line*. Jackson: University Press of Mississippi, 2005.

Mullen, Harryette. "Optic White: Blackness and the Production of Whiteness." *Diacritics* 24.2–3 (Summer–Autumn 1994): 71–89.

Murphy, Gretchen. *Shadowing the White Man's Burden: U.S. Imperialism and the Problem of the Color Line*. New York: New York University Press, 2010.

"National Negro Academy." *Colored American* (Washington, DC), January 6, 1900: 11.

"The Negro Academy." *Christian Recorder* (Philadelphia), January 4, 1900: 2.

"Negro Deserter Beheaded." *New York Times*, December 9, 1901: 3.

"Negro Troops Are Asked to Revolt." *Atlanta Constitution*, November 2, 1899: 2.

Ngai, Mae M. *Impossible Subjects: Illegal Aliens and the Making of Modern America.* Princeton, NJ: Princeton University Press, 2004.

Ngô, Fiona I. B. *Imperial Blues: Geographies of Race and Sex in Jazz Age New York.* Durham, NC: Duke University Press, 2014.

Nicholson, Stuart. *Billie Holiday.* Boston: Northeastern University Press, 1995.

Nugent, Richard Bruce. *Gay Rebel of the Harlem Renaissance: Selections from the Work of Richard Bruce Nugent*, ed. Thomas H. Wirth. Durham, NC: Duke University Press, 2002.

Obrecht, Jas. "'Dust My Broom': The Story of a Song." *Jas Obrecht Music Archive.* May 8, 2011. Web, July 1, 2013.

O'Brien, Colleen C. "'Blacks in All Quarters of the Globe': Anti-Imperialism, Insurgent Cosmopolitanism, and International Labor in Pauline Hopkins's Literary Journalism." *American Quarterly* 61.2 (June 2009): 245–70.

O'Brien, Edward J., ed. *The Best Short Stories of 1932* and *The Yearbook of the American Short Story.* New York: Dodd, Mead, 1932.

Onishi, Yuichiro. *Transpacific Antiracism: Afro-Asian Solidarity in 20th-Century Black America, Japan, and Okinawa.* New York: New York University Press, 2013.

Ontal, Rene G. "Fagen and Other Ghosts: African-Americans and the Philippine-American War." In *Vestiges of War: The Philippine-American War and the Aftermath of an Imperial Dream, 1899–1999*, ed. Angel Velasco Shaw and Luis H. Francia. New York: New York University Press, 2002. 118–33.

Otis, Johnny. *Listen to the Lambs.* New York: W. W. Norton, 1968.

———. *Upside Your Head! Rhythm and Blues on Central Avenue.* Hanover, NH: Wesleyan University Press, 1993.

Ottley, Roi. *"New World A-Coming": Inside Black America.* 1943. New York: Arno, 1969.

"Our Monthly Review." *Voice of the Negro* 1.5 (May 1904): 169–70.

Pace, Harry H. "The Philippine Islands and the American Negro." *Voice of the Negro* 1.10 (October 1904): 482–85.

Park, Robert Ezra, comp. *East by West: Our Windows on the Pacific.* Special issue, *Survey Graphic* 9.2 (May 1926).

———. *Race and Culture.* Glencoe, IL: Free Press, 1950.

Payne, James Robert. "Afro-American Literature of the Spanish-American War." *MELUS* 10. 3 (Autumn 1983): 19–32.

Pedroche, Conrado. "The Man Who Played for David." 1938. In *Philippine Short Stories, 1925–1940*, ed. Leopoldo Y. Yabes. Quezon City: University of the Philippines Press, 1975. 398–403.

Peery, Nelson. *Black Fire: The Making of an American Revolutionary.* New York: New Press, 1994.

———. *Black Radical: The Education of an American Revolutionary.* New York: New Press, 2007.

Perry, Jeffrey B., ed. *A Hubert Harrison Reader*. Middletown, CT: Wesleyan University Press, 2001.

Petersen, William. "Success Story, Japanese-American Style." *New York Times Magazine*, January 9, 1966: 20+.

Petry, Elisabeth. *Can Anything Beat White? A Black Family's Letters*. Jackson: University Press of Mississippi, 2005.

"Philippine Stories." Review of *Footnote to Youth*, by José Garcia Villa. *New York Times Book Review*, October 8, 1933: 7.

["A placard written in Spanish . . ."] *Richmond Planet*, November 11, 1899: 8.

Ponce, Martin Joseph. *Beyond the Nation: Diasporic Filipino Literature and Queer Reading*. New York: New York University Press, 2012.

——. "On Becoming Socially Articulate: Transnational Bulosan." *Journal of Asian American Studies* 8.1 (February 2005): 49–80.

Posadas, Barbara M. "The Hierarchy of Color and Psychological Adjustment in an Industrial Environment: Filipinos, the Pullman Company, and the Brotherhood of Sleeping Car Porters." *Labor History* 23.3 (Summer 1982): 349–73.

Prashad, Vijay. *Everybody Was Kung Fu Fighting: Afro-Asian Connections and the Myth of Cultural Purity*. Boston: Beacon Press, 2001.

Puente, Lorenzo Alexander L. "Anti-U.S. Imperialism as Assertion of Black Subjectivity at the Turn of the Last Century." *Kritika Kultura* 5 (December 2004): 55–69.

"The Race War That Flopped." *Ebony* 1.8 (July 1946): 3–9.

Rafael, Vicente L. *White Love and Other Events in Filipino History*. Durham, NC: Duke University Press, 2000.

Raphael-Hernandez, Heike, and Shannon Steen, eds. *AfroAsian Encounters: Culture, History, Politics*. New York: New York University Press, 2006.

Reed, Ishmael. *Mumbo Jumbo*. 1972. New York: Scribner, 1996.

REgenerations Oral History Project: Rebuilding Japanese American Families, Communities, and Civil Rights in the Resettlement Era. Vol. 1. Los Angeles: Japanese American National Museum, 2000.

Richardson, Claiborne T. "The Filipino-American Phenomenon: The Loving Touch." *Black Perspective in Music* 10.1 (Spring 1982): 3–28.

Rizal, José. *El Filibusterismo*. Trans. Ma. Soledad Lacson-Locsin. Ed. Raul L. Locsin. Manila: Bookmark, 1997.

——. *Noli Me Tangere*. Trans. Ma. Soledad Lacson-Locsin. Ed. Raul L. Locsin. Honolulu: University of Hawai'i Press, 1997.

Robinson, Greg. "The Life and Times of Hisaye Yamamoto: Writer, Activist, Speaker." *The Great Unknown and the Unknown Great. DiscoverNikkei.Org*. March 14, 2012. Web, September 13, 2015.

Robinson, Michael C., and Frank N. Schubert. "David Fagen: An Afro-American Rebel in the Philippines, 1899–1901." *Pacific Historical Review* 44.1 (February 1975): 68–83.

Rogin, Michael. *Blackface, White Noise: Jewish Immigrants in the Hollywood Melting Pot*. Berkeley: University of California Press, 1996.

Rusling, Gen. James. "Interview with President William McKinley." *Christian Advocate* 78 (January 22, 1903): 17. In *The Philippines Reader: A History of Colonialism, Neocolonialism, Dictatorship, and Resistance*, ed. Daniel B. Schirmer and Stephen Rosskam Shalom. Cambridge, MA: South End Press, 1987. 22–23.

Russell, Timothy Dale. "African Americans and the Spanish-American War and Philippine Insurrection: Military Participation, Recognition, and Memory, 1898–1904." PhD diss., University of California, Riverside, 2013.

Said, Edward. *Orientalism.* 25th anniversary ed. New York: Vintage, 2003.

Salman, Michael. *The Embarrassment of Slavery: Controversies over Bondage and Nationalism in the American Colonial Philippines.* Berkeley: University of California Press, 2001.

San Buenaventura, Steffi. "The Colors of Manifest Destiny: Filipinos and the American Other(s)." *Amerasia Journal* 24.3 (Winter 1998): 1–26.

San Juan, E., Jr. *Carlos Bulosan and the Imagination of the Class Struggle.* Quezon City: University of the Philippines Press, 1972.

———. "An African American Soldier in the Philippine Revolution: An Homage to David Fagen." *Cultural Logic* (2009): 1–36. Web. July 9, 2010.

Saroyan, William. "An Informal Introduction to the Short Stories of the New American Writer from California, Toshio Mori." In *Yokohama, California*, by Toshio Mori. Seattle: University of Washington Press, 1985. 1–4.

Scarborough, W[illiam] S. "The Negro and Our New Possessions." *Forum* 31.3 (May 1901): 341–49.

———. "Our New Possessions—an Open Door." *Southern Workman* 29.7 (July 1900): 422–27.

Schubert, Frank. "Seeking David Fagen: The Search for a Black Rebel's Florida Roots." *Tampa Bay History* 22 (2008): 19–33.

Schweik, Susan. *A Gulf So Deeply Cut: American Women Poets and the Second World War.* Madison: University of Wisconsin Press, 1991.

Scruggs, Charles. *Sweet Home: Invisible Cities in the Afro-American Novel.* Baltimore: Johns Hopkins University Press, 1993.

See, Lisa. "PW Interviews: Cynthia Kadohata." *Publishers Weekly* 239.35 (August 3, 1992): 47–48.

Seniors, Paula Moore. *Beyond "Lift Every Voice and Sing": The Culture of Uplift, Identity, and Politics in Black Musical Theater.* Columbus: Ohio State University Press, 2009.

Shankman, Arnold. "'Asiatic Ogre' or 'Desirable Citizen'? The Image of Japanese Americans in the Afro-American Press, 1867–1933." *Pacific Historical Review* 46.4 (November 1977): 567–87.

Shepperson, George. "Notes on Negro American Influences on the Emergence of African Nationalism." *Journal of African History* 1.2 (1960): 299–312.

Sherrard-Johnson, Cherene. "'A Plea for Color': Nella Larsen's Iconography of the Mulatta." *American Literature* 76.4 (December 2004): 833–69.

Shilliam, Robbie. *The Black Pacific: Anti-Colonial Struggles and Oceanic Connections.* London: Bloomsbury Academic, 2015.

Slotkin, Joel. "Igorots and Indians: Racial Hierarchies and Conceptions of the Savage in Carlos Bulosan's Fiction of the Philippines." *American Literature* 72.4 (December 2000): 843–66.

Smith, Shawn Michelle. "In the Crowd." *African American Review* 42.1 (Spring 2008): 41–46.

Solberg, S. E. "Bulosan—Theseus—Villa: A Cryptography of Coincidence." *MELUS* 15.2 (Summer 1988): 3–25.

Sone, Monica. *Nisei Daughter*. Seattle: University of Washington Press, 1979.

Son of Kong. Dir. Ernest B. Schoedsack. Exec. prod. Merian C. Cooper. 1933. Warner Bros., 2005. DVD.

Spence, Eulalie. "A Criticism of the Negro Drama, as It Relates to the Negro Dramatist and Artist." *Opportunity* (June 1928): 180.

———. *Her*. 1927. In *Black Female Playwrights: An Anthology of Plays before 1950*, ed. Kathy A. Perkins. Bloomington: Indiana University Press, 1989. 132–40.

———. *The Whipping*. 1934. *Black Drama*. Web, May 31, 2008.

Steen, Shannon. "Racing American Modernity: Black Atlantic Negotiations of Asia and the 'Swing' Mikados." In Raphael-Hernandez and Steen, *AfroAsian Encounters* 167–87.

Steward, Charles. "Manila and Its Opportunities." *Colored American Magazine* 3.4 (August 1901): 248–56.

Steward, Frank R. "The Men Who Prey." *Colored American Magazine* 6.10 (October 1903): 720–24.

———. "Pepe's Anting-Anting: A Tale of Laguna." *Colored American Magazine* 5.5 (September 1902): 358–62.

———. "'Starlik': A Tale of Laguna." *Colored American Magazine* 6.5 (March 1903): 387–91.

———. "Three Stories." *PMLA* 126.3 (May 2011): 784–97.

Steward, Theophilus G. "Two Years in Luzon: I. Filipino Characteristics." *Colored American Magazine* 4.1 (November 1901): 4–10.

———. "Two Years in Luzon: II. Filipino Characteristics." *Colored American Magazine* 4.3 (January–February 1902): 164–70.

———. "Two Years in Luzon: III. Preparations for Civil Government." *Colored American Magazine* 5.4 (August 1902): 244–49.

Strong, Edward K., Jr. *The Second-Generation Japanese Problem*. Stanford: Stanford University Press, 1934.

Suisman, David. "Co-workers in the Kingdom of Culture: Black Swan Records and the Political Economy of African American Music." *Journal of American History* 90.4 (March 2004). Web, April 11, 2004. http://www.historycooperative.org/journals/jah/90.4/suisman.

Tabios, Eileen, ed. *The Anchored Angel: Selected Writings by José Garcia Villa*. New York: Kaya, 1999.

Taketani, Etsuko. *The Black Pacific Narrative: Geographic Imaginings of Race and Empire between the World Wars*. Hanover, NH: Dartmouth University Press, 2014.

———. "The Cartography of the Black Pacific: James Weldon Johnson's *Along This Way*." *American Quarterly* 59.1 (2007): 79–106.

———. "Colored Empires in the 1930s: Black Internationalism, the U.S. Black Press, and George Samuel Schuyler." *American Literature* 82.1 (March 2010): 121–49.

Tate, Claudia. "Nella Larsen's *Passing*: A Problem of Interpretation." *Black American Literature Forum* 14.4 (Winter 1980): 143–46.

Thornbrough, Emma Lou. *T. Thomas Fortune: Militant Journalist*. Chicago: University of Chicago Press, 1972.

"3 Die in Blaze after Threat." *Chicago Defender*, December 29, 1945: 10.

"'Trial by Fire' Opens: Rev. G. H. Dunne's Documentary Put On by Blackfriars' Guild." *New York Times*, December 5, 1947: 31.

Thurman, Wallace. *Infants of the Spring*. 1932. New York: Modern Library, 1999.

"The Training of Teachers." *Southern Workman* 29.7 (July 1900): 390.

"T. Thomas Fortune's Philippine Appointment." *New York Times*, November 30, 1902: 12.

Udansky, Margaret L. "Counting Heads: The 1990 Census; Nation's Minorities Surge in '80s; Diversity Foreshadows Major Changes." *Atlanta Journal-Constitution*, March 11, 1991: A1.

"Under Fire." *Richmond Planet*, November 30, 1899: 4.

United States. Bureau of Insular Affairs, War Dept. *What Has Been Done in the Philippines: A Record of Practical Accomplishments under Civil Government*. 1904. Rpt. in *African American Perspectives: Pamphlets from the Daniel A. P. Murray Collection, 1818–1917*. Web, May 31, 2008, http://memory.loc.gov/ammem/murraybibquery .html.

Vaz, Mark Cotta. *Living Dangerously: The Adventures of Merian C. Cooper, Creator of King Kong*. New York: Villard, 2005.

Villa, José Garcia. *Doveglion: Collected Poems*. Ed. John Edwin Cowen. New York: Penguin, 2008.

———. *Footnote to Youth: Tales of the Philippines and Others*. New York: Charles Scribner's Sons, 1933.

———. *Selected Stories*. Manila: Alberto S. Florentino, 1962.

———. "Untitled Story." *Story* 1.4 (November–December 1931): 45–53.

"Voices from the Philippines: Colored Troops on Duty—Opinions of the Natives." *Richmond Planet*, November 30, 1899: 1.

Volpp, Leti. "American Mestizo: Filipinos and Antimiscegenation Laws in California." *UC Davis Law Review* 33 (Summer 2000): 795–836.

Wagner, Bryan. "Disarmed and Dangerous: The Strange Career of Bras-Coupé." *Representations* 92 (Fall 2005): 117–51.

Wald, Elijah. *Escaping the Delta: Robert Johnson and the Invention of the Blues*. New York: Amistad/HarperCollins, 2004.

Wall, Cheryl A. *Women of the Harlem Renaissance*. Bloomington: Indiana University Press, 1995.

Waseda, Minako. "Extraordinary Circumstances, Exceptional Practices: Music in Japanese American Concentration Camps." *Journal of Asian American Studies* 8.2 (June 2005): 171–209.

Weheliye, Alexander G. *Phonographies: Grooves in Sonic Afro-Modernity.* Durham, NC: Duke University Press, 2005.

Weinbaum, Alys Eve. "Reproducing Racial Globality: W. E. B. Du Bois and the Sexual Politics of Black Internationalism." *Social Text* 67 (Summer 2001): 15–41.

Weiss, Myra Tanner. *Vigilante Terror in Fontana: The Tragic Story of O'Day H. Short and His Family.* Los Angeles: Socialist Workers Party, 1946.

Wells-Barnett, Ida B. *Lynch Law in Georgia.* Chicago: Chicago Colored Citizens, 1899.

Widener, Daniel. " 'Perhaps the Japanese Are to Be Thanked?' Asia, Asian Americans, and the Construction of Black California." In A. Jones and Singh, *Afro-Asian Century* 135–81.

Williams, Patricia J. "The Rules of the Game." In Gooding-Williams, *Reading Rodney King* 51–55.

Winters, Yvor. *The Selected Letters of Yvor Winters.* Ed. R. L. Barth. Athens: Swallow Press / Ohio University Press, 2000.

Woodson, C[arter] G[odwin]. 1915. *The Education of the Negro prior to 1861.* North Stratford, NH: Ayer, 2002.

———. "John Henry Manning Butler." *Journal of Negro History* 30.2 (April 1945): 243–44.

———. *The Mis-education of the Negro.* 1933. Mineola, NY: Dover, 2005.

———. "Walter Howard Loving." *Journal of Negro History* 30.2 (April 1945): 244–45.

Yamamoto, Hisaye. "A Fire in Fontana." 1985. In *Seventeen Syllables and Other Stories.* Rev. and expanded ed. New Brunswick, NJ: Rutgers University Press, 2001. 150–57.

———. Introduction to *The Chauvinist and Other Stories*, by Toshio Mori. Los Angeles: Asian American Studies Center, 1979. 1–14.

———. "Las Vegas Charley." In *Seventeen Syllables and Other Stories.* Latham, NY: Kitchen Table Women of Color Press, 1988. 70–85.

Yoshida, George. *Reminiscing in Swingtime: Japanese Americans in American Popular Music, 1925–1960.* San Francisco: National Japanese American Historical Society, 1997.

Young, Kevin. *The Grey Album: On the Blackness of Blackness.* Minneapolis: Graywolf, 2012.

Yu, Henry. *Thinking Orientals: Migration, Contact, and Exoticism in Modern America.* New York: Oxford University Press, 2001.

Yu, Timothy. "Asian/American Modernisms: José Garcia Villa's Transnational Poetics." 2004. Web, May 31, 2008, http://www.meritagepress.com/yu.htm.

———. " 'The Hand of a Chinese Master': José Garcia Villa and Modernist Orientalism." *MELUS* 29.1 (2004): 41–60.

INDEX

ABOUT THE AUTHOR

Vince Schleitwiler is Acting Assistant Professor in the Department of American Ethnic Studies at the University of Washington.